Social work field education and supervision across Asia Pacific

Edited by Carolyn Noble and Mark Henrickson

SYDNEY UNIVERSITY PRESS

Published 2011 by SYDNEY UNIVERSITY PRESS
University of Sydney Library
sydney.edu.au

Sydney University Press
Fisher Library F03
University of Sydney NSW 2006 AUSTRALIA
Email: sup.info@sydney.edu.au

National Library of Australia Cataloguing-in-Publication entry

Title: Social work field education and supervision across Asia Pacific
           / edited by Carolyn Noble and Mark Henrickson.
ISBN: 9781920899691 (pbk.)
Notes: Includes bibliographical references.
Subjects: Social work education--Pacific Area.
           Social work administration--Study and teaching--Pacific Area.
           Social sciences--Study and teaching--Pacific Area.
Other Authors/Contributors:
           Noble, Carolyn.
           Henrickson, Mark.
Dewey Number:
           361.3

Cover image by Carolyn Noble
Cover design by Miguel Yamin, University Publishing Service

Contents

Preface

In 2009 the then President of the Asia-Pacific Association for Social Work Education (APASWE), Professor Soung-Yee Kim from Korea, in partnership with the Korean Association of Social Workers and the Korean Council on Social Welfare Education sponsored a Dean's forum on social work education and practice development in the Asia-Pacific region. This forum brought together key scholars to gather ideas, share information, and have in-depth discussions on social work curricula and developments in the Asia-Pacific region. Countries represented included Australia, Bangladesh, Cambodia, Hong Kong, India, Malaysia, Mongolia, Nepal, Philippines, Singapore, South Korea, Sri Lanka, Thailand and The People's Republic of China. Topics explored included accreditation standards and licensing requirements; social work curricula and its structure, continuing education; field practica and supervision; and indigenous models of education and practice.

An important session on social work global standards spontaneously appeared as social work educators enthusiastically met to share, debate and learn from each other. What was remarkable were the similarities in accreditation standards and licensing requirements as well as in the structure and content of social work curricula, field education and student supervision practices. Most countries took the International Association of Schools of Social Work (IASSW) global standards as a model to adopt in designing and delivering their programs. While there were many similarities, the section on indigenous models of education and practice identified the cultural challenges that the spread of social work programs across the region brings with it. It also identified how the local voices of each country are beginning to adapt these standards so as to make their programs reflect their cultural, social and political priorities and as a result are shaping new ideas, new curricula and new responses to issues of imperialism, socioeconomic privilege, paternalism and goodwill.

In many ways this forum inspired the APASWE book series beginning with the first book in 2009 *Social work education: voices from the Asia Pacific*, which then led to this book on field education and supervision across Asia-Pacific. As did the first book, this book draws together stories from social work beyond our individual borders and experiences. Also, like the first book we have worked across languages and cultures to produce this exciting and vibrant collection of research, experiences and debates about field education and supervision. No longer can social work field education be regarded as sitting on the periphery of social work, but must be considered an integral part of the education of social workers. It is in the field education experience that students explore the various ways to integrate knowledge, skills and experiences into their beginning practice.

In this volume we continue to acknowledge that English is the colonial language in the region, and have, as an attempt to address this issue, included several chapters in the author's own language. We have kept the same format where each chapter has abstracts in English, Chinese, Japanese and Korean in an attempt to increase the accessibility of this scholarship, and to help to continue building scholarly bridges in this vast region. All contributions have been peer-reviewed and each makes a unique and valuable contribution to social work scholarship across the region.

This book is the result of the hard work of many people. A special mention goes to our South Korean colleague Professor InYoung Han who helped enrich this volume by coordinating the chapters from colleagues in Japan, South Korea and Taiwan. This edition is much richer for her efforts. A special thank you goes to the absolutely invaluable work of our translators, most of whom are postgraduate social work students or recent graduates. This group of people enthusiastically responded to the call for translation assistance as a way to participate in what they saw as an important undertaking and to contribute to the international development of social work education. It is with profound thanks that the editors acknowledge the hard and dedicated work of these translators: Shuguang Jiang, Milly Zhang, and Dr Polly Yeung (Massey University, New Zealand), Yayoi Ide (Massey University, New Zealand), Takae Itakura (D.Phil. student, Kyoto Prefectural University, Japan), and Keisuke Yuasa (D.Phil. student, Osaka University, Japan), Japanese; Jeawoo Jung and Young Im Lee Park (Massey University, New Zealand). The global community truly became local as these language teams worked together to produce the best possible result.

We are grateful also to the contributors to this book, who took time they did not have to write new work that contributes to the scholarship in this field. It has been our privilege as editors to work with committed and insightful international scholars who are dedicated to developing the Asia-Pacific regional perspective on social work field education. A significant development in this scholarship is the increasing number of cross-institutional exchanges that are happening across the region. We are entirely confident that international field education placements along with staff exchanges will only increase in the future. It is our hope that this book will encourage educators, supervisors and students to develop and undertake those experiences in an informed, thoughtful, and critical way.

Postscript to this edition

The editors want to acknowledge that during the development of this book we were reminded with brutal ferocity once again how interconnected the Asia-Pacific region is. The region is connected not only by human constructs such as technology and trade, but by the very structure of the earth and its oceans. The earthquakes in the Canterbury district in the South Island of Aotearoa New Zealand and the catastrophic earthquake and tsunami off the northeast coast of Japan profoundly affected the lives of tens of millions of people throughout the region, including a number of contributors to the book you are now reading.

We acknowledge those who lost their lives, those whose fate is unknown, those whose lives are irrevocably changed, and those who continue to work tirelessly for the recovery and rebuilding of our region.

Carolyn Noble and Mark Henrickson
April 2011

Setting the scene

From theory to context

Chapter One

Field education: supervision, curricula and teaching methods

Carolyn Noble

Increasingly field education is acknowledged as the crucial component in the education of social workers. This is true for all programs and across all countries where social work as a discipline exists. Importantly field education is the place in the social work curricula where students develop their professional selves and integrate their knowledge and skills under the supervision of expert practitioners. The rich diversity of its pedagogy is explored in this chapter, with particular attention to its philosophy, its goals, its framework, its content and important elements that make for good, effective supervision. The process of supervision is set with framework of adults as learners and uses a critically reflective stance to guide the students in the process of becoming professional practitioners. Teaching and learning strategies are discussed in the context of how to ensure effective learning outcomes for each student. Its usefulness across the Asia-Pacific region is highlighted, where social work programs are flourishing.

实习教育：督导，课程体系以及教学方法

作为社会工作者教育的一个重要组成部分，实习教学日益得到承认。这种情况适用于所有社会工作教学计划以及社会工作能够作为一个独立学科所存在的所有地区。

在社会工作教学大纲里面，实习教育占有一个非常重要的位置，因为学生们可以在经验丰富的从业人员的督导下发展他们的职业自我概念并将他们的知识和技能与实践相结合。这一章将通过重点分析有助于实现有效督导的理念，目的，结构，内容及其重要组成部分来探索实习教学法所具有的多样性。这种督导的过程是建立在以成年人为初学者的构架之上并从审慎反思的角度来引导学生成为专业的社会工作者。本章还讨论了如何保证每一个学生都获得有效学习成果的教学策略。突出强调了实习教育在社会工作项目日益繁荣的亚太地区的有效性。

現場教育とスーパービジョンについての考え方

本章は、社会正義や人権の観点から啓発される批判的視点がどのように現場教育のカリキュラムの中に取り込まれうるのかについて、とりわけスーパービジョンのプロセスとの関連において述べる。批判的視点から得られたこの洞察は、いかに知識が生み出され、伝達され、ある幾つかの文化グループに特権を与え、他の文化に不利益を与え、そしてそのことで困難に立ち向かうことを目的とした批判的教育を啓発し、そうすることによって社会の不利益を呼びかけ、社会変革戦略を啓発するのかについて探求する。現場教育のカリキュラムにおいて差異を呼びかけることの影響や複数の声を取り入れることは、議論されており、現場プログラムが発展して要件を満たすという方法に基づいて文化的な関連づけを探求するソーシャルワークのプログラム内においての利用に適している。

현장 교육 : 감독, 교육 과정 및 교수법

점차적으로 현장 교육은, 사회 복지사 교육에 있어서의 가장 중요한 구성 요소로 인식 되어지고 있다. 모든 프로그램과 사회 복지가 하나의 과정으로 존재하는 모든 나라

에 있어서 이것은 사실이다. 중요하게도 현장 교육은 사
회 복지 교육 과정에 자리잡고 있다. 학생들은 이 과정을
통하여, 그들의 직업적인 자신들을 개발하고, 전문 실무
자들의 지도아래 그들의 지식과 기술을 통합한다. 그 교
수법의 풍부한 다양성은, 그것의 철학, 목표, 구성, 그것
의 내용및 중요한 요소를 특별한 관심을 가지고 이 장에
서 탐구되며, 그것은 영구적이며 효과적인 감독을 생성한
다. 감독의 과정은, 성인을 학생으로 하는 체계로 편성 되
어지며, 학생들을 전문가적인 실무자가 되도록 지도하기
의하여, 비판적이고 반영(反映)적인 입장을 사용한다. 가
르치고 배우는 전략은, 각 학생에 대한 효과적인 학습 효
과를 보장하는 방법의 맥락안에서 설명되어진다. 사회 복
지 프로그램이 활성화되는 아시아 태평양 지역에서 그것
의 유용성은 강조되어 진다.

What is interesting in reviewing the scope and breath of social work programs across the region as presented in the 2009 Deans forum, sponsored in part by Asia-Pacific Association for Social Work Education [APASWE] was that there was almost unanimous agreement that field education and student supervision was the crucial component in the development of professional practice, not only in the region but also globally. Given its agreed underlying significance for the successful education of social work practitioners, and given the increase in international staff, knowledge exchanges, student placements, and the permeable borders between countries as well as the the desire for graduate social workers to practice internationally (Cox & Pawar 2006; Dominelli 2010; Razack 2002) it is important to explore the common features of field education and assess them for their continuing usefulness for this diverse region's social work programs. This introductory chapter, then, considers what is agreed in the literature and in the experiences of field educators to see what is (and is not) useful the Asia-Pacific region.

In all social work courses field education is the primary subject where students have the opportunity to link, and then test, campus-based theory with the professional and organisational aspects of the workplace (Cleak & Wilson 2007; Cooper et al. 2010; Maidment & Egan 2009; Razack 2002, Trevithick 2006; Tsui 2005). In particular, Schneck (1995, p8) refers to field education as the 'nexus of influence', since it has one foot in academia and the other in practice. It is here that students see firsthand that social work is practiced in highly charged social, economic, political and cultural environments where values and context influence social work continuously. In most programs students on placement (another term for field education) experience the highly charged nature of the world of practice in a variety of human and community service agencies, aid agencies and government and non-governmental organisations, large and small. It is in these settings that students not only discover the 'what and why' of the practice context but also the 'how to' of practice interventions (Noble & O'Sullivan 2009). Students are expected to absorb practitioners' 'inside knowledge' which gives meaning and direction to social work practices for their own learning, despite the variety of practice settings and the opportunities they present.

As active and self-directed learners, social work students undertaking their practica are expected to contribute to the learning process as well as to learn from the experience. In being in the midst of its realities students as would-be professionals have an opportunity to reflect on their abilities to undertake this role, as well as develop and extend new practice skills and new knowledge about how to work in the field. They are expected, not only to learn about the practical knowledge and wisdom from experienced social workers as they go about their daily work *in situ* but also to reflect on and review this knowledge and experience at the same time. Placement is often the only opportunity that students have to foster a critical and reflective approach to social work before entering the profession as qualified practitioners. It is on placements that students are identified as either suitable or unsuitable for professional practice, underscoring its importance for the profession as a whole. The importance of field education's role in the formation of beginning social workers includes its educational and professional role in preparing students for competent and ethical practice. Underpinning the effectiveness of field education is students having access to good, quality supervision. Supervision that teaches them what social work is, how to perform social work tasks, how to build relationships, and how to integrate theory and practice and reflect on its efficacy and develop the necessary awareness for effective practice (Cleak & Wilson 2007; Noble & Irwin 2009).

The question guiding this chapter, then, is what are the common elements embedded in field education? That is, what is its knowledge base, its goals, its content and educational framework, and important elements that make for good, effective supervision? The focus of this chapter is on students and their supervisors in the field, but the ideas discussed are equally relevant for practitioners seeking professional supervision as they navigate the challenges of practice.

FIELD EDUCATION: ITS KNOWLEDGE BASE

Field education provides students with the opportunity to integrate theory with practice in the workplace with all the complexities and competing demands associated with contemporary social work. The knowledge that informs practice is referred to in the literature as prac-tice knowledge, an important element in the education of social work professionals. This knowledge can be used in many practice situations to produce sound judgments and effective decision-making, and to give meaning to interventions. It is important to have theoretical under-standings of the world but it is equally essential is to know how to apply this knowledge to real-life situations in the workplace and consequen-tially to know what knowledge is useful and how to acquire it (Noble 1999). To do this requires emotional and social intelligence; self and professional reflection and opportunities for transformational learning.

Emotional and social intelligence

Emotional intelligence requires students to understand how their emo-tions, attitudes and beliefs influence emotional responses to service users, to workers, to supervisors and to other colleagues. This is true for practitioners and workers in the agency where understanding emotions as they unfold is an important part of effective practice. Social work is demanding work, dealing with poverty, violence, abuse, depression, grief and loss, social exclusion, oppression and discrimination. These are all situations that evoke emotional responses. An emotionally intelligent person is someone who knows how to manage their reactions to these situations, and also to keep disruptive emotions in check (Giles et al. 2010). Being emotionally responsive also requires the learner to be motivated by their emotional responses to strive to improve and reach goals (Giles et al. 2010). Emotional intelligence needs a social intelligence to achieve self-awareness that extends from the internal, personal world into the social world, as social work is not just concerned with individual responses to social problems but clearly locates itself within the social, economic, cultural and political contexts that frame these problems (Noble & O'Sullivan 2009). Combining emotional intelligence with a social awareness of the sociopolitical, economic and cultural context enhances opportunities for insightful and socially aware practice (Giles et al. 2010).

Self and professional awareness

Trevithick (2005) identifies self-awareness, that is, the professional use of self, as the underlying element in developing a useful knowledge base for practice. Gathering together the rich and diverse experiences of individual students' lives and using these to reflect on how they can formulate a unique sense of themselves and their relationship to the world can help students, as Trevithick says working 'from our best selves' (p44). This self-reflection must also include professional reflection, which is, constantly reviewing the assumptions, values, reasoning, behaviours and theories that underlie practice. According to Bolton (2005) practitioners are required constantly to think through current practice methods, theories, frameworks and guidelines in order to let new ideas, new theories, and new ways of working emerge. This self-knowledge and professional awareness help answer the questions 'What are we doing? Why are we doing it? How are we presenting ourselves to the agency, to the service users and to the professional community?' (Trevithick 2005). To acquire the answers to these questions and then to continue to develop this knowledge also requires the capacity to be self-critical. Fook (2002) argues that a reflective approach to practice can assist in transforming practice in a way that allows the integration of theory and practice to be more responsive, creative and to achieve change, especially important in today's unsettled and ever changing world. By this she means that by using a critical lens practitioners can evaluate their world views no matter how cherished they are and choose alternatives so as not to become complacent, ineffective and resistant to change.

Transformational learning

Giles et al. (2010) name this integration of experiential knowledge with critical reflection *transformational learning.* Based on Mezirow's (2000, as cited in Giles et al.) ideas about compassionate interaction with others and the acceptance of difference in value positions, transformational learning enables students to move beyond factual knowledge to being challenged emotionally in such a way that old knowledge, values and ideas are shifted, so that new knowledge can take its place. Central to its transformative aspect is the opportunity for students to challenge their beliefs and ideas and to make genuine leaps forward in acquiring a compassionate and informed understanding about people, their lives and the broader aspects of the global world. It is expected that this new knowledge and these new ideas and values are more open, discriminating, differential and reflective (Giles et al. 2010).

Thinking about how to start: stages and steps in planning field education

While there are many different ways universities, training institutions and agencies might set up their field education program, Table 1 below outlines a general overview.

Table 1: Stages and steps in planning the practicum

Stages	Steps
Pre-placement	Identify the focus of agency
	Select student
	Establish educational goals
Beginning	Allocate educational tasks – learning plan
	Clarify roles and responsibilities for all those involved
	Arrange supervision
	Identify backup supervision and options
Middle	Identify desired level of students competence at end of placement
	Review learning plan
	Arrange liaison visits
Final – evaluation and termination	Assess student competence against learning goals and achievement.

For the successful implementation of field education experience, the student, the supervisor, the university (or training institution) and the agency, all need to be actively involved and supportive of the process. Although much of what is learnt in placement happens as a result of careful planning and through modelling supervisors' behaviours as well as other workers in the agency, it is crucially important to also take time to prepare and think about what learning opportunities and practice experiences are available, what learning is attached to these experiences, and what is needed to help with each stage of the learning process. So it is crucial for the student to be cognisant of what the specific goals of field education are so they can incorporate this learning into their developing framework.

FIELD EDUCATION: LEARNING GOALS

Sending students into human and community services agencies to work with and learn from experienced practitioners has to have clear educational goals as well as benefits. Because students go into settings such as large government organisations, large and small NGOs and faith-based agencies that deal with income and emergency support, statutory protection for the mentally ill, the physically and intellectually disabled and vulnerable children, troubled teens and families in crisis as well as in community settings and social action/advocacy groups, there must be clearly defined advantages for all participants.

Student learning goals should be carefully thought through before students embark on their practice learning and sign up at an agency. That is, students should have some ideas as to what they want to learn, how and where this learning will take place, and what is needed to achieve these goals. Other considerations include what context will be best for the learning process, who will be useful to guide or supervise, and how will the student know that this learning has happened – all important considerations that need to be settled before the placement begins. Setting learning goals is the first step towards articulating the learning experience. Some things that might be useful to think about are:

- What are the requirements of the training institution and the course?
- What knowledge and skills do I want to test out in practice?
- What theoretical approaches do I want to explore in specific fields of practice?
- What personal growth do I want to explore?
- What type of agency or organisations interest you?
- What type of service users do you want to work with and learn about?
- What social and cultural issues interest you? Are the issues too complex for a student?
- What are the interests, skills and abilities of the supervisor?
- What are the agency's structures, policies and guidelines?

11

- What are the teaching and learning styles of the supervisor and your particular ways of learning?
- What practical considerations do you need to consider?

The setting of these goals most often occurs in a collaborative arrangement with the student, the supervisor and the academic responsible for the field education program. Therefore some goals will reflect what the student wants – personally and professionally, what the supervisor can offer with her expertise and what the academic institution requires for that level of placement. The goals can change as the learning progresses and the student grows in confidence about articulating what s/he wants to learn and experiment with.

LEARNING CONTENT

As practice learning can occur in many different organisational settings and across many different approaches, the student needs to be proactive in order to capture the opportunities available for their professional growth. A list of contents essential for students growth can be found in Cleak and Wilson's text (2007, p41) where they specify seven key areas that students should cover in their practice learning. The first area concerns *values, ethics* and *professional practice*. This includes framing interactions with service users, colleagues, supervisors and other students on principles of social justice, human rights and non-discriminatory behaviour. All human interaction should place human wellbeing and respect above all other principles (Giles et al. 2010). In the second area, the focus should be on *processes, skills* and *relationships*. This requires the application of knowledge into action. Skills, for example, can vary from basic skills such as providing information on resources, listening, paraphrasing and contracting, to intermediate skills such as working with depressed or socially isolated individuals or families to advanced skills such as being able to work with multifaceted and intractable problems and in situations involving conflict and high levels of distress and stress (Trevithick 2005). The third area concerns having an opportunity to *apply campus-based knowledge* in practice settings. Placement is an opportunity for students to use their knowledge from psychology, sociology, social policy, law and philosophy and organisational theories (i.e. campus-based knowledge) to help in identifying and explaining their judgment and decision-making with service users. Linking the 'ideal' with the 'real' world enriches students learning and provides a language to describe their work and the framework to analyse the situation from a broader structural perspective (Cleak & Wilson 2007). The fourth area concerns *self-learning and professional development* which should be clearly defined in the learning contract with the supervisor. The fifth area concerns the *organisational context* where personal problems are viewed as public and structural issues. The sixth and seventh areas concern the opportunity to learn about the *value of research* and to use this research to *inform social policy* (Cleak and Wilson 2007).

Linked to the acquisition of key knowledge areas is the opportunity to experiment with actual skill development. Depending on the level of placement, i.e. first (beginner) or second (advanced) placement, there are essential skills needed for professional work. These include self-management; interviewing and communication skills, informal and formal transfer of information and knowledge, information gathering and documentation of evidence, appropriate intervention and engagement skills, and evaluation of the helping process. In addition, students need to be able to manage their own learning and direct their own activities. To be self-motivated and proactive enables students to grab all the opportunities the placement can offer. Practice methods associated with skill acquisition can include:

- Observation/participation
- Direct service user contact
- Case management
- Project work
- Group work
- Community action and engagement.

THE LEARNING AGREEMENT

As already indicated the main placement goals are the integration of theory and practice skill development, and experimental use of new knowledge and skills. To prepare for the learning experiences both the supervisor and student need to outline what is to happen, identify relevant tasks and activities, and specify its purpose and relationship to students' learning. There are learning opportunities everywhere on placement: with the supervisors, other colleagues/students in the agency, and with service users. To capture these experiences, students need to have a full understanding of the agency – its purpose, context, goals, its services and activities, its funding source and the legislative and social policies that influence its functioning (an example of how to set a learning agreement can be found in Cleak & Wilson 2007, pp43–44).

THE EDUCATIONAL FRAMEWORK

The integration of theory and practice needs an educational framework – a methodology to guide the process. Many educational methodologies can be used to facilitate experiential/transformational learning in practice. These methodologies include: issue-based learning, problem-based learning; critical reflection; critical incident analysis; constructive learning, which includes the use of narratives; autobiographical texts; journaling; storytelling; life-writing, and other creative artistry and poetics which emphasise process and authorship. Incorporating learner experiences as part of the educational process needs to be placed centrally in this process that is, the student and supervisor should explore what the student is experiencing and provide many different opportunities for students to express this in a way that enables their voice to come through. Students learn to determine and frame their own learning processes. Seeing students as adult learners means valuing their existing skill and knowledge and encouraging their incorporation in evaluating and reflecting upon the current learning opportunities. In addition these methodologies are complimented by applying a solution-focused approach to adult learning as a means of further facilitating the development of knowledge and skills for practice (Cleak & Wilson 2007; Noble 1999). Lastly the role of critical reflection in extending opportunities for significant learning must be addressed. When reflection on what has just happened, how and then why, is given a critical lens, the learning process extends from a more pragmatic and simplistic approach to addressing larger more complex socioeconomic, cultural and political issues. Developing a critical focus for use in field education means focusing on the interactive aspects of practice experiences and situations in the context of sociopolitical relations of power. It enables students to learn skills and techniques to adjust to the demand of a rapidly changing environment and the unspecified challenges this change brings (Cooper et al. 2010). Critical reflection is increasingly informing the pedagogy of field education curricula.

CRITICAL REFLECTION AND CRITICAL QUESTIONING

Reflection assumes a critical dimension when the reflection includes an analysis of the present social structures and current sociopolitical, economic and cultural relations (Brookfield 2005). It is assumed that through this reflection process the student confronts and then works towards resolving the dilemmas, contradictions, and significant issues identified in such a way that s/he is cognitively or affectively changed. Viewed as the means by which transformational or deep learning is possible, critical reflection involves a continuous reflective cycle in which experience and reflection is inextricably linked (Brookfield 2005). The push to apply a critically reflective pedagogy in the education of social work practitioners comes from the belief that reflective processes should be linked to the emancipatory project of human and community service practice. Social work is concerned with promoting social change, as well as problem solving in human relationships and the empowerment and liberation of people to enhance wellbeing uncovering power relations and questioning dominant structures and relations forms also forms an integral part of its educational work. In identifying, challenging and drawing up new strategies to tackle existing power relations that are discriminatory and exploitative of marginalised groups, critical reflection focuses directly on the teaching and learning from 'the inside' (McLaren 2005). Starting with a description of a particular incident, the next step is to reflect on it with the intention of coming to new understandings. New understandings emerge by unpacking hidden assumptions, values, ideologies, interpretations, conclusions, and biases to expose how discriminatory behaviour is embedded in the *status quo*. In so doing it becomes possible to focus on the interactive aspects of practice experiences and situations in the context of sociopolitical relations of power. In particular this process includes reflecting on the influence of the practitioner in the particular situation and her/his interactions as well as particular interpretations, behaviours, hidden assumptions associated with the work being done with service users and how these are also affected by power relations (Fook 2002; McLaren 2005). Possible social change strategies can be identified so that broader change is also an outcome.

To apply critical reflection to the learning process requires the supervisors (in this case) to encourage students to become critical thinkers. A critical thinker doesn't only think about and then interrogate assumptions and interpretations of the social world, but also explores their adequacies and then the consequences. Critical thinking informs the epistemology of transformational learning (McLaren 2005). This requires the supervisor to incorporate critical questioning into the core curriculum. In encouraging students to probe beneath the surface of current situations, circumstances and practices, students are freed to discover their own interpretations of events, discover their own ideas and develop their own strategies for action and change. As a result students have the opportunity to make new learning available to themselves and others; make new claims to knowledge; discover new ways of viewing the world and construct new ways to help address issues of poverty, discrimination, oppression and exclusion (Bolton 2005).

Some examples of critical questioning that might be useful to begin the process of critical inquiry and reflections include students asking these questions when thinking about the agency.

- What is the structure of the organisation?
- What is its purpose?

- Describe and identify key aspects of the culture?
- What are its goals?
- Who has the power – how is this used?
- Where is decision-making focused?
- How do decisions get made?
- Who sets the direction for the organisation?
- What do you hope to achieve and receive while working in the organisation?

Critical questioning should focus on both outside and inside knowledge by including reflection on the influence of student interactions as well as particular interpretations, behaviours, and hidden assumptions that are guiding their work, and how these might be complicit in reproducing inequalities based on gender, class, and ethnic relations (Bolton 2005; Fook 2002). It requires that both the student and the supervisor pay attention to the process of making student assumptions and judgments, and not just focusing on the product (action).

So what are the *teaching and learning tools* that can facilitate this experiential/transformational learning to take place? Table 2 (below) provides a comprehensive coverage of educational tools that when used together can offer students a more collaborative, interactive, thoughtful and empowering approach to their learning.

In summary then, field education provides students with the opportunities to:

- Experience the benefits of a rich and transformational learning experience
- Integrate theory and practice
- Develop competencies in a range of skills, approaches and practice methods
- Learn about their ability as future social workers and their ability to develop self-efficacy
- Observe skilled workers and model and reflect on what they see
- Interact with real people in real situations with real ideas that have emerged from a critically reflective process.

Table 2: Teaching and learning tools

Discussion tools	Observation tools	Activities
Narratives	Modelling	Role plays – Games
Process records – log books	Direct observation	Simulation
	Videotaping	Skills training
Care plans	Audio taping	Presentations
Intake summaries	One-way screens	Co-working
Journals – diaries	Observing work in	Agency visits
Log books	practice	Committee meetings
Critical incident reports		Contact with individual
Concept maps – policy docs		and groups
Films, books & articles		

SUPERVISION AND THE SUPERVISORY RELATIONSHIP

Student supervision is the educational or teaching relationship which makes it possible to explore the link between theory and practice in order to develop a professional script. Traditionally supervision has been discussed as providing a supportive, educational, meditative and administrative functions for effective practice (or likewise providing personal, administrative, organisational and professional development for supervisees to carry out their work as professionally and successfully as possible (Kadushin 2002). Establishing a structure for mutual planning, goal setting, designing and implementing learning activities has clearly defined personal, interpersonal and organisational advantages. O'Donoghue (2003) describes supervision as instrumental in providing a teaching and learning dyad where the student in relationship with a supervisor can explore, reflect upon, and make new connections with current knowledge and practice methods as well as make changes in theory and practice and organisational management. Peer or group supervision, regular one-to-one meetings, setting clear and measurable goals and establishing a personal performance plan are strategies suggested to maximise the benefits of effective supervision.

In general, the purpose of supervision has been identified as providing the student with support, encouragement, opportunities for skill sharing, knowledge and information exchange within a structured relationship that draws out the students' strengths and encourages the testing and evaluation of their theory and practice abilities. The mandate is drawn from the organisation, the training institution, the profession and the student. Establishing a structure for mutual planning, goal setting, and designing and implementing learning activities has additional personal, interpersonal and organisational advantages. The successful use of supervision occurs when the student is encouraged to analyse and reflect on his/her performance and progress as a means by which the quality and competence of his/her practice can be measured.

Within this context much is written about the supervisee/supervisor match or mismatch in learning styles. Cleak and Wilson (2007, pp19–20) for example, have developed a framework for applying different learning style theory to supervisory practice stressing the importance of recognising how and in what context learning occurs as being of similar importance to the supervisor's social work knowledge, skills and practice experience. Equally important is the need to make teaching and learning approaches flexible, responsive, reflective and evolving in order to bring as much variety as possible into the relationship to avoid ritualistic, superficial and automatic responses. Creating a safe and supportive learning environment can encourage different approaches to learning and questioning and can set the scene for becoming a socially aware practitioner.

Creating a safe learning environment where, for example, issues associated with gender, class, sexual orientation, age, ethnicity, biases and prejudices that form barriers or result in discriminatory practices, values or beliefs can be safely explored is paramount to good, effective supervisory practice (Noble & Irwin 2009). Both the student and the supervisor need to feel safe in undertaking the critical reflection and critical questioning identified above so that unpacking and exploring issues of power and meaning in the social milieu can occur without judgment or fear of failure (Irwin & Napier 2004). A safe learning environment should also include consideration of ethical, legal and liability issues and professional concerns about performance, accountability, and professional misconduct (O'Donoghue 2003).

CONCLUSION

Social work is viewed as an international profession mainly as a result of its existence in all developed countries and its emergence in most developing countries. Its rapid growth across the region, although clearly significant, is under explored. Razack (2002) reminds us that in particular field education with its international students and shared international curricula maintains its relevance and influence by constantly responding to the needs of diverse societies and the influences from an increasingly globalised world. Further Razack (2002) in quoting Nimmagadda and Cowger's (1999 in Razack 2002) study argues that

> those who might believe that (Western) social work knowledge might be destructive because of cultural incongruity give too much credit to the power of such knowledge and too little credit to the power of local cultures and local practitioners (and educators). (Razack 2002, p127)

The ideas expressed in this chapter are not meant to be definitive or adapted without critique and critical reflection. They are a summary of common elements and understandings about field education and supervision currently in vogue. The challenge is to take these ideas as ideas and *adapt,* not adopt, the useful and relevant ones to programs across the region. The more pressing challenge is to review these ideas with a cultural lens and assess their relevance to the many emerging social work programs across the region, all with different histories, cultures and opportunities for adaptation. That is, to have confidence that whatever program is developed its relevance will be meditated through the cultural influences of each country as they build up their own social work programs.

Lastly this chapter is presented not to discredit or inhibit locally inspired forms of pedagogic practices or fill the space so that there is no room for other cultural perspectives, beliefs and structures to emerge. Oppression and hegemony is a trap for all cultures, and ethnocentrism is not only a problem for the West: celebrating difference and seeking inclusiveness is a task for all peoples. However in the final analysis adaptive work of this material will be done by the reader. Using self, group and/or collective reflection of the material presented will allow a more conscious critique of its usefulness and relevance in other cultural settings and locations from both an educational, cultural and language perspective. It is not my intention in presenting these ideas of creating and promoting a standardised format for undertaking field education and supervision uncritically, but to contribute to the egalitarian educational processes with colleagues across the region who, like me, are immersed in the ongoing education of 'would be' social work practitioners, and who would like this process to be as open, engaging and as egalitarian as possible.

REFERENCES

Bolton G (2005). *Reflective practice: writing & professional development.* (2nd edn). London: Sage.

Brookfield S (2005). *The power of critical thinking for adult learning and teaching.* Maidenhead, UK: Open University Press.

Cleak H & Wilson L (2007). *Making the most of field placement* (2nd edn). South Melbourne, VIC: Thomson.

Cooper L, Orrell L & Barden M (2010). *Work integrated learning: a guide to effective practice.* London: Routledge.

Cox D & Pawar M (2006). *International social work: issues, strategies and programs.* Thousand Oaks, CA: Sage.

Dominelli L (2010). *Social work in globalizing world.* Cambridge, UK: Polity.

Fook J (2002). *Social work: critical theory and practice.* St Leonards, NSW: Allen & Unwin.

Giles R, Irwin J, Lynch D & Waugh F (2010). *In the field: from learning to practice.* South Melbourne, VIC: Oxford University Press.

Irwin J & Napier L (2004). (Re)Forming field education: creating opportunities to maximize students' learning on placement. *Women in Welfare Education*, 7: 106–17.

Kadushin A (2002). *Supervision in social work*. NY: Columbia University Press.

Maidment J & Egan R (Eds) (2009). *Practice skills in social work & welfare: more than just common sense*. (2nd edn). Crows Nest, NSW: Allen & Unwin.

McLaren P (1995). *Critical pedagogy and predatory culture: oppositional politics in a postmodern era*. London: Routledge.

Noble C (1999). The elusive yet essential project of developing social work education as a legitimate area of inquiry. *Journal of Social Work Education*, 3(1): 2–16.

Noble C & Irwin J (2009). Social work supervision: an exploration of the current challenges in a rapidly changing social, economic and political environment. *Journal of Social Work*, 9(3): 345–56.

Noble C & O'Sullivan J (2009). Is social work still a distinctive profession? Students, supervisors and educators reflect. *Advances Journal*, 11(1): 89–108.

O'Donoghue K (2003). *Re-storying social work supervision*. Palmerston North, NZ: Dunmore Press.

Razack N (2002). *Transforming the field: critical antiracist and anti-oppressive perspectives for the human services practicum*. Halifax, NS: Fernwood Publishing.

Schneck D (1995). The promise of field education in social work. In G Rogers (Ed). *Social work field education: views & visions* (pp3–16). Dubuque, IA: Kendall/ Hunt Publishing. Co.

Trevithick P (2005). *Social work skills-a practice handbook*. (2nd edn). Berkshire, England: Open University Press.

Tsui MS (2005). *Social work supervision: contexts and concepts*. Thousand Oaks, CA: Sage.

Chapter Two

Current Australian programs for international field placements

Helen Cleak and Mim Fox

The social work profession has become more attentive to its international dimension through raising students' awareness of how global issues influence local concerns and by developing their awareness of cultural competencies. This educational focus on international issues, as well as increased student mobility and interests and overseas employment opportunities, has seen an increasing demand for international placements by social work students in recent years. The first section of this chapter outlines the effects of globalisation on the organisation and delivery of social work services domestically, as well as its increasing importance within the social work curriculum. The second section briefly outlines the educational standards and principles that underpin field education programs and processes in Australia, and how the Australian Association of Social Workers Accreditation Standards are incorporated into international field placement programs in the Asia-Pacific region operating in some Australian universities.

澳洲社会工作专业系列课程中的海外实习

社会工作学习提倡进一步深化学生对全球化问题影响当地事件的认识和加强学生的跨文化交际能力。藉此，社会工作在全球范围内受到越来越广泛的关注。近年来，越来越多的社工系学生把目光投向海外实习。本章节讨

论亚太地区的海外社工实习。海外实习应该与社会工作的本质相融，透析实习地区的文化背景和实习安排。本章第一部分将探析海外社工实习的理论基础以及这些理论基础与澳洲社会工作者协会认证标准的关联。第二部分介绍两所澳洲的大学提供的海外社工实习项目，并讨论实习的组织过程，教育意义及实践要求。这些要求涉及到实习督导，学习任务，外联方面的支持和实习过程中的交流。

オーストラリアのソーシャルワークプログラムにおける国際現場実習について

ソーシャルワーク専門職は、国際問題がいかに地元の問題に影響を与えているのかについて学生の意識を高めることを通して、そして学生の多様なカルチュアル・コンピテンスを開発することによって、国際規模でもって気を配るものとなってきている。この国際問題への焦点化は、近年ソーシャルワークを学ぶ学生による国際実習への需要の高まりにおいて見られる。本章では、学習の背景およびアジア・太平洋地域において実施された国際現場実習の構造を強調する、ソーシャルワークのプログラムに含まれる実習教育の不可欠な本質について議論する。まず、国際的な背景において現場教育実践を支持するという理論や、これらの概念とAASW評価基準(2009)間との関係性を分析するという理論について探求する。次に、国際現場実習プログラムを運営しているオーストラリアの二つの大学の実践例を報告し、これらの実習先の機関、およびスーパービジョン、学習課業、切れ目の無い支援、そして連絡調整手配といったこれら大学の教育や実習要件について議論する。

호주 사회복지학 프로그램 중의 해외 현장 실습

얼마나 세계적인 사안들이 현지 현안들에 영향을 주는

지에 대해 학생들의 의식을 고취시키고, 문화적 측면
에서의 적합성을 높이기 위해 사회복지 분야는 사회복
지의 국제적인 면에 더욱 주의를 기울여 오고 있다. 이
글은 국제적인 현안들에 초점을 맞추고 있는데, 이 현
안들은 최근 몇 년간 사회복지를 공부하는 학생들로부
터의 해외 현장 실습에 대한 증대되는 요구와 관련되
어 있다. 이 장에서는 아시아 태평양 지역에서 실행된
해외 현장 실습의 학습 맥락과 체계를 강조하면서, 사
회복지학 프로그램 안 에서의 현장 교육의 필수적인
본질을 논의할 것이다. 첫 번째 절에서는 국제적인 맥
락 안에서 현장 실습 교육을 뒷받침해주는 이론들에
대해 검토할 것이다. 그리고, 이러한 개념들과 호주 사
회 복지사 협회 인정 기준(2009년) 과의 관계에 대해
분석할 것이다. 두 번째 절에서는 해외 현장 실습 프로
그램을 운영하고 있는 호주의 두 대학교의 사례를 소
개할 것이다. 또한, 이러한 실습을 담당하는 기관들과
그 기관들의 교육적이고 현실적인 측면에서의 필요요
건들, 즉 감독, 학습 과제, 연락 지원 및 의사 소통 방식
에 대해 논의할 것이다.

INTERNATIONAL SOCIAL WORK AND FIELD EDUCATION

Globalisation is a process that leads to the growing interdependence of the world's people (Seitz 2008, p27). Although globalisation has been largely dominated by economic interests, the impact of new forms of international governments, and the creation of a world culture and technical forces, such as information and transportation systems, also play a role in this growing interdependence. Healy (2008) adds security and social welfare interdependence and suggests that migration and HIV/AIDS are examples of social welfare interdependence. Healy also highlights poverty, the status of women, street children and the adoption of local social policies internationally, as some of the issues that are 'global in nature in that they are shared by many or all nations and require multinational action' (Healy 2008, p119).

As some social issues are indeed global in nature, then it follows that training social work students to practice in an international context is acutely relevant (Nagy & Falk 2000). For example, widespread civil war and international conflicts has seen a change in family dynamics with families becoming further divided by mass migration and displacement (Lyons 2006, p374). This is turn impacts on Australian social and immigration policies as well as local health and welfare services for refugees and newly arrived migrants. Therefore social work services in both the statutory and voluntary sectors must now take into account regional, international and global influences on national policy directions and implications for practice developments (Lyons 2006, p370). Migration to, and within most Western communities, either by choice or as a destination by displaced refugees, is also impacting on social work interventions which require them to have more knowledge of 'transnational' practice and cultural competence (Lyons 2006, p373). However, much of the literature on cultural competence is presented in a descriptive way that assumes the existence of uniform features of those belonging to the same cultural group and little analysis of diversity and power differences between cultural groups (Williams 2006).

When discussing a relationship between social work and the modern understanding of globalisation, the history of colonisation and social work's role in professional imperialism cannot be ignored. Cox and Pawar point out that although the emergence of social work globally did occur largely in parallel, the actual nature of the professional practice was different, 'in part because their sociocultural and political economy contexts were different' (Cox & Pawar 2006, p7). However, it appears clear that the various national social work structures recognise each other as sharing much in common, such as the same ethical principles and similar social problems (Cox & Pawar 2006; Healy 2001, p100).

If a consequence of globalisation is that what occurs in one country has a potential impact on the population of another, then it's an educational imperative that social work students need training in international social issues. Some writers advocate for all students and practicing social workers to be oriented to an international analysis of a situation (Cox & Pawar 2006, p40) and specifically in social development as a method of social work practice. To this end Razack and Haug argue for an anti-colonialist and anti-oppressive social work education that begins in the classroom and is replicated in the international field placement experience (Haug 2005, p127; Razack 2009, p10).

As globalisation has affected the nature of social work, it also has affected the modern student. The world is now significantly easier to travel and navigate and international experiences are increasingly becoming a valued resumé inclusion. Students are also realising that an international placement is desirable and within their reach. Wehbi provides some insight as to the various motivations a student may have to undertake an international field placement: a fascination with other cultures; liking people of another country; the desire to make a difference and the desire to give something back (Wehbi 2009, p52). Students also are seeing that the choice of future employment now includes specialising in refugee work, natural disasters and work in humanitarian organisations such as the United Nations, Red Cross and Amnesty International and thus knowledge of international social work and ideally, a placement in an overseas country, is important for enabling a social worker to plan his or her career path (Cox & Pawar 2006, p64). Considering the importance of international field placements in social work education, there is relatively little that has been published on the topic in academic journals (Pawar et al. 2004). In particular, there has been a paucity of research into the critical cultural aspects of this emerging area of social work education but one argument has been that social work exchanges have often been characterised by students' beliefs that they are going to help others, as opposed to learning through their placement experience about the danger of perpetuating oppressive colonial relations (Abram et al. 2005; Wehbi 2009).

AUSTRALIAN INTERNATIONAL PLACEMENTS PROGRAMS IN THE ASIA-PACIFIC REGION

There are 29 social work degree programs in Australia that are subject to accreditation by the Australian Association of Social Work (AASW) (Healy & Lonne 2010). The newly revised Australian Social Work Education and Accreditation Standards (2010) has set national minimum standards for teaching field education subjects as well as other social work subjects and are reviewed by the AASW every five years. Most Australian universities reflect strong similarities in defining and describing their field education curriculum (Australian Learning and Teaching Council 2010), which has been shaped by social work's historical relationship with the human service industry and by the requirements stipulated by the AASW. These principles form the framework under which international placements are arranged in order to be assessed as an accredited placement that can count towards a student's social work qualification in Australia.

Access to field placements in Australia and many other Western countries, such as the US and Ireland, are predominantly secured through a voluntary partnership between the university and the individual social worker or agency team, an approach known as the 'grace and favour' model by Irish academics (Wilson et al. 2009). This contrasts with other models used in England where supervisors are paid to take students but must adhere to a strict code of educational practice (Wilson et al. 2009). The Accreditation Standards require students to complete a minimum of 980 (140 days) hours of field education, taken over at least two placements with each placement being a minimum of 290 hours (40 days) duration and typically, the placement requirements are split relatively evenly between two placement periods (Healy & Lonne 2010, p22). This minimum number of hours is comparable to programs taught in the US but considerably less than hours required by English courses that have three placements over 185 days (Wilson et al. 2009).

Negotiation of international field placements

The Accreditation Standards (2010) allow a student to undertake half of their allocated placement hours (70 days) in an overseas placement. Most social work programs in Australia have organised overseas placements on a year-to-year basis for students who demonstrate a keen interest and/or have appropriate contacts in another country. Some programs rely upon offers made by international agencies and the staff's knowledge and contacts with possible overseas placements, or students may put forward suggestions and contacts for overseas placements that the school then negotiates on the student's behalf. For example, international students who have undertaken their social work course in an Australian university may request to return to their homeland to complete one of their field placements. Students are not permitted to negotiate their own overseas placement without university involvement.

Over the years, a pool of suitable agencies has been established and placements are approved only when the schools or staff have a pre-existing affiliation with either an agency or a particular university, where a formalised relationship has been developed (in some instances through a Memorandum of Understanding) and where the school is confident about the quality of the learning experience for the student. Sometimes, the relationships between overseas agencies and the tertiary institution are more fluid and dependent upon offers made by international agencies and the school's knowledge and contacts with possible overseas placements. Students may also put forward suggestions and contacts for overseas placements that the school may then negotiate on the student's behalf.

One advantage of establishing long-term partnerships with international field placements is that the school is more aware of the specific needs of the partner organisations and to ensure that students are able to make meaningful contributions. Ideally, student placements should be demand driven, where the host organisation requests specific skills or abilities, which sending programs can then strive to provide (Lough 2009). For instance, staff matching student interests with international placements may request that students have some language capacity and other skills that will allow them to make a significant and meaningful contribution (Lough 2009). An example is short language courses in the Khmer language being a useful way that students can prepare themselves for an international placement in Cambodia.

Preparing students for an international field placement experience

The background and reasoning of a students' initial choice to undertake an international placement is crucial in determining the successful outcome of the experience. In order to foster the internationalisation of social work without reproducing inequitable North-South power relations these motivations need to be explored and critically examined (Wehbi 2009, p49). Individual interviews can be used to explore with students why they want to an overseas placement, to describe previous travelling experiences and their special professional interests. Students sometimes link their interest to a typically colonial notion of wanting to make a difference in an international placement, which reinforces a benevolent perspective (Wehbi 2009). Or the student may connect their interest in an overseas country to the idea that they can make a difference, whereas they feel they may not be able to in a local placement. This motivation hints at the charity perspective that reinforces the belief that they can intervene to 'save' them (Abram et al. 2005). Careful screening and pre-placement briefing can enable students to explore their expectations of their student role on placement and to critically examine the structural realities that limit the contribution they could make in an overseas placement (Abram et al. 2005). After exploring student motivations, a primary role of social work educators in the preparation phase is to encourage students to explore international/ cross-cultural practice and the impact on themselves. The development of strategies for handling cross-cultural work and foreign situations, such as language and daily exposure to poverty, can be confronting for students. This exploration should occur prior to departure through formal briefing and debriefing sessions organised by the school, and offers the students the opportunity to share their experience with other students upon return. Other topics covered can include cross-cultural awareness, standards of dress and respect for local culture.

Students travelling in pairs or as a group is encouraged so that the students are ensured a support network in an otherwise challenging environment. This can also be beneficial to foster group responsibility by allowing students to undertake as much preparation work as possible themselves, such as exchanging information and supporting each other in buying tickets, obtaining visas, getting vaccinations and finance, and sharing tasks amongst the group (Magnus 2009).

During the pre-placement phase, clarity is required around the nature of a social work task or supervision expectations. The agency sometimes may differ from the Australian university as to their understanding of our requirements (Cleak & Wilson 2007). These elements are tested even more when the student is geographically distant to their educational institution as it becomes difficult for university field educators to monitor the students learning, skill development and overall wellbeing. Students capacity for flexibility, initiative and resilience requires an assessment prior to acceptance to an international placement, and supervisors interest and experience with students' needs should be equally determined (Magnus 2009).

Supervision of international field placements

Field education in social work grew out of the apprenticeship model of teaching where students learnt by 'doing' and the social work supervisor acted as a role model and as a gatekeeper to the profession (Cleak et al. 2000). Each student must therefore be supervised by a qualified social worker that is able to expose them to appropriate social work tasks, who assumes responsibility for the placement and guides professional practice learning (AASW 2010). The field educator must be a qualified social worker with a minimum of two years full-time practice experience, or its part-time equivalent (AASW). In addition, the student must receive a minimum of one and a half hours of supervision per week (AASW). Much of a student's learning on placement is mediated through this student–supervisor relationship. This relationship helps to define and structure the range of student learning tasks and experiences and the expectations on the provision of supervision does not differ whether the student is undertaking a local or international field placement.

Other supervision arrangements have become more commonly used as an alternative to the traditional model. This includes task supervision, group supervision, external supervision and shared supervisory arrangements. A task supervisor is an experienced human service worker who is not social work qualified or a social worker with less than two years practice experience (ALTC 2010, p45). The task supervisor is usually employed at the same agency as the student and provides the day-to-day direction to the student. In this instance an external field educator, who is qualified but is usually not a staff member of the agency where the student is placed, offers formal social work supervision. This can be a difficult role as the external supervisor does not have access to agency information and is unable to participate in the day-to-day activities of the student (ALTC 2010, p44).

Given the above requirements and the geographical distance of international field placements, organising appropriate supervision can be the most challenging aspect of the placement experience. The AASW requirements regarding length of placement and supervision arrangements can restrict the availability of international placements. This is particularly true in countries where there is a lack of supervisors who would be recognised by the AASW. External supervision is more common in overseas placements where a staff member from a local university or a qualified social worker from another agency is engaged to supervise the student on placement.

Other identified concerns regarding supervision include agency uncertainty about the home school's expectations of them, the unpredictability of social work supervision, the dependency upon task supervisors and staff reluctance to engage in reflective models of teaching with the student (CSSW international placement paper 2006). It has been the experience over many years of placing students in Asia-Pacific agencies that many of their staff who have been trained locally, are not so familiar with the postmodern concepts that promote a more collegial and reflective approach to teaching and learning and which encourage self-directed learning and adult learning styles of interaction. In addition an agency accepting a student on an international placement may have a different interpretation of what a social work task is or what the supervision expectations are at the home school (Cleak & Wilson 2007). Magnus (2009) states that some students report that supervisors do not live up to their expectations to give individual attention and opportunity for critical discussion, and suggests that students must be prepared to realise that cultural differences might become explicit in this process (p381). Social work programs should therefore seek clarity about the exact nature of the learning tasks and the supervision arrangements before the student travels. Students are challenged to be open-minded and, as guests, to be less expectant and open to understanding different ideas of supervision. Ultimately the responsibility for successful supervision rests with both parties and students are encouraged to be proactive in their contribution.

Communication

Maintaining regular communication and following the accreditation standards for liaison contact (Cleak & Wilson 2007) is a demanding aspect of an overseas placement, especially if problems arise. Technology has enabled regular contact to be maintained via email, telephone and video conferencing using Skype facilitates the face-to-face requirement. In some programs, visits to the overseas placement agency can be achieved by planning around other academic commitments, such as conferences and teaching locally. Where formal relationships have been established with an overseas university the responsibility for regular monitoring of the placement and liaison support has sometimes been delegated to the local overseas university. This has proved beneficial as they are often the educational body with the history and knowledge of the agency and therefore can smoothly navigate cross-cultural issues as they arise. In this instance, the home university would have email contact with the student and the overseas university regularly to ensure smooth progression of the placement, assess all placement learning tasks (and provide additional tasks to further learning if necessary) and finally, to debrief the student upon arrival back in Australia.

Principles of learning and assessment

There are many different ways of supporting teaching and learning on field placement and the Accreditation Standards (2010) require programs to use a range of learning activities to ensure that students can use a variety of interventions in their own practice. In addition the standards ensure a more equitable way of making more aspects of a student's performance available for evaluation. Doel and Shardlow (1996) suggest that a successful and balanced placement ought to contain a significant number of different methods to optimise the development of

33

knowledge, skills and values (p117). Cleak and Wilson (2007) describe a range of teaching and learning tools which provide various ways in which the student's performance is made accessible to the supervisor, enables the quality of the learning to be identified and therefore evaluated, and provides written documentation of the progress of learning and any issues that may arise. These tools include discussion with the supervisor, process recording, clinical observation, role playing and reflective journals. These tools and techniques for learning do not differ according to the geographical location of the placement as the Australian social work expectations of the principles of learning and assessment are deeply ingrained in Australian field education. What differs though is how long students are orientated to their tasks during placement before there is an expectation to perform, and how the outcomes of these tasks are communicated to the home university. An example is that students may find themselves very quickly being involved with communities and individuals on an international placement at a pace that is faster than their peers on a local placement. The communication to the home university therefore becomes paramount because this process is not being discussed in a timely manner with the students own field education staff (making the relationship with the on-site supervisor that much more crucial) thereby making the reflective journals a more important learning tool.

Debriefing upon return

A final area of emphasis in the literature on international field placements is the work that needs to occur with students upon their return (Heron 2005; Pawar et al. 2004). There is importance attached to appropriate debriefing and re-entry for returning students and it is argued that students need a framework to help them make sense of their experiences upon their return as well as a space to critically reflect on the learning that has occurred (Abram et al. 2005; Heron 2005). In addition, students undertaking international field placements often miss out on the integration seminars that coincide with the local placements. Integration seminars are an opportunity for students to be supported educationally on their placement, to connect the classroom content with the workplace, and to gain both formal and informal support from their peers. Due to geographical distance overseas, students are unable to attend these seminars and hence debriefing upon return is often the only opportunity for this additional support and integration of their learning experiences.

CASE EXAMPLES OF INTERNATIONAL FIELD PLACEMENTS

Two case examples are now presented of social work students undertaking international field placements in the Asia-Pacific region within their social work degree. The first is of a student on placement in Indonesia. This case example highlights a situation where the student has excellent learning opportunities and skill development but is inadequately supported in her learning. The second is of a student on placement in Manila. This case example highlights the benefits of a formalised agreement with an overseas agency in order to provide strong educational support for both the student and the supervisor.

CASE STUDY OF A STUDENT ON AN INTERNATIONAL PLACEMENT IN NORTH SUMATRA, INDONESIA

Marie is a final year Bachelor of Social Work student who was placed in North Sumatra, Indonesia, working with internally displaced people as a result of a tsunami. A large aid and humanitarian NGO informed the university of student placement vacancies and this was advertised to the student body. Marie had always been professionally interested in humanitarian work and had enrolled in the Bachelor of Social Work with the aim of entering this field upon graduation. Prior to her studies she had travelled extensively both as a tourist and having undertaken development work as a volunteer. For one of her core subjects she had previously written an essay on the topic of displaced peoples as a result of natural disaster and so had developed an interest in this area. When the placement in Indonesia was advertised Marie happily applied via her university. She then had an interview with the NGO after which she was accepted for the placement. The NGO then organised for in-house training before her departure. At this training Marie was taught survival skills, professionalism as a representative of the NGO, and cultural competency.

Placement arrangements and progress

When Marie arrived she found out that her main task on placement was to be direct client work with internally displaced people who had lost their homes and livelihood as a result of a tsunami. Marie was able to conduct home visits to assess clients (mainly women), situations and circumstances to explore how well-integrated they were with local communities, in the aim of rehousing these individuals into other surrounding communities. While on placement Marie also had opportunities to liaise with other aid agencies and local supports, as well as to work in a multidisciplinary team.

University contact

Marie had task supervision from the manager of the agency she was placed with who was not from a social work background, as well as informal supervision from colleagues on the placement. There were however no social workers in the team she was working with. Marie was offered long distance supervision from her home university field educator, but this proved to be sporadic and difficult due to poor communication technology. A liaison visit was conducted halfway through the placement on the telephone and Marie had other email contact throughout the placement with her university field educator.

Throughout the placement Marie engaged in cross-cultural comparison with her supervisor and colleagues, as well as completing regular journal entries online. Overall Marie felt that her international placement experience had provided her with strong direct practice experience, experience working with disaster and trauma victims and insight into the reality of working in the humanitarian and international aid field. However, Marie highlighted upon her return that the lack of social work supervision had made it difficult for her to link the social work theory to practice in the humanitarian field and when working in a multidisciplinary team she had had difficulty developing a specifically social work identity.

CASE STUDY OF STUDENT ON AN INTERNATIONAL PLACEMENT
IN MANILA

Bill was placed in a humanitarian-based organisation in Metro Manila, Philippines. The population of the Philippines is 78.6 million people with average household size being five members and one-third of the population is defined as living in poverty. The organisation approaches their work from a holistic and structural way by introducing programs that build capacities of families and communities, such as micro financing, housing cooperatives, entrepreneurial ventures, health, nutrition and educational projects. It receives funding from UNHCR, UNICEF, World Food Program (WFP), AusAID as well as engaging local services and members of the community in providing assistance and services to these vulnerable populations. Bill is a mature final-year student who was placed at the organisation for a 70-day placement with two other students. Bill had his first placement in an aged care, case management facility and he has worked part-time as a carer in a disability service and has travelled to countries in Europe and South America.

Placement arrangements

This organisation offers the university up to four social work placements each year in a number of their programs and have qualified social workers who work in all of these areas. At the start of the academic year, the university liaised with senior staff at the agency to discuss which staff were available to supervise and individual students' learning needs were matched to the various programs. Bill's learning tasks had primarily a community development focus and he spent time in communities in Northern Luzon undertaking a survey and involvement in a 'cash for work' (CFW) project. The CFW program works directly with communities that have been affected by typhoons and works toward empowering community members, building on established strengths within the community in order for communities to better educate and prepare themselves for another possible natural disaster.

Progress of placement

In the first few weeks, Bill had a thorough orientation, which included learning about the agency through reading a comprehensive student manual that had been prepared by agency staff. The manual gave a detailed overview of the agency's strategic plan, policies and procedures as well as material relevant to security awareness, agency protocols and cultural understanding. The project coordinators of the various programs spent individual time with Bill, giving an overview of their target groups, work responsibilities, funding streams, etc. The student had the opportunity to conduct interviews, focus group discussions, home visits, and attend community assembly meetings in these first few weeks. Bill used group work and teamwork skills, applied strength-based interventions and kept a journal to reflect on his activities. The agency helped to organise safe, student accommodation in an afford-able apartment which was a short train ride from the agency which Bill shared with another student.

University contact

Contact between Bill and the university was maintained through regular emails and Skype and there were two formal, liaison contacts via teleconferencing when both Bill and the field educator were present.

THE BENEFITS OF THE INTERNATIONAL FIELD PLACEMENT

There are a number of identifiable benefits of the international place-ment program for students, the placement agencies and the social work program:

1. The overseas placement program offers social work students the opportunity to experience another culture and perspective, to develop knowledge and skills in working in developing countries, to use this experience to work in a range of international settings in their career (for example humanitarian and aid work), and with international client groups (for example refugee and migrant populations in Australia).

2. Many universities around the world now have an international mandate and encourage international student exchange. The international placement program allows these links to thrive due to constant positive outcomes.

3. Social work staff are able to broaden their experience in negotiating appropriate learning opportunities for students who wish to improve their understanding of cross-cultural practice and cultural competency as well as to become more reflective about students notions of culture and to seek an understanding of how power operates in defining cultural norms and relations between cultural groups.

4. Students have been able to contribute in both welfare and humanitarian ways to the various agencies where they are placed. They have provided essential work such as counselling, case management and community development and their involvement in bigger projects have helped to mobilise large-scale operations for refugees, internally displaced persons and survivors of human-made disasters. When projects have operated over a number of years students have been able to work consecutively in them over time and the impact that the students are able to make is multiplied.

5. One of the exciting aspects for students undertaking a placement overseas is the opportunity to undertake social work roles and have exposure to fields of practice that are unavailable in an Australian-based placement. Projects such as poverty alleviation, capacity building, income generation, responding to natural disasters and other meso-level interventions are some of the social work practices in developing countries and are usually more appropriate for Australian social work students that do not have the local language needed for direct work with client groups.

Reflecting on the organisation of the international field placement

Students are often positioned between several cultures and find it difficult to find the right words to describe and interpret experiences. They are often in remote geographical and technological spaces where they are unable to 'bounce' their ideas and impressions around. Magnus (2009) suggests that students are encouraged not to wait for the right words, inspiration or a fitting break to start writing, but to start and keep writing what they see, hear and think at all times. Students' assignments, journals and other reflective tools are important vehicles for critical reflection of their daily experiences.

Here is an excerpt from a student's journal that highlights the challenge of working in a cross-cultural setting, but also the need for critical reflection by students. The student was undertaking an international field placement at a Cambodian NGO that offered services to people with HIV/AIDS and their families:

> Confidentiality is a relatively new concept in Cambodia and most people are not aware that they may have the right to counselling in a private environment without other people hearing or knowing what was discussed. Also there are many topics in Cambodian culture that are just not discussed by anyone. Therefore it may take time to build up a trusting relationship with the client before topics such as sex and abuse may be discussed successfully. The other main difference in social work practice is the actual concept of counselling. Counselling in Cambodia is also a new concept and, from my experience, clients have a hard time understanding abstract questions regarding their feelings or visualizing what has happened in the past or what they would like to happen in the future. Many times my questions regarding their past experiences were met with limited response or a change in topic. Many people feel uncomfortable discussing personal feelings. For Cambodians 'losing face' may be their main concern, so they may avoid questions that invite emotional responses so as not to show any negative emotions. Also during my time counselling people with HIV in Cambodia I noticed that many people feel uncomfortable discussing many topics, such as illness, death or sex, and respond by laughing. Laughter seems to be the norm for Cambodians when they feel embarrassed or awkward in social situations. This can be quite disconcerting for the western counsellor, seeing the client laughing and then finding out that they are talking about a time when their husband

was abusive or that they lost a child to AIDS. Yet the topics they are talking about are of a serious nature and deserve more discussion and it can be hard to get the client to open up about the topic when they continue to laugh or respond by saying they have said enough about that topic and wish to say no more. In this situation I found it best to respect the feelings of the client and slowly discuss the topic over a number of visits. I found it best not to ask direct questions in regard to uncomfortable topics, but to ask related questions, allowing the client more time to adjust their train of thought to the discussion. (Kleeman 2007)

CONCLUSION AND THE WAY FORWARD

Western social work education models, including Australian, have a long way to go to address both local and global challenges such as poverty, mass migration, ethnic conflict and human rights violations. To this end, social work programs around the world are embracing internationalisation both within their curricula and in their field education programs. In order for social work programs to appropriately internationalise their educational program, they need to move from sporadic and opportunistic involvement of staff to a more formalised program that emphasises social development theory and international social work (Healy 1986). Undergraduate social work programs in Australia have been providing students with the opportunity to undertake international field placements for many years and have seen benefits emerge for both students and the programs themselves. In order to maintain professional learning goals for students on an international field placement from Australian universities, the Australian Association of Social Workers Accreditation Standards are used to guide requirements for supervision, working models of international placements and learning tasks. In the past these international placements have often been organised *ad hoc*. This chapter has discussed a framework for supporting students learning on international placements in the context of an internationalised educational program, via the Australian Association of Social Workers Accreditation Standards. Lessons learnt by experienced university social work educators have also been presented using two case examples that highlight how both direct and indirect social work tasks can be achieved on an international placement, ultimately supporting an anti-oppressive placement experience. Unfortunately, Australian international placements are usually unidirectional and rarely engage in multilateral exchange (Wehbi 2009) with a large number of Australian students (ie. students from the global North) undertaking their field placements in the Asia-Pacific region (i.e. the global South) (Lough 2009). Further research is required as to the ability to provide international field placements without reproducing the paternalism and colonialism often associated with interventions originating from the global North.

Acknowledgement

The authors would like to acknowledge Associate Professor Elizabeth Fernandez for her work with international field placements at the University of New South Wales over the last eighteen years.

REFERENCES

AASW (2010). *Accreditation standards.* Kingston, NSW: Australian Association of Social Work. [Online]. Available: www.aasw.asn.au/publications/ethics-and-standards [Accessed 13 May 2011].

AASW (2010). *The AASW Code of Ethics.* Kingston, NSW: Australian Association of Social Work. [Online]. Available: www.aasw.asn.au/publications/ethics-and-standards [Accessed 13 May 2011].

Abram FY, Slosar JA & Walls R (2005). Reverse mission: a model for international social work education and transformative intra-national practice. *International Social Work,* 48(2): 161–76.

Australian Institute of Primary Care (2004). *Clinical education review: final report.* Bundoora: La Trobe University, Faculty of Health Sciences.

Australian Learning and Teaching Council (2010). *A guide to supervision in social work field education.* (Revised edition). Strawberry Hills, NSW: Australian Learning and Teaching Council.

Bocage M, Homonoff E & Riley P (1995). Measuring the impact of the fiscal crisis on human service agencies and social work training. *Social Work*, 40(5): 701–05.

Cleak H, Hawkins L & Hess L (2000). Innovative field options. In L Cooper & L Briggs (Eds). *Fieldwork in the human services* (pp160–74). St Leonards, NSW: Allen & Unwin.

Cleak H & Wilson J (2007). *Making the most of field placement*. Melbourne, VIC: Cengage.

Combined Schools of Social Work (2006). International placement paper. Unpublished. Available from RMIT, 80 Victoria St, Carlton, VIC, 3000, Australia.

Coulton P & Krimmer L (2005). Co-supervision of social work students: a model for meeting the future needs of the profession. *Australian Social Work*, 58(2): 154–66.

Cox D & Pawar M (2006). *International social work*. Newbury Park, CA: Sage Publications.

Department of Human Services (DHS) (2008). *Clinical placements in Victoria: considering a clinical placement agency*. Melbourne, VIC: Workforce Branch, Victorian Government.

Haug E (2005). Critical reflections on the emerging discourse of international social work. *International Social Work*, 48(2): 126–35.

Healy L (2008). *International social work: professional action in an interdependent world*. (2nd edn). Oxford, UK: Oxford University Press.

Healy L (2001). *International social work: professional action in an interdependent world*. New York: Oxford University Press.

Healy L (1986). The international dimension in social work education: current efforts, future challenges. *International Social Work*, 29: 135–47.

Healy K & Lonne B (2010). *The social work and human services workforce: report from a national study of education, training and workforce needs*. Strawberry Hills, NSW: Australian Learning and Teaching Council.

Kadushin A (1992). *Supervision in social work*. New York: Columbia University Press.

Lough B (2009). Principles of effective practice in international social work field placements. *Journal of Social Work Education*, 45(3): 467–81

Lyons K (2006). Globalization and social work: international and local implications. *British Journal of Social Work*, 36: 365–80.

Magnus P (2009). Preparation for social work students to do cross-cultural clinical practice. *International Social Work*, 52(3): 375–85.

Maidment J (2003). Problems experienced by students on field placement: using research findings to inform curriculum design and content. *Australian Social Work*, 56(1): 50–60.

Maidment J & Egan R (Eds) (2009). *Practice skills in social work and welfare.* Crows Nest, NSW: Allen & Unwin.

Nagy G & Falk D (2000). Dilemmas in international and cross-cultural social work education. *International Social Work*, 43(1): 49–60.

Razack N (2009). Decolonizing the pedagogy and practice of international social work. *International Social Work*, 52(9): 9–21.

Seitz JL (2008). *Global issues: an introduction.* Melbourne, VIC: Blackwell Publishing.

Wehbi S (2009). Deconstructing motivations: challenging international social work placements. *International Social Work*, 52(1): 48–59.

Wilson G, O'Connor E, Walsh T & Kirby M (2009). Reflections on practice learning in Northern Ireland and the Republic of Ireland: lessons from student experiences. *Social Work Education*, 28(6): 631–45.

CHAPTER THREE

COLLABORATION BETWEEN FIELD EDUCATION FACULTY AND FIELD SUPERVISOR IN KOREA

실습담당교수와 현장수퍼바이저의 협력

Soo Mi Jang

장수미

실습은 사회복지교육의 핵심요소로서, 이론과 실천의 통합에 중요한 역할을 담당한다. 이 장은 실습교육의 효과성을 높이기 위해 실습담당교수와 현장수퍼바이저의 협력방안을 논하고 있다. 그동안 실습교육은 현장수퍼바이저의 수퍼비전에 거의 의존해 왔으며, 실습의 목표와 실습의 내용에 대해 대학과 현장간 논의가 원활하지 않았던 것으로 보인다. 본 연구에서는 실습교육의 양축을 담당하는 실습담당교수와 현장수퍼바이저의 협력방안을 모색하는 것을 목적으로 하여 조사연구를 실시하였다. 이를 위해 첫째, 실습의 현황과 문제점을 살펴보고, 둘째, 현장실습에 대한 대학과 현장의 인식 및 상호기대를 고찰한 후 셋째, 성공적인 실습교육을 위한 대학과 현장의 협력방안을 제시하였다. 본 연구는 사회복지실습교육을 효과적으로 수행하기위해 대학과 현장간의 상호이해를 도모하고 효과적인 실습프로그램을 구성하기 위한 기초자료를 제공할 수 있을 것이다.

45

This chapter focuses on collaborative work between the field education faculty and the field education supervisor. Effective field education needs collaboration between educational settings and the field. We include various suggestions to promote the collaboration of both parties based on research. This chapter includes field education contents of Korean schools, expectations of professors and supervisors, and various suggestions. Schools should offer well-prepared orientation, continuing education for supervisors, in- and out-of-class seminars on practice methods, various meetings with supervisors, agency exposure for students, and curriculum revision. Agencies should offer a well-prepared orientation, balanced supervision, promote electronic communications online, attend continuing education, and exchange professional experience with educational settings. The chapter discusses various suggestions for effective field work education in Korea.

┌┌的社工┌┌┌育机┌和┌┌┌┌的合作

本章节重点讨论社工系教育单位和实习导师的相互合作情况。两者的紧密合作是学生实习获得成功的重要因素。在研究报告的基础上，我们提出几点建议。本章节谈论到的内容涉及到韩国社工系学生的实习目标，学校教授和实习导师对学生的期望，以及针对实习的几点建议。就与实习导师合作而言，社工教育单位应该做到以下几点：全面介绍学生实习，提供在职持续进修培训，开展有关实践方法的课内课外研讨会，安排实习导师与课程教学人员会面，讨论实习机构能在多大程度上协助学生和修订实习内容。就与教育单位合作而言，实习机构也应该做到以下几点：全面介绍实习机构，提供及时的督导，使用互联网络沟通，参加持续进修培训，以及相互交流实践经验。本章节以韩国社工实习为背景，为成功的社工实习提出了几点建议。

韓国における現場教育職員と現場スーパバイザー間の
協力

本章では現場教育教員と現場スーパバイザー間の協力
的作業について焦点を置く。効果的な現場教育のため
には教育環境と現場間の協力が必要である。我々は本
章において研究を基とした両者の協力を促進させるた
めに多様な提案を行っている。本章の内容は韓国の学
校における現場教育の内容、教授やスーパバイザーの
期待感、そして多様な提案を含んでいる。学校側は十
分に準備されたオリエンテーション、現場でのスーパ
バイザーのための継続教育、実習方法についての授業
内外のセミナー、学生のスーパバイザーとの様々なミ
ーティング、関係諸機関による学生への仕事の開示、
そしてカリキュラムの見直しを提供するべきである。
関係諸機関は、十分に準備されたオリエンテーショ
ン、バランスのとれたスーパービジョン、インターネ
ットを利用したコミュニケーションの促進、継続教育
への参加、教育環境での専門的な経験の交流を提供す
べきである。本章では韓国における効果的な現場教育
のために様々な提案について議論する。

현장실습은 사회복지교육의 핵심요소이다. 이는 실천학문으로
서의 사회복지학의 특성상 실습은 이론과 실천을 통합하고, 전문
성과 현장성을 증진시킬 수 있는 기회가 되기 때문이다. Larger
& Robbins (2004)는 실습의 미션에 대해 다음과 같이 정의하였
다. '학생들은 실습을 통해 교실에서 배웠던 것을 현장에서 시험
해보고, 이론과 실천을 통합하고, 개입의 효과성을 평가하고, 사
회적, 정치적, 경제적으로 불평등한 현실을 경험하고, 문화적 민
감성과 유능성을 기르기 위해 노력하며, 윤리적 딜레마로 인해
무엇을 선택할 지를 고민하고, 전문성을 키우며, 정체성을 확립
시킨다'. 이와같이 사회복지교육에서 중요한 위치를 차지하고 있
는 실습교육은 학교에서 개설되며, 교과목의 운영과 책임은 실습
지도교수가 맡고 있지만, 학습은 현장에서 이루어지며 기관수퍼

47

바이저의 수퍼비전이 주요 학습의 도구가 되는 특성을 갖고 있다. 따라서, 성공적인 실습교육을 위해서는 대학과 현장이 실습의 목표를 공유하며, 상호협력 및 연계를 통하여 실습생의 실천수행능력을 발달시키도록 도와야 할 것이다. 이에 본 chapter에서는 첫째, 한국 사회복지 실습교육의 현황을 전반적으로 살펴보고, 둘째, 현장실습에 대한 사회복지 대학과 기관의 기대를 탐색한 후, 마지막으로 대학과 기관간 협력방안을 제시해 보았다.

I. 한국의 사회복지실습교육

전통적으로 사회복지실습은 한국 사회복지교육의 현장성과 전문성 증진을 위한 핵심교육과정이었다. 더구나 실습 교과목이 1급 사회복지사 국가시험의 필수이수과목으로 지정됨에 따라 대학에서는 실습교과목의 책임있는 운영이 더욱 중요해졌다고 할 수 있다. 한국사회복지교육협의회에서 발행하는 교과목지침서에는 사회복지현장실습 교과목의 목표, 주요내용 및 교육지침을 소개하고 있다. 또한 한국사회복지사협회에서는 현장실습지침서를 개발하여 실습교육의 기준으로 제시하였고, 계속해서 그 내용을 개정해오고 있다. 다음에 소개하는 한국 사회복지실습교육의 현황은 2010년에 수정보완된 지침을 기초로 소개하였다.

1. 현황

사회복지현장실습은 「사회복지사업법」에 따라 실습기관, 실습지도자, 실습시간이 규정되어 있으며, 이외의 사항은 대학과 기관의 상황에 따라 세부규정을 만들어 유동적으로 실시하고 있다.

1) 실습의 구조적 측면

○ 실습기관

「사회복지사업법」에서 규정하고 있는 실습기관은 사회복지사업과 관련된 법인·시설, 기관 및 단체가 해당된다. 먼저 사회복지사업과 관련된 기관 및 단체로는 사회복지사업을 목적으로 하는 사단법인·재단법인이 있으며, 공공기관으로는 지방자치단체, 중앙정부, 국회, 자원봉사센터 등이 있다. 또한 사회복지서비스를 제공하는 병원, 상담소, 학교, 교정기관, 조사연구기관, 시민사회단체 등 다양한 사회복지실천현장이 실습기관이 된다.

○ 실습지도자

실습기관에는 반드시 법적 기준에 따른 실습지도자가 있어야 한다. 실습지도자의 자격은 다음과 같으며, 아래의 기준 중 어느 하나라도 만족하면 실습지도가 가능하다.
  - 사회복지사 1급 자격증을 소지한 자로서 3년 이상 실무경험이 있는 자
  - 사회복지사 2급 자격증을 소지한 자로서 5년 이상 실무경험이 있는 자

○ 실습시간

현재 현장실습교과목은 최소 3학점을 이수해야 하며, 학교 및 학제(학부 및 대학원)에 따라 심화실습 I, II 등이 추가되어 6~9학점 체제로 이루어져있다. 하지만, 각 교과목의 실습시간은 반드시 최소 120시간 이상을 시행해야한다. 학기중 실습과 방학중 실습이 모두 가능하며, 실습시간은 다음과 같다.
  - 학기중 실습 : 주당 8시간 실습기관에 출석하여 최소 120시간 이상 실습시행
  - 방학중 실습 : 1일 8시간 주 5회 실습기관에 출석하여 최소 120시간 이상 실습시행

○ 실습지도교수, 실습생의 자격

실습지도교수와 실습생의 자격기준은 법적으로 규정되지는 않았다. 하지만 일반적으로 실습지도교수는 사회복지사 1급 자격증 소지자이어야 하며, 대학은 현장 실무경험이 풍부한 실습지도전임교수를 채용하여 가능한 한 전임교수가 실습지도를 담당하도록 권장하고 있다.
  실습생의 경우 실습전 선수과목을 이수하되, 사회복지개론, 인간행동과 사회환경, 사회복지실천론, 사회복지실천기술론, 지

역사회복지론, 사회복지정책, 사회복지윤리와 철학, 사회복지조
사, 프로그램 개발과 평가 등에서 4과목 이상 이수하도록 권장하
고 있다. 또한 실습기관의 특성에 따라 선 이수과목을 필수로 규
정하고 있는데, 예를 들어 병원 실습전 의료사회복지론을, 학교
실습전 학교사회복지론을 수강하도록 한다.

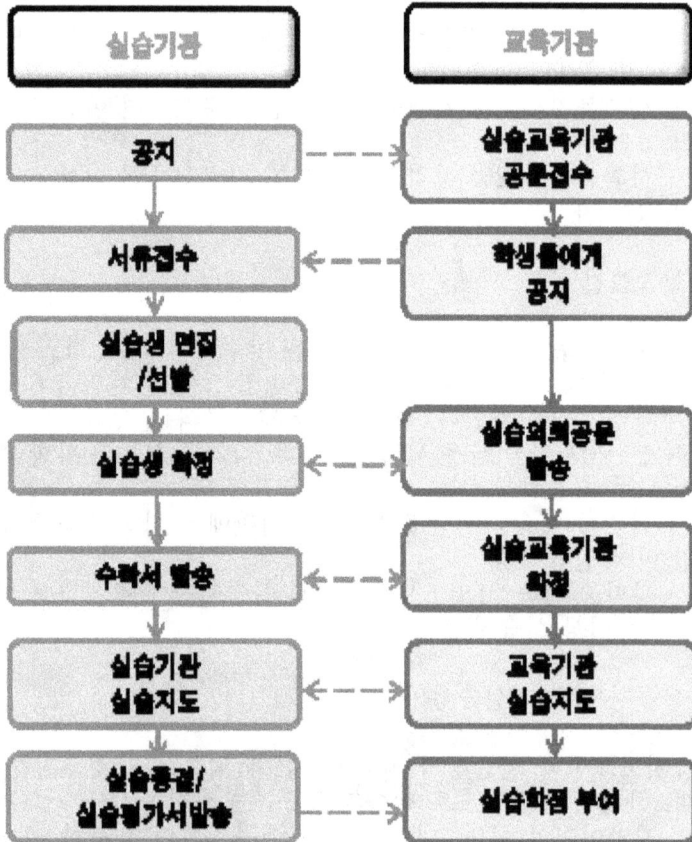

<그림 1> 실습진행절차
(한국사회복지사협회 2010)

○ 실습 진행 절차

실습기관과 교육기관은 실습의 시작에서부터 평가에 이르기까지 다음의
절차를 밟으며 상호협력하게 된다<그림 1>. 먼저 실습기관은 기관홈페이
지, 한국사회복지사협회 홈페이지 등 인터넷을 통해 실습생모집을 공지
하며, 각 대학에 공문을 발송하기도 한다. 학생들은 이를 보고 필요한 서류
를 접수하며, 기관에서는 서류전형 및 구술 면접을 통해 실습생을 선발한
다. 이후 실습활동에 대한 실습지도를 하며, 마지막으로 종결평가서를 작
성하여 대학에 보내는 것으로 실습이 종료된다.
　　한편 대학에서는 실습기관으로부터 온 공문을 학생들에게 공지하며,
실습의뢰 공문을 기관에 발송함으로써 실습을 확정한다. 현장에서 실습
이 진행되는 동안 학교에서도 실습지도가 이루어지며, 기관의 평가서를
참조하여 학점을 부여한다.

2) 실습의 내용적 측면

다음은 한국사회복지사협회(2010)에서 제안한 구체적인 실습
내용이다. 실습내용은 실습기간동안 모든 실습생이 이수할 것을
권장하는 필수공통내용과 필수선택내용이 있고, 자유선택내용
은 기관의 특성에 따라 가능한 활동을 이수하도록 구성되어있다.

<표 1> 실습내용

구분	실습내용
필수 공통 내용	1. 오리엔테이션 1) 기관소개 및 지역소개 2) 대상 집단의 이해 3) 실습생의 자세와 역할 4) 실습일정과 과제 안내 2. 행정업무 1) 훈련목적 하의 각종 기안서 2) 기관운영과 관련된 규정검토 3) 예·결산서 작성 연습

구분	실습내용
필수 선택 내용	3. 사례관리 1) 사례접수(intake) 2) 사례회의 3) 자원연결 4) 개입 5) 사후관리 4. 집단지도 1) 소집단지도 2) 대집단프로그램 5. 지역복지 및 정책개발 1) 지역사회조직 2) 정책개발 및 평가 3) 사회행동, 홍보, 옹호 등
자유 선택 내용	1. 개별상담 2. 가족상담 및 치료 3. 프로포잘 작성 4. 사회조사 5. 타기관방문 6. 지역탐방

　　수퍼비전은 실습내용이 학습으로 이어지도록 돕는 주요 학습 기제라고 할 수 있다. Powell (1993)은 수퍼비전에 대하여 '원리를 실천기술로 이전되도록 돕는 훈련 및 교육과정'으로 정의하였는데, 실습수퍼바이저는 학생을 전문직으로 사회화시키고, 전문직의 핵심지식, 기술, 가치를 전수하는 역할을 담당한다(Abram et al. 2000; 재인용). 실습이 진행되는 동안 대학과 현장은 실습수퍼비전을 제공함으로써 학생이 성공적으로 실습목표를 달성하도록 도와야 한다.

　　실습기관은 기관 소개, 실습의 의미 및 목표 수립, 실습생의 자세 및 태도, 실습일지 등 각종 기록작성 방법 등에 대한 오리엔테이션을 실시하고, 실습활동에 따라 정기적인 수퍼비전이 제공된다. 이상적인 실습지도 인원은 실습지도자 1인당 최대 5명의 실습생으로 권고하고 있다.

교육기관에서도 실습이 진행되는 동안 실습세미나 수업을 통해 학생의 실습활동에 대한 개별 및 집단 수퍼비전이 제공되어야 한다. 또한 실습기관과의 정기적인 의사소통을 통해 실습목표 수립 및 실습내용에 대한 피드백이 원활하게 이루어져 학생의 실습을 원조한다.

2. 한국 사회복지실습교육과 관련된 문제점

한국의 사회복지실천이 다양화, 전문화됨에 따라 사회복지실습 현장도 다양화되고 있으며, 실천학문으로서의 사회복지학의 특성상 실습교육의 중요성은 더욱 커지고 있다. 한국 사회복지교육체계의 발달과 함께 실습교육도 발전도 지속되고 있지만 최근 한국 대학의 사회복지학과의 급증과 매년 배출되는 사회복지사 수의 증가, 통합방법론을 중심으로 한 교과과정의 개편 등으로 실습교과목의 내실 있는 운영과 관련하여 몇 가지 문제점이 제기되고 있다.

첫째, 실습시간의 부족이다. 현재 한국의 실습시간은 학부와 석사과정 모두 최소 120시간 이상으로 규정되어 있다. 이는 학교에서 배운 지식을 실천에 적용시켜보고, 사회복지사로서 가치를 경험하며, 구체적인 실천기술을 훈련하기에는 매우 부족한 시간이다. 한국의 사회복지 교과과정의 변천에서 실습과목에 대한 비중은 통합방법론을 중심으로 임상과 정책의 절충적 모색을 추구하면서, 오히려 더 감소하는 경향을 보였으며, 이는 이론과 실천교육의 괴리를 초래하게 되었다(조흥식 1997). 사회복지현장 실습은 비단 임상과목에만 해당되는 것이 아니라 정책이나 행정과 같은 거시적 접근, 지역사회복지와 같은 중범위접근은 물론 조사와 같은 간접 실천방법 과목에도 해당되는 것이다. 특히, 현재 한국의 사회복지교육에서 학부과정의 목표가 기본적인 자질과 실력을 갖춘 일반주의(Generalist) 실천 사회복지사 양성이라고 할 때, 실습에서는 직접 실천뿐 아니라 간접 실천도 경험할 수 있어야 할 것이다. 따라서 현재 120시간의 실습시간은 시수면에서 절대적으로 부족하므로 실습시간의 확대가 필수적이다.

둘째, 실습교육의 질적인 측면의 강화가 필요하다. 현재 한국의 사회복지학부생 및 대학원생의 수는 급증하고 있는 반면, 이들을 실습교육시킬 수 있는 사회복지기관수는 상대적으로 적다. 이러한 현실에서는 자격을 갖추지 않은 사회복지사가 수퍼바이저가 되기도 하며, 이는 수퍼비전의 질적 문제를 초래하는 요인이 된다. 현장의 다양한 활동을 교육과정으로 전환시키지 않은 채 실무현장을 있는 그대로 경험하게 하는 것 자체를 실습이라고 생각하는 경향이 있어 실습이 구조적인 교육의 형태를 갖추지 못하고 있다. 따라서 비전문성의 문제는 실습교육의 비표준화, 실습수퍼바이저의 부재, 실습시킬 업무의 부족, 실습시킬 사례의 부족 등을 야기한다. 실습교육의 비전문성을 초래한데에는 대학의 책임도 있다. 4년제 대학에서는 학부제실시에 따라 전공학점의 이수학점이 축소되고 있어, 실습교육도 충분하지 않은 점이 문제가 된다(양옥경 2005).

셋째, 대학과 현장의 유기적인 관계형성의 부족이다. 그동안 실습은 이론과 실천을 양분하는 형태로 교육이 제공되어 왔다. 현장에서는 대학에서 배우는 이론이 적용가능성이 없다고 기피하고, 대학에서는 현장에서 전문성을 볼 수 없다고 비판하고 있다(양옥경 2005). Homonoff (2008)는 기관의 수퍼바이저들이 '학생들이 이론에 대한 지식이 부족하다' '현장에 대한 학교의 이해가 부족하다' 라고 언급하고 있어 실습에 대한 학생의 준비부족을 지적하였다. 이러한 비판에도 불구하고 대학과 현장에서는 실습기간동안 학생이 무엇을 해야 하는지, 어떤 실습활동이 보다 강조되어야 하는지, 수퍼비전 내용을 무엇이어야 하는지 등에 대한 체계적인 연구는 없었고, 현장에서의 학교와의 연계노력도 부족하였다.

II. 현장실습에 대한 대학과 기관의 인식

사회복지대학과 현장은 실습의 목표를 달성하기 위해 지속적으로 의사소통해야하며, 협력 및 연계가 필요하다. 하지만 주로 실습교육은 기관의 책임이 되어 버리며, 기관수퍼바이저의 수퍼비전에 전적으로 의존하는 경향을 보인다. 이러한 현실은 대학과 기관의 상호불만을 초래하여 결국 실습교육의 효과성을 저해하는 요인이 된다. 다음에는 실습지도교수와 기관수퍼바이저를 대상으로 실습지도에 대한 인식를 조사, 비교하기 위해 실시된 실증연구를 소개하였다. 연구방법으로는 특정주제 및 자극에 대한 주관적 의견이나 인식의 구조를 확인하는 데 유용한 Q방법론(Q-methodology)을 활용하였다.

조사의 대상은 서울 및 충북지역 실습지도교수(25명)와 기관수퍼바이저(30명)이다. 우선 연구자는 Fortune (1994)의 틀에 따라 핵심실습내용에 관한 진술문을 23개 선정하였다. 이 틀은 일반주의 사회복지실천에서 필요한 실습내용을 포괄적으로 담고 있는데, 전문적 발달측면, 기관 및 조직의 이해 등의 행정적 측면, 지역사회 및 정책, 서비스 전달체계 측면, 기본적 대인관계 측면, 클라이언트 체계개입을 위한 일반적 실천기술 측면 5가지 범주로 이루어져있다(예: 전문적 발달측면에는 사회복지가치 및 전문가 윤리의 내면화, 인간다양성에 대한 존중, 사회경제정의 증진, 자기인식, 전문적 성장을 위한 노력, 사회복지실천과 효과성이 포함됨). 한인영 등(2002)는 학부실습에서는 주로 일반주의 실천을 다루며, 이를 토대로 다양한 세팅과 클라이언트 집단에서 각기 다른 문제에 다양한 개입수준으로 적용할 수 있는 본질적 기술을 이해해야 하는 것을 강조한 바 있다. 따라서 Fortune의 개념이 학부실습의 내용을 잘 반영한다고 판단되었기 때문에 연구의 틀로 사용하였다.

연구자는 23개의 실습내용에 대한 진술문을 조사대상자들이 중요하다고 생각하는 정도에 따라 순위를 매기도록 하였고, 이렇게 분류된 자료를 PQ Method 2.11.을 이용하여 요인분석을 실시하였다. 그 결과 실습수퍼비전에 대한 실습지도교수의 인식유형은 3가지, 기관수퍼바이저의 인식유형은 2가지로 구분되었다. 이와같은 유형화작업은 실습지도교수와 기관수퍼바이저들이 실습을 어떻게 인식하고 있는지, 인식유형에는 차이가 있는지, 있다면 양자의 특성은 무엇인지에 대한 논의를 이끌어내는 기초자료가 될 수 있다. 다음은 주요 연구결과이다.

1. 실습지도교수와 기관수퍼바이저의 인식유형

실습지도교수는 실습수퍼비전에 대해 3가지 유형으로 인식하고 있었다. 즉 사회복지사의 태도 및 마인드 강조형, 전문지식 및 실습생의 자기이해 강조형, 다양한 체계개입에 필요한 실천기술 강조형이다. 한편, 기관수퍼바이저는 사회복지가치 및 자기이해강조형, 전문지식 및 실천기술 강조형의 2가지 인식유형으로 도출되었다.

실습지도교수 인식유형		기관수퍼바이저 인식유형
A. 사회복지사의 태도 및 마인드 강조형	VS	I. 사회복지가치 및 자기이해 강조형
B. 전문지식 및 실습생의 자기이해 강조형		II. 전문지식 및 실천기술 강조형
C. 다양한 체계개입에 필요한 실천기술 강조형		

<그림 2> 실습지도교수와 기관수퍼바이저의 실습수퍼비전 인식유형

2. 실습지도교수와 기관수퍼바이저 인식유형의 비교

이상의 결과를 바탕으로 실습지도교수와 기관수퍼바이저의 실습수퍼비전에 대한 인식의 공통점과 차이점을 살펴보면 다음과 같다.

먼저 공통점으로는 실습지도교수와 기관수퍼바이저는 실습에 대해 완전히 상반되거나 대조적으로 생각하기보다는 부분적으로 중복되는 시각을 가지고 있다는 것이다. 즉 양 측은 사회복지실천의 지식, 가치, 기술의 측면이 실습에서 공히 강조되어야 한다고 생각하였다. 또한 양 측이 실습에서 모두 강조하는 것은 직접 실천분야로서 개인, 가족, 집단에 대한 미시적인 실천을 중요하게 여겼다. 따라서, 대학과 현장에서는 직접 실천분야에 대한 수퍼비전을 강화해야 할 것이며, 무엇보다 질적인 수퍼비전을 위해 수퍼바이저의 재교육에도 관심을 가져야 할 것이다.

한편, 차이점으로는 실습지도교수가 실습수퍼비전의 내용을 세분화하여 생각하는 반면, 기관수퍼바이저는 보다 포괄적인 영역에 대한 수퍼비전을 중요하게 여겼다는 점이다. 예컨대, 실습지도교수에서 나타나는 2가지 유형이 기관수퍼바이저 1가지 유형에 모두 포함되어 있었다. 이는 수퍼바이저들이 실습에서 더 기대하는 것이 많으며, 이에 따라 더 많은 실습목표를 설정할 수 있음을 시사한다. 따라서 대학에서는 실습에 앞서 기관이 실습생에게 요구하는 것을 파악하기 위해 기관과 실습전에 의사소통

하는 기회를 마련하고, 이를 실습오리엔테이션에서 학생들에게
주지시키는 등 사전준비가 필요할 것이다.

III. 사회복지대학과 기관의 협력방안

다음에서는 한국의 실습교육 현황, 실습지도교수와 기관수퍼바
이저의 실습에 대한 기대를 살펴본 결과를 바탕으로 사회복지대
학과 실습기관간 실습교육에 대한 협력방안을 구체적으로 제시
해보았다.

1. 사회복지대학의 역할

1) 학교 실습오리엔테이션의 강화

실습오리엔테이션은 기관뿐 아니라 대학에서도 반드시 필요하
다. 학교에서 실시하는 실습오리엔테이션은 실습교과의 전반적
목표를 소개하고, 실습교과의 진행과정과 실습의 의의, 실습분야
와 기관소개, 실습에 필요한 기초지식을 전달하는 것이다(김선
희, 조휘일 2000). 선행연구에서는 학교의 준비가 많을수록(강
희자 2003), 실습에 대한 사전교육여부(오승환 2005)가 학생의
실습만족도에 영향을 미침이 나타났다. 하지만 선행연구에 의하
면 교수의 93%, 기관실무자의 96%가 오리엔테이션이 필요함에
는 동의하지만, 실제로 오리엔테이션이 그리 도움이 되지 않았다
고 보고하고 있어(박지영 외 2009) 오리엔테이션의 내용을 보완
할 필요가 있음을 알 수 있다. 대학에서 실시하는 실습오리엔테
이션에는 실습의 의의 및 목표 확인, 실습생의 태도와 자세, 실습
에 대한 학생의 기대와 불안을 다루어 주는 것이 좋다. 특히, 학
생들은 학교와는 다른 낯선 환경인 사회복지기관에서 처음으로
조직생활을 하기 때문에 불안하며 스트레스를 경험하므로, 미리
사회복지조직에 대한 이해가 필요하다. 이때 실습오리엔테이션
은 실습 2-3주 전에 실시함으로써, 학생이 실습에 대해 준비할
시간을 여유있게 주는 것이 좋다.

2) on-off linc 실습세미나 수업의 실시

실습세미나 수업에서는 실습과 관련된 고충, 어려움 등을 나누

고, 이에 대한 실습지도교수의 수퍼비전이 수업을 통해 정기적으로 제공되어 학생의 실습을 돕게 된다. 또한 다양한 기관에서 실습중인 여러 동료들의 실습경험을 수업에서 나누게 되므로, 사회복지 자원에 대한 이해의 폭이 넓어지고, 또래 수퍼비전(peer supervision)을 활용할 수 있는 이점도 있다. 이때 실습세미나 수업은 실습이 진행되는 기간에 병행하여 실시되는 것이 가장 좋은데, 실습과정중에 실습지도교수의 수퍼비전 내용이 반영되도록 하는 것이 중요하기 때문이다.

수업시간은 학기 중인 경우 주 1회 3시간을 제공하는 것으로 하고, 방학 중에는 학기의 15주를 기준으로 45시간 제공하는 것을 원칙으로 한다(한국사회복지사협회 2007). 만약 실습이 방학 중에 진행되거나 실습기관이 전국적으로 흩어져있어 수업이 어려우면 인터넷을 활용한 online 수업을 적극적으로 활용하는 것이 좋다. online site를 만들어 실습일지 및 기타 실습과제를 정기적으로 탑재하면 실습지도교수의 실시간 수퍼비전이 가능하며, 그 이외 실습에 대한 고충, 어려움, 질문사항 들에 대한 피드백을 적시에 줄 수 있는 장점이 있다. Roberts-DeGennaro et al. (2005)의 연구에서는 online support site를 활용한 실습교육에 대한 학생의 만족도 및 활용정도가 매우 높은 것으로 나타났으며, 구체적인 활용방법이 제시되어 있어 유용하다. 실습지도교수의 실습지도는 1인당 30명 이내의 학생으로 하는 것이 좋다.

3) 실습박람회 및 간담회 개최

대학에서 개최하는 정기적인 실습기관 박람회 및 실습지도자 간담회는 대학-현장간 의사소통 기회를 제공할뿐더러 대학과 현장 간 협력의 통로가 될 것이다. 실습박람회는 실습을 준비하고 있는 학생들에게 실습기관에 대한 정확한 정보를 제공할 수 있다. 학생들은 개인적으로 선배, 동료들에게 실습기관에 대한 정보를 구하므로 정확하지 않은 정보를 접할 수 있고, 또 최신의 정보수집에는 한계가 있다. 이때 학교가 기관의 참여를 유도하여 실습박람회를 개최한다면 학생들의 실습기관 선정에 상당한 도움이 될 것이다. 실습박람회에 참여한 기관은 기관소개책자, 사진, 실습프로그램 등을 소개하고, 즉석에서 Q & A 시간을 마련함으로써 실습생의 궁금한 점을 해소시켜 줄 수 있을 것이다.

실습지도자 간담회는 실습지도교수와 기관수퍼바이저가 직접 만나는 것이 이상적이며, 만남이 어려울 경우 전화, 온라인 등의 방법으로 실습기관과 긴밀한 관계를 유지하도록 한다. 간담회에서는 기관수퍼바이저와 실습생별 목표를 협의하거나, 목표 성취정도와 실습 상황을 검토하며, 실습과 관련된 문제발생을 예방하거나 중재하는 기회를 갖게 된다(한국사회복지사협회 2010).

4) 기관수퍼바이저 교육프로그램 개발 및 보상제도 마련

한국사회복지사협회(2007)는 실습지도자 자격증 취득과정을 제안한 바 있다. 먼저 이론교육(40시간)에서는 수퍼비전 이론, 실습행정, 실습지도계획서 작성법, 실습지도자의 자세와 역할, 사례관리, 프로그램 개발과 평가, 비영리조직 자원개발, 조직관리 및 행정, 재무회계규칙 등을 다룬다. 다음으로 워크샵을 통해 실습지도사례에 대한 수퍼비전(10시간)을 개별(6시간), 집단(4시간) 수퍼비전으로 나누어 교육받는다. 이상과 같은 교육프로그램은 관련 인적자원을 가지고 있는 대학에서 개발, 실시함으로써 기관수퍼바이저의 역량을 강화시키는 데 도움이 될 수 있다.

다음으로 수퍼바이저에 대한 보상제도의 도입 및 실시가 요구된다. 사실 실습지도는 바쁜 실무자들에게는 부담이 되는 업무이다. 일부 사회복지기관에서는 선임 사회복지사가 되어야 실습지도를 맡게 되므로 학생 실습지도가 전문직의 승진기회로 여겨지기도 하고, 실제로 교육 및 업무역량을 제고 할 수 있는 기회가 되기도 한다(Peleg-Oren et al. 2007). 하지만 대부분의 경우 실습지도는 어느 정도의 자기 희생이 필요한 업무로서 후학에 대한 애정 및 사회복지사 양성의 사명감이 절대적으로 필요한 일이다. 따라서 학교에서는 이에 대한 감사의 표현으로 기관수퍼바이저에 대한 다양한 보상을 제공함으로써 실습교육을 원조할 수 있다. 보상제도로는 기관수퍼바이저에게 교과목 수강권이나 대학도서관 출입증과 같은 재교육 기회를 준다거나 best supervisor를 선정하여 시상식을 하는 등 감사표현 기회를 지속적으로 가지는 것이 좋다.

2. 실습기관의 역할

1) 실습프로그램의 구축 및 수퍼비전 강화

기관에서는 실습전에 학생과 대학의 욕구에 맞는 실습프로그램을 개발하여 실습시작 전에 대학에 제시할 수 있어야 할 것이다. 실습기관수의 부족과 기관의 바쁜 업무 환경으로 인해 대학과 현장간 실습계획서의 공유 및 실습계약 등의 구조화된 절차 없이 실습이 시작된다면, 결국 실습생의 혼란을 가져올 것이고 이는 실습교육의 효과성을 저해하게 될 것이다. 예컨대, 실습지도교수와 학생의 경우 실습에서 기대하는 바가 다양한 클라이언트 체계에 대한 직접적인 실천기술의 습득인 반면, 현장수퍼바이저는 실천기술의 적용보다는 사회복지사의 가치 정립을 우선으로 하는 경우도 발생할 수 있다. 실습생을 모집할 때 실습프로그램을 함께 공지하고, 실습계약에 실습내용에 대한 부분이 포함된다면 이러한 불일치를 막을 수 있을 것이다. 또한 실습오리엔테이션을 통해서 구체적인 실습내용을 소개하는 것이 반드시 필요하다.
    수퍼비전은 실습교육의 주요 도구로서, 현재 실습교육은 수퍼비전에 의해 이루어진다고 해도 과언이 아니다. 실제로 기관 수퍼바이저는 학생을 전문직으로 사회화시키고, 전문직의 핵심 지식, 기술, 가치를 전수하는 역할을 담당하므로(Abram et al. 2000), 수퍼바이저의 수퍼비전은 사회복지교육에서 중요한 위치를 차지함은 물론 실습교과목의 성공적인 운영에 절대적임을 알 수 있다(장수미 2010). 하지만 현실적으로 많은 기관에서 수퍼바이저의 바쁜 업무로 인해 실습수퍼비전에 충분한 시간을 투여하지 못하고 이는 실습생의 실습만족도를 저하시키는 직접적인 원인이 되고 있다. 따라서, 기관에서 실습지도를 중요하게 인식하고, 실습지도를 맡은 사회복지사의 경우 업무조정을 해주는 배려도 필요할 것이다.

2) 기관수퍼바이저 재교육을 통한 자격강화

현재 실습기관의 절대적 부족으로 자격을 갖추지 않은 수퍼바이저가 실습지도를 하는 경우가 종종 발견된다. 최근 한국사회복지교육협의회에서는 실습기관인증제를 도입하여 이 문제를 해결하려는 움직임이 있어, 조만간 수퍼바이저 자격강화와 이를 위한 재교육과정이 마련될 것으로 기대된다. 사실 실습교육은 기관의 자발적인 참여를 통해 이루어지는 것으로써 기관의 교육에 대한 헌신(committment), 조직의 자원을 기꺼이 제공하고 학생의 학습을 지지하려는 노력 등이 필수이다(Bogo 2005). 하지만 사회복지현장을 둘러싼 환경의 변화는 물적, 인적 자원의 부족을 초래하여 자격을 갖춘 우수한 수퍼바이저의 확보가 쉽지 않은 것이 현실이다. 따라서, 수퍼바이저의 자격강화를 위한 재교육 프로그램이 대학과 연계되어 개발되고, 기관에서는 사회복지사들이 재교육 프로그램에 참여할 수 있도록 격려하는 것이 중요하다.

3) 대학과의 활발한 의사소통체계 구축

사회복지대학과 실습기관간의 관계는 실습교육의 발전과 강화를 가져오는 데 결정적인 요소이며, 현장수퍼바이저의 만족도는 실습지도교수와의 연계와 관련이 있는 것으로 보고되었다(Bennett & Cole 1998). 이 연구에서 기관수퍼바이저의 만족을 예측하는 요인은 실습지도교수와의 총 접촉횟수, 의뢰가능성 등이었다. 실습기간 동안 실습지도교수는 기관방문 등을 통하여 간담회를 가지며 실습의 전반적 사항을 논의하게 된다. 반대로 기관수퍼바이저도 대학에서 마련한 특강 등에서 현장경험을 나눌 수 있으며, 이를 통해 대학은 사회복지현장의 최신 이슈를 접할 수 있다. 또한 산학협력 연구프로젝트를 통해 서로의 전문경험을 나눔으로써 이론과 실천의 통합을 통한 사회복지 지식을 발전시킬 수 있다.

<참고문헌>

김선희, 조휘일(2000) 사회복지실습, 경기: 양서원.

강희자(2003). '사회복지전공학생의 실습만족도에 관한 연구'. 이화여대 석사학위논문.

박지영, 심경순, 최말옥(2009). '부산지역 사회복지 현장실습교육의 현황과 개선방안에 관한 연구', 한국사회복지교육, 10: 143-69.

양옥경(2005). '사회복지현장실습 교육모델 개발연구'. 한국사회복지교육, 1(1): 97-127.

오승환(2005). '사회복지실습만족도 결정요인에 관한 연구'. 한국사회복지교육, 1(2): 105–21.

장수미(2010). '사회복지현장실습 수퍼비전에 대한 실습지도교수의 주관적 인식유형 연구'. 한국사회복지학, 62(2): 235–55.

장수미(2011). '사회복지 실습지도교수와 현장수퍼바이저의 실습수퍼비전 내용에 대한 인식 비교'. 사회복지연구, 42(1): 373–400.

조흥식(1997). '사회복지교육제도와 현장실무의 연계' 사회복지연구, 9: 101–32.

한국사회복지사협회(2007). 현장실습지침서.

한국사회복지사협회(2010). 사회복지현장실습안내서.

한인영, 박인선, 김미옥(2002). 사회복지실습, 서울: 이화여자대학교 출반부.

Abram F, Hartung M & Wernet S (2000). The non-MSW task supervisor, MSW field instructor, and the practicum student: a triad for high quality field education. *Journal of Teaching in Social Work*, 20(1/2): 171–85.

Bennett L & Col S (1998). Social work field instructor satisfaction with faculty field liasons. *Journal of Social Work Education*, 34(3): 345–52.

Bogo M (2005). Field instruction in social work: a review of the research literature. *The Clinical Supervisor*, 24(1/2): 163–93.

Fortune A (1994). Field education. In F Reamer (Ed). *The foundations of social work knowledge* (pp121–30). NY: Columbia University Press.

Fortune A & Abramson J (1993). Predictors of satisfaction with field practicum among social work students. *Clinical Supervisor*, 11(1): 95–110.

Homonoff E (2008). The heart of social work: best practitioners rise to challenges in field instruction. *The Clinical Supervisor*, 27(2): 135–69.

Larger P & Robbins V (2004). Field education: exploring the future, expanding the vision. *Journal of Social Work Education*, 40(1): 3–11.

Peleg-Oren N, Macgowan M & Even-Zahav R (2007). Field instructors' commitment to student supervision: testing the investment model. *Journal of Social Work Education*, 26(7): 684–96.

Powell D (1993). *Clinical supervision in alcohol and drug abuse counseling: principles, models and methods*. CA: Jossey-Bass.

Roberts-DeGennaro M, Brown C, Min J & Siegel M (2005). Using an online support site to extend the learning to a graduate field practicum in the United States. *Journal of Social Work Education*, 24(3): 327–42.

Placement Experiences
From Indigenous to
International

Chapter Four

Indigenous[1] social work education and training in Australia

Sue Green and Eileen Baldry

The Australian Association of Social Work (AASW) Code of Ethics contains a statement of commitment to addressing Indigenous disadvantage and working with Indigenous people. It is imperative that social workers are provided with education and training that allow them to develop the knowledge and skills to meet this professional obligation. University social work undergraduate programs have only been grappling seriously with including Indigenous Australian social work in their core teaching since the late 1990s. This chapter reflects on developments in Indigenous social work, including emancipatory and decolonising practices, and discusses social work undergraduate and professional courses building this theory and practice. It is argued that Indigenous and non-Indigenous students alike need to decolonise their hearts and minds to be able to engage with Indigenous social work effectively.

澳洲土著社会工作学

澳洲社会工作协会的伦理法规有一段声明提供怎样去支援澳洲当地土著人士所受到不公平的民生对待。对於社会工作者来说，具备对土著文化的认知和接受相关教育

---

1 We use the terms Indigenous and Aboriginal interchangeably in this chapter to denote the Aboriginal and Torres Strait Islander peoples of Australia.

培训是保持社工专业资格的一项极具重要的条件。直到1990年尾，大学本科学位课程才开始引入针对土著人士的社会工作科目。透过这篇文章，两位作者反映了土著社会工作课程在澳洲当地的的发展。内容包括怎样将'人性解放'和'去殖民化'融入社会工作，以及讨论社工学生因此和讨论社工学生所需要运用的专业理论和实习教育学。文章指出，土著和非土著学生均需要使自己的内心及思想脱离殖民主义的定式，以便能够有效地从事土著社会工作。

オーストラリアにおける固有のソーシャルワークの教育

オーストラリア•ソーシャルワーク協会　(Australian Association of Social Work)の倫理綱領は、生まれながらの不利益や、原住民との協働への解決のための努力ついて述べている。この倫理綱領は、ソーシャルワーカーにとってこの専門的な義務を満たすための知識や技術を発展させることを可能とするような教育や研修が提供されるために不可欠であると述べている。大学のソーシャルワークの学士号プログラムは、1990年代後半以降、授業の核となる教えに地元オーストラリアのソーシャルワークを取り込み、それを厳格に守ってきた。本報告は、地元のソーシャルワークにおける発展を反映させたものである。解放と自立を許すような実践を含み、この理論の実践を組み立てる学部と専門家コースのソーシャルワークについて議論する。また、原住民に対しても原住民でない学生に対しても同様に、地元独自のソーシャルワークに効果的に従事することを可能にさせるために彼らの精神を自律させることが必要であるということを主張している。

호주 원주민관련 사회복지학 교육

호주 사회복지협회 윤리 규정은 원주민으로서 겪는 불리한 점들을 신중히 다루고 그들과 일하는데 있어 전심을 다해야 한다는 진술을 포함하고 있다. 이와 같은 전문가로서의 의무사항을 충족시키기 위해, 사회복지사는 관련 지식 및 기술 개발을 위한 훈련과 연수를 반드시 받아야 한다. 호주 원주민관련 사회복지 분야를 사회복지학 학부 프로그램의 주요 교수 과정으로 포함시키는 것에 대한 진지한 논의는 겨우 1990년대 후반에서부터야 시작되었다. 이 발표는 해방적이고 탈식민지적인 실습 방식을 설명하면서 원주민관련 사회복지학의 발전을 되새겨 볼 것이다. 그리고 이 이론과 실습을 발전시킬 수 있는 사회복지학 학부 및 전문가 과정에 대해 논의할 것이다. 원주민 학생과 원주민이 아닌 학생 모두 원주민관련 사회복지학을 효과적으로 습득하기 위해 그들의 마음과 정신에서 식민지적인 요소를 제거하는 것이 필요하다고 주장된다.

Since the British invasion of what was to become known as Australia, non-Indigenous people have impacted, usually detrimentally, upon Australian Aboriginal and Torres Strait Islanders' lives, cultures and societies. This has been a common experience for indigenous and first nation peoples around the world. Australian Aboriginal and Torres Strait Islanders have resisted in many ways including physical retaliation, hiding children, handing on knowledge orally and symbolically and using non-Indigenous education, policy and law to regain land and be afforded full citizenship and rights. Social work, even though a relatively new profession, has been and is deeply implicated in many of the social policies and practices that have affected Aboriginal and Torres Strait Islander peoples. The Australian Association of Social Workers' (AASW 2010) Code of Ethics clearly sets out its recognition of this history and its obligation to Australian Aboriginal and Torres Strait Islanders:

- Social workers acknowledge the Aboriginal and Torres Strait Islander peoples, the First Australians, whose lands, winds and waters we all now share, and pay respect to their unique values, and their continuing and enduring cultures which deepen and enrich the life of our nation and communities.
- Social workers commit to acknowledge and understand the historical and contemporary disadvantage experienced by Aboriginal and Torres Strait Islander peoples and the implication of this for social work practice.
- Social workers are responsible for ensuring that their practice is culturally competent, safe and sensitive. (p5)

These principles are applicable in any society where indigenous or first peoples are facing challenges to their human rights, culture and wellbeing. Although this chapter focuses on Indigenous Australians much of the discussion will have relevance to societies that have been colonised and where first and indigenous peoples are faring worse than non-indigenous people. Social work in these countries needs to come to grips with a range of social work theory and practice in relation to indigenous and first nations peoples. In this chapter we discuss the place of the indigenous practicum.

So far most practice in keeping with the Code of Ethics has been without the benefit of professional education grounded in Indigenous Australian social work theory and practice. This is largely because there has been very little work done in this area in Australia. This paper considers what social work students need in preparation for working with Australian Aboriginal and Torres Strait Islander peoples, what this might mean for social work practicums, and matters that can arise for students whilst undertaking a practicum. It recognises the profession's obligation to ensure all social work students and practising social workers participate in professional education that will assist them to work respectfully and in genuine partnership with Aboriginal and Torres Strait Islander peoples and communities. It also recognises at least two aspects of Indigenous social work education: that for Indigenous persons preparing to be social workers and that for non-Indigenous persons. Prior to attending placement it is important that students have some Indigenous social work knowledge. So, before focusing directly on Indigenous issues in the social work practicum, we discuss some initiatives that have been developed at the University of New South Wales (UNSW) to prepare social work students for working with Aboriginal and Torres Strait Islander peoples and communities.

INDIGENOUS SOCIAL WORK COURSES AND PRINCIPLES

Over a decade ago we began to develop Indigenous social work courses culminating in a core (compulsory) course in the UNSW social work program, 'Aboriginal People and Social Work' and an elective in the postgraduate Social Development program, 'Working with Aboriginal People'. These courses were and are founded in a number of principles and perspectives – emancipation, de-colonisation, self-determination, anti-discrimination and social justice - from both the AASW Code of Ethics (2010) and Indigenous critical analysis of past and contemporary policy and practice. These are discussed in earlier papers (Baldry & Green 2002; Green and Baldry 2008) and summarised below.

Emancipatory social work practice, which emerged from the radical turn in social work theory and practice of the late 1970s (Pease & Fook 1999, p8), rejects an approach that casts persons as problems. It engenders a critical appraisal of circumstances and structures, empowerment of and respect for those with whom social workers work and it supports social action leading to structural change (Adams et al. 2002). Smith (1999, p167) argued that in Indigenous social inquiry, emancipation from the control of non-Indigenous experts should be an aim and outcome, and that Indigenous peoples should own and control their research to that end. Similarly Indigenous social work practice should aim for such emancipation.

Decolonisation is a process of recognition of past and present cultural, community and spiritual strengths of and by Indigenous Australians independent from, and in spite of, the colonial oppression they have suffered. It is also the process of inner change from the colonised mindset viewing Aboriginal peoples as irrelevant to the colonising project and therefore expendable, or as inferior and in need of saving. This process is an emancipatory or empowering one and one

71

that is building Indigenous Australians' capacity to draw strength from social and cultural knowledge and to determine a path and place in 21st century Australia as self-determining peoples (Smith 1999; Watson 1994).

Decolonising of both Indigenous and non-Indigenous social workers and other professionals, is a prerequisite and an ongoing necessity to create a respectful framework for working together. It also results in an appreciation, a valuing of and a respect for Aboriginal ways of knowing. The linking of Aboriginal knowledge with Western social work theory and practice is essential to the development of Indigenous social work practice (Bennett et al. 2011, pp30–31). The principle of self-determination has particular import in Indigenous Australians' lives and communities as the ongoing legacies of colonisation have forcibly suppressed Indigenous Australians' freedom as self-determining peoples. This principle recognises that Australian Indigenous peoples have the right to reclaim this freedom and to participate fully in decisions about how they develop their personal, social and cultural lives and their communities (AASW 2010; Watson 1994).

Anti-discrimination fosters an approach to social work practice, which seeks to reduce, undermine or eliminate discrimination and oppression (Thompson 1997). This is crucial in Indigenous social work as Australian society in general and human services in particular display racist attitudes and practices towards Indigenous Australians (Baldry et al. 2006). Gilbert's (1993) call is as relevant in the twenty-first century as it was when made almost twenty years ago:

> [N]on-Indigenous Australians [must] recognise the racism inherent in society and address the disadvantage [faced by Indigenous people] that is reflected in social, economic and cultural poverty. (p45)

Social justice is a core social work philosophy but, in a first peoples, and in particular, an Indigenous Australian context, requires that indigenous and first nations peoples should not only be entitled to the same rights and services as other citizens but should also be afforded particular support and resources to overcome the theft of land, language and children as well as the historically gross inequitable distribution of and unfair access to such services and benefits (AASW 2010; Commonwealth of Australia 1992).

These principles, that are central to an emerging Indigenous social work theory in Australia and elsewhere, such as in New Zealand, USA and Canada (Connolly 2001; National Association of Social Workers 2009; Sinclair 2004; Weaver 1999), informed and continue to inform the development of the core Indigenous social work course mentioned earlier. The course is further directed by a number of intentions that are logical outcomes of these principles. These are:

1. To bring non-Indigenous students face-to-face with the effects of Australia's colonial past upon Indigenous Australians so that they understand the contemporary context and to support Indigenous students' unique and valued place as future social workers. But it is also to affirm the possibilities for positive and fruitful collaborations.

2. To provide an experience of Indigenous culture, communication and ways of living in community. As Weaver (1999, p221) notes it is impossible to work positively with others if there is no understanding of culture, tradition and belief systems.

3. To model how Indigenous and non-Indigenous can work together for their mutual benefit.

4. To incorporate Indigenous methods of teaching and learning, especially the use of the self (Bennett & Zubrzycki 2003, p66), the use of narrative and symbol and of direct experience.

The core course, 'Aboriginal People and Social Work', occurs in the second session of the second year of the social work degree and before the students undertake their first practicum in year three. This course sequencing was designed to ensure that students have essential and basic preparation to work alongside Aboriginal people and communities, before commencing their practicum. Although very few students will have the opportunity to work directly with Aboriginal people and communities, many will have contact with Aboriginal clients during their practicum. These undergraduate and postgraduate Indigenous social work courses work towards an integrated Indigenous tertiary social work education offering that attempts to open up Indigenous social work to students and equip them to meet social work professional obligations as set out in the Australian Association of Social Workers' Code of Ethics. Applying social work learning has always been central to the social work student experience and we have worked towards this education aspect of Indigenous social work by providing a social work practicum experience within the Indigenous unit (Nura Gili) at UNSW. These students have been supervised by an Aboriginal social worker. We reflect on these practicum experiences below.

INDIGENOUS SOCIAL WORK PRACTICUM

Fourteen social work students (both from UNSW and other universities, half of who had not done the core Aboriginal social work course), over ten years have undertaken a practicum at Nura Gili. The major task in the practicum has been to work in programs that the Indigenous Unit runs, such as: the Indigenous Women's Academic Mentoring Program for Indigenous Female Students undertaking an undergraduate degree aiming to foster these young women into postgraduate degrees and academic careers; the Indigenous Winter School for Indigenous High School students aiming to increase Indigenous high school completion and subsequent enrolment in a university degree; and Walama Mura, a student volunteer program working in an Indigenous community. The practica, as well as working directly with Aboriginal students in the programs, required the practicum students to keep a self-reflective diary, in which they recorded their experiences, reactions, thoughts and feelings. They were required to analyse their diary notes critically and discuss them with their supervisor and their mentor if they had one (use of mentors is discussed later). They were also required to read specific social work theory and identify the strengths and weakness of the theory in terms of working with Aboriginal people, and read articles on working with Aboriginal people, consider the strengths and weakness of the approaches and how they could incorporate helpful aspects into their own practice.

These practica have been undertaken by both Aboriginal (6) and non-Aboriginal students (8). A range of issues regarding social work students' preparation for working with Indigenous Australian peoples have arisen and we consider these here.

All students on practicum at Nura Gili shared common learning experiences such as those mentioned above as well as the role of social work (both historically and contemporaneously) with Indigenous Australian peoples and communities, working alongside Aboriginal colleagues, the needs of Aboriginal students, and examining how their own cultural background might impact upon their work with Aboriginal clients. There were, though, some marked differences between Indigenous and non-Indigenous students and amongst Indigenous students. Many of these experiences will have parallels for indigenous and non-indigenous students internationally.

ABORIGINAL STUDENTS

The Aboriginal students can be divided into two groups: those who had grown up knowing of their Aboriginality and culture and having strong connections with Aboriginal communities, and those who grew up with very little or no experience of Aboriginal communities. Some of these latter students had not known of their Aboriginality while growing up. The non-Indigenous students can also be divided into two groups: those students who already had either a relationship with Aboriginal peoples or experience with Aboriginal peoples and communities and those students who said that they had no previous experience with Aboriginal peoples and communities. The majority of the students, who undertook their practicum with the Aboriginal unit at UNSW, had elected (and in some cases actively sought) to do their placement with the unit. Five of the six Aboriginal students and six of the eight non-Indigenous students had elected to do their practicum with the unit. For the small number of non-Indigenous students who had not chosen this placement, only one expressed a desire to have a placement elsewhere and eventually left for a different practicum.

In general, the practicum experience for the students, staff and the client group was positive, with many of the students staying in contact with staff and visiting the centre for social events for years after they graduated. There were, though, challenges the social work students faced that they may not have faced had they not been placed within an Aboriginal unit. As is often the case in a practicum, having to deal with difficult situations and value conflict produced some of the most effective learning processes for the students and these are discussed below.

Identity

Identity, for groups who have been dispossessed, is a fundamental concern the world over. All those in the second group of Aboriginal students, those who had not grown up with a strong sense of their Aboriginality, were confronted with issues to do with their identity. These included students who had recently found out that they were Aboriginal as well as those who had elected to do their practicum within an Aboriginal organisation to develop their understanding of their Aboriginality and make connections with other Aboriginal people. Complicated issues arose for these students.

There was a question about whether they could even consider themselves Aboriginal, not having grown up within Aboriginal communities, not knowing Aboriginal culture and not having directly experienced discrimination as an Aboriginal person. As Bennett et al. (2011, pp26–27) point out, Aboriginal social workers benefit greatly from being able to link to their country and family of origin. The role of the supervisor in these situations was to sit down and explore with the student why they might not have known about their Aboriginality. This meant that the supervisor and the student needed to explore the history of Australia, how it was colonised and the policies that impacted upon Aboriginal peoples' lives such as the removal of Aboriginal children from their families and the impact and continuity of these policies into 21st century Australia. These discussions allowed the student to consider the many different strategies that Aboriginal people used to avoid having their children removed such as denying their Aboriginality and moving from place to place to avoid the reach of the Aborigines' Protection Board (the government agency that removed

Aboriginal children from their families). Exploring the variety of ways of splitting Aboriginal families and stealing or removing children and other family members, including contemporary Indigenous over-incarceration and child removal practices, gave these students a current perspective on their own experiences. Students then understood why, in many cases, the stolen individual and their children did not know they were Aboriginal. This afforded a perfect opportunity to highlight how individual personal experiences were linked to the political, in this case the linking of their own experience to previous and current government policies regarding Aboriginal people. Most of the students experienced feelings such as loss, sadness and anger in regard to what their families might have experienced but also what they themselves had been denied. Furthermore, it gave this group of students a sense of having a right to call themselves Aboriginal. For the first time they experienced being Aboriginal and they developed a connection with other Aboriginal people.

In working with this group of students, a supervisor would need to have an understanding of Australian history and how past policies and practices have resulted in people having an Aboriginal background but not knowing that. Supervisors need to work with the student to address such a life changing experience. This may include assisting them to link their family history (and thus their recent ancestors) to the racist policies and practices of the past. Separation and disinheritance are ubiquitous experiences for Indigenous Australians, as they are for many first nations and indigenous peoples across the region, and the implications are extensive. The denial of Aboriginality has an intergenerational effect on many Australians. The discovery of Aboriginality for current and future generations of Australians and the trauma arising from this discovery has the potential to become one of the largest areas of trauma work Australian social workers may face. The discovery that your family was subjected to genocidal policies and practices and that you have been lied to about who you are, is a traumatic experience for most. Dealing with identity and the task of finding one's community and family are not resourced adequately. Supervisors with students who are dealing with such identity and transgenerational trauma should direct them to an appropriate counsellor whilst providing a supportive environment.

Ethics of working with family and community

Aboriginal students faced the ethical dilemma of working with a client with whom they had family and community relationships. Due to the nature and the small size of Aboriginal communities in Australia, it is almost inevitable that Aboriginal social workers will work with Aboriginal people and communities with whom they have some sort of relationship and/or cultural obligation. Tom Calma, an Australian Aboriginal social worker and previous Aboriginal and Torres Strait Islander Social Justice Commissioner at the Australian Human Rights Commission, highlighted this point when he said:

> Social work is a demanding job for anyone and requires personal resources to help people in great need. I'd argue that for Indigenous social workers it is especially hard. Because we often work in our own communities, with our own families, it is a 24 hour job where you are always unofficially on call. This can be exhausting and also creates its own challenges when a 'tough call' needs to be made because it can be hard to separate the personal from the professional. (Calma 2008)

As Calma points out, many Indigenous social workers work within their own communities, and have clients with whom they have a family or community relationship. In order to begin to address this dilemma, the Indigenous students on placement at Nura Gili were asked to consider what the most appropriate way to deal with this issue was. Most students said that they should not work with their relative and that the person should be referred to another worker. In the setting of the practicum it was always possible for this to occur. However, students were asked to consider how to deal with this matter when it was not possible to refer the client to another worker or agency. Students considered matters such as confidentiality, conflict of interest and the fact that Indigenous clients frequently had little access to culturally competent and culturally safe services. All students recognised that they needed professional supervision in that circumstance so understood how important it would be, in their future practice, to establish such a professional relationship.

However, it was difficult for students to consider how they would say no to family and community or how they could work within the boundaries of the workplace and within work hours when community members, some of them senior people, expected them to be available all the time. This is a problem for almost all Indigenous social workers, not just students, because they have high obligations to their families and communities, they are in such demand and the need is so great. This matter deserves greater discussion amongst Indigenous social workers and the social work community in general but is not something we have the space to consider further in this chapter.

Identifying with trauma

Some Aboriginal social work students on practicum found it difficult to separate the personal from the professional when confronted with the trauma being experienced by their clients. In some instances this brought to the fore their own personal experiences, such as being a member of the stolen generation, and their experiences of abuse and racism.

Aboriginal students had to deal with the issues and crises that their communities and families were facing during the period of their practicum and whilst this could and indeed did affect non-Indigenous students, it occurred at a much higher rate for Aboriginal students. As is the case with many indigenous and first nations peoples across the world, Aboriginal Australians have poorer health and in general more complex health issues than the general population. This aspect of being Aboriginal impacts on Aboriginal students' ability to undertake and complete their practicum. Health issues facing their families will often mean that students will be required to look after family members, sometimes having to travel to home communities away from the location of their practicum. Given the lower life expectancy, Aboriginal students in general experience a higher rate of familial and community deaths than non-Aboriginal students, requiring their attendance at cultural matters, sometimes for many weeks.

Aboriginal students experience much higher rates of social problems and acute crises than the non-Indigenous student population. These include legal matters, child protection issues, housing and homelessness and abuse. In many instances, whilst the student might not be facing the crisis, a close family member may be, but the impact for the student is likely to be the same as if she or he was facing it personally, such are the obligations and responsibilities to their family and community. Furthermore once an Aboriginal student commences their tertiary education, particularly in the helping professions, the expectations of the student and their own feelings of obligation to provide assistance to others, increase dramatically. In instances where this occurred, students were strongly encouraged to attend appropriate services, such as family reconnection, legal and counselling services. We have found that it is not appropriate for the practicum supervisor to provide anything other than general support in this context. If the supervisor does take on such a trauma counselling role, it compromises the supervisor's capacity to address performance issues and act effectively as a social work educator.

Non-Aboriginal students

Whist non-Indigenous students experienced some of the issues that Aboriginal students faced including issues of identity (as migrants and in one case as a refugee) they did face some different challenges. Two of the non-Indigenous students found the lack of resources such as having to share a desk, phones and computers, office space with other staff and the common room with the client group (Indigenous Australian students) very difficult. They struggled to understand that this was an issue for services (and not just Aboriginal services) and that it was an excellent opportunity to enhance their experience and learning of what it is like for people from disadvantaged communities and for those people who work with communities facing extreme poverty and alienation. In fact one student left the placement at the unit stating that it was their right as a social work student to be provided with the sole use of a desk, phone, computer and to have an office that if shared, was only shared with other students. Despite much discussion about the reality of many Aboriginal and Torres Strait Islander organisations and many community organisations being similarly under-resourced, the student moved to another placement.

Being in a minority

Non-Indigenous students from Anglo-Australian backgrounds faced being in a minority group, most for the first time in their lives. Over two-thirds of the Nura Gili staff members were and are Aboriginal or Torres Strait Islander persons as are all of the clients. The majority of students on practicum were willing to explore and to reflect upon what it meant for them at both the personal and the professional level to be in a minority. In some cases though, it was necessary to provide them with a non-Indigenous staff member as a mentor. It was important for the student to have someone with whom they could speak about their feelings and experiences of working within an Aboriginal organisation and being a minority. Having a non-Indigenous staff member act as a mentor meant that the non-Indigenous student could explore some of the issues they were experiencing without the fear that they might offend an Aboriginal person. It was less threatening for the student to have someone, who was not an Aboriginal person, explore with them whether their feelings were in fact racist or had a racist basis, (discussed further below). The majority of non-Indigenous students explored their whiteness – this was the first time many had become aware of the concept – by considering what Bennett et al. (2011, p25) describe as the privileges of white cultural identity. Some students used the opportunity to consider how belonging to the dominant group in society gave them certain privileges and power and to consider how this would impact on their role as a social worker. Some struggled so much with this shift that the focus was on how to deal with the problem of being in a minority in the unit, rather than their future social worker role. This did though give them tools and strategies to begin to address such feelings in the future.

Racism

A central concern was racism. Some students had racist attitudes that had prevailed despite having already completed at least two years at university and for the majority of UNSW students, despite having completed the core Aboriginal social work course. For most, these racist attitudes came as a shock. They had not realised that they held them or that the views were, in fact, racist. Whilst none of the students demonstrated overt racist attitudes, many had formed an idea that the problems facing Aboriginal people were due to deficits that Aboriginal people held; that Aboriginal people needed to get over the past; and that the problems would be resolved if only Aboriginal people would assimilate into the wider society. This position, that indigenous people and their behaviour are the problem, is evident on many levels in Australian society, as well as in other colonial societies, and can be clearly seen in government policies both historically and currently. Policies have continuously focused on forcing Aboriginal people, rather than the structural inequities that exist within Australian society, to change (Baldry & Green 2002).

Some non-Indigenous students appeared to need Aboriginal people to affirm them and by doing so confirm they were not racist. This need could and indeed did, hinder the development of relationships between the social work student and staff within the unit as well as with the client group because it inappropriately focused on the social work student's need rather than on the needs of the clients. This was made more challenging by the fact that their supervisor (a social worker) was an Aboriginal person and these students sought this affirmation from her. In all but one case, the students were able to accept this as an important opportunity to work through their hitherto unrecognised racist attitudes and thinking. This challenge was also evident for some students during the Aboriginal social work courses mentioned earlier.

FRAMEWORK FOR PREPARING TO WORK WITH INDIGENOUS PEOPLE

One need these experiences highlight is that of preparation for social work students to engage with Indigenous social work approaches prior to their first practicum, a need we tried to address with the core Indigenous course. We did see a difference between those students on practicum at Nura Gili, who had done the core course and those who had not. Those who had completed it understood at least some of the principles of Indigenous social work we outlined early in this chapter and had a foundation in the history of Indigenous dispossession. They were, for example, less likely to 'blame' Aboriginal peoples for Aboriginal peoples' 'problems' than students who had not completed the course. The practicum we are discussing here was one based in an Indigenous unit with the majority of staff and all the clients being Aboriginal so the learning and challenges arose directly and immediately out of Indigenous Australians' historical and contemporary experiences.

Of course it is not realistic that even a small fraction of social work students will have the opportunity to undertake one of their practica in an Aboriginal organisation or community, or have an Aboriginal social worker as a supervisor or advisor. It is though essential to prepare students to work with Aboriginal people regardless of where they undertake their practicum or their future practice. Neither is it realistic to expect that students will have access to an Aboriginal social work supervisor or advisor. However when students undertake a practicum within an Indigenous organisation or a service for Indigenous people, the practicum and the supervisor should be prepared to address the sorts of issues we have raised in this paper.

The Indigenous social work practicum experiences discussed and analysed above suggest that a core social work course, such as 'Aboriginal People and Social Work', is an essential but not sufficient preparation for Indigenous and non-Indigenous social work students alike to work with Aboriginal Australians. The course may equip students with some fundamentals like decolonisation, anti-oppressive, anti-discriminatory and emancipatory principles, respect for Indigenous knowledge and effects of colonisation, but these need to be put to the test. The numerous challenges specific to social work in first nations, and in this particular case, Indigenous Australian contexts, that emerged for the students on practicum required deep reflection, mature development, determined change, skilled supervision and an array of other support services. Supervision that inspires students to grapple with emerging Indigenous social work challenges is vital to this indigenisation of practicum. Social work supervisors, Indigenous and non-Indigenous, may need professional development to assist them to do this.

Our experience, as explored earlier, suggests that a framework for preparation for Indigenous social work practice requires the integration of academic and field education curricula. These bring together for social work students, the theory and practice of Indigenous social work and include:

- A core Indigenous social work course to provide a grounding in Indigenous social work.
- During both the course and the practicum:
    - Self-reflection exercises exploring students' own relationships to and with Indigenous people and communities. These reflections should be undertaken by both Indigenous and non-Indigenous students.
    - An exploration of how mainstream social work values and principles intersect and interact with Indigenous social work practice.
    - The fostering of an appreciation and respect for Indigenous knowledge systems.
- Culturally aware supervision.
- The availability of appropriate support outside the practicum, for Indigenous and non-Indigenous students facing difficult questions about Indigenous matters raised in the practicum.

THE FUTURE FOR INDIGENOUS SOCIAL WORK PRACTICE

Wilson (1995) suggested at the end of last century, that the social work profession needed to learn from the fact that many Indigenous Australians 'regard social workers and other helping professionals with, at best, deep suspicion and mistrust and, at worst, contempt' (p10). He concluded that the social work profession can, 'in *coalition* with Aboriginal people, play a useful part in assisting Indigenous people to gain access to the resources and life chances that all other Australians take for granted' (p14). We would take his suggestion further. Energetic attention to social work students' preparation for practice working with and alongside Indigenous Australians will provide a good foundation for ongoing professional development and for the indigenisation of the social work profession. More social work programs, including the practicum, encompassing Indigenous social work approaches, will assist to build better social work practice. Understanding of and empathy and respect for first nations and indigenous communities and understanding of the powerful trans-generational effects government and non-government policies and practices have had and still have upon them, are being considered increasingly as core learning goals in Australian and other colonial nations' social work degrees. These goals must be extended to social work practica for this learning to begin to take root as practice. The courses, and in particular the development of practica reflecting Indigenous social work practice discussed here, are but small steps towards this.

REFERENCES

AASW (2010). *AASW Code of Ethics*. Kingston, NSW: Australian Association of Social Workers [Online]. Available: www.aasw.asn.au/publications/ethics-and-standards [Accessed 13 May 2011].

Adams R, Dominelli L & Payne M (Eds) (2002). *Critical practice in social work*. Hampshire: Palgrave Macmillan.

Baldry E & Green S (2002). Indigenous welfare in Australia. *Journal of Societal & Social Policy*, 1(1): 1–14.

Baldry E, Green S & Thorpe K (2006). Urban Australian Aboriginal peoples' experiences of human services. *International Social Work*, 49(3): 364–76, doi: 10.1177/0020872806063410.

Bennett B & Zubrzycki J (2003). Hearing the stories of Australian Aboriginal and Torres Strait Islander social workers: challenging and education the system. *Australian Social Work*, 56(1): 61–70, doi: 10.1046/j.0312-407X.2003.00054.x.

Bennett B, Zubrzycki J & Bacon V (2011). What do we know? The experiences of social workers working alongside Aboriginal people. *Australian Social Work*, 64(1): 20–37, doi: 10.1080/0312407X.2010.511677.

Calma T (2008). The role of social workers as human rights workers with Indigenous people and communities. [Online]. Available: www.hreoc.gov.au/about/media/speeches/social_justice/2008/20080212_socialwork.html [Accessed 13 May 2011].

Commonwealth of Australia (1992). *Aboriginal deaths in custody: overview of the response by governments to the Royal Commission.* Canberra, ACT: Australian Government Publishing Service.

Connolly M (Ed) (2001). *New Zealand social work: contexts and practice.* Oxford: Oxford University Press.

Gilbert S (2001). Social work with Indigenous Australians. In M Alston & J McKinnon (Eds). *Social work: fields of practice* (pp62–72). Oxford: Oxford University Press.

Gilbert S (1993). The effects of colonisation on Aboriginal families: issues and strategies for child welfare policies. In J Mason (Ed). *Child welfare policy: critical Australian perspectives* (pp37–50). Sydney, NSW: Hale & Iremonger.

Green S & Baldry E (2008). Building an Australian Indigenous social work. *Australian Social Work,* 61(4): 389–402, doi: 10.1080/03124070802430718.

National Association of Social Workers (2009). Code of Ethics of the National Association of Social Workers. [Online]. Available: www.socialworkers.org/pubs/code/code.asp [Accessed 13 May 2011].

Nicoll F (2004). Are you calling me a racist?: Teaching critical whiteness theory in indigenous sovereignty. borderlands e-journal, 2. [Online]. Available: www.borderlands.net.au/vol3no2_2004/nicoll_teaching.htm [Accessed 13 May 2011].

Nipperess J (1998). *Indigenous Australian content in BSW degrees.* Sydney: School of Social Work, University of New South Wales.

Payne M, Adams R & Dominelli L (2002). On being critical in social work. In R Adams, L. Dominelli & M Payne (Eds). *Critical practice in social work* (pp1–12). Basingstoke, UK: Palgrave.

Pease B & Fook J (1999). Postmodern theory and emancipatory social work. In B Pease & J Fook (Eds). *Transforming social work practice* (pp1–24). St Leonards: Allen & Unwin.

Saskatchewan Indian (1973). College Trains Social Workers. Saskatchewan Indian, 3(12): 9. [Online]. Available: www.sicc.sk.ca/saskindian/a73dec09.htm [Accessed 13 May 2011].

Sinclair R (2004). Aboriginal social work education in Canada: decolonizing pedagogy for the seventh generation. *First Peoples Child and Family Review*, 1(1): 49–61.

Smith LT (1999). *Decolonizing methodologies: research and indigenous peoples*. New York: Zed Books.

Thompson N (1997). *Anti-discriminatory practice*. (2nd edn). Basingstoke, UK: Macmillan.

Watson L (1994). Developing women's services along indigenous lines. In W Weeks. *Women working together: lessons from feminist women's services* (pp91–102). Melbourne, VIC: Longman Cheshire.

Weaver HN (1999). Indigenous people and the social work profession: defining culturally competent services. *Social Work*, 44(3): 217–25.

Wilson J (2002). Social work practice and Indigenous Australians–notes from a remote region. In PA Swain (Ed). *In the shadow of the law: the legal context of social work practice* (pp7–15). 2nd edn. Leichhardt: Federation Press.

CHAPTER FIVE

INTERNATIONAL STUDENT PLACEMENTS: WORKING WITH THE CHALLENGES AND OPPORTUNITIES

Deborah West and Dan Baschiera

Charles Darwin University (CDU), Darwin, Australia, offers a Bachelor of Social Work and a Bachelor of Humanitarian Studies. The two are closely linked with a clear focus on cultural competence and social justice within a humanitarian paradigm. Both provide the opportunity for students to undertake placements overseas. The Bachelor of Humanitarian Studies in particular, has created unique opportunities for student placements in a variety of environments, many of which have limited infrastructure and can change rapidly in terms of political stability. These placements offer fabulous learning environments but also create some challenges and risks for students and the University. This chapter explores both the challenges and opportunities of organising, administering and undertaking international placements from the perspectives of students, supervisors/agencies and academic staff. It provides an overview of the guiding philosophy, the elements that have been embedded within the program and the processes put in place to address student safety and security.

社会工作学生在海外实习的挑战和机遇

澳洲查理达尔文大学开设了社会工作学士学位和人道主义学士学位。在人道主义的範畴上，这两个学位具有共

89

同的焦点：跨文化交流的能力和社会公义感。两个学位
课程都给学生提供了海外实习的机会。特别是人道主义
学士课程塑造了特别多的机会给学生在不同环境下进行
实习。这些实习环境包括基础设施不完善和政治不稳定
的国家。

对于实习学生和大学来说，海外实习创造了各种宝贵的
学习机会，但与此同时，也产生一系列的挑战和风险。
这篇文章从学生，实习机构/实习机构导师和大学讲师的
角度去探索海外社工实习在组织，管理，以及在实际操
作中遇到的机会和挑战。本文将提出一个海外实习的指
导方法和讨论有关海外实习的各个要点。与此同时，本
文也会将讨论怎样确保学生在海外实习过程中的人身安
全。

学生のために実施される国際実習

チャールズダーウィン大学ではソーシャルワークおよ
び人道主義学の学士号を授与している。この２つの学
士号は、人道主義学の理論的枠組の中でカルチャルコ
ンピテンスや社会正義に明確な焦点が置かれたものと
して密接に関わり合っている。両学士号は学生に海外
での実習の機会を提供している。特に人道主義学の学
士号は、多くの場合経済基盤に制約があり、また政治
的安定性という意味において急速に変動するような多
様な環境の中で学生の実習のためのユニークな機会を
生み出している。

これらの実習は驚くべき学習環境を提供するだけでは
なく、同時に一方で学生や大学側にいくつかの困難や
危険を生み出すこともある。本章では学生、スーパバ
イザーあるいはスーパバイズ機関また教育機関側のス
タッフのそれぞれの視点から組織化、管理、さらには
国際実習を実施することの困難性と、その機会を創出
していくことの両方について検討している。それは、

ガイドとなる方針を概観できるものを提供しており、その構成要素は、学生の安全と安心について取り組むために配置されているプログラムとプロセス内に組み込まれている。

해외에서의 학생 현장 실습 교육: 도전과 기회들

Charles Darwin University 는 사회복지학 및 인도주의학 학사 과정을 제공하고 있다. 이 두 과정은 인도주의적 인식 체계 안에서, 문화적 측면에서의 적합성과 사회 정의에 분명하게 초점을 두고 있으면서 서로 밀접하게 연관되어 있다. 또한, 학생들에게 해외에서 현장 실습을 할 수 있는 기회를 제공하고 있다. 특히, 인도주의학 학부 과정은 다양한 환경 속에서 학생 실습을 할 수 있는 독특한 기회를 주고 있는데, 많은 경우 한정된 사회 기반 시설과 정치적 안정측면에서 급속히 변할 수 있는 곳에서 이루어진다. 이러한 현장 실습은 굉장히 좋은 학습 환경을 제공하기도 하지만, 학생들과 학교측에 몇 가지 도전과 위험을 불러일으키기도 한다. 이 장에서는 해외 현장 실습을 체계화하고, 실행하며, 관리하는데 있어 어려운 점들과 기회들을 학생, 감독관/기관, 학교 당국 관점에서 살펴볼 것이다. 그리고 지도철학, 프로그램 안에 자리잡고 있는 요소들, 그리고 학생들의 안전과 보안을 다루기 위해 도입된 과정들에 대해 간략히 소개할 것이다.

Globalisation has brought with it an increasing awareness and curiosity about the world beyond our local borders. Globalisation is defined by Holmes, Hughes and Julian (2007, p454) as 'A complex set of social, economic, political and cultural processes that cut across national boundaries, increasing levels of interconnectedness such that the world is reconstituted as a single social space'. Key elements of globalisation according to Macionis and Plummer (2008) include permeable borders particularly around economic transactions, media and popular culture; global communication systems based on ICT networks and infrastructure; the development of a 'global culture' or 'global village' where urban areas look similar; increased awareness of common problems such as environmental and security issues. Other theorists add to this list a growing sense of risk and the rise of transnational corporations that operate outside of local boundaries (Bryman 2004; Cohen & Kennedy 2000; Hawkins 2006).

Globalisation translates into increased opportunities to become aware of, and gain insight into, a myriad of cultures, places, events and knowledge. Opportunity for increased cultural awareness and insight brings with it both positive and negative impacts. It can foster a greater sense of understanding and respect for various cultures, encourage travel and exploration, open up new horizons, increase empathy for the plight of others and make us critically conscious of the impact that we have on each other. However, sources such as popular media and tourism, through which we are exposed to different cultures and environments, can generate distorted views and lead to a false sense of security around our own levels of understanding and cultural awareness. This can also result in a superficial desensitisation to the impact of things such as armed conflict, natural disasters and absolute poverty.

Pervasive media coverage of humanitarian disasters and world events, whether these are environmental or political, has increased public and professional awareness about the need to prepare for disasters. While we acknowledge catastrophic disasters have occurred historically, the number of disasters and the people affected by disasters has been increasing. The United Nations International Strategy for Disaster Reduction stated in a media release on 28 January 2010 (UNISDR 2010) that 'The number of catastrophic events has more than doubled since the 1980–1989 decade'. Within the global context, these disasters are complex humanitarian emergencies often featuring a compounding series of problems, including: armed conflict and war, ethnic conflict, famine, natural disasters, human rights breaches and breaches of the political contract.

Aid agencies have started to respond to this complexity with higher levels of training being required. Increasingly those with skills in social work, psychology, and technical/logistical humanitarianism are in demand. The connection of social work to the field that is referred to as 'humanitarianism' is appropriate as social work is underpinned by the same key ethical frameworks. In fact, the IFSW (2000) states that 'Social work grew out of humanitarian and democratic ideals, and its values are based on respect for the equality, worth, and dignity of all people'. The international definition of social work as outlined below easily fits within the frame of the humanitarian field.

> The social work profession promotes social change, problem solving in human relationships and the empowerment and liberation of people to enhance well-being. Utilising theories of human behaviour and social systems, social work intervenes at the points where people interact with their environments. Principles of human rights and social justice are fundamental to social work. (IFSW 2000)

As such the humanitarian field and social work are closely linked with perhaps the context and role of the worker being the main distinguishing features.

Changes in the global context also mean that human service practitioners must understand the broader impacts of globalisation, including the North-South divide. While a somewhat antiquated definition, it has relevancy in drawing attention to concerns around economic and potentially colonial value bases. Therefore it is important that future human service practitioners are able to identify latent colonial cognitions while learning to bridge the individualism and collectivism as evidenced in North-South divisions. In the context of international placements it is an issue critical to comprehending some of the interactions between global changes and local environments. This interaction is often referred to as 'glocalisation' (Macionis & Plummer 2008) which forms a key theoretical construct for humanitarian work.

Glocalisation is a complex matter, as Hall and Hall (1990, p6) point out. They state that 'Context is the information that surrounds an event; it is inextricably bound up in the meaning of that event. The elements that combine to produce given meaning – events and contexts – are in different proportions depending on the culture'. This reminds us that how and what we consider context is also culturally bound and needs to be questioned. Therefore we need to integrate the mix of North-South issues into the professional role and function within a given agency context as a *glocal* understanding of an event, be that a crisis or a chronic issue. This type of understanding requires a variety of knowledge and skills that are underpinned by values, empathy and sensitivity.

Situations presented in times of crisis and disaster are challenging and dangerous and require a heightened set of skills in order to live and work in such threatening environments. While in the past the recruitment of aid workers was not an issue, recent indicators show shortfalls for international aid relief, donor fatigue is increasing and now combined with high attrition rates it is becoming increasingly difficult to recruit professionally trained and resilient aid workers (Hearns & Deeny 2007). The net effect is a diminishing workforce. As Hearns and Deeny (2007, p28) state:

> [T]his does not bode well for the future of aid relief work, especially in complex emergencies. NGOs and government agencies involved in disaster relief must ensure that those deciding to work in this field are well supported and relate positive experiences that will stimulate recruitment and retention.

The humanitarian field is a specialised field of practice requiring a mix of technical and logistical competencies and more traditional social work practice skills. It is here that universities can step in and provide the training and the skills that aid workers in contemporary contexts need. Developing resilience in the field requires in-depth training integrating theory and practice within a course design featuring in context and realistic learning tasks. It is our view that this type of training must include international placements. There are risks associated with international social work/humanitarian placements and these must be addressed if such excellent learning opportunities are to be maximised. In these placements students can be exposed to the rigour of absolute poverty and a learning experience often further complicated by a mix of cultural diversity that directly and intrinsically impacts upon, or even seriously challenges, the student's North-South worldview. We will talk more about working with student experiences of culture shock later in this chapter.

Overall, we believe that globalisation has increased awareness of the need for work in the humanitarian field and increased the complexity of the work. As Cleak and Wilson (2007) note, students are now more aware of the international environment and the burgeoning need for social development workers, or wish to respond to urgent humanitarian crises following wars and natural disasters. In addition they observe that the advantages of a global environment, including the technological capacity to communicate easily, have also made overseas placements a more viable option for students. For some this means a desire to work specifically in this field, while for others it sparks an interest in what might be thought of as international social work.

It is not acceptable to take advantage of such interest and opportunity without a clear theoretical, pedagogical, ethical and administrative framework to prepare students adequately. Key constructs such as social justice, globalisation, cultural competence and the ability to work in areas with reduced infrastructure form the basis of what we term the humanitarian paradigm which flavours our programs. However, such a paradigm is in its infancy, both in terms of the existing materials and our own thinking which in turn is intended to respond to and influence the emergent thinking. The paradigm is therefore intertwined with the courses in a myriad of ways and influences the research we choose to do and how we do it. Our approach to the preparation for placements and subsequent work in the sector also informs our own processes as it ameliorates risk, while influencing how we approach the teaching, the type of resources provided and, of course, the placements that our students undertake. As such this is a work in progress.

In the following sections we explore the key challenges and risks that we face and how we address them based on our own reflections and feedback from students, field supervisors and agencies. It is our intention that this exploration will provide a framework for others to think about and compare their international placement experiences. We begin this section by looking at how this paradigm is embedded in the content of the programs to provide the theoretical and pedagogical framework. We then go on to consider the key challenges and our strategies for reducing risk at critical points in the process: organising placements, in transit and on arrival, in country and returning home. In the final section we draw this together, highlighting some key themes that have emerged to discuss the lessons learned.

DEVELOPING THE PARADIGM

In the business that is higher education, all universities develop a brand identity through their marketing, strategic plans, their specialisations and subsequently the programs they offer. With Charles Darwin University's location in remote northern Australia, our programs are reflective of the needs of the region and the resources that we have available. This emphasis on working in and responding to the needs of people in areas of limited or reduced infrastructure is a core part of the challenge of human services in the Northern Territory and in many parts of the Asia-Pacific region. It links to the North-South economic development paradigm and therefore the environment that we aim to prepare students to work in. However, we also recognise that this is a specialist area and not for everyone.

As such we offer both an accredited Bachelor of Social Work (BSW) program with a humanitarian/international flavour and a more specific humanitarian and community studies program, the Bachelor of Humanitarian and Community Studies (BHCS). Both prepare students for, and offer the opportunity to undertake placements in diverse locations from remote Australia to Africa and the Asia-Pacific region as well as the more traditional local placements. As both of the programs are fully accredited through professional bodies (the BSW being accredited by the Australian Association of Social Workers and the BHCS through the Australian Institute of Welfare and Community Workers), the core skills and knowledge of social work and community studies are incorporated as it would be in any other professionally accredited program. As such, students undertake a range of units which incorporate: communication skills; models and skills for direct practice with individuals, families and groups; community work; social policy; organisational theory; ethics; research methods; and, legal issues.

However, it is our position that this curriculum alone is insufficient to send students into the diversity offered by international placements.

The additional information that is needed, a key part of our humanitarian paradigm, is a focus on social justice, globalisation, cultural competence and specific skills for working in challenging environments. These elements are included in two ways: first, there are specific units which focus on relevant theory and practical skills; and second, content within what might be considered core knowledge and skills units is flavoured with relevant material and assessment.

Examples of specific units include the requirement for all students to undertake a unit on global sociology. This gives them a theoretical grounding in the concept of globalisation and the associated North-South impacts. It challenges many of their assumptions about Western culture and provides a framework for looking at the world in a different way. Another example is a unit that is compulsory for BHCS students prior to placement and a strongly recommended elective for social work students who may want to undertake overseas or remote placements. This two week 'live in' intensive includes technical/mechanical skills, safety strategies, security knowledge and the experience of applying and extending core skills in relation to working with people in difficult environments. It provides students with a range of 'what if' and 'chaos' scenarios. It tests cognitive management in mission security, and intelligence gathering skills embedded within the assessment and practical application.

In one of the key learning activities within this unit students are assigned a 'mission' to survey and design a 15,000 displaced persons camp on a remote outstation where they are camped with only a bore hole as infrastructure. Student resiliency is tested with a 'real' situation where they have only a four-wheel drive, and a number of all-terrain vehicles (quad bikes) to accomplish the mission. They sleep outside in sleeping bags, and use a bush toilet and a bucket shower. It is a scenario as tough, if not tougher, than what they would experience on mission and in the context of their international placement. The removal of all the luxuries of home, being placed in a challenging situation and having to live and work as a group requires students to adjust and re-evaluate their priorities while applying a range of theory to strategically solve a major tactical problem.

As previously indicated, the second way the humanitarian paradigm is incorporated is within core units (e.g. group work, organisational theory, legal issues, social policy) which include a global perspective on the given topic. This requires a collaborative approach on the part of staff and a clear pedagogical framework to include content, readings, case studies and assessment which covers the content and allows choices for students in contextualising assessment to their professional focus. For example, readings from the humanitarian field (some required and some optional) are included in all units and assessment includes such things as an agency analysis of a humanitarian aid organisation.

This approach has its own challenges in terms of sourcing relevant material and including such assessment and teaching in an inclusive manner in all units. There is limited material available particularly coming from a human service framework. While ongoing review of literature is essential, the other strategy is to ensure that we, as academics, contribute to the development of this field and humanitarianism through writing and research.

Additionally, the articulation of such an approach and philosophy to students who have various foci of practice (including what might be deemed more traditional social work, international social work, remote area community work and in humanitarian aid work) is also an ongoing challenge. Student evaluations have reflected this where some want a very specific focus on their area of interest in all units (rather than choices) and others can't see the relevance of units such as social policy or research methods to the humanitarian field. While the idea of students not seeing the relevance of specific units to their overall program is not unusual, it is concerning. Our approach to reconciling this has been to do additional work in articulating the framework, providing material, seminars etc. on course structure and continuing to work as a team to reinforce the messages to students in all units.

This issue is very much related to and resolved through the integration of theory and practice and within the actual placement experience. It is often on placement where students recognise the value and application of core skills. This recognition we believe will now be driven deeper with a new online unit students will complete while on placement. This unit is designed to integrate their learning to deal with chaotic, uncertain, practical and pragmatic issues that will often confront them unpredictably on a placement that is in a totally different cultural environment to what they are accustomed. It is also an environment that often carries with it the experience of a totally new language and as such challenges the student to reflect and act on how to communicate across the language barrier.

The integration of theory and practice into a cohesive framework for practice in any given setting has always been a challenge in human service education for both the students and the educators. This is the case regardless of the field of practice a student might be interested in but perhaps becomes more challenging when trying to move beyond the more traditional borders or less emphasised fields of practice. For example, it is easier to find information on and discuss the application of theory and practice in the field of mental health, justice or child protection than anything around international social work or humanitarian aid. The challenge then is to assist the student to conceptualise, translate and integrate material into the context and role of the worker in the humanitarian field. Several approaches to dealing with this have been developed – the contextualisation of assignments, the two week remote 'live in unit' and the development of a new unit directed at integrating the material covered in the course with a student's chosen field of practice and offered online while students are undergoing placement.

Such preparation for field does of course take place in all programs to varying extents. It is the development of the humanitarian paradigm within the program that provides additional support to those students who will go into international placements. Feedback from students indicates a need to focus curricula on such a paradigm to include globalisation, de-colonisation, social justice and practical skills. However, the effectiveness of such preparation is only tested once a student embarks on the experience. At the same time there are number of more practical considerations involved from a University perspective in relation to the administrative aspects of organising and maintaining any placement. These issues are explored in the next section.

CHALLENGES AND OPPORTUNITIES IN ORGANISING PLACEMENTS

While all placements carry an element of risk, such factors are amplified in the international setting particularly when these are undertaken outside of major urban areas or within countries that are very different than the home setting. The challenge of safety in these settings pervades all elements of placement. It relates to the physical and emotional safety of the student both during and after placement as well as the duty of care to those that the student will work with and the agency more generally. In the context of humanitarian or international social work placements we see this as a constant which requires critical analysis. It is an ongoing process that combines student and agency feed back into our risk management planning and program development for every stage of the process. The following sections reflect this process of ongoing development around risk management based on feedback from students, supervisors, agencies and our staff under the headings of organising placements; student preparation for placement; in transit and on arrival; in country and returning home.

ORGANISING PLACEMENTS

Central to safety and risk management is the importance of locating appropriate placements within the international scenario. This involves research and liaison to get an effective mix of cross-cultural, relevant, and mixed projects and with humanitarian students in particular, technical and people skill exposure. Agencies available for placement are identified and assessed for suitability. This is done in liaison with the potential agency's management. The assessment includes an evaluation of the level of professional training and project work that is available (if in the case of a social work student the supervisor has to have a recognised degree with two years experience) and that the agency will provide a measure of security and protection for the student. This will often include accommodation and keep, often a home stay with a staff member, which at local costs always makes the placement cost effective for the student.

The placement coordinator will regularly monitor the Department of Foreign Affairs and Trade (DFAT) travel warnings while at the same time establishing a liaison with the student's future supervisor. Once the placement is agreed upon a specialised supervisor's handbook is emailed to the supervisor. Critically all placements also need to have suitable email capacity to ensure ongoing communication and in particular teleconferencing during official placement liaison sessions. In Tanzania, given the distance, we also support a voluntary coordinator in country who assists in monitoring student needs and safety. At this stage the countries that we provide international student placements in are Cambodia, India, Tanzania, and Thailand. We are currently assessing potential placements in Nepal, Timor L'Este, and the Philippines. The stability of the country, safety and the professionalism of in country agency staff are key criteria.

The second part explores the interests of students and how the agency might fit with their interests, knowledge and skills. Sometimes this can be challenging even for the agency supervisors as while they are open to students they often need some guidance on potential projects. This issue is reflected in this correspondence with an agency supervisor, 'Do you or he have any ideas for projects – as I think we said before we definitely welcome non medical students but it can be tricky coming up with good projects!' University field staff spend considerable time in negotiating and suggesting ideas that will fulfil the requirements of a learning placement.

Once a potential project is identified that fits with the agency and student needs, preliminary links are made between the student and the agency and planning begins. Students are warned at the beginning of the process about the country's stability and that a negative DFAT report will result in the immediate cancellation of the placement.

STUDENT PREPARATION

As outlined above the academic program is designed to provide students with a range of skills and knowledge to undertake placement. However there are also some more practical considerations such as immunisations, health management, appropriate clothing and specific information for the student about to embark on an international placement. All students are required to have appropriate immunisations and be able to effectively monitor and manage their personal health issues. They are provided with a list of items that they will need to take with them on their placement including sturdy boots, long pants, insect repellent, and money belt. In the specialist 'live in' unit students are given substantial information and training to develop situational awareness, how to protect against illness, what to avoid and look out for and to ensure critical requirements such as medicines, money and passport are all secured, and that passports and visas are up to date.

One-to-one briefing sessions are provided to all students who are going on international placements. These sessions are based on key lists of information that agencies such as Medecins Sans Frontières recommend. In this session information is again recapped about clothing, health and other issues but also incorporates current placement country requirements around personal safety and security and travel documentation is checked. Students are provided with a comprehensive field education manual which includes all such risk management information and are also insured with the University's travel and health insurance. Key messages are reinforced to ensure students understand the link between their behaviour and safety. As Medecins Sans Frontières (2003, p22) states, 'More importantly, your individual behaviour in the field will affect how well you integrate and therefore your safety … There is very little distinction between your professional and private life when you are on a mission'. This is a very important lesson which is often challenging for students. The opportunity to fully brief students on a one-to-one basis enhances learning where students working with a fully experienced staff member are made fully aware that they have to shoulder a substantial self-responsibility for risk management as it is their health and wellbeing that is on the line and that the environment they are going into is very real and unforgiving.

While we do not put students into situations of immediate crises or disaster, many of the placements they go to are in countries where there are underlying political and environmental issues and tensions. Confronting such issues is much different than going to a local area which is much more stable and culturally/linguistically familiar. This type of environment, University supervisors have noted in student reports, has sharpened their reflection and intensified the learning. While students are made fully aware of the risks involved we have to acknowledge they are in training for this profession and are likely to work in such conditions.

Students taking responsibility for pre-placement preparation is noted and appreciated by the agency supervisors. One supervisor who provided a very positive report on a student explicitly commented on this aspect saying that the student 'was well prepared as she had gathered all the useful information about the Centre from the website before coming to the Centre'.

IN TRANSIT AND ON ARRIVAL

While in transit students are required to provide updates on travel. They are required to carry a cellular telephone (mobile phone) that is fully operational and with international roaming capacity, thus are able to SMS (text) or email the coordinator at each stage and as the need arises. In turn the coordinator will also remind them of this responsibility and it is suggested that this is done while waiting in transit. On arrival at the agency the student is to provide the coordinator with an arrival email. This process is also repeated on the return journey. If a scheduled message does not come through, the coordinator then liaises with the prospective agency in order to establish contact. To date the system has worked well as students are aware that this is part of the assessment process and they generally appreciate the security of being monitored in transit.

The agency is briefed on the student's departure, expected arrival time and both the agency and coordinator have a copy of the student's itinerary.

In country

Despite the intensity of the one-to-one briefings and focused cross-cultural and community training, the complexity of humanitarian and international social work still challenges students. The need for this type of placement training is well demonstrated in the following comment from a student who did her placement with the This Life Cambodia Agency:

> So many questions; questions that I had previously not even thought about. This is my first understanding of why it is so imperative to be immersed in a culture to become culturally appropriate and safe. Things such as this and the questions that experiences generate cannot really be taught, you need to experience to understand fully.

The intensity of thinking while being in a hard placement environment is well demonstrated by this reflection from a student who recently returned from a placement with a medical agency working on the Thai-Myanmar border:

> However, there is a very real threat that malaria could resurface in resistant forms if it is not permanently eradicated in the near future. A focus on promotion and awareness of resistance and the causes of resistance is needed within the population but is a difficult one to deliver.

In the early stages of placement students often find themselves feeling a little out of depth particularly if the agency has a specialisation for which they are not trained, such as medicine. It takes a little time for students to realise that their competencies do fit albeit in a unique way and to reflect on some of the significant issues that really do impact in the humanitarian field. We see this as a truly challenging yet enhanced learning experience and well reflected in the following comments that were a few days apart by another student who also did her placement on the Thai-Myanmar border.

> In terms of ethical considerations … my curiosity means I am happy to attend (Medical) consults and learn but in consideration to the patients and their families – I have no medical knowledge to impart so is it unethical that I join in?

> Coming into the field – I feel like a fraud – under informed and under prepared. I thought today … how great it was to be researching and working on something that actually 'meant something' and wasn't just another assignment. It's scary to think that people can come here with no training and begin working in the humanitarian field. I'm sure that many are very good at what they do but I feel like there is a cross-cultural understanding that is lacking in many people. On one hand, people don't strive to understand the context of the situation they are living and working/volunteering in (social, political, economical) and on the other, people don't strive to understand the context of themselves and the situation they have come from. People come to teach English and expect that students will want to learn what they have to say – they don't think about the ramifications of their actions and then see fit to whinge about how tiring their days are. Sometimes I wonder if I would be able to handle the other people who chose to work/volunteer in this field.

Conversely what presents in pre-placement as a professional organisation can prove the opposite when tested by the student. This can be quite frustrating for both student and placement coordinator as a lot of work goes into researching the placement to try and ensure a good learning experience but given the complexities of culture, distance and differing perspectives, placements sometimes do not meet the criteria set by the University, the Australian Association of Social Work, the Australian Institute of Welfare and Community Workers [AIWCW], and the student. This was the case for one student who had previous significant international working experience and is well demonstrated by comments in her journal again over a several days:

Reminded (supervisor) about supervision session. Sent her an email saying that if supervision did not take place, my placement would be pulled. Can't believe I have to resort to this!! (Supervisor) was very quick to respond.

First supervision – ok. Think (supervisor's) idea of supervision is to tick off the learning contract objectives. Can't see (supervisor) providing constructive feedback if it's slightly negative – it's the whole saving face Philippino cultural nuance.

I have been discussing the best way to handle the lack of supervision and general lack of work within the agency – we have too much time on our hands, despite asking (supervisor) to be involved in activities. I feel I am seriously wasting my placement time.

This then brings us to the challenge of living and working in a different culture. While a lot of training is delivered in cross-cultural training, colonial imposition and the multiple divides between individualism and collectivism, it appears that with our experience actual on-the-ground integration is an intrinsic reality that a student can never be cognitively fully prepared for. This has been the case for all our students, and is demonstrated by a comment from a student in Tanzania:

The first two weeks were really overwhelming – there was so much to take in – I think I certainly experienced culture shock – I don't think you can totally avoid it no matter how well prepared you think you are and of course I've not travelled overseas in eight years and the first time to Africa I am sure it will be easier from now on!

Here a similar comment from student on placement in India:

I must admit that integrating into the community is not as easy as I thought it would be.

Followed two weeks later this further comment:

Still integrating into the community. I wonder if this is going to be a reoccurring theme and process of my field placement?

While we were aware there were going to be issues with cultural integration on an international placement the actual intensity caught us by surprise both going in and on return to Australia. As one University coordinator indicated this is an important part of our own reflective practice.

The feedback gave me some opportunity on what to add when briefing new students. There were some cultural misunderstandings; not knowing the culture of Tanzania, the tribe and the Roman Catholic religion which is another culture of its own.

Supervisors have commented that students have an initial difficulty in integrating and communicating and have identified culture shock in the students. While there are language difficulties in the first weeks the students are overwhelmed by the environment, values and difference and it takes some time to start managing the difference and to realise their competencies. An agency supervisor captured this element in his report:

[The student] felt much more comfortable after her first initial weeks in Sadhana Forest, where she was very shy and lacking in confidence with her work. I have seen her communication within the community and organisation develop and strengthen throughout her placement.

Supervisors though have been both supportive and quick to note the difference in our placement students in that they come to grips with the placement a lot quicker than other volunteers and students.

Health issues are however a key issue for students and supervisors and can undermine the placement. This affects all aspects of placement including agency supervisors. For example one placement was delayed due to health issues on the part of the agency staff as indicated in this correspondence, 'Sorry for the delay in getting back to you both Paul and I have been laid up with dengue – up and about now!!' Many of the student and agency reports are scattered with references to the impact of the environment on a student's health. As one agency supervisor commented, the student 'also needs to ensure her health is maintained. India is a very hard country to stay well all of the time!' Such challenges to health can be quite confronting for students.

Feedback from supervisors has been positive and all have requested more students from CDU. The following comments from agency supervisors indicate that the program content is very relevant and valued in the field:

> The values and practices within the culture of the Tanzanian society and some of the subcultures (tribal/nuns) are quite different. However, [the student] had respect for these differences and as a result there was a mutual respect from both sides. We had not anticipated that [the student] would be so capable, not only in getting the technical project done but in bringing in the community to support her as well. Many workers and some nuns could not speak English well, but this did not deter [the student] from communicating with them. Some workers think they also learnt English from her. I was very impressed with her attitude. Her sanitation audit report is extremely professional and we will be able to make very good use of the data in the camps, she has done an excellent job here, I hope you can send us more of your students.

It is evident that many have been pleasantly surprised with the capacity of the student for service delivery and the quality of that service delivery.

RETURNING HOME

On return to Australia students however find themselves caught in the surreal of transiting from the resource poor environments they have adapted to into the opulence of urban Australia. This 'reverse culture shock' in fact has been more distracting, has caused delays in providing assessment materials and has generated a need for the coordinator to debrief the student in full and in detail. These debriefs can and do continue into several sessions, are very helpful to the students and provide us with a fuller insight to the student experience. This in turn enables the development and research toward a pre-placement psychological inoculation for students so that they can improve their cognitive perception and in turn management. Humanitarian agencies also find this to be the case with staff returning from their international missions and provide regular debriefs as required. Interestingly the entry and return culture shock is not so intense for some students who adapt well and quickly both ways.

Certainly on return lecturers and field educators always find students reflecting on whether this work is for them. The international placements give them a real experience in the field and in this context there is significant value in this sound training and self-realisation of career path. To date all but one of our humanitarian graduates have continued and returned into the field.

Key lessons

There are a range of lessons and ongoing challenges that arise from reflection on the international placement experience from the perspective of students, supervisors, agencies and University staff. Such lessons are likely to apply to any institution that seeks to send students on a placement outside of their home country.

The most frequent issue that arises is around culture shock – both on arrival in the host country and on return to the home country. Despite building this into the programs in theoretical and practical terms it remains the most discussed issue. As outlined in the opening section, this is likely related to some extent to the impact of globalisation. Many people assume because they know something of another country or that the country is similar on the surface that they will be comfortable in the surroundings. They might also assume because they have visited as a tourist that they have a good understanding of the culture and what they will face. However, for our students, this was not their experience. Their reflection journals and debriefing sessions highlighted this as a major issue which impacted on their ability to adjust and carry out their tasks. Most students though planned strategies to deal with this after they got through their initial stages of settling in.

This suggests that there is a great need to thoroughly prepare students. Preparation must deal with the ideas, concepts and issues that arise around cross-cultural social work and humanitarian work including the vast differences that arise in thinking, models and actions from various cultural standpoints. This includes both the broader aspects of North-South divides and developmental paradigms and Eastern–Western philosophical bases. Ensuring that they understand the various ways that this takes shape is essential so that when they are confronted with differences and contradictions, they have the skills to work through them.

However, the preparation must go beyond cross-cultural work to explore the concept of safety in different cultures and the practical skills and behaviours to deal with this. What is safe to do or considered safe in one place is not in another and can have dire consequences. They must understand both the reality of this and the need to find out about and respect local customs to keep themselves safe. Practical skills for living and working in areas where the infrastructure is more limited is essential to reduce some aspects of culture shock and the direct first time exposure to and working with extreme poverty. If they are prepared and have experienced living without many of the 'normal' conveniences of their home country, they will be less confronted by these aspects of difference and can invest in understanding the less obvious but more important elements.

The match between skills and placement again becomes more critical as does a constant re-assessment of the situation at hand. The student/agency fit is an essential component of any placement but to withdraw from an international placement is more complex at all levels and puts the student, agency and University at greater risk. Ongoing monitoring of the suitability of any given placement is vital. Politically, countries can go from quite stable to unstable in the time it takes for a student to board a flight. Having clear processes and contingencies in place is essential to deal with such outcomes. There is a fine line between a challenging placement that prepares a student to work in international situations and one that is unsafe either physically or emotionally.

It is also essential that they have the support to carry out a placement. This raises issues in terms of the supervisory process and the need for ongoing support from the home institution throughout the placement. In terms of supervision, there are many issues that arise – assumptions about time, use of self, health standards, work expectations etc., differences in models of practice, even the nature of supervision itself can all vary. Vetting supervisors and ensuring that the supervisor/student fit is appropriate to meet the learning goals then becomes even more vital yet more difficult. Clear processes, planning and preparation are essential.

Students need the tools to be able to safely explore and learn about their placement setting and agency while integrating theory and practice. The integration of theory and practice was another element that the students struggled with while in country. This is related to the supervision provided but still remains the key task of the student which is more challenging on international placement. They are essentially trying to become familiar with a *glocal* practice model that is outside of their own *glocal* experience. As such it adds another layer to the integration of theory and practice. This requires additional knowledge, frameworks and skills to come to terms with the task and to begin to tackle it. Without such a framework students can become overwhelmed with the process.

CONCLUSION

The balancing act is to provide a challenging and relevant placement that prepares the graduating student to operate as a beginning practitioner in the field while providing a 'safe' learning environment. The issue here is what constitutes safe in a variety of cultural contexts and what can provide the opportunity for development without overwhelming the student. If the balance is achieved, students struggle but learn and thrive. The idea is not to eliminate the cultural, health and safety risk but rather to reduce and manage the risk to a level that is challenging but negotiable with the appropriate knowledge, skills and behaviours. The next step is to provide training that clearly identifies and covers these core elements and to place it within an appropriate framework. We have found with our students, exposure to such controlled risk does indeed produce both resilience and excellence, given the agency feedback received to date. These are two of the qualities that make them employable to the humanitarian aid sector.

Critically as in any student placement, there is an element of risk, and while in a standard urban setting the risk relates predominantly to student failure, the risk is much broader when placements are undertaken in more distant locations that are very different from their home environment. This applies equally to those students going from any country to another whether it is from Australia to Thailand or Japan to New Zealand. As such, to send students into international placement requires preparation beyond the basic social work skills that are culturally bound and in a *glocal* framework. To not provide such preparation is unethical and puts the student at risk. Critically the students are working intrinsically with a different culture and in places with the real stress and trauma of poverty. This is significantly different to being a tourist on holiday and visiting 'from a distance'. Our challenge and responsibility as educators is to minimise the risk while providing rewarding very real and relevant opportunities for learning and development.

REFERENCES

Bryman A (2004). *The Disneyization of society*. London: Sage Publishing.

Centre for Research on the Epidemiology of Disasters (CRED) (2009). *Emergency events database* (EM-DAT). [Online]. Available: www.emdat.be [Accessed 2 March 2011].

Cleak H & Wilson J (2007). *Making the most of field placement*. Melbourne, VIC: Thompson Press.

Cohen R & Kennedy P (2000). *Global sociology*. New York: New York University Press.

Corey G, Schneider CM & Callanan P (1998). *Issues and ethics in the helping professions*. 5th edn. Pacific Grove, CA: Brooks/Cole.

Hall ET & Hall MR (1990). *Understanding cultural differences: Germans, French, and Americans*. Yarmouth, ME: Intercultural Press.

Hawkins M (2006). *Global structures, local cultures.* South Melbourne, VIC: Oxford University Press.

Hearns A & Deeny P (2007). The value of support for aid workers in complex emergencies: a phenomenological study. *Disaster Management & Response,* 5(2): 28–35, doi: 10.1016/j.dmr.2007.03.003.

Holmes D, Hughes K & Julian R (2007). *Australian sociology: a changing society.* Frenchs Forest, NSW: Pearson Longman.

IFSW (2000). Definition of social work. Berne: International Federation of Social Work. [Online]. Available: www.ifsw.org/f38000138.html [Accessed 5 March 2011].

International Federation of Red Cross and Red Crescent Societies (IFRC) (2008). World disasters report 2007. Geneva: Author. [Online]. Available: www.ifrc.org/en/publications-and-reports/world-disasters-report [Accessed 9 March 2011].

Macionis J & Plummer K (2008). *Sociology: a global introduction.* London: Pearson Prentice Hall.

Medecins Sans Frontières (2003). Carnet de route MSF: practical information to read before during and after your mission. Paris: Medecins Sans Frontières.

United Nations International Strategy for Disaster Reduction Secretariat (UNISDR) (2010). Earthquakes caused the deadliest disasters in the past decade. [Press release].[Online]. Available: www.unisdr.org/archive/12470 [Accessed 13 May 2011].

CHAPTER SIX

AUSTRALIAN SOCIAL WORK STUDENTS IN VIETNAM: THE COLLISION OF CULTURAL DIFFERENCE

Peter Garrity

Social work students undertaking their field education placements are meant to further develop their skills; integrate social work practices and principles as well as cultivate an individual professional identity beyond the backdrop of social work theory and knowledge. Four students from Cairns, Australia undertook their final field education placement in Vietnam, in which the complexities of difference between Western knowledge and understandings of social work and the realities of the cultural and contextual environment contrasted markedly. This study suggests many benefits are gained by social work students undertaking culturally dissimilar field education placements; for example, developing, adapting and integrating linkages between cultural difference and social work practice and/or knowledge, integrating cultural nuances influencing and/or changing the student's own social work knowledge base and, by implication, their practice of social work, and contextualising student's own social work professional identity.

社会工作专业实习：文化差异的碰撞

社会工作专业实习有三个目的：强化学生专业技能，结合理论和实践，以及在教授社工理论和知识的过程中塑

造学生独特的个人专业风格。四位来自澳洲凯恩斯的社工系学生选择了越南作为他们最后一个实习的地点。越南的文化，社会背景与西方社会迥异，当地对社会工作和西方社工理论也有着不同的理解。本论文认为社工系学生选择与他们文化背景相异的国家作为实习地点，将会获益良多。例如，在异国实习的过程中，学生可以加强，采用和结合文化差异和社工工作实践的理论和知识。实习也有助于学生更深层次地总结出细微文化差异给社会工作所带来的影响，并用之扩大和改变自己对社会工作的认知。此外，社工系学生将会深化对社工专业身份的认识。

ソーシャルワーク現場実習：異文化間の衝突

ソーシャルワークを学ぶ学生が現場実習を実施することは、彼らの技術を発展させること、すなわち、ソーシャルワークの理論と知識の背景を超えた個人の専門家としてのアイデンティティを育成させること同様に、ソーシャルワーク実践と原則を統合することを意味している。オーストラリアのケアンズからの四人の学生は、西洋の知識とソーシャルワークや文化的、背景的な環境が顕著に対照的である現実の理解との間の違いの複雑さのあるなかで、彼らのベトナムでの最後の現場実習を実施した。本研究では文化的に異なる現場教育実習を実施したソーシャルワークを学ぶ学生が得た多くの利益について奨励します。その実習とは例えば、発達し、順応して、文化的な相違やソーシャルワーク実践、あるいは知識間の関係を結びつけること、そして文化的ニュアンスや学生の独自のソーシャルワーク知識のベースに影響を与えたり変えたりすること、あるいは彼らのソーシャルワーク実践を、そして、学生独自のソーシャルワークの専門家としてのアイデンティティを背景づけることによって結びつける実習である。

사회복지 현장 실습: 문화적 차이에 따른 충돌

사회복지를 공부하는 학생들은 현장 실습 교육을 통해 그들의 기량을 한층 더 발전시킬 수 있다. 예를 들어, 사회복지 실습과 이론적 원리들을 통합할 수 있을 뿐만 아니라, 사회복지 이론과 지식적 배경 너머로 각자가 전문가로서의 정체성을 기를 수 있다. 케언스 출신인 4명의 호주 학생들은 마지막 현장 실습 교육을 베트남에서 받았다. 그곳은 사회복지에 대한 서구적인 지식 및 이해와 이것과는 현실적으로 극명하게 대비되는 문화적, 상황적 환경 사이에서 비롯되는 차이들이 복잡하게 존재하고 있다. 이 연구는 사회복지를 공부하는 학생들이 문화적으로 다른 곳에서 시행되는 현장 실습 교육을 통해 많은 혜택을 얻을 수 있다는 것을 알려주고 있다. 예를 들어, 문화적 차이와 사회복지 실습 또는 지식간의 연계를 발전, 조정, 통합할 수 있다. 또, 학생 자신의 사회복지 지식 기반과 사회복지 실습에 영향 또는 변화를 주는 문화적으로 미묘한 차이를 융합할 수 있으며, 각자가 사회 복지 전문가로서의 정체성을 확립할 수 있다.

Social work students undertaking field education are expected to develop their professional application of social work values, principles, practices and techniques to meet the social work practice standards of the Australian Association of Social Workers (2003). In so doing, one of the important things we expect students to learn is the difference between what they know and what they don't know.

The student's own knowledge, understanding, practice and abilities are challenged by the context of field education. This can be a difficult process that requires critical self-reflection by students. Ways that this reflection can occur include self, peer and supervisor evaluations. Journals are an important way for students to reflect, and to present those reflections to an experienced social work supervisor for review, comment and discussion. The journal fixes the thoughts, feelings and understandings of the student at a moment in time. It provides an opportunity for students to record their lived experiences, and to reflect on those experiences from a distance. The student observes what is written and reflects on it. The recorded discourse creates a reflective cognitive stance which enables the reader to create meaning and understanding of the reflective experience. Journaling allows students to 'transform [their] lived experience into a textual expression of its essence in such a way that the effect of the text is at once a reflexive re-living and a reflective appropriation of something meaningful' (van Manen 1997, p36).

This chapter is written with the assistance, acknowledgement and permission of these students to utilise written journal recordings of their experiences to gain some insight, understanding and knowledge of the students' journey whilst on field placement in Vietnam. In doing so and to capture the progress made, Edmonds' (2010) framework, from her analysis of the journals of nurses who were studying internationally will serve as a model in this chapter for considering the students thoughts, feelings and experiences recorded in their journals whilst on field placement in Vietnam.

Edmonds (2010) named recognising, encountering, adapting and mastering as key features of her model, though not mutually exclusive or linear, these key features assist to map the student's journey. As students experience and interact with their contextual environment, they begin a process of critical reflection (i.e. recognising) of the actual experience (i.e. encountering), attempting to make sense of or adjust to the experience (i.e. adapting) and therefore increase their sense of personal and professional stability and security; whilst finally, gaining ascendancy and/or control, in the form of increased knowledge, for example, over the experience (i.e. mastering).

Placement beginnings

The four social work students undertaking their field education placement were, Ali, Kate, Lauren and Hannah. They were single, young, White females, resident of Australia and having the Western customs, mores, norms and values of the dominant culture within Australia.

118

These students self-selected to be considered for this placement after the University field education placement team had been approached and informed by a local experienced social worker. She was undertaking some volunteer work in Vietnam and would welcome the opportunity to supervise social work students in Vietnam. This particular social worker had previously supervised social work students locally and had contacts already in place in Vietnam. The field education team was informed the social worker had previously travelled to Vietnam and discussed with several agencies possibilities of social work students undertaking their field placement with them. It was agreed to further this matter firstly by the social worker contacting those agencies and verifying, in writing, their interest in providing a field placement opportunity for social work students. Secondly, the field education team explored the legal and ethical responsibilities of such a placement as well as gauged the interest of social work students in undertaking their second field placement of a placement in Vietnam.

Preparation to undertake this type of placement was undertaken over a period of months, whereby negotiation between various agencies in Vietnam, the social worker who would be the field supervisor and the university field education team had to be completed. Discussions were held about the proposed sites, including agency and location, the learning environment, safety and support of students, and logistics, such as accommodation and travel. Once some of the logistical and feasibility details were addressed satisfactorily the University undertook due diligence in terms of its 'duty of care' to students, the legal contracts and procedural matters were completed.

During this period, the basic organisational arrangements such as medical and travel requirements were considered. Discussion, clarification and negotiation with the social worker and field education team members were undertaken to establish general learning expectations and compatibility of relationships. The usual student and field supervisory boundaries were also articulated and clarified and the matter of 'on the ground' personal support addressed. This was done to avoid any complication of the supervisor's responsibilities in terms of the professional support role/function and personal support role/

function. Role and responsibilities were further clarified around this matter, and students identified their own support networks external to each other and the supervisor.

To further their own understanding, the students undertook some research into the historic, cultural and political history of Vietnam along with the contextual environment and service provision of the agencies they would be potentially joining. This was complemented by the supervisor and a member of the field education team being able to share their personal experiences of Vietnam, and in particular the differences between their usual living arrangements and lifestyle in Australia and what they would experience in Vietnam. Learning expectations as well as medical and travel plans were discussed, clarified and agreed to and personal and professional supports were made clear, including confirmation of student, supervisor and University role and responsibilities.

In providing the requisite formal support to students it was agreed one member of the field education team, namely this author, would be the liaison person for all students. The liaison person's role was to maintain communication with the students and supervisor on behalf of the Field Education Program of the Department of Social Work and Community Welfare at James Cook University. The liaison person had the responsibility to ensure students were provided with the opportunities to develop the knowledge and skills necessary for effective social work practice. In undertaking these tasks the liaison person received and responded to student journals, time logs, student learning statements as well as the evaluation outcome of the placement with each student and field supervisor. It was further agreed, given the circumstances of distance, that communication via Skype, telephone and/or email would be formalised on a regular basis, as well as putting emergent contacts in place.

These students, like all students undertaking their field placement also attended a two-day intensive workshop to review the practicalities of field placement, including support mechanisms, assessment criteria, expectations and role responsibilities, ethical practice and behaviour and managing or responding to difficult circumstances.

PLACEMENT IN CONTEXT

Two of the social work students, Ali and Kate, undertook their social work field education placement at the Office of Genetic Counselling and Disabled Children (OGCDC) in Hue City. This agency provides assistance to sick and disabled children and their families in central Vietnam and the central highlands and was founded by the Hue College of Medicine and Pharmacy in 1999 (OGCDC 2004). These two students were involved in several program areas including the Job Training and Creation program, which had established a craft-making workshop for people with disabilities, and the Healing the Wounded Heart Shop that displayed and sold the craft products to support these people in Hue City. Students also became involved with the Adaptive Equipment and Transportation program, which assisted people with disabilities with greater options for mobility, along with the Rehabilitation program, an activity and therapeutic centre for children with functional disabilities.

The other two social work students, Hannah and Lauren, undertook their social work field education placement at Giving It Back To Kids (GIBTK), an agency founded by an American couple in 2002 to assist children to reach their maximum potential through education, medical care, nutrition and love (GIBTK 2010). These two students were mainly involved in two programs, the Orphanage Support program, caring for orphans, street kids, and children whose families are unable to care for them due to poverty; and The Father's House program which cared for young unmarried mothers.

LOCALE IN CONTEXT

The two agencies were located within a cultural, social and political landscape which had some bearing on the student's actions or reactions within the contextual environment of the agency.

In 1986 Vietnam began a process of economic reform called *doi moi*, meaning renovation or renewal (Hugman et al. 2007). The *doi moi* policy entailed new forms of management, reorganisations of the administrative sector, reconsiderations of the state and market, and increased globalisation (Rydstrøm 2003). The next 20 years saw

Vietnam enter a rapid period of transition, making substantial progress as indicated by the rise in the material living standards for an increasing proportion of the population (Hugman et al. 2007).

The growth in the economy improved capacity to further develop infrastructure in education and health, even as social problems continued to grow and new ones develop. These problems were categorised within social policy as, 'social protection' – for example, people in poverty – and 'social evils' – for example, trafficking of children and young women (Hugman et al. 2007). In response to some of these problems Vietnam enacted legislation prohibiting the use of any physical violence against women and children, including the Law on Marriage and Family, 1986, and the Penal Code of the Socialist Republic of Vietnam, 1989 (Rydstrøm 2003).

These changes, though a progressive response to social problems, have been moderated by the historical significance of Confucian reminiscence in Vietnamese society influencing perceptions and customs based on gender and which also exists alongside the official communist ideology. In consequence, there remains a dual tension of the past and present and a persistent struggle for equality of the sexes which impacts on the position, rights and interests of women (Rydstrøm 2003).

The discipline of social work is contextually relevant within the social structure environmental overlay of Vietnam, even though there is no 'systematic framework for the recognition of professional social work' in Vietnam (Hugman et al. 2007, p204). The social welfare workforce is qualified (Hugman et al. 2007) though most often qualified at a tertiary level in other disciplines different to social work, such as, teaching or nursing. The cultural and social context in Vietnam can create limitations and potential barriers for the effective implementation of responses social work and social workers can bring. Equally, the environmental landscape appears to engender opportunities for social work and therefore social work students to undertake meaningful learning. It is this potential for growth promoting options for improving social work students' own practice frameworks and capacity which is pursued, as it also has the potential to add to the wellbeing of people they are in contact with and perhaps, in this case, to the social fabric in Vietnam.

CULTURES COLLIDE

The students' initial journal entries exposed students' preconceived expectations and views of what the field education placement would be like. What emerged were unfamiliar and painful realisations which challenged the students' own understandings of their personal and professional identities.

The students, initially exhilarated and excited by the differences they encountered, began to adjust to the reality of the purpose of being in Vietnam. Those differences became markedly positioned in their minds. The students experienced uncertainty, beginning with marked differences in agency structures and ways of working within their assigned agencies, to what they had previously experienced. Language, values, social and political underpinnings came to the fore, changing students responses from one of curiosity to one of heightened anxiety. One student wrote, 'I began to have a mini meltdown, going through the thought process of, why did I come here? I'm not ready for this … overall I felt abandoned' (Hannah's journal). The students' reactions appeared markedly similar to those described as 'culture shock' by Munford (2000), Hashim (2003) and Pyvis and Chapman (2005); though equally they could just have been 'settling in' to a completely new experience.

These students had ready and regular access to their supervisor. However, their dissatisfaction, impatience, anger, and sadness, as well as some feelings of uselessness and ineffectiveness, were in evidence. Individual supervision, coupled with peer group supervision and support, collective social outings, as well as written and verbal communication with the liaison person, failed to resolve students' unease. These students may have adapted better, at least emotionally, to their situation if they had, in their words, been able to 'communicate' effectively within this environment (students' journals); it seemed though this new experience was so overwhelming that effective communication had been sidelined or overtaken by the student's emotional state.

It seemed the changes experienced by these students resulted in their usual means of coping being ineffective as a means of handling this new experience and contextual environment. The strain and anxiety resulting from contact with a new culture and feelings of loss, confusion, and impotence resulting from loss of accustomed cultural cues and social rules were having a profound impact (Brown & Holloway 2008; Reynolds & Constantine 2007; Pyvis & Chapman 2005; Hasim 2003).

Collectively and individually these students were in a state of culture shock rather than experiencing settling in difficulties. Culture shock occurs when there is a loss of predicted family cues, difficulties with interpersonal communications and there is a crisis of identity (Pyvis & Chapman 2005).

In the early days of their placement, students clearly felt quite overwhelmed: 'the sights, the sounds, the smells!' coupled with noticing 'so much poverty' as well as 'seeing the glaring disparity between those with money, and those without' the 'massive mansions next to little tin shacks; a Mercedes next to a rusty bicycle' (Ali's journal). This feeling of being overwhelmed occurred alongside the frustrations of being unable 'to easily communicate' and discovering 'an organisation that seems to have very little organisational structure, no ideas of what they want us, as students, to do, and has a very different idea of what social work is' and the feeling of being somewhat lost (Hannah's journal).

> Personally (I felt) many emotions ... such as, anger, confusion, frustration and I was mostly scared that I was going to get nothing from this placement. (Lauren's journal)

> I'm feeling frustrated ... I'm feeling like I'm talking about things I have been thinking about for years now and while I have a larger, more academically appropriate vocabulary, my understanding of where to go with it all become murkier the more I know. (Kate's journal)

Moving from awareness and understanding, that is, a knowing, to an action, where there is a sense of being overwhelmed and/or experiencing feelings of powerlessness, became crucial for the students' sense of personal and professional identity. The truism of 'the more you know the less you actually know' begins to emerge; the unknowns, if left unattended, create uncertainty and give rise to feelings of frustration, sadness and anger.

Students were confronted by many limitations, some that were expected, like language and communication (Hannah's journal) and some which came with an element of surprise, such as a 'lack of understanding about the cultural values which may drive people' (Kate's journal). Students also needed to 'facilitate an existential freedom without imposing my own values and definitions of free' (Kate's journal) whilst gaining clarity as 'I also questioned my own role here' (Ali's journal).

Identifying themselves as wanting to be useful and to make a difference, these students questioned their 'usefulness or (to make a) difference to and/or for whom?' (Ali's journal) Searching for answers to establish her worth as a person as well as a social work practitioner, one student stated she wanted to

> make a difference for others ... I also want to make a difference for myself too. Is there such a thing as absolute altruism? Or in doing something solely for someone else, are you actually doing it for yourself as well? And why does this immediately conjure up negative feelings, that it is not okay to do something for myself ... [Therein is found] a great importance in giving something of myself ... [as well as] taking something for myself too. Perhaps ... it is not taking something for myself but giving something to myself. Maybe I can do that. I am in a bit of a black hole at the moment; still questioning what I'm doing here. What my role is? Do I belong here? Where do I belong? ... [There are] so many questions which I have no answers to and have absolutely no idea where to find the answer. I've been feeling a lot of self-doubt this week. Questioning what I can give. And then questioning why I feel like I have to give. I think it's possible that being a Westerner here puts a certain amount of pressure on me to be useful, to help; to give. (Ali's journal)

The ebb and flow of these feelings and thoughts developed into role confusion, uncertainty of expectations, questioning of personal values and challenges to self and/or professional identity. Overall, students felt a sense of loss manifested, to some degree, in terms of uselessness and questioning their own personal abilities and those as a social work practitioner. This brought into prominence the matter of cultural and contextual difference, which, in some instances, led to feelings of impotence as students struggled to cope with the contextual environment.

The feeling of impotence can arise in many forms. In one instance a student remarked:

> I have been attending the workshop [for people with disabilities] every morning, and it is starting to get a bit weird. Every morning we just sit and chat, working with them on whatever handicraft item they want us to try to make. At times it's fun. And then I remember that this is their job, their livelihood. And I am a clumsy Westerner sitting on the floor in the middle of their workspace, probably getting in the way, feeling hot and bothered, and asking for help because I am unable to do the weaving. (Ali's journal)

This student felt overwhelmed and frustrated and began to wonder 'what the hell am I doing here?' and went on to identify:

> knowing any social work [I] might do at the workshop [will] later on require trust and relationships to be built; and knowing this takes time and patience, but all the time feeling like an intruder and an impostor. An intruder, because I felt I had no right to be there [and] an impostor because I wondered if they're expecting something from me which I am unable to give. I suppose in a way I positioned myself as a learner, they were the experts; [whilst I attempted] to build rapport and friendship. But that is not enough. I figured that I am unable to just sit around weaving every morning for the rest of my placement, for both my sanity's sake and my learning experience. (Ali's journal)

Moving through this morass of conflicting and turbulent emotions and thoughts, students noticed a magnification of their surroundings and circumstances. These experiences were heightened by an assault on students' senses resulted in a continuous pendulum swing of emotions from euphoria to depression. This led, in some instances, to inertia and thoughts of a lack of professional progress within the placement.

The students had found themselves in an unfamiliar cultural environment, where their previous awareness, knowledge and understandings were inadequate for coping fully with the situation, causing some disequilibrium and emotional disturbance. The degree of disturbance varied and ranged from minor to severe, and fluctuated over time. The actual impact on each student depended largely on the student's own resilience, the extent of dissonance with the culture, the contextual environment and the personal and professional stake involved along with the actual and/or perceived personal supports for each student. Even through this dissonance, acculturation was beginning to emerge as the students' interactions and interrelationships developed with the agency, agency colleagues and the service users of their respective field placements as well as with people they met from the general populace.

THE LEARNING JOURNEY

Initially, the students' knowledge base was challenged, with them facing an internal tussle in integrating their previous knowledge and understandings with an acceptance of a new cultural and contextual reality. This changing experience involved the recognition and struggle both with a sense of loss of their professional identity and the added potential of gaining new knowledge and new understandings and a new identity.

Grief responses to loss are integral parts of life, but how the loss is experienced can be quite distressing and even devastating. The students' own emotional, physical and spiritual connections to their relationships bounded by the experience of loss shaped their grieving processes. Other factors, such as age, gender, level of maturity and/or psychosocial development, previous histories of resolving loss issues along with support networks and strengths gained from present and past relationships also played a part and influenced the grieving process and the outcome.

Grieving entails the consolidation of all is valuable and important from the past and preserving it from loss, whilst simultaneously re-establishing meaningful patterns of relationships in which the loss can be accommodated (Goldsworthy 2005). A sense of continuity can then be restored by detaching the familiar meanings of life from the relationship in which they were embodied and re-establishing them independently of it.

In this instance, students faced either making adjustments in order to make sense of the learning experience or to resist and remain within their own perceived safety and/or comfort boundaries and lose the experiential learning opportunities presented. In essence, to resist 'invites questions about the individual's capacity to make the adjustments' (Pyvis & Chapman 2005, p24) and therefore to change.

The students, in adjusting to a new reality, including coming to terms with the culturally unfamiliar as well as resolving cultural incongruities and dissimilarities, were faced with responding to their emotional turmoil by actioning some inner strategy or strategies of resolution and/or change. This was finally accomplished through a thematic process of recognising, encountering, adapting and mastering (Edmonds 2010), which occurred naturally, whilst implicitly interwoven into the students' own resilience and desire to achieve a creditable outcome from their experience and so, confirm or affirm their own personal and professional identity.

Recognising

Recognising is a process of critical self-reflection.

One student observed 'our dynamic identity (the surface) is always shaped in relation to our context' (Kate's journal) and reflected that

> The boundaries apparent between humans seen so starkly when travelling; this divide is what I don't like about the culture of travel; travel to find understanding, but often we are over standing ... a culture bending to meet the needs of foreign currencies. (Kate's journal)

Place becomes a reflective paradigm of challenges to nuances of social work, including values, standards and ethics, in that

I have a constant awareness of my whiteness, of being a foreigner. These feelings spurs two main understandings; insight into being a minority (and questioning) how transferable could this experience be? (Kate's journal)

These experiences provide an opportunity to walk in another's shoes, of acknowledging the difference. There is a heightened awareness of, and including, vulnerability, powerlessness, difference, empathy, compassion along with values and cultural competence, in particular, in relation to the inner reflection of one's own culture.

Although cultural differences are discussed, debated and reviewed throughout the social work curriculum, with which these students had been inculcated, the practical experience created an assault on students' senses; stripping, in a sense, the students' own safety apparatus bare and from which students were effectively forced into questioning the fundamentals of their own personal and professional identity and own specific place within social work.

Encountering

The immediate effect of encountering the sights and sounds of cultural diversity was that students were enthralled by the excitement of the new. As experience upon experience of both the scheduled and unexpected overwhelmed their senses, this thrill changed into something less benign. The disequilibrium arose as the excitement of the emerging and enfolding experience merged with the student's emotional unease coupled with self-doubt about their own knowledge and capabilities. An internal struggle to integrate the new and the different developed.

Students reflected on the question of poverty and the appearance of a divide between rich and poor as well as the agency responses which were markedly different from what they had previously known and accepted as reasonable (student journals). Why did these matters, at least initially, catch students' attention? Their seemingly ordered thoughts had a basis that orientated them in terms of social work practice. Their experiences were viewed through a specific cultural lens, sometimes to the exclusion of other possibilities and/or other viewpoints, thereby creating certain pathways to the exclusion of others. There is no difficulty in this as long as the social work student is conscious and aware of this and is able to place all the information at hand through a critically reflective lens prior to making judgements or comments and/or undertaking purposeful actions.

'Capitalism is to blame' wrote one student (Ali's journal), which may be apt in terms of the descriptive experience and thoughts flowing from this; however, did this actually capture the processes inherent within the experience? What stopped the student from viewing capitalism or socialism in terms of people? The context, when viewed in relational terms, may avoid the pitfall of blaming a system by focusing energies on potential responses that may be of benefit to people.

The impact of capitalism on people in Vietnam is worthy of the student's critical reflective processes, and perhaps embedded within the statement 'capitalism is to blame' is the underlying question, 'does capitalism keep people in poverty?' Or perhaps, since Vietnam is a socialist country, what is the purpose or reason for embracing some vestiges of capitalism? Or, what are the benefits and/or limitations of this approach? (Student journals).

Encountering the broader environmental spectrum and these perceived structural disadvantages the students took stock, making comparisons with what is known and/or who the student is personally and/or professionally. This comparison may, in turn, skew reasoning and/or analysis. The students struggled with difference and a desire to understand from a known perspective or understanding.

> I have to wonder whether I would be saying the same thing if I lived here, grew up here, and had to spend the rest of my life here. It is easy for me, as an outsider, to be critical (and) to presume I know what is going on. (Ali's journal)

The journey undertaken by students was reflected by the key aspects of the placement experience and the contextual environment within which it was imbedded.

Adapting

Adapting to overwhelming new experiences takes time. It began slowly at first and gathered momentum as students found their place in their living arrangements and within their assigned agency as well as in the tasks they became involved in.

The initial steps taken were tentative. Students tended to ebb and flow between the prevailing emotional tides of their experiences. Change became increasingly evident from the struggles of language, culture, agency differences, people's perceptions and/or expectations, as students began to adapt and adjust to their experiences.

Students needed to find effective ways to engage in meaningful communication; from conversing non-verbally, using gestures and sign language as well as single word statements to becoming more verbally interactive in somewhat halting or broken English to having Vietnamese colleagues assisting as interpreters. One student commented,

> It is important I remember that interpretation is a much more complex process than is word for word translation. Rather than the simple substitution of one language for another, it calls for the deciphering of two linguistic codes each with its own geographical, cultural, historical and linguistic traditions. (Lauren's journal)

As the students became more active and interactive, joining in activities like craft-making and in engagement with agency service users, there was a realisation the roles of service provider and service user were increasingly blurred. Students, apart from having their social work knowledge and capabilities to impart to others, became more aware they were the recipients in some situations. A transference and realisation took place as the students began to accommodate to the cultural and environmental milieu enabling them, in turn, to become more proactive. The students consciously began to engender meaning in their placements, fulfilling the requirements of the social work degree and developing further their practice skills, knowledge and abilities.

In one instance, two students met with a group of young unmarried mothers (Hannah's and Lauren's journals) and with the assistance of a Vietnamese colleague acting as an interpreter, gained an indication these young mothers wanted to learn more about how to care for their children. The students, in the context of strengthening the maternal/child bond, developed bilingual strength cards, with written phrases on each one, one side in English and the other side in Vietnamese. These cards provided the impetus and the means for group engagement with these young mothers, in which the context varied and changed as conversations developed (Hannah's and Lauren's journals).

The students' identification of themselves within this construct of cultural difference forged the integration of emotional dissonance into a change orientation reinforced by the activity of group work engagement. The students began to move from a sense of being the other, an outsider, to being as one within their environment. Though never insiders, they began to experience less, at least within themselves, the sense of being an outsider. This gradual response to the emotional dissonance they had been experiencing allowed the movement from a static immobilisation to one of personal and professional growth and development.

Mastering

Edmonds (2010) saw mastering as largely dependent on how students perceive and/or engaged with the challenges they faced. Like the cyclic grieving interplays of cumulative losses, these challenges can be viewed and responded to by the student as a threat or challenge. If they view the presenting experience as a challenge, the student has sufficient confidence and personal resources to engage with the situation to achieve a positive outcome. If, on the other hand, the student views the experience as a threat, their reactions will tend to be a reflective response of flight/fight: in this instance, withdrawing from the experience whilst fighting an internal emotional battle of negative self-talk.

It was noted by one student:

> Now, I am humbled by the amount I have to learn, and am becoming more mindful, observing myself, integrity; the definition of which being, the state of being unimpaired; soundness ... [and the] ... quality or condition of being whole or undivided; completeness. (Kate's journal)

The analogy of the glass half empty or half full begins to emerge as a way of understanding and moving from a static to an action position. This inner emotional realisation forces the student to face the reality of their experience and the circumstances they face. In focussing on the deficits in problems I created, an opportunity to be critical, to be serious and to be negative. The arms of optimism are the best place for me to live ... there is always a solution, a better way. Translating this perspective to micro and macro practice contexts I am likely to be in; understanding the empty is important but maintaining a space for visions to be realised, for the extra things that make a difference to be sought out and done. (Kate's journal)

In mastering, the student seeks inspiration and questions the foundations of their own sense of self as well as their own competence as a potential social work practitioner. Does this occur as a result of the student's own culture and frame of learning/practice, or are they open to cultural relativism?

Tesoriero (2006) suggests reflexivity concerns moving from absolute and dualistic thinking to an appreciation of relativity and ambiguity. In this way, the student shapes her own understanding through a process of awareness, critical reflection and analysis in bridging the macro and the micro thereby 'shifting from defining myself as a bigger picture person and seeing that the small things make up the whole' (Kate's journal).

BRIDGING THE CHALLENGES

The emotional ebb and flow of managing new experiences and the student's perceived or real fears and/or losses created a cyclic overture of recognising, encountering, adapting and mastering responses and the resultant emotional collision between the personal and the professional.

Over time, the integration of uncertainties into certainties became more profound; though for these students there was no complete satisfactory integration; rather there was an interweaving of the personal and the professional into a more cohesive and positive whole.

Cultural dissonance, communication, knowledge, understanding of social work, financial and material resource deficits challenged students' views of social work practice and purpose as well as of themselves, giving rise to feelings of anger, confusion, frustration as well as thoughts of field placement failure (student journals). The task, therefore, was to process, identify, understand and accept, and/or adjust to, these emotions, whilst attempting clarification of the effective contribution of social work and social work practice to the field placement agency.

The students noted the differences of social work practices, which in turn, raised their own awareness of agency and cultural differences and elicited questions of how Western social work could possibly be effective within a culturally different context and/or as a result of the mix of the cultural ethos within an agency based on, for example, Christian ideology, charity and volunteerism (student journals).

There were several moments of enlightenment experienced by students, where a moment of clarity illuminated their thinking, as they weaved the cultural context within their own world viewpoints. This included, for example, undertaking a community development approach to practice rather than being solely focused on a direct service delivery mode. It meant taking less of the initiative by allowing the experience to unfold within the parameters of the service user's world view (Student journals). This reality of spending long periods of time in taking small steps became a struggle of meaning, value and understanding. The implication was that time is of the essence, field placement is time limited, and small steps may lack worth, or make no tangible difference. Time and small are relative terms. Effective change, no matter how small or time constrained provides a building block without which the next building block is unable to be laid.

The students' search for meaning was, sometimes, a tortuous journey as they struggled to integrate the environmental and contextual stimuli into what they readily knew and understood. In the example of the impact of capitalism on people in Vietnam, students engaged in a process of critical reflection through their observations of people as they went about their daily activities, to find understanding and/or meaning of this within the cultural and social environmental context (Ali's and Kate's journal).

These social work students, having been inculcated into the social mores and norms of a Western, democratic and capitalist country, that is Australia, raised pertinent questions about their experience of Vietnam, a socialist country. These questions included, 'What is the purpose and reason for embracing some vestiges of capitalism?' or, 'What are the benefits and/or limitations of this approach for people in Vietnam?' It is from this, the following query arises: 'Does the influence of capitalism in Vietnam keep (some) people in poverty? Or, are there other reasons?' (Ali's and Kate's journal)

Structural disadvantages can be more evident when the differences to one's own view of the world is markedly challenged and in making comparisons to what is being experienced with what students know and/or in terms of their personal and/or professional identity can skew reasoning and/or analysis. So when one student stated:

> I have to wonder whether I would be saying the same thing if I lived here, grew up here, and had to spend the rest of my life here. It is easy for me as an outsider to be critical, to presume I know what's going on. (Ali's journal)

This student identified a key aspect of the field placement experience and contextual environment in her search of meaning.

Another student experienced many children in one orphanage sharing the same room for sleeping; however the dwelling was in need of repair and had a leaking roof, so when it rained all the children and their bedding became wet:

> The orphanage, I later found out belongs (in true socialist fashion) to the people of the community. Responsibility for repairs, however, is up to the NGO [non-government organisation] funds, not the community members. The government takes too long to do repairs so if you entice them with paying for it the process may hasten, or it may be a donation to the government. What does this represent to the local community, a shifting of responsibility, to overseas donors? [Perhaps] the first hints at the challenge of sustainability. (Kate's journal)

The shift from family, village and community responsibility towards external resources could be viewed as the shift or adaptation of socialism within or through a developmental capitalist agenda.

It seems students need to be more aware of terminology and/or meaning of terms within the environmental context to effectively make sense of the experience; for example, in 'Vietnamese the term for social work, *cong tac xa hoi*, also refers to a charitable and/or voluntary effort' (Hugman et al. 2007, p198). Hence, service responses may be viewed as less a matter of community responsibility and more whether a non-government agency has, in this situation, the interest, time or financial resources as well as the volunteers to respond.

Meanings are also culturally placed within the contextual environment and students must navigate the potential maze of difference, whilst continually being critically reflective and analytical of the experiences they encounter. How does the divide come together?

JOINING AND INTEGRATION

The human boundaries across and between cultures are 'so stark' when travelling; the differences are 'in your face' and the divide, from a student perspective, requires a bridge, one of 'understanding' though maybe this, in turn, creates 'over-standing' with the culture being, in some respects, twisted to meet the needs of 'foreign susceptibilities and sensibilities' (Kate's journal).

Professional boundaries are also highlighted through differences of cultural norms. Human interaction, as a result of Western professional boundaries, may be kept, at least physically, at a reasonable distance. 'I was hurting for her' (Hannah's journal): the student saw a women in pain and responded from that part of her which had been touched, the story resonated deeply and quite 'naturally I just hugged her' as she 'cried in my arms for what felt like 20 minutes' (Hannah's journal).

The student and the woman shared their stories through this embrace. Their worlds collided and a mutuality of understanding was met through the woman's tears of anguish; from her immediate emotional circumstance to the student's controlled feelings as they rose to the surface. Professionalism with its Western boundaries in place fails to detract from the raw emotion and the unique relationship enveloping through the form of being human. The resultant change, 'a different woman' (Hannah's journal), began to smile, expressing thanks for the sharing of stories; this unique human interaction provided the catalyst for the future, in that the woman was the first one to the gate to greet me, she had a smile from cheek to cheek and came up and hugged me straight away. She thanked me for hugging her and it was what she just needed most. (Hannah's journal)

In undertaking social work field placements in Vietnam these students experienced the collision of the respective cultural differences, whilst struggling; at least initially, before they began to create a different understanding of social work and its implications for practice. The cultural experiences produced many challenges, though these students, through their determination, time and perseverance coupled with their reflections and analysis of and on practice, melded and joined this experience into their own social work understandings, knowledge and practice base. They did this whilst simultaneously adding to and developing further their understandings, knowledge and practice of social work. The cultural worlds collided and came together: balancing what students knew at the beginning of placement with the knowledge gained from their practical placement experiences.

IMPLICATIONS FOR SOCIAL WORK PRACTICE AND EDUCATION

This study suggests there are many benefits gained by social work students undertaking their field education placements in another country including, being able to undertake and/or adapt social work practice where difference permeates the contextual environment; develop and integrate further the nexus between cultural difference and social work knowledge; and develop an effective integration of the cultural nuances which influence and/or change the student's own social work knowledge base and by implication their practice of social work.

Preparedness for social work practice

The practice experience of these students was culturally defined, and though expected, it had its own challenges. These challenges provided a context for students to connect and reconnect with their social work knowledge, skills and abilities. It also provided an opportunity to further develop their professional identity within this context through a process of critical reflection during supervision; through personal contemplation; in peer group interactions as well as in their written journals.

The students in their written journals also began to identify their beliefs, thoughts, constructs and imaginings; including their personal and professional expectations, which they reconciled through their behaviours and wants, whilst engaging with their physiological changes and psychological responses that individually impacted upon them (Barrett 2006; Lindquist & Barrett 2008).

Although initially the students struggled for meaning, in terms of their placement experience and their view of social work practice, as the placement progressed the students' engagement with their experiences enabled them to construct and embed meaning of their actions and emotional responses, and thereby to define their social work practice within an understanding of the contextual environment.

The students, in turn, began to identify and explain the significance, purpose and consequence of the cultural experience as an opportunity to view the cultural differences by merging and integrating them into their own culturally competent social work practice.

Cultural nuances, difference and social work knowledge

Cultural competence is a fluid and evolving concept with many elements rather than a homogeneous concept with a defined composition (Davis 2007). Sawrikar and Katz (2008) grouped the terms culturally aware, culturally sensitive and culturally competent together in capturing the essence of cultural competence. McPhatter (1997) described cultural competence as having three components, namely; enlightened consciousness, grounded knowledge base, and cumulative skill proficiency. Campinha-Bacote (1999) defined cultural competence as the ongoing process of seeking cultural awareness, cultural knowledge, cultural skill, and cultural encounters.

The Australian Association of Social Workers (2010) Code of Ethics, 5.1.2 states that culturally competent, safe and sensitive practice requires social work students and practitioners to

> develop culturally sensitive practice by acknowledging the significance
> of culture in their practice, recognising the impact their own ethnic and

cultural identities, views and biases can have on their practice and on culturally different clients and colleagues. (AASW 2010, p17)

Cultural awareness is about 'being aware of or knowing what are the (common) cultural norms, values, beliefs and practices' (Sawrikar & Katz 2008, p13), whilst cultural sensitivity is concern with being more familiar with 'how diversity expresses itself' (Sawrikar & Katz 2008, p13). Students engaged in becoming more aware of their own cultural norms, mores values and beliefs, whilst simultaneously being more cognisant of difference without making people feel different (Sawrikar & Katz 2008). As a result, students made further advancement in avoiding any reliance on stereotypical information to inform their viewpoint.

Even though these students would have experienced some bias embedded within their formal and informal social work education, which is culturally and contextually bound within a Western worldview, their critical analysis and reflection enabled them to view and review their existing understanding and knowledge base to formulate a new culturally rooted knowledge base (McPhatter 1997). It was this process of enlightened consciousness which restructured the students' primary worldviews and shifted their consciousness. Cumulatively, the students' skill proficiency was extended by maintaining a 'focused, systematic, reflective and evaluative' (McPhatter 1997, p272) practice rather than by indiscriminate selection, thereby developing further their cultural awareness and competence.

In essence, cultural competence is a journey rather than a destination, it is

> a process of striving to become increasingly self-aware, to value diversity, and to become knowledgeable about cultural strengths and vulnerabilities experienced by families. (Bonecutter & Gleeson 1997, p111)

It is this ability to engage a person from a culturally different group and create a climate of acceptance, equality, and considerateness for the interaction that highlights a culturally competent social work student. This is equally true whether the social work student is part of the dominant culture or in the minority within another culture.

CONCLUSION

In undertaking their fieldwork practice placements in Vietnam, these social work students expected to be challenged by the social, structural and cultural difference they would encounter. The challenges, however, exceeded their conscious ability to formulate a true understanding what these challenges would mean both personally and professionally.

Preparation for placement requires knowing some pertinent information usually concerning who, what, when and where in terms of roles, responsibilities and expectations within the contextual framework of the field education placement. In undertaking fieldwork practice, specifically in a different culture, students need to be more appraised of, and cognisant about, any additional factors that could present themselves before entering into a commitment to undertake this contextual field placement. In this instance preparedness could have entailed students' participating in practical experiential exercises to engage their critical reflective analysis through Edmonds (2010) 'recognizing, encountering, adapting and mastering' process. Although different to the actual experience students will face, such rehearsal provides the opportunity to explore differences in a supportive environment. In so doing, students can become more aware of the nexus between contextual differences and their social work knowledge.

It is also incumbent on academic mentors to prepare students for field education placements by ensuring pre-placement educative processes include students'

- being aware and have an understanding of their own specific cultural mores, values, beliefs and norms;
  - having contextual knowledge of the cultural mores, values, beliefs and norms of the potential host field education placement agency, people and/or country;
  - having knowledge and understanding of any social, structural, political and cultural differences and therefore potential clash between the
- contextual environments of the host agency/country and the student's university/country; and

140

- the students' own practice orientation and/or theoretical underpinnings and the ideology and/or values and orientation of the placement agency;
  - field education expectations of, or about, the contextual and cultural implications of the fieldwork learning environment;
  - being aware of supports they can expect, both formally and informally, that will be realistically possible in the particular field placement circumstance.

Once these matters have been appraised, clarified and better understood, social work students and their academic mentors are in an improved position to maximise the learning potential of the fieldwork placement and minimise any adverse impact or effect that may occur, particularly in culturally diverse field education placements where a collision of cultural difference is more likely.

It is important for social work students to undertake their field education placements with open hearts and minds, including having appreciation of what it is to be human and, as shown in this case, the cultural nuances and overlays that define the person, the context and the place.

There are also particular benefits in social work students' engaging, participating and embracing the experience of culturally diverse field education placements. These include developing further the nexus between difference experienced in the field and social work knowledge, preparedness for social work practice within culturally diverse environs, and the integration of cultural nuances within the students' own social work knowledge base. In so doing, students will become more complete social work practitioners.

Acknowledgements

This chapter would have been impossible without the assistance and consent of social work students, Lauren Bacon, Hannah Baker, Alison Duncan and Kate Samuels from James Cook University, in sharing their written documented field placement journals. I am indebted to these students' generosity in sharing their lived experiences openly and honestly with the author and their contribution is gratefully acknowledged.

REFERENCES

Australian Association of Social Workers (AASW) (2010). *Code of Ethics.* Canberra, ACT: Australian Association of Social Workers.

Australian Association of Social Workers (AASW) (2003). *Practice standards for social workers: acheiving outcomes.* Canberra, ACT: Australian Association of Social Workers.

Barrett LF (2006). Solving the emotion paradox: categorization and the experience of emotion. *Personality and Social Psychology Review,* 10(1): 20–46, doi: 10.1207/s15327957pspr1001_2.

Bonecutter FJ & Gleeson JP (1997). Broadening our view. *Journal of Multicultural Social Work,* 5(1): 99–119, doi: 10.1300/J285v05n01_08.

Brown L & Holloway I (2008). The adjustment journey of international postgraduate students at an English university: an ethnographic study. *Journal of Research in International Education,* 7(2): 232–49, doi: 10.1177/1475240908091306.

Campinha-Bacote J (1999). A model and instrument for addressing cultural competence in Health Care. *Journal of Nursing Education,* 38(5): 203–06.

Chang W (2007). Cultural competence of international humanitarian workers *Adult Education Quarterly,* 57: 187–204, doi: 10.1177/0741713606296755.

Churchman A & Mitrani M (1997). The role of the physical environment in culture shock. *Environment and Behavior,* 29(1): 64–86, doi: 10.1177/001391659702900103.

Clandinin DJ (2006). Narrative inquiry: a methodology for studying lived experience. *Research Studies in Music Education,* 27: 44–54.

Davis TS (2007). Mapping patterns of perceptions: a community-based approach to cultural competence assessment. *Research on Social Work Practice,* 17: 358–79, doi: 10.1177/1049731506295103.

Edmonds ML (2010). The lived experience of nursing students who study abroad: a qualitative inquiry. *Journal of Studies in International Education,* 14(5): 545–68, doi: 10.1177/1028315310375306.

Giving It Back to Kids (GIBTK) (2010). Mission. [Online]. Available: givingitbacktokids.com [Accessed: 18 November 2010].

Goldsworthy KK (2005) Grief and loss theory in social work practice: all changes involve loss, just as all losses require change. *Australian Social Work*, 58(2): 167–78, doi: 10.1111/j.1447-0748.2005.00201.x.

Hashim IH (2003). Cultural and gender differences in perceptions of stressors and coping skills: A study of Western and African college students in China. *School Psychology International*, 24(2): 182–203, doi: 10.1177/0143034303024002004.

Hugman R, Nguyen TTL & Nguyen TH (2007). Developing social work in Vietnam. *International Social Work*, 50(2): 197–211, doi: 10.1177/0020872807073985.

Lindquist KA & Barrett LF (2008). Constructing emotion: the experience of fear as a conceptual act. *Psychological Science*, 19(9): 898–903, doi: 10.1111/j.1467-9280.2008.02174.x.

Mattner M (2004). Power to the people? Local governance and politics in Vietnam. *Environment and Urbanization*, 16(1): 121–28, doi: 10.1177/095624780401600110.

McPhatter AR (1997). Cultural competence in child welfare: what is it? How do we achieve it? What happens without it? *Child Welfare*, 76(1): 255–78.

Mumford DB (2000). Culture shock among young British volunteers working abroad: predictors, risk factors and outcome. *Transcultural Psychiatry*, 37(1): 73–87, doi:10.1177/136346150003700104.

Office of Genetic Counselling and Disabled Children (OGCDC) (2004). About us. [Online]. Available: www.ogcdc.org [Accessed: 18 November 2010].

Peshkin A (2000). The nature of interpretation in qualitative research. *Educational Research*, 29(9): 5–9, doi: 10.3102/0013189X029009005.

Polkinghorne DE (2005). Language and meaning: data collection in qualitative research. *Journal of Counseling Psychology*, 52(2): 137–45.

Pritchard R (2010). Re-entry trauma: Asian re-integration after study in the West. *Journal of Studies in International Education*, 20(10): 1–19, doi: 10.1177/1028315310365541.

Pyvis D & Chapman A (2005). Culture shock and the international student 'offshore'. *Journal of Research in International Education*, 4: 23–42, doi: 10.1177/1475240905050289.

Reynolds AL & Constantine MG (2007). Cultural adjustment difficulties and career development of international college students. *Journal of Career Assessment*, 15(3), 338–50. doi:10.1177/1069072707301218.

Riessman CK & Quinney L (2005). Narrative in social work: a critical review. *Qualitative Social Work*, 4(4): 391–412, doi: 10.1177/1473325005058643.

Rydstrøm H (2003). Encountering 'hot' anger: domestic violence in contemporary Vietnam. *Violence Against Women*, 9: 676–97, doi: 10.1177/1077801203009006004.

Sawrikar P & Katz I (2008). Enhancing family and relationship service accessibility and delivery to culturally and linguistically diverse families in Australia. *Australian Family Relationships Clearinghouse*, 3: 1–20.

Scott S (2003). Gender, household headship and entitlements to land: new vulnerabilities in Vietnam's decollectivization. *Gender Technology and Development*, 7: 233–63, doi: 10.1177/097185240300700205.

Tesoriero F (2006). Personal growth towards intercultural competence through an international field education programme. *Australian Social Work*, 59(2): 126–40, doi: 10.1080/03124070600651853.

van Manen M (1990). *Researching lived experience: human science for an action sensitive pedagogy*. Ontario: The Althouse Press.

Chapter Seven

A Vietnamese and Australian Cross-Cultural Field Placement Using Community Arts to Heal and Prevent Child Trafficking

Amanda Nickson, Catherine Briscoe, Skye Maconachie
and Michael Brosowski

This chapter reports on the overseas placement of an Australian social work student from James Cook University (JCU) with the Blue Dragon Children's Foundation in Vietnam. It discusses why it worked well; what learning opportunities and supports were available; the benefits of an external supervisor located in Vietnam; the role of technology and the student attributes that contributed to the placement's success. The context of the placement was a community arts partnership between the Blue Dragon Children's Foundation, Red Cross and James Cook University where the student worked with children who had been trafficked or were at risk of being trafficked in two rural villages. The Theatre for Social Change project involved drama workshops and provided experience in cross-cultural work involving interpreters and producing plays, videos and a blog site, *The Right to Shine*. The experience is discussed from the viewpoint of the main stakeholders.

越南和澳洲的跨文化社工实习：利用社区艺术项目治疗儿童心理创伤和遏制儿童贩卖行为

本章讨论一位来自澳洲詹姆斯库克大学的社工系学生在越南蓝龙儿童基金会做海外实习的情况。内容涉及以下几方面：海外实习顺利的原因；学生在实习过程中获得的学习机会和支持；派驻越南校外实习导师的好处；电脑科技和学生的个人能力也促成海外实习获得成功。蓝龙儿童基金会，红十字会和詹姆斯库克大学三方合作组织了一个社区艺术项目。一位来自詹姆斯库克大学社工系学生以本项目为实习背景，与来自越南两个农村地区的一些孩子共同完成此艺术项目。在这些孩子中，   有些有被人口贩卖过的经历，也有些曾经面临被贩卖的风险。'社会变迁表演项目'为跨文化社工实习提供了宝贵的参考经验。此项目涉及到与当地翻译的合作，戏剧的编排和录影，   同时创建了一个'人人发光发亮'的博客网站。此外，有关参与方将会从不同角度讨论本次海外实习的情况。

子どもの人身売買を解決して防ぐためにコミュニティー・アートを使う

本章は、ベトナムにあるブルードラゴン児童基金に海外現場実習に行ったジェームスクック大学のオーストラリアのソーシャルワークの学生の海外現場実習について報告する。本章では、なぜこの実習が成功したのか、どういった学習機会や支援が利用可能であるのか、また、ベトナムでの外部のスーパーバイザーの利点、現場実習を成功させるのに貢献したと考えられる技術と学生の役割について議論する。本実習の背景としては、二カ所の田舎の村ですでに人身売買された経験があるか、あるいは人身売買のリスクのもとにあった子どもたちと実習を行った学生が実習を行ったブルードラゴン児童基金、赤十字、そしてジェームスクッ

ク大学間におけるコミュニティー・アートのパートナ
シップであった。社会変動のための演劇プロジェクト
は、ドラマ・ワークショップを含んでいたり、演出家も
参加させ、「輝く権利」という劇、ビデオやブログサ
イトを製作したりした異文化交流事業における経験を
提供した。この経験は、主たる当事者の観点から議論
されている

어린이 인신매매 치유 및 방지 목적으로서의 지역사회
예술을 이용한 베트남과 호주간 문화 교류적 현장 실습

이 장은 James Cook University 에서 사회복지를 공부
하고 있는 호주 학생의 해외 현장 실습에 관해 보고 하
고 있는데, 그것은 베트남에 있는 청룡 어린이 재단 (the
Blue Dragon Children's Foundation) 에서 실행되었다.
이 장에서는 현장 실습이 왜 잘 될 수 있었는지에 대해 설
명하고 있다. 어떠한 배움의 기회와 지원이 있었는지, 베
트남에 주재한 외부 감독관으로부터의 혜택, 과학 기술의
역할, 그리고 현장 실습 성공에 기여한 위 학생의 자질을
논의하고 있다. 이 현장 실습의 주요 맥락은 청룡 어린이
재단, 적십자사, 그리고 James Cook University간의 지
역 사회 예술에 관한 동반자적 관계에 관한 것이며, 이를
통해 위 학생은 두 시골 마을에 사는 인신매매 경험이 있
는, 또는 인신매매 위험에 처해있는 어린이들과 같이 일
을 할 수 있었다. 사회 변화 프로젝트를 위한 모임에는
드라마 워크샵이 포함되었고, 다른 문화 안에서 일하면
서 겪은 경험들이 제공되었다. 이것은 연극, 비디오, 그리
고 블로그 사이트, 빛을 발할 수 있는 권리(The Right to
Shine), 의 소개와 통역관의 참여를 통해 이루어졌다. 이
경험들은 주요 이해 관계자들의 관점에서 논의될 것이다.

This chapter describes a successful community theatre project which
involved children who had been trafficked from rural villages in Hue
province, central Vietnam, to the garment factories and streets of Ho Chi

Minh City and who had returned to their homes. It was a community education project providing information to families and communities about what really happened to these children as a way of preventing further children being trafficked. It also provided therapeutic outcomes for participants. The project provided an opportunity for a social work student to do an overseas placement in community work. The key learnings are the importance of a placement being well planned; for an experienced field educator to be available to the student; the willingness of each stakeholder to cooperate and make it work and the availability and use of technology. The chapter is written in a way that gives the perspectives of four key stakeholders around these learnings. The stakeholders are the James Cook University [JCU] social work student, Skye Maconachie; the CEO of the Blue Dragon Children's Foundation, the non-government organisation with whom the student did her overseas placement, Michael Brosowski; the external Field Educator, Catherine Briscoe, a social work adviser and consultant with Voluntary Service Overseas (VSO); and the Field Education Co-ordinator and liaison person for the placement from James Cook University, Amanda Nickson. The chapter concludes with the key factors that contributed to the success of this project and placement. These factors are recommended as areas to be considered by others looking at implementing successful overseas social work student placements.

The field education coordinator and liaison person's experience

The placement came about after the student requested the opportunity to work on a new, time-limited project with the Blue Dragon Children's Foundation, in Vietnam. The student had previously done voluntary work for the Blue Dragon Foundation and was able to speak some Vietnamese. The project was to do drama workshops with children who had been trafficked into working away from their villages to financially support their families and had later returned to their homes.

In considering an overseas placement, a requirement by the JCU Field Education program was that there must be a suitably qualified supervisor in Vietnam and that it was up to the student to find the supervisor. Where one is not available in the placement agency, someone in another agency or university could be suitable. Other factors to consider include need for the placement to be well planned by the Field Educator; a clear learning plan and assessment process as outlined by the university; an experienced and available Field Educator to provide professional supervision; availability of basic technology such as a phone and computer for the student and the university liaison person to have regular and timely link ups and feedback; maturity and flexibility of the student in working in a new culture/cross-culturally; the willingness of the student to learn a new language whilst doing placement; and the willingness of all the stakeholders to work collaboratively together. (Nickson et al. 2009).

The student was able to find a suitably qualified supervisor in Vietnam. Catherine Briscoe was working for a different organisation and willing to be involved in supervision of the student placement. Catherine was available to provide some face-to-face supervision; some regular phone supervision and was also available to travel to the student for the mid placement and end of placement review. Before the placement began, the student and supervisor met face-to-face which was helpful and planned well how they could maintain regular contact and supervision. The dates and times for the initial contact with the liaison person, the mid placement liaison contact and end of placement contacts were also arranged between all parties prior to the start of the placement. These were to be teleconference phone calls. The placement agency, Blue Dragon Children's Foundation, appeared very supportive of having the student placement and was keen for the project to go ahead.

The student's reflective journals were emailed regularly to the liaison person and feedback was given promptly, also by email. Phone contacts to touch base and ensure that the student was allright were also arranged early in the placement and at regular intervals as the placement progressed.

Initially, as the Field Education Coordinator, I had some concerns about the student's safety and the university's duty of care to a student on placement. Several characteristics of the student put my mind at ease. The student had lived in Vietnam before; was familiar with the culture and knew some Vietnamese; was familiar with the organisation with which the placement was planned and seemed to have the flexibility and maturity to manage this confronting yet exciting proposed community development placement.

Purcell (2009) explores community development as a process both for individual and for community empowerment. He suggests that using material such as photographs, drawings, poems and short plays facilitate community members to reflect on the current circumstances in their lives. The proposed drama workshops with children would provide a means of community education for the whole village communities and it was hoped, prevent further trafficking of children.

THE BLUE DRAGON CHILDREN'S FOUNDATION CEO'S EXPERIENCE

Blue Dragon Children's Foundation began in late 2002 by a group of volunteers seeking ways to help Hanoi's street children return to school and training. The Foundation registered as an Australian organisation in 2003, and finally as an International Non-Governmental Organisation (NGO) in Vietnam in 2004.

With support from other agencies and many volunteers – both Vietnamese and expatriate – Blue Dragon grew into a well-reputed NGO, providing a range of services to street kids, including a legal advocacy service, residential homes, a social work program, psychology, and school fee relief.

Background and context to the placement project

In late 2005, when Blue Dragon staff happened to meet a trafficked boy on the streets of Ho Chi Minh City, they were well placed to find a way for that child to escape from the traffickers and return home to his village in Hue, central Vietnam. That boy, a 13-year-old named Ngoc, was illiterate, having never been to school, and came from a family that lived in a tin shack on a beach. Having grown up in such extraordinary difficulty, Ngoc was a very easy target for child traffickers who took him to the south of the country with the promise of a free education and care in return for some minimal help selling flowers in a shop. However, once in Ho Chi Minh City, Ngoc was put to work on the streets selling roses to foreign tourists and outside night clubs. He was beaten for failing to sell enough, and all of the money he made – including 'tips' and gifts from well-meaning tourists – were taken by the traffickers. Ngoc worked through the night, every night, and the promised education never materialised.

Ngoc's return home was a very happy event, but it also enabled Blue Dragon staff to learn of a hitherto unknown, but widespread, problem of children being trafficked from remote rural villages in Hue province to the south of Vietnam. Almost no government agency or NGO seemed to be aware of this happening, and so no agencies had developed any interventions. The exception to this was a local NGO based in Ho Chi Minh City which offered English classes to the trafficked children, with the backing of a UK based charity.

Having met with the families of several dozen trafficked children, Blue Dragon started a process of rescuing and returning children and teens aged under 16, and established a program called 'Safe and Sound' which seeks to not only bring the children home to their families, but also provide ongoing support for returnees and prevent more children from being trafficked.

To really make 'Safe and Sound' a lasting success, it was this last goal that needed to be realised: the prevention of new cases of trafficking. Otherwise, Blue Dragon would be bringing children home only to have traffickers take children from neighbouring families to fill the vacancies.

In Vietnamese culture, families and individuals will rarely acknowledge having made mistakes or bad choices. Thus, when trafficked children returned to Hue, their families were talking openly about the 'large sums of money' that the traffickers had paid the children – in reality a pittance – but were not telling their community about the terrible working conditions and dangers of life in Ho Chi Minh City. It became clear to Blue Dragon staff that we needed to convey warnings to families, to let them know that allowing their children to be taken to the south to work was a bad choice.

In 2008, a former volunteer and long time friend of Blue Dragon, Skye Maconachie, approached us with a concept to teach drama to formerly trafficked children in Hue. The idea was very attractive for several important reasons. Firstly, Skye knew Blue Dragon well and understood our philosophies and values. This was important as working with trafficked children in Vietnam is an understandably sensitive undertaking. Second, the idea of a drama program met multiple goals of 'Safe and Sound'. A final performance held in villages would help to educate the communities about the realities of child labour in Ho Chi Minh City: drama is, after all, an excellent mode of communication and could easily be harnessed to raise awareness of an issue. The children would be given a voice to tell their families and communities about their experience in a safe, non-threatening way: through performance and play rather than through direct conversation. We expected that this would be empowering for the children, giving them a voice to say through drama what they could not otherwise express. And third, we believed that, on a simpler level, a drama program would be an excellent summer activity for children in rural Hue, where recreation for children is the lowest priority for struggling families. One reason that children sometimes go willingly with traffickers is that they are bored at home; this program would be anything but boring.

Despite the benefits of the program – all of which were realised over the ten week period – there was one significant challenge to the success of what became known as 'The Right to Shine'. Skye was coming not as a volunteer, but as a social work student, and so needed professional supervision and support. At that time Blue Dragon had no staff member qualified to provide such supervision; and Skye would be working 600 km from Blue Dragon headquarters in Hanoi, which meant that she would be largely 'on her own'. This was not an ideal situation for her to achieve the goals of her social work study. Fortunately a solution was quickly found. Catherine Briscoe, a social worker attached to Voluntary Service Overseas (VSO), was willing and able to take on the role of supervisor, and agreed to travel to Hue over the course of the program to visit Skye and ensure she was developing her social work skills.

Although Skye had previously volunteered with Blue Dragon (particularly through AusAid's Australian Youth Ambassador program), she was now coming with new skills, underpinned by academic theory, which she could apply to her work with the children. This helped ensure that 'The Right to Shine' was more than just a drama program; it also contained elements of a therapeutic intervention.

Skye's concept of a drama program for returnee trafficked children became a detailed plan, and finally a reality. Support from Catherine to offer professional supervision was very important to the success of 'The Right to Shine', allowing Skye the opportunity to debrief during difficult times (facilitating trafficked children to open up about their sometimes-harrowing experiences is itself an emotionally demanding task) and to routinely reflect on her own learning as she implemented her ideas.

The final result was a resounding success. A total of 42 children took part in a very worthwhile drama program (27 in Hai Tien and 15 in Phuong Dien); an estimated 1700 community members learned about the dangers of child trafficking; Blue Dragon's 'Safe and Sound' program was supplemented with an outstanding summer activity; and Skye grew and learned through her hands-on role in implementing the project.

THE STUDENT'S EXPERIENCE

Setting up my international student placement

From 2004 until 2009 I was involved as a volunteer with Blue Dragon Children's Foundation (BDCF) in Hanoi, Vietnam. With a strong focus on community and social development, Blue Dragon was the perfect host organisation for my placement. Through my volunteer work I had already established the key foundations of: good rapport, alignment with philosophies and a contextual understanding of Blue Dragon's work.

In order to mobilise this placement, thorough planning and preparation was required on my behalf. With social work only recently emerging as a recognised profession in Vietnam, I had the task of securing an in-country supervisor with Australian Association of Social Work equivalent qualifications. Following negotiations with Blue Dragon and my university emails were sent out to contacts within Vietnam. With perseverance we eventually received the contact details of Catherine Briscoe, a Social Work Advisor and Consultant with VSO in Hanoi. Catherine was the perfect candidate and was willing to support my placement. Her experience in international development and involvement in Vietnam enriched my entire placement.

Another element of the pre-placement planning included the successful application for funding for the Right to Shine project through Art Action, Singapore.

'Right to Shine'

'Right to Shine' was the principal project of my placement. The conceptualisation began in Hanoi eight months prior to the placement over cups of jasmine tea on the floor of Van Ta Ngoc's house (Blue Dragon's lawyer and 'Safe and Sound' co-coordinator). Reflecting on this incredible journey, it is difficult to find words to express the transformation, emotion and solidarity which occurred during the 'Right to Shine', which began as a such a small seed that evening in Hanoi. Van discussed the challenges of the 'Safe and Sound' program, which works directly with children in the province of Hue who are at high risk or are victims of trafficking. Despite Blue Dragon's successes in rescuing victims, traffickers were continuing to prey on the same villages. Parents continued to consent to their children being taken (for the first time or repeatedly).

Through ongoing discussion concerning 'breaking the cycle' of trafficking, two specific risk areas of the program were identified:

- School holidays were an extremely high-risk period for traffickers to prey on children and youth as they were not safely engaged in supervised activities
- There was a lack of awareness and understanding of how trafficking impacts the individual and the community.

These areas became the motivation behind developing a Theatre for Social Change project which would:

- positively engage and empower youth who had been trafficked or who were at high risk of being trafficked over the school summer holidays
- create community awareness of the issues of trafficking by compiling the youths' stories into a theatrical performance which not only presented the issue but also explored alternative solutions and options.

The framework for the 'Right to Shine' was primarily based on Augusto Boal's Theatre of the Oppressed (2000): theatre of the people, by the people, and for the people. Theatre of the Oppressed encompasses a range of theatrical techniques as a means to explore the knowledge of the people and transform reality in the social and relational field. Boal (2000) speaks of theatre being a new language, which allows participants to see their past experiences in a new way. 'By learning a new language, a person acquires a new way of knowing reality and of passing that knowledge on to others' (Boal, p121). In this way, the participants were able to engage in re-enactments of their experiences by using a new language, theatre. This tool of theatre opened up many dialogues between the victims of trafficking, their families, schools, community leaders and local government. It shifted 'the oppressed' from being spectators of their own lives to being actors, making action and re-creating their lives.

Boal speaks of Theatre of the Oppressed as 'offering everyone the aesthetic means to analyse their past, in the context of their present, and subsequently to invent their future without waiting for it'. (International Theatre of the Oppressed Organisation n.d) This is exactly what the 'Right to Shine' aimed to do. The ten weeks of workshops were mapped into three phases: community development; consciousness raising; and performance creation. Within these phases, opportunities were created for self-expression, reflection, solidarity, life skills, daring to dream and exploring alternatives to the issues impacting their lives.

This process culminated in two performances which utilised the experiences of the youth to create awareness, break down stigma and open up dialogue on the issues of trafficking within their communities.

Getting started

With all of the support elements of my field placement organised: agency, supervisor, project plan, funding, and target group. I headed off to Hue, Central Vietnam to meet my direct team, partners, representatives of local government, the communities, and of course the youth. This was when I surrendered to the pace and procedures of local operations and protocol. Blue Dragon's 'Safe and Sound' manager supported me during the first week as we made official government introductions, completed paperwork and gained permission for a foreigner to work in the two communities of Hai Tien and Phuong Dien. After all the official business was over, I was then able to recruit an interpreter/co-facilitator, train up my small team of three comprising the Blue Dragon local worker, Linh (not a real name); an interpreter and co-facilitator, Ngoc (not a real name) and myself, meet the youth and plan a schedule of workshops with them for the upcoming 12 weeks.

The weeks that followed were more incredible than I could have ever imagined or planned. Facilitating the youth was an absolute honour. Hearing their stories and witnessing their process and transformation shift led to greater awareness and respect. My mornings involved motorbike trips at the crack of dawn to both villages in order to complete our three hour workshops before the intense heat of the midday sun wiped us out. Afternoons were spent documenting the group work process, blogging, reflecting with my team, updating my supervisor and Blue Dragon, and planning for the next workshop.

The youth completely engaged in the program as it was such a new concept. Not only did they thrive on this empowering approach but it was also an opportunity for them to have a voice, share their stories, break down stigma and create change for their communities. Daily attendance was excellent with very few children missing any of the program. No words can really express the magic that occurred in those workshops and the impact it had on the lives of all who were involved.

The messages of 'Right to Shine' directly reached over 1,700 people through the community performances.

Collaborative processes with external stakeholders

This project worked effectively as a field placement due to the following factors: relationships; support; shared vision; local resources; preparation and planning. Different stakeholders contributed and collaborated on many different levels throughout this placement and were essential to the success of 'Right to Shine'. The Blue Dragon Children's Foundation has worked for years to break down barriers and gain support for their projects against human trafficking. Without their tireless commitment to social change and human rights this placement and project would not have been possible. Blue Dragon and the 'Safe and Sound' manager were integral in mobilising this project in the communities, through their relationships with partners, local government, and community leaders. Blue Dragon supported me throughout the placement, both professionally, emotionally and personally. Blue Dragon also committed valuable resources and time to support this project as a placement, including a project manager, Nadine Ziegeldorf. Nadine travelled weekly to the project site to provide support, especially focusing on project administration, production of performances and debriefing.

The Red Cross in Hue was the key local partner for the 'Safe and Sound' program. All proposals must go through the Red Cross for approval and support, as they are directly connected with local government. The Red Cross guided us through the correct political protocols in order to be able to work in these communities. Red Cross took a leap of faith, due to their strong relationship with Blue Dragon to trust in the project and me. Red Cross had a shared vision of child rights. The timing of this program coincided with a local government movement against child exploitation. This created enough support to allow us to operate in this usually conservative and restricted region. Red Cross is also invested in, and has a shared vision with Blue Dragon to stop child trafficking in their province.

Project funding from Art Action Singapore allowed Blue Dragon to: employ a co-facilitator/translator, and a local Theatre Director to organise political and theatrical logistics of performances; hire equipment for performances, make costumes, transport youth and their families to different communities; purchase healthy and nutritious snacks and meals for the youth; and employ two local mothers to prepare food.

This funding was put back into local resources and the community economy by purchasing all possible supplies locally before having to go to the city. BDCF's local staff member, Linh, was invested in the wellbeing of the youth, as they were from his community. He had essential relationships amongst the communities, which made our work successful. Ngoc, my interpreter/co-facilitator, was a vital element to the success of this project. He contributed to every level of the project: facilitation; negotiations; organisation; and cultural advisor.

We developed a very strong team dynamic from an early stage by facilitating training to introduce these new ideas of theatre and social change, as well as creating a shared knowledge base from which we worked. I continued to have weekly meetings to introduce workshop plans in order to empower Linh and Ngoc with the tools and experiential knowledge to facilitate the majority of the workshops. Each staff member had strengths and expertise, which enriched the project. We all had a shared vision with the best interest of the youth as our priority.

The availability of a Community Mentor/Professional Theatre Practitioner assisted the project. Through networking we developed a connection with Tuan, a local Theatre Director who had years of experience negotiating the political restrictions on 'theatre' in Vietnam. Tuan was able to navigate this process for us, including screening the scripts and making adjustments to the performances so as to fit within certain restraints. Tuan became a valuable mentor for the youth and without his participation and willingness, we may never have been able to do the community performances.

Other factors that contributed to the success of the placement from my perspective included the external supervisor, Catherine Briscoe, whose cross-cultural awareness and experience in working in Vietnam brought depth and relevance to her supervision. Catherine's familiarity with the political climate of Vietnam in context to this project was also very beneficial. She supported my ideas and passion whilst guiding me with pertinent questions that informed my reflective practice. Supervision occurred weekly via Skype. Weekly plans and group feedback were emailed to Catherine prior to our Skype sessions helping to enhance her understanding of the weekly occurrences. This gave both of us an opportunity to prepare questions, reflections and feedback to maximise on our time. Catherine was able to schedule two on-site visits for both mid placement and end of placement assessment. These visits provoked reflections and discussions that were essential for further development of practice.

Technology was fundamental in supporting the field placement. An internet connection was vital. Skype opened channels for communication between my supervisor, university liaison, BDCF head office and me. Maintaining a blog site was an effective means of keeping all stakeholders up to date with the projects' progress.

I found that I brought a number of attributes to this project which I feel led to its success. Among these were: a willingness to understand and learn from different cultures; an openness to acknowledge and utilise the skills and expertise that already existed in the community; flexibility and a sense of humour when things don't go the way you plan; problem solving skills, creativity; initiative and resourcefulness; a willingness to share all that you know and to learn from those around you; being organised with planning as well as being flexible in implementing back up plans; a genuine desire to contribute to the host country and the work of the placement organisation; and using skills in developing and maintaining supportive relationships.

THE FIELD EDUCATOR'S EXPERIENCE

In 2009 I was working in Hanoi for Voluntary Service Overseas (VSO, a British NGO) to promote training and practice skills development in social work in Vietnamese and NGO social services. I had good contacts with the Blue Dragon Children's Foundation. When I was asked to supervise an Australian student doing a placement project with Blue Dragon I liked the sound of both the project and of the challenges it presented. I was interested in the idea of working with children and through them with communities to confront the realities of trafficking children in Vietnam. I was also intrigued by the use of drama activities with which I had experimented in my early group work days but never taken any further than skill-practice role plays.

The challenges presented by this placement were different than any I had encountered before. We were working at a distance from one another with Skye working in Hue in central Vietnam while I was based and working in Hanoi at a distance of more than 500 kms so that most of our supervision had to take place by email and phone. I was not part of the management structure of Blue Dragon so the main supervisory functions I could undertake for this placement were educating and enabling/supporting the student (Hawkins & Shohet 2000). Responsibility for managing the student within the organisation remained with Blue Dragon, although I retained some responsibility for the wellbeing of the clients and the quality of the work done with them. The drama activities, which were the main focus of the student's placement, were a personal expertise that she was bringing in to her placement so that the focus of my supervision was on the goals, values, manner and impact of her activities rather than on the content of those activities.

The student worked through and with Vietnamese collaborators who mediated her interventions with the children with whom she was working. Although the student spoke some Vietnamese, it was not sufficient to convey her ideas directly to the children nor to understand their feedback and comments exactly. Working with Skye to understand the cultural context of the work with both the children and with the collaborators was crucial as was thinking with her about how to share and agree with the collaborators the aims, values and appropriate behaviours for facilitators and children in the activities.

Relationship development

I had some concerns about the feasibility of providing useful supervision with these unusual aspects to the placement but was relieved in meeting Skye, prior to her starting her placement, to realise that we could communicate easily. We shared a respect for and interest in Vietnamese culture and values. We were both enthusiastic about the country and about the resilience and strengths of Vietnamese people while being aware of the hardships with which so many families and their children struggled. We shared common values about people's dignity, how to help people develop their own goals and work towards these, and not imposing agendas. These values are very much part of the Blue Dragon ethos (www.streetkidsinvietnam.com/learn-about-blue-dragon/our-values/) so I was pleased though not surprised to find that Skye, through her previous experience of work with Blue Dragon, was committed to them.

I was also happy to find that Skye was eager for input from me and did not feel that her expertise in theatre and in the use of drama activities was all that was needed for the placement. She wanted to use these as tools for social work. Given the nature of the placement and the distant contact it demanded, starting out with a sense of mutual respect and an interest in sharing learning and experience was very important.

Contracting and supervision structure

Our initial sense of rapport helped us to agree to a contract for working together, although it was demanding for both of us. We agreed that we would meet by Skype every week at 7 p.m. on an agreed day. The day was flexible depending on our calendars but was always agreed in advance and the session happened every week.

We set aside an hour for the phone meeting. Prior to the meeting, Skye sent me a plan of the workshop activities to be undertaken with each group of children and a summary of the feedback, given by the children for each session. She wrote an agenda for our discussion, explaining what had happened that caused her to raise these particular issues. Skye also developed a blog 'The Right to Shine' reporting on the project and on the reactions of the children, which I read before sessions.

I went to visit Skye in her placement twice, once mid-placement and once near the end of the placement, staying overnight, visiting the children's groups and meeting the collaborators. These visits allowed for longer supervision sessions face-to-face, to take stock and to think through some of the theoretical issues we had discussed. They also gave me a much clearer idea of the student's physical working environment, of the reactions (and enthusiasm) of the children, of the collaborators and their attitudes to the student and to the children and of the surrounding stakeholders, including parents and community leaders, whose resources, views and attitudes had to be identified and fully considered in plans for the work. The visits also clarified the intensity of the work the student was undertaking and of her commitment to it.

Supervision content

I found that the issues that surfaced in supervision were more heavily focused on support and enabling with some issues combining both elements of educating and enabling/supporting. Much of the educational work I did undertake was about validating the student's own very intensive learning in the placement and approving her efforts to ensure that her collaborators were able to keep pace with her fast developing understanding and skills. I stressed and asked for specific thinking and reading about group work processes including developing group rules and procedures and helping children own and reinforce them, and identifying the roles different children played in the group, and how each affected group dynamics. With community work processes, I put emphasis on recognising the values held by community members and learning how to work within these (Ife & Tesoriero 2006).This arose from the recognition following discussion in the workshop sessions, that the children regarded work and going to the big city to work, apart from their families, as normal and even something to look forward to. They had a strong sense of duty and commitment to contributing to the family income. The student had to cope with her own commitment to children's rights and her organisation's anti-trafficking stance. She used an external newspaper story to help the children open up about what they knew about bad things that could happen if they worked away from home. Eventually the children developed storylines for their performances that looked at the dangers of bad employers but did not condemn working.

In considering the termination processes, the project built up to the climax of presentations for the community with a heavy load of organisational work as well as rehearsal and planning work with the children. There was also emotional reluctance to consider finishing work with the children and with the collaborators who built up very strong relationships with the student. Planning for and working on termination was a struggle.

Skye acknowledged that her placement was so active that she struggled to focus on theory. She accepted that her learning pattern tends to focus first on active experimentation and learning from reflection on the experience of the action (Kolb 1984, in Cleak & Wilson 2007). She did however respond to our theoretical discussions and undertook the related work.

In supporting/enabling the student, we worked on issues such as self-care including agreeing on a manageable workload, where an initial plan for three workshops in each village per week was reduced to two still requiring a total of four half-day sessions every week. Skye also needed to accept her own right to be assertive in asking for certain standards of work and cooperation. The collaborators quickly became very keen and involved in the project but did not always recognise the student's need for clear and legible translations of discussions with the children or for quick, accurate interpretation during the actual work sessions with the children. The student was hesitant about being more insistent given the good will of the collaborators but with discussion recognised that she could see and explain her needs as essential tools for the project and therefore part of the required structure.

Support and learning were both important in working on diplomacy in discussions with authority in the local environment. While the local Blue Dragon staff helped, the student also had to meet with village leaders and district officials whose approval and cooperation was needed for every stage of the project. Support was needed to help cope with the uncertainty and delays in getting the project's needs met.

The reactions from the local village communities also caused varying problems. In one village the sessions took place in a public area in the centre of the village. Villagers sat around the area and chatted watching the children, which only became a problem when male youths started commenting on some of the older girls, just on the verge of adolescence, causing immediate self-consciousness and withdrawal by the girls. The male collaborator, with prompting, had a few friendly words with the young men and they disappeared but it took a little time to restore the confidence of the girls.

In the second village the setting was inside a building and more isolated and the staff here were more concerned about the indifference of parents and other community members. The only spectators for the activities here were the younger children of the village. For this village, supervision discussions focused more on the situations of the families and the work the parents did to support their numbers of children. Avoiding being judgmental about parental neglect was discussed.

Coping with emotional issues

Support was needed too at different emotional moments in the project. The situations and needs of children and their families were acted out and commented on as normal life by the children in the drama sessions but caused distress for the staff team. Again the student had to cope with her own distress and that of the collaborators. Support here meant giving permission to acknowledge distress, to discuss it openly with the collaborators in the staff debriefings and to use it to plan support for the families during the project and subsequently.

Distress was also felt when a case history from a news story of a trafficked child was used as the basis of a role play and one group of children acted out the violence meted out to the child at length and with very strong emotions. Coping with personal and collaborator reactions and fears needed time and discussion.

Overall, I found this placement experience very rewarding and believe that it brought real benefits for the children and for the villagers and local representatives who watched the final performances by the children. The children gained self-understanding and self-esteem and the community opened up to the exploration of the dangers the children might meet in going so far from home to work. The placement seemed to work well as a learning experience for the student who learnt both her abilities and about her need to conceptualise and use theory in her work.

CONCLUSION

This field placement was successful and a positive experience for all stakeholders, and we believe, for the children and communities of the two villages who participated in the Right to Shine project. The key factors which contributed to the success, which are recommended in considering overseas placements, are for the placement to be well planned; for an experienced field educator to be available to the student; the willingness of each stakeholder to cooperate and make it work and the availability and use of technology. Student attributes that are essential include: a willingness to understand and learn from different cultures; an openness to acknowledge and utilise the skills and expertise that already exists amongst the community; flexibility and a sense of humour when things don't go the way you plan; problem solving skills, creativity; initiative and resourcefulness; being willing to share all that you know as well as being willing to learn from those around you; being organised with planning as well as being flexible in implementing back up plans; having a genuine desire to contribute to the host country and the work of the placement organisation; and having skills in developing and maintaining supportive relationships. The blog site Right to Shine (2009) includes comments from some of the child participants:

- 'Don't exploit children, help them if you see them in bad situations'.
- 'I used my real emotion when performing. I think I am luckier than other people, because other people are still in worse situations than my family. Even though, I feel like my family's conditions are very poor'.
- 'You need the children for the future of the country'.

Finally, in a speech given at the end of one of the performances one child proclaimed:

My name is Tuat, I am 14 years old ... For me, this was a very meaningful summer holiday as I was lucky to attend the Right to Shine program. This program has bought many opportunities to make friends with the others in my community and especially brought the knowledge about drama, and an understanding of life values. Through our performance, we would like to send a message to all of the children in the commune and our peers, that Saigon is not a suitable place for us to work. Although I have not been to Saigon, I have learnt a lot about the reality through the stories of my other friends who have been trafficked. I now understand the risks and dangers which lie beneath the beautiful surface of the big city which fascinates so many young people. I also understand that there are many alternative options to get safer jobs around our community so that we can not only earn money to support our families but also protect ourselves from trafficking and exploitation. In my opinion, going to school is the best way to make our dreams come true. I am so grateful to this program which brings to us such a precious time this year. Thank you.

Acknowledgment

The authors would like to thank Art Action Singapore, Red Cross and Blue Dragon Children's Foundation for making this program possible.

References

Blue Dragon Children' Foundation Website (2011). [Online]. Available: www.streetkidsinvietnam.com [Accessed 2 February 2011].

Boal A (2000). *Theatre of the oppressed.* (New Edition). London: Pluto Press.

Cleak H & Wilson J (2007). *Making the most of field placement.* (2nd edn). Melbourne, VIC: Thompson

Hawkins P & Shohet R (2000). *Supervision in the helping professions.* (2nd edn). Maidenhead, UK: Open University Press.

Ife J & Tesoriero F (2006). *Community development: community-based alternatives in an age of globalization.* (3rd edn). French's Forest, NSW: Pearson.

International Theatre of the Oppressed Organisation (n.d). *Declaration of principles.* [Online]. Available: www.theatreoftheoppressed.org/en/index.php?useFlash=1 [Accessed 13 May 2011].

Nickson A, Kuruleca S & Clark M (2009). *Fijian and Australian social work learning through field education*. In C Noble, M Henrickson & IY Han (Eds). *Social work education: voices from the Asia Pacific* (pp50–72). Carlton, VIC: Vulgar Press.

Purcell R (2009). Images for change: community development, community arts and photography. *Community Development Journal,* 44(1): 111–22.

Chapter Eight

Violence against women: critical feminist theory, social action and social work in the Philippines

Annalisa Enrile and Jennifer Nazareno

Recognising the importance of expanding teaching and field education practice to a more globalised context, our research focuses on global education of social workers. Established in 2006, this course draws from feminist and complex systems theories to examine violence against women, feminist theory and social action from a global perspective. The course is based on a partnership between the University of Southern California School of Social Work (USC SOWK) and the University of Philippines, Diliman-College of Social Work and Community Development (UP CSWCD). The three-week program includes daily instruction that combines lectures with professors and guest speakers and agency visits from the community, discussion panels on labour issues, land ownership, poverty, prostitution, legislative process, healthcare and other relevant topics.

针对女性的暴力：菲律宾的女权主义论，社会行动论和社会工作

全球浸入式研究课程

在全球范围内，社工理论的教学和社工实习的重要性受

到越来越广泛的关注。本研究主要讨论社工教育的全球化。浸入式研究课程创立于2006年，利用女权主义论和复杂系统论全面探讨针对女性受暴力，女权主义论和社会行动论。本研究课程是与菲律宾大学蒂利曼分校的社会工作和社区发展学院共同合作创立的。课程为期三周，学院教授，客席演讲者就不同论题发表他们的意见。论题包括劳工问题，土地归属权问题，贫穷问题，娼妓问题，立法程序问题，健康医疗以及其他相关问题。除此以外，课程参与者亦会参访各个社区服务机构。根据此研究课程，我们提出三个论点。　第一，社区发展和政策执行时所面临的挑战。第二，教学单位和社工系学生的不同经验。第三，作为社工系的教学人员，我们从此研究课程中总结出的合作经验和如何深化跨文化/国际化的社工实践。

女性に対しての暴力：フィリピンにおけるフェミニスト理論、ソーシャルアクションとソーシャルワーク

―グローバル化の浸透プログラムに関する一考察―

よりグローバル化した状況へと教育や現場教育実習を拡大することの重要性を認識することから、本研究はソーシャルワーカーのグローバル教育に焦点をおいている。2006年に設立して以来、本コースは、グローバルな視点から女性に対する暴力、フェミニスト理論やソーシャルアクションを調査するための、フェミニスト理論や複雑なシステム理論から情報が得られている。このコースは、フィリピン大学、ディルマン、ソーシャルワークおよびコミュニティ開発学部との提携に基づいている。この3週間のプログラムは、教授、ゲストスピーカー、地域の関係機関の訪問者、などに加え、労働問題、土地の所有権、貧困、売春、法制過

程、健康管理や他の関連問題に関する討論助言者による講義を組み合わせた日々の教育が組まれている。本研究は、(1)開発と実施における課題 (2)教職員と学生の様々な経験 (3) 異文化間•国際ソーシャルワーク実践にさらに影響を与えるためのもう一つのソーシャルワークのプログラムとの協同の中で教育者として得た洞察力、の3点について要点を述べる。

여성에 대한 폭력: 남녀평등주의 이론, 필리핀의 사회적 행위 및 사회복지학. 글로벌 집중 프로그램에 대한 연구

사회복지학 교습과 현장 교육에 있어 좀 더 세계적인 맥락으로 뻗어나가는 것이 중요하다는 것을 인식함에 따라 우리의 연구는 사회복지사의 글로벌 교육에 초점을 맞추고 있다. 2006년도에 설립된 이 과정은 남녀평등주의 이론과 복잡 조직 이론을 바탕으로 하고 있다. 이 과정은 여성에 대한 폭력, 남녀평등주의 이론, 그리고 사회적 행위를 세계적 관점에서 조명하고 있다. 이 과정은 University of the Philippines Diliman 과 University of the Philippines College of Social Work and Community Development 와의 동반자적 관계를 기반으로 하고 있다. 3주 과정의 프로그램은 매일매일의 교육을 포함하는데, 이것은 교수 및 초청 연사 강의, 지역 사회 기관의 방문, 그리고 노동 문제, 토지 소유권, 가난, 성매매, 입법 절차, 의료 및 다른 관련된 주제에 대한 공개 토론으로 이루어 진다. 우리는 다음과 같은 영역에 대해 간략히 기술할 것이다. (1) 이 과정을 개발하고 실행하는 데 있어서의 도전 과제들 (2) 교수진과 학생들이 겪은 다양한 경험 (3) 문화간/국제적 사회복지 실습에 더욱 큰 영향을 주기 위해 다른 사회복지학 프로그램과의 협력하는 과정에서 교육가로서 얻은 통찰.

Educating and preparing students to become social workers within an international context is a daunting challenge. It is no longer sufficient to establish cultural sensitivity or culturally competent social work standards. As more social workers engage in international work abroad or in their home countries, the need to understand globalisation, transnational patterns, economics and political power is imperative. Without this context and background, students are unable to grasp the full scope of global social work. (Murphy et al. 2009).

Recognising the importance of expanding teaching and field education practice within a more globalised framework, this case study focuses on one way of transmitting global education of social workers through a global immersion program. Though globalisation is not a new phenomenon, the increasing infiltration of globalised economic markets have created many new social inequalities and vulnerabilities that impact societies and populations around the world, particularly women. Thus, the program draws from critical feminist and complex world systems theories to examine social, economic, and political injustices against women and ways to elicit social action from a global perspective. Established in 2006, the course goes beyond the traditional notions of a 'study abroad' program and creates a learning space where students are able to gain hands on experience within a specific country's environment while providing skills that could be used in both international and domestic circumstances. Praxis is carried out by the infusion of both theory- and action-based strategies. The main course objective is for students to gain globalisation and critical feminist viewpoints in social work. With these knowledge bases, students may better develop social action strategies that integrate a theoretical lens and gain a better understanding of other models of social service in an international setting. Further, the question of how best to prepare students for work in these international settings, transnational agencies, and/or international populations is also addressed in this course.

This article will outline (1) theoretical frameworks and discourses to better illuminate the urgency for building a critical knowledge base as it relates to international social work; (2) various US experiences of students and faculty; (3) the challenges of development and implementation of this program; (4) recommendations to influence cross-cultural/international social work praxis.

DEVELOPING A GLOBALISATION AND CRITICAL FEMINIST DISCOURSE FOR US SOCIAL WORK PRAXIS

Globalisation has created a growing range of social and economic problems with increasingly diverse types of clients, requiring today's social workers to gain critical knowledges of international populations, exposures to alternative methods of service delivery and international networking skills more than ever before. In response, the University of Southern California School of Social Work (USC SOWK) offers a series of cross-cultural study-abroad seminars that combine classroom instruction with experiential learning to help students understand different cultural perspectives through firsthand interactions with host cultures. Yet, it is integral for social work students to have a critical understanding of various frameworks around globalisation and feminist theories to better assist them in conceptualising their positionalities and roles as social workers in the United States (US). Additionally, the aim is to develop critically conscious social workers able to engage in social work praxis in international social settings.

In essence, globalisation means the flows of capital, commodities, ideas and people across borders. Popular and dominant perceptions of globalisation often elucidate the novel view that the world is now a 'single place'. Some scholars assert that we are entering a global age and that a whole new world order has emerged (Albrow 1997; Held et al. 1999; Robertson 1992). Within classroom discourse, debates over the term globalisation and whether it is something to celebrate or have a growing concern for, occur. For some, the 'global age' represents a new birth of freedom, new connections occurring at a global scale via the advancements in technology, transportation and communications that have brought US closer as a global community (Albrow 1997; Held et al. 1999; Robertson 1992). Those with similar views may suggest that such breakthroughs deserve much celebration due to exposures to free market capitalist trade and democratic institutions, new ideas

173

and products that have become universally available and can in turn improve and create more prosperous lives for more people around the globe (Friedman 1999).

Yet there is another side. As opposed to the ahistorical, glamorised, simplistic notion of the term globalisation, critics argue that this process encompasses more than the new sources of wealth and prosperity that are often celebrated. Due to today's rapid forces of globalisation, what remains invisible are the vast new vulnerabilities that have been created and felt around the world, mostly by women. Certain feminist scholars have examined how globalisation has increased specific types of labour provided by racial, ethnic minority, immigrant and recent migrant women from less industrialised countries. More specifically, these scholars interrogate how social inequities around gender, class, race, ethnicity, histories, wars, nationality and citizenship play a significant roles in the social realities these women currently find themselves in (Anderson 2000; de la Luz Ibarra 2000; Glenn 1986, 1992; Guevarra 2009; Hondagneu-Sotelo 1994, 2001; Kousha 1995; Mohanty 1991; Momsen 1999; Parreñas 2001; Rollins 1985; Romero1999; Thornton Dill 1988).

Critics argue that there is nothing new or trendy about globalisation. Utilising a world systems lens, Wallerstein (1974, 1984) and Sassen (2008) postulate that undergirding globalisation is age-old capitalism in post-industrialised, rich nations that have penetrated to other parts of the world (often through wars and occupations) in order to create a capitalist, neoliberal world economy. Such critics postulate that political leaders and corporations of industrialised regions have infiltrated less 'developed' countries to exploit their labour and natural resources in order to retain economic domination and greater profits in a purportedly integrated world (Portes & Borocz 1989; Sassen 2008; Wallerstein 1974). In fact, the gap between the richest and poorest in the world is approximately four times bigger than it was a century ago (UNDP 2008).

These growing issues directly impact marginalised populations, especially women who are most often represented in all categories of oppression and discrimination. Thus, it is integral for social work students to be critically conscious and knowledgeable about the social implications of globalisation. However, in order to work with such populations, it is more relevant than ever that social workers have an understanding of the globalised processes of world economic systems. Sassen (2008) articulates that the world economy is divided between the Global North and the Global South. She describes the Global North consisting of a small number of global cities found in the core regions of the world in which banking, finance, administration, professional services, and research are concentrated. Particular to the US, these global cities include places like New York, Chicago, Los Angeles, and Miami and dominate much of the world economy.

These divisions symbolise the merging and consolidation of power and have created huge concentrations of wealth. Thus, globalised capitalist development creates high-paying professional jobs in wealthy nations, higher levels of income inequality, and a higher demand for low-wage service workers around the globe (Sassen 2006, 2008). As Hochschild (2004, p17) notes, the growing split between the North and South means that 'the middle class of the Third World now earns less than the poor of the First World'. Without this macro viewpoint, mezzo and micro practitioners are unable to fully comprehend or treat their clients past the point of superficial interventions. This course, as part of a larger global immersion project emphasises the importance of all three aspects of social work within a global praxis. The global restructuring of the political economy has created often unnoticed social inequalities and disadvantages that are endured and embodied in the sense that it has become an everyday social reality for so many women. Consequently, the course not only focuses on conventional issues relating to violence against women (i.e. domestic violence and sexual assault), but ventures beyond traditional concerns. Women continue to make up the majority of low wage service workers, exported labour, and carry the main burdens of poverty.

Critical feminist scholars have argued that gender is an invaluable resource for capital and labour markets that depend on women's labour, particularly in production work, domestic work, and care work. In addition, women are most vulnerable to prostituted exploitation (Choy

2003; Enloe 2000; Fernandez-Kelly 1989; Guevarra 2009; Hondagneu-Sotelo 2001; Hossfeld 1990; Mies 1982; Misra et al. 2006; Momsen 1999; Ong 1987; Parreñas 2001; Safa 1995). Thus this course examines aspects of violence against women such as women's labour, trafficking of women and children, impact of militarisation, and barriers to health and reproductive health care. Such exploitations and violations against women can be linked to the continual presence of patriarchical, dominant views that subordinate women and a Westernised capitalistic profit motive that obscure the historical, social, economic and cultural forces that have led to the devaluation of women as well.

Globally, there are an increasingly disproportionate number of racially ethnic migrant women engaged in labour as domestic workers, sex workers, nannies and health care workers around the globe. While making life easier for their employers, Romero (2002) argues that these women earn extremely low wages, rarely receive benefits if at all, labour long hours doing physically demanding work and grappling with trying to provide care for their own families as well. Thus, these women comprise a significant group of vulnerable, feminised labour in the lowest wage sectors among the world economies (Foner 2000; Kwong 1998; Mahler 1995; Sassen 1998). Case in point, Filipino women represent one group of feminised labour that work as domestic workers, caregivers and entertainment hostesses in Los Angeles and Rome. They supply the undervalued services indispensable to maintaining both the structures and symbols of global economic power and privilege (Parreñas 2001).

Embedded in the phenomenon of the global feminisation of migrant labour is the disturbing trend that these numbers shroud the numbers of women who are trafficked for labour and/or sexual reasons. Currently, there are 95 million women migrants worldwide (UNFPA 2006). Of these numbers, the amount of women and girls trafficked each year into the sex trade (often through coercion or abduction) and labour enslavement varies widely, ranging between 700,000 and 4 million (US Dept of State 2002). According to Nikolic-Ristanovic (2002), uneven distribution of wealth has constantly been among the key factors of sex trafficking but only in the past several decades has sex trafficking become a global problem.

Enloe (2000) further emphasises the exploitation of women as it relates to the global politics engaged in certain themes of militarisation and promotions around tourism. Irrespective of whether a war is currently going on in a certain region or not, violence against women has been correlated with the very presence of militarisation (Nikolic-Ristanovic 2002). The US military presence in the Philippines has existed for over 100 years, first in the form of the largest US military bases in the Pacific until 1986 to the formation of 22 ports through the US-Philippines Visiting Forces Agreement (Marigold 2003). Around each of these ports and in the place of the former US bases, most notably in Angeles City and Subic Bay, a red light district and sex tourism continues to thrive. This provides an interesting backdrop for students to learn about the role of militarisation and the complicated relationships between the US and those countries where they place their military installations. Thus, war and post war conditions can serve a significant role in the expansion of sex trafficking and prostitution on both local and global scales. Countless women continue to be subjected to numerous abuses and forms of violence including rape, battery, and a legacy of sexually transmitted disease (Marigold 2003). Widespread abandonment of the Amerasian children they have fathered is not uncommon.

Various research on women against violence stresses that such abuses cause poorer physical and mental health, physical injuries and a more significant need for medical resources than non-abused women (Campbell 2002; Heise et al. 1999). Additionally, sexual abuse in the form of forced sex not only produces physical and mental trauma but causes anatomical damage to various organs, and can result in sexually transmitted infections (STIs), including HIV/AIDS (Campbell, 2002). Gender-based violence impacts women's reproductive and sexual health as well and may lead to chronic pelvic pain, vaginal bleeding, painful menstruation, sexual dysfunction and infertility (Campbell 2002).

Students are exposed to how globalisation directly impacts the issues of violence towards women on these varying levels. To this end, this course develops methodology within which to discuss the larger issues of poverty; the balance of political and personal power; and micro-macro intervention techniques in the context of globalisation. Hence, a theoretical lens becomes all the more necessary to analyse practice standards.

Providing a transnational feminist lens in social work

Feminist scholars provide a critical lens on gender roles in society as they relate to the household, economic and labour markets, geopolitics and international conflicts and how these themes link to women's everyday lives. Students are exposed to these knowledge bases during their foundation courses (Gilligan 1982; Kessler-Harris 1975 Mohanty 1991, 2003; West & Zimmerman 1987). However, even within feminist theory, there is a broad range of perspectives. Thus, the 'feminist' label is too overarching and must be further refined if students are to understand and utilise such theory in praxis. In the case of this course, transnational feminist theory is utilised as it is the most accurate lens for viewing global feminist movements. These types of transnational feminist frameworks have been developed to challenge the simplistic, ahistorical and celebratory narratives around 'global sisterhood'. (Grewel & Kaplan 1994; Mendoza 2002; Mohanty 1991, 2003). Further, while there are a number of different ways to approach the subject, the ability to provide students with concrete examples is a powerful method for students' learning processes. Therefore, the Philippines and its vibrant, ever-shifting women's movement was chosen for the site of this course.

Transnational feminist writings expose the historical roots of imperialism, occupation and subjugation that have structurally shaped the lives of millions of Filipino women scattered around the world (Espiritu 2003). Similar postcolonial trajectories can be applied to Caribbean women in New York (Colen 1995); Mexican and Latina women in California and other parts of the US (Hondagneu-Sotelo 2001; Romero 1992) and Sri Lankan women in Saudi Arabia (Gamburd 2000). In the early twentieth century, US colonisation and occupation of the Philippines included the infiltration of their governments, militaries, economic systems and health care systems (Ong & Azores

1994). Without a complex understanding of the colonial and imperialist relationship between the US and the Philippines, a historical amnesia of an imperialist past takes place or what Matthew Jacobsen has called the 'modern art of forgetting' (Jacobson 1999, p117) and in part has led to the celebratory notions of globalisation.

'Although imperialism is most often treated as a matter of economics and diplomacy, it has an embodied presence in the lives of people from colonized nations' (Espiritu 2003, p48). As such, Espiritu (2003), Guevarra (2009) and Parreñas (2001) claim that the culture of US imperialism and the racialised, gendered, class-based social hierarchies does not cease with Philippine independence from the US, but endures today and continues to influence how Filipino women in the Philippines and the US are perceived. Pre-existing imperialistic, colonial, cultural and economic relations play a critical role in the constant exodus of migrants from the Global South to the Global North (Castles & Miller 1998). Transnational feminist writings have attempted to expose these differences, asymmetries and these longstanding inequities between women. As such, the transnational feminist perspective resists utopic ideas about 'global sisterhood' but instead focus on laying the groundwork for more equitable social relations among women across borders and cultural contexts (Mendoza 2002). In doing so, it provokes social workers to re-evaluate the dominant discourses and constructed knowledges around the role of globalisation, migrant women from less industrialised countries and immigrant women of colour in the US.

CRITICAL IMPORTANCE OF GLOBAL IMMERSION

Given the complexities around this social phenomenon that attribute to violence experienced by women, the question still remains as to the best way to address the issue of teaching students to become global practitioners, operating from a distinct theoretical perspective and engaging in action-based models of intervention that are empowering. In other words, how does social work education create social workers who are transformative in their work? This global immersion course is concerned with that objective and constructed to address the needs of closing the gap between theory and practice in education (Lerner

1997). Students that choose to travel and study in the Philippines can gain critical insight and awareness around the impacts of colonialism and militarism on women and feminist movements that illuminate and protest violence against women. Indeed, there were several measures designed to address the role of social workers in social change paradigms operating from a transnational feminist perspective around the issues of violence against women within the Philippines context. First, pragmatic areas that must be considered are: structure of the course within the unique aspects of the host country (in this case the Philippines), equal partnerships with like-minded institutions, and relevant assignments to validate the global immersion process.

As stated earlier, the Philippines provide a unique backdrop for the global immersion. A strategic part of the Pacific Rim, the Philippines is located close to China, Vietnam, Malaysia, and Indonesia. Unlike its Asian neighbours, a more than 500-year legacy of Spanish colonialism and over 50 years of American neocolonialism has made the Philippines the only Roman Catholic Asian country, and one of the few Asian countries where English remains a dominant language (English only ceased being the medium of instruction in 1996). This is not to say that the Philippines does not share any similarities with other Asian countries, and this is reflected through cultural values such as *hiya* (shame), *pakikisama* (the betterment of the group over the individual), and *bahala na* (fatalism). On the outside, the culture may seem very egalitarian with the people of the Philipines having elected two female presidents. As is often the case, there is more than the surface would suggest. The mix between indigenous and colonial influences has created a patriarchal societal structure wherein women are given certain liberties such as education and job advancement, but where male power paradigms are upheld. Notably, however both female presidents have lacked the support of the broader women's movement in the Philippines. To teach feminism in an area such as the Philippines is to also give a vibrant, tangible example to students of different aspects within a women's liberation movement. (Agbayani & Enrile 2003; Aquino 1994).

Structure of the program

The overall global immersion program is open to all USC graduate students, with priority given to those students in the School of Social Work obtaining their Masters in Social Work. If there are any spaces open, then students from other universities are welcome to apply. Students are asked to fill out an application which is then reviewed by the course instructors and the director of the global immersion program. When there are a number of applications, instructors may choose the option of in-person and phone interviews to determine which students are selected for the program. Students are selected on a number of criteria such as international experience, area of interest, and study plan. Upon submission of their application, students must also place a deposit on the program (which is returned to them if they are not selected). Once they are selected, students may opt to use their financial aid to pay for the global immersion. Costs of the global immersion are covered by students who are responsible for summer school enrolment (the course is a four-unit offering) as well as program costs which include their board, lodging, and in-country transportation.

The Philippines serves as a prime example for students interested in learning about the impacts of militarism, the complex relationship with the US based on its shared military history as well as the physical vestiges of former military bases. As stated earlier, the Philippines women's movement is a fitting backdrop that accommodates a number of feminist paradigms and international work in which students are able to gain firsthand experiences that relate to their course work. The program attempts to address the balance between theory and practice. An ideal program provides a sufficient amount of time for students to engage in distinct and various cultures of the host country and at the same time account for the confines of work demands and financial limitations of a typical social work student. The course begins in the US with a one week orientation and discussion of theoretical content. This occurs at the home campus of the USC SOWK usually toward the end

181

of the academic year. Students are instructed on packing appropriately for realistic weather conditions and are instructed on taking appropriate medical precautions. The on-site Student Travel Center is used as a tool toward achieving these goals.

The second part of the course takes place in the Philippines. Several versions of the program were created to address the needs of students: standard two weeks (this is the official schedule of coursework), optional third week (usually occurring before the trip where students can experience an out-of-town trip to the famed Philippine Rice Terraces and indigenous tribal culture), or an optional fourth week (usually occurring after the course work where students may choose to do an in-depth field experience with one of the partner agencies). The optional third week allows the course to include areas of interest that are timely to the Philippines but do not necessarily fall under the umbrella of 'violence against women' such as environmental issues (mainly, deforestation and mining) and indigenous rights. Since the bulk of the course is situated within the capital city Manila, students who are able to arrive early can visit and experience various provinces and take in the nature and environmental landscapes of the Philippines. For those students that may never have the chance to return to the Philippines again, these areas can serve as an educational opportunity for the interface between the indigenous cultures and capitalist influences that are reconstructing the sociopolitical landscapes.

Almost all of the students choose the optional third week as it also allows them to ease into the Philippines and get acclimated to certain factors such as the time-zone change, climate and various cultures. The optional fourth week allows students the opportunity and choice to further explore an area that they are interested in as well as to create further networks and cultivate experiences in that area. For example, in 2007, several students became interested in transnational feminist organising and opted to stay in Manila to attend an international women's conference. They engaged in this conference as interpreters and provided documentation support. In doing so, this opportunity provided further educational and advocacy related experiences through working closely with agencies and organisations involved in conference planning. Other logistical considerations include staffing the immersion program and figuring out where students will stay, which will be addressed in the next section.

The actual course is structured to contain several parts: topic area content, field experiences, and student process/advisement sessions (also known as debriefings). Each topic area is served as a daily theme, which then was substantiated by a lecture given by a prominent researcher in that area as well as a field experience. Field experiences took the form of field trips to agencies, organisations, and communities. As much as possible, coordinators worked to create field experiences that would be exemplary in the specific topic area of the day but that would also provide the most engagement with actual social workers, community organisers, and when possible, clients and communities. These field experiences ranged from visits to agencies such as the Women's Crisis Center (which serves women survivors of rape, sex trafficking and prostitution), the Sanctuary Center (which treats women with mental illness due to trauma from physical and sexual abuse), the Buklod Center (a women's advocacy organisation that exposes human rights violations against women and children), to urban poor communities. In many instances, several field experiences had to be designed as the class size of students (some years more than 25) could not be accommodated. Most agencies and organisations felt comfortable with the entire class. However, field experiences such as sharing with community members, home stays, or participation in interventions worked best with small groups of six to eight students.

Students and team members were required to attend a daily debriefing, or student process and advisement session. The sessions were mostly conducted in the morning before the day's program began, although some sessions had to be scheduled for later times to accommodate the program. During overnight field experiences, sessions were held on the bus. The need for flexibility is crucial but more importantly, an appropriate amount of time must be allocated to ensure that consistent debriefings occur. For some of the students, this was their first experience travelling overseas. For most of the students, this was their first encounter with topic areas such as poverty or sexual exploitation. The entire process of transitioning from reading an article and understanding the components theoretically takes on a whole new meaning when students come face-to-face with the stark and startling realities of most communities they visit. For instance, one can read about the presence of slums in the city, but to actually walk through ankle high human excrement, mud, and dirty laundry water that compose the gutters that small children play in surrounding the dirt floors of their makeshift homes, is quite another story. These sessions of student process and advisement provide students with a space for discussion and debate, connecting the issues to the experiences, or simply a space where they can express their emotional responses. Depending on the topic area, instructors also offered private office hours for added support. In mixed gender settings, sometimes process groups were gender specific to provide an added level of sensitivity and support. For example, after a sharing with domestic violence and rape survivors, a separate 'women's only' group was held in order to provide a safe space for women to talk about their feelings and experiences.

Partnership with the University of Philippines, Diliman

The course, first designed in 2006, partnered with various grassroots women's organisations. However, during the first assessment, it was clear that a university partner would be beneficial to the program. It was an easy decision for the USC SOWK to partner with the University of the Philippines, Diliman Campus because of their renowned College of Social Work and Community Development [UP CSWCD], both because of former connections between faculty members and the reputation of the school's social work program. A team from the USC SOWK (instructors and global programs director) met with a representatives of the UP CSWCD composed of the Dean of the College, several tenure line instructors and field instructors. A memorandum of agreement was created that outlined the designation of responsibilities and tasks. It cannot be overemphasised how important a demarcation of duties is necessary to the smooth handling of the course. To this end, it was decided that the main instructor of the course from USC SOWK and a designated instructor from UP CSWCD be considered the coordinators of the overall program. In addition to the coordinators of the program, a program team was assembled that would work together before and after the duration of the course. Team members that had a background in social work were preferred. From the USC SOWK side, team members included:

- one co-instructor whose main role was to provide administrative assistance to the main instructor and facilitate daily debriefing sessions with students
- one doctoral level student whose main role was to provide academic and social support to graduate student (MSW) participants
- one or two community workers to work with students and provide additional support when needed by the instructors. Community workers are usually selected because of their work with the Filipino community either in the Philippines or abroad. Community members did not always have to have a social work background, though it was preferred.

Team members from the UP CSWCD side included:

- one liaison to UP CSWCD who was on site at the hotel and stayed with the students during the entire program. This person served as the main connection with the school and provided everyday types of supports such as making sure daily logistics (transportation, communication to the agencies, etc.) were taken care of
- one administrative support person, who provided support for clerical needs such as photocopying, making sure students had access to banks, emergency health care, etc.
- one or two additional support persons who provided translation assistance and general student support.

The teams were essential in creating an efficient program operation. A good ratio of team members to students is roughly five or six students per team member. This assures constant student contact and the ability to make sure that student needs are met. In this type of intensive immersion program, it is necessary to make sure that students are processing information on a cognitive as well as emotional level. One of the ways to ensure that academic and social support for the course is adequate is by providing an adequate proportion of support members and resources per student.

The coordinators of the program designed a syllabus that included the daily instruction and combination of lectures with professors and guest speakers from the community and discussion panels. Such topics included the historical and contemporary interconnections between the US and the Philippines, migration and labour issues, land ownership, poverty, prostitution, legislative processes, and women's health issues in addition to home stays and field trips to such places as a women's prison and a red-light district. Coordinators from both schools provided balanced input on designing and finalising the syllabus. It is important to note that a true partnership was achieved in creating the syllabus by which instructional needs from USC SOWK were balanced with the local expertise and informed opinions of UP CSWCD. Striving for a mutually beneficial arrangement was a goal for the duration of the project. The partnership also allowed for the students to be housed at the UP Diliman Campus at the UP Hotel. The setting was ideal due to its location within the host site campus The university was located outside of the main city (making it easier to keep track of students' whereabouts), increasing student contact with UP students (school was in session at the time), and providing security (the campus is guarded 24 hours a day).

Students were exposed to a number of experiences that were invaluable in translating theory into practice. In order to further challenge them and to help them articulate their experience, relevant assignments and activities were created. Students were asked to keep a journal. They were encouraged to write more than just their initial feelings and reactions but also to incorporate the course readings, theoretical frameworks and lectures with their experiences. The journal composed the foundation of a global portfolio that students turned in at the end of summer. Journal prompts were provided to students to stimulate their thinking processes through experiential and reflective exercises and group-based assignments. Students were also prompted to understand issues from a range of perspectives, including discussing alternative viewpoints after conducting site visits to women's social service, community and human rights organisations; and cultural excursions. Students were encouraged to reflect on how to better engage in social work praxis in international social settings. They also were prompted to explore the similarities and differences found in relation to social work praxis in the Philippines versus the US.

Students were also assigned a final project, composed of two parts. The projects were partner based and partners were told to choose a population of interest that they would further study and develop during the course. The first part of the project was a formal, academic paper which required students to provide a description of their topic and the population affected; the status of that population within (possibly outside of) the Philippine context, main issues of the population, social action (if any) that the population is taking, implications to social work practice, and challenges and recommendations. In addition to the formal papers, students created a photo essay depicting the Philippines from the viewpoint of the population their project was based on. Both the photo essay and paper were presented upon return to the US in community and campus-based forums.

Student experiences and insights gained as educators

The success of the global immersion programs is perhaps best measured by the number of students that continue to sign up for them and participate. The program, which began in 2006 with the Philippines global immersion has since expanded to other countries including the United Kingdom, Amsterdam, Puerto Rico, India and Israel. While students generally believe that the program is 'extremely intense', they have an almost unanimous reaction to their experiences as being 'life altering'. At the end of the course, students are given a lengthy evaluation packet to fill out. The evaluation is composed of open ended questions in addition to university evaluation standards. Notable responses include:

- I always knew that social work was about being able to empower your clients but I have been able to really see what that means concretely here [in the Philippines]. Yesterday, we had one on one time with a group of little girls who had been victims of sexual exploitation – they had been sold into the sex trade. And, we spent time with them and did an art intervention that we read about. It made me realise that what we are learning we can also put in to practice.

- This experience has changed my life. I never really thought about how different things are when you are out of your comfort zone. I have never been so uncomfortable in my life but I've never felt stronger or more capable either. The best part was the experience of our home stays in the country side and we spent the day working with the farmers. It made me not just appreciative of my own life but also made me realise that you have to take all of this into account when you are working with different communities.

- I thought this was going to be a peek into how another country is, but it really honestly has been a reflection on myself as a social worker and what it means to do global social work. I came because I wanted to be an international social worker. I realise now that I have a long way to go and there are a number of things that I have to learn like economics, and politics, and UN policies.

- I am from the military and I actually came to the Philippines several times during my tour of duty. I have to say that I am ashamed to admit that I came here for 'rest and recreation' and I won't go into detail about what that means but I came to terms with it during the time we were at the former military bases at Subic Bay. We had a sharing with prostituted girls and women. The woman we spoke to was barely 19 and she was supporting her whole family. She was misled into believing she was going to be a salesgirl at a department store. But in actuality, she was forced into prostitution. I always thought prostitution was about choice and being there – I realise there was nothing further from the truth, I am rethinking all that. It's made me rethink a lot of things. It's like opening my eyes for the first time.

In order for students to gain a more comprehensive understanding of the foundational tenets of the course, ongoing collaboration with social work institutions like the University of the Philippines, Diliman along with the critical involvement and partnership with grassroots women's organisations is both crucial and essential. Global immersion programs that attempt to infuse theory and practice not only better prepare social workers students for work here and abroad; but provide a space for more critical engagement and provocative analyses around the global interconnections that create the social realities of our clients and populations we seek to serve. Witnessing the transformations of thought and perspectives in students through first-hand exposures to other social work institutions, various communities and women's grassroots organisations served as substantiation for such programs. Such courses serve as a catalyst for instructors to continue to create innovative ways to engage the classroom around the impacts of globalisation and transnational feminist frameworks toward strengths-based social action strategies.

Challenges in development and program implementation

Challenges experienced in the development and implementation of this course centered around logistical matters and minimal issues around program content. Logistically, the challenge of coordinating a program in another country for a group of students can be overwhelming. As coordination efforts are being pursued, instructors must rely on program partners to be able to execute plans accordingly. For the most part, one way to mitigate any problems that may arise is to have clear expectations. It is important to clarify even what might be considered the most nominal of things, such as what is considered 'adequate' standards. For example, instructors from USC SOWK indicated that a hotel would have to be reserved for students and that students would be able to share two to a room. UP CSWCD complied and reserved rooms that housed two students but in some cases the rooms only had one large king size bed. The expectation was that there would be no problem for students to share; however, this turned out to be a significant problem as USC SOWK had policies against that. All of this could have been avoided if clearer guidelines were laid out.

Like many other global immersion programs, certain logistical challenges we also encountered included issues of student conduct and oversight and the question of drawing boundaries with students (i.e. curfew issues, alcohol consumption) as well as making sure students were kept adequately safe. Students were required to be present during the formal program of the course but otherwise they were free to go where they pleased. For the most part, this did not pose any problems but there were instances where students were late to the morning session and had to make up those times during office hours. Further, making sure that students were sensitive, respectful, and engaging was also a challenge. Students did not knowingly or even consciously act in a disrespectful way, but there were times where instructors had to make sure to provide guidelines of acceptable behaviour either due to cultural differences or to a particularly sensitive situation they would encounter. These challenges were discussed during the student process and advisement sessions and generally the topic of discussion and debate during such sessions. Finally, logistics in the area of handling student emergencies prompted team members to make sure that contingency plans were in place. For instance, the need to have an adequate medical emergency plan (each year, there are inevitably one or two students who have to go to the emergency room, usually for stomach related illnesses) and an plan to return students to the US for emergency reasons (for instance, one year a student had a death in the family and had to return to the US right away).

Program-wise, once the decisions and compromises around the syllabus were made, there were very minimal challenges. The biggest challenge was making sure that the content addressed the issue of transnational feminism. While this is a growing paradigm of social work praxis in the US, that is not the case in the Philippines. In many instances, there were no overt or blatant examples of transnational feminism as a driving theory for intervention. Though this was unfortunate, it was not detrimental to the program. USC SOWK instructors had to provide added lectures and reading materials that gave students the tools to make the connections between theory and the coursework. USC SOWK instructors encouraged the recognition of the need for more transnational studies, spaces and dialogues that would enable social work programs involved in global immersion to discuss varying feminist perspectives that emphasise the global interconnectness and need for collaboration. In some ways, this challenge served to increase discussion around theory and ultimately around the ways in which transnational feminism could be construed as being translated (or not) into plausible interventions and practice methodologies.

CONCLUSION

In examining various violences against women at a transnational level, it is imperative that US social work discourse continue to be more inclusive of the theoretical frameworks that elucidate the complexities around transnational studies as they relate to globalisation and trans-national feminist thought. Given the advancements in technologies, communications and transportation, social work praxis in an interna-tional context has become all the more crucial to addressing violence against women that can be attributed to the complex impacts of glo-balisation. We must further prepare social work students to go beyond the understanding of cultural sensitivity or culturally competent social work standards. As more social workers engage in international work abroad and work with recent migrant families and individuals in the US, the need to provide global immersion programs and curriculum that provide an understanding of globalisation, transnational patterns, economics, and political power becomes all the more apparent. We need to constantly address the following question: How do we become more transformative in our work as social workers? Critically illuminating the interconnections and contexts that shape the violences imposed on women is key. By providing critical theoretical frameworks to provoke further in-depth analyses around the violences endured by women in this context and continually collaborating with other social work institutions and grassroots women's organisations in the international setting is one integral way to building a more inclusive social work model that can begin to combat some of the challenges of globalisation.

Recommendations

Programs such as this course and the overall global immersion framework are the first steps to constructing educational experiences for social work students interested in cross-cultural or international social work praxis. In order to refine the course work, the following recommendations are provided

- Ongoing partnerships between institutions solidified through long-standing memorandum of agreements
- Partnerships should begin with the course and program itself but have the potential to expand into shared research, publications, and exchange experiences between faculty members
- The program itself has the potential to expand to a longer course of study – up to one semester that could accompany a concentration of study focusing on international social work and/or global social work
- Use of the course or program to create the development of international field placements
- Integrate curriculum as it relates to global social work that are used in social work institutions in other countries in order to further expose students to other social service models in international settings
- Become a host social work institution for social work students from other countries to gain a better understanding of the social service models and social work needs and practices found in the US.

REFERENCES

Agbayani P & Enrile A (2003). Filipino American children and adolescents. In J Gibbs (Ed). *Children of color: psychological interventions with culturally diverse youth* (pp229–64). 2nd edn. San Francisco, CA: Jossey-Bass.

Aquino B (1997). Philippine feminism in historical perspective. In B Nelson & N Chowhurdy (Eds). *Women and politics worldwide* (pp590–607). New Haven, CT: Yale University Press.

Anderson B (2000). *Doing the dirty work?: The global politics of domestic labour*. London: Zed Books.

Anderson B (1997). Servants and slaves: Europe's domestic workers. *Race+Class*, 39: 37–49, doi: 10.1177/030639689703900104.

Campbell J (2002). Health consequences of intimate partner violence. *The Lancet*, 359: 1331–36, doi: 10.1016/S0140-6736(02)08336-8.

Castles S & Miller MJ (1998). *The age of migration: international population movements in the modern world*. (2nd edn). London: Macmillan.

Choy CC (2003). *Empire of care: nursing and migration in Filipino American history*. Durham, NC: Duke University Press.

Colen S (1995). Like a mother to them: stratified reproduction and West Indian childcare workers and employers in New York. In FD Ginsburg & R Rapp (Eds). *Conceiving the new world order: the global politics of reproduction* (pp78–102). Durham, NC: Duke University Press.

de la Luz Ibarra M (2000). Mexican immigrant women and the new domestic labor. *Hum Organ*, 59: 452–64. [Online]. Available: findarticles.com/p/articles/mi_qa3800/is_200001/ai_n8885859 [Accessed 12 May 2011].

Enloe C (2000). *Maneuvers: the international politics of militarizing women's lives*. Berkeley and London: University of California Press.

Enloe C (1989). *Bananas, beaches, and bases: making feminist sense of international politics*. Berkeley, CA: University of California Press.

Espiritu YL (2003). *Home bound: Filipino American lives across cultures, communities, and countries*. Los Angeles, CA: University of California Press.

Fernandez-Kelly MP & Garcia AM (1989). Informalization at the core: Hispanic women, homework and the advanced capitalist state. In A Portes, M Castells & LA Benton (Eds). *The informal economy* (pp247–64). Baltimore, MD: John Hopkins University Press.

Foner N (2000). *From Ellis Island to JFK: New York's two great waves of immigration*. New Haven, CT: Yale University Press.

Friedman TL (1999). *The lexus and the olive tree: understanding globalization*. New York, NY: Farrar, Straus and Giroux.

Gamburd MR (2000). *The kitchen spoon's handle: transnationalism and Sri Lanka's migrant housemaids*. Ithaca: Cornell University Press.

Gilligan C (1982). *In a different voice*. Cambridge, MA: Harvard University Press.

Glenn EN (1986). *Issei,nisei, war bride: three generations of Japanese American women in domestic service*. Philadelphia, PA: Temple University Press.

Glenn EN (1987). Racial ethnic women's labor: the intersection of race, gender and class oppression. In C Bose, R Feldberg & N Sokoloff (Eds). *Hidden aspects of women's work*. New York, NY: Praeger.

Glenn EN (1992). From servitude to service work: historical continuities in the racial division of paid reproductive labor. *Signs* 18: 1–43. [Online]. Available: www.jstor.org/stable/3174725 [Accessed 15 February 2011].

Grewel I & Kaplan C (1994). *Scattered hegemonies: postmodernity and transnational feminist practices*. Minneapolis, MN: University of Minnesota Press.

Guevarra AR (2009). *Marketing dreams, manufacturing heroes: the transnational labor brokering of Filipino workers*. New Brunswick, NJ: Rutgers University Press.

Heise LL, Ellsberg MC & Gottemoeller M (1999). Ending violence against women. *Population Reports L*, 27: 1–43. [Online]. Available: www.nnvawi.org/pdfs/alo/Campbell_1.pdf [Accessed 12 February 2011].

Held D, McGrew A, Goldblatt D & Perraton J (Eds) (1999). *Global transformations: politics, economics and culture*. Stanford, CA: Stanford University Press.

Hochschild AR (2004). Love and gold. In B Ehrenreich & A Hochschild (Eds). *Global woman: nannies, maids, and sex workers in the new economy* (pp15–30). New York, NY: Metropolitan Books.

Hondagneu-Sotelo P (2000). Feminism and migration. *Annals of the American Academy of Political and Social Science*, 571: 107–20.

Hondagneu-Sotelo P (1994). *Gendered transitions: Mexican experiences of migration*. Berkeley, CA: University of California Press.

Hossfeld K (1990). Their logic against them: contradictions in sex, race, and class in Silicon Valley. In K Ward (Ed). *Women workers and global restructuring* (pp149–78). Geneva: ILR Press.

Jacobson M (1999). Imperial amnesia: Teddy Roosevelt, the Philippines, and the modern art of forgetting. *Radical History Review,* 73: 117–27, doi: 10.1215/01636545-1999-73-117.

Kessler-Harris A (1975). The debate over equality for women in the workplace: recognizing differences. In A Kessler-Harris. *Gendering labor history* (pp191–207). Urbana, IL: University of Illinois Press.

Kousha M (1995). African American private household workers, white employers and their children. *International Journal of Sociology of the Family,* 25: 67–89.

Kwong P (1998). *Forbidden workers: illegal Chinese immigrants and American labor.* New York, NY: New Press.

Lerner G (1997). *Why history matters.* New York, NY: Oxford University Press.

Mahler SJ & Pessar P (2006). Gender matters: ethnographers bring gender from the periphery toward the core, gender and migration revisited, special issue, *International Migration Review,* doi: 10.1111/j.1747-7379.2006.00002.x

Marigold J (2003). Women, violence, and the reinvolvement of the U.S. military in the Philippines. *Human Rights Dialogue,* 2: 10. [Online]. Available: www. carnegiecouncil.org/resources/publications/dialogue/2_10/online_exclusive/1071. html [Accessed 6 March 2011].

Mendoza B (2002). Transnational feminisms in question. *Feminist Theory,* 3: 295–314, doi: 10.1177/146470002762492015.

Mies M (1982). *The lace makers of Narsapur: Indian housewives produce for the world market.* London: Zed.

Misra J, Woodring J & Merz S (2006). The globalization of carework: immigration, economic restructuring, and the world-system. *Globalization,* 3: 317–32, doi: 10.1080/14747730600870035.

Mohanty CT (2003). *Feminist without borders: decolonizing theory, practicing solidarity.* London: Duke University Press.

Mohanty CT (1991). Under Western eyes: feminist scholarship and colonial discourses. In C Mohanty & A Russo (Eds). *Third world women and the politics of feminism* (pp51–80). Bloomington, IN: Indiana University Press.

Momsen JH (1999). *Gender, migration and domestic service.* London: Routledge.

Murphy Y, Hunt V, Zajicek AM, Norris AN & Hamilton L (2009). *Incorporating intersectionality in social work practice, research, policy, and education.* Washington, DC: NASW Press.

Nikolic-Ristanovic V (2002). *Social change, gender and violence: post-communist and war affected societies* (Social indicators research series Vol.10). Norwell, MA: Kluwer Academic Publishers.

Ong A (1991). The gender and labor politics of postmodernity. *Annual Review of Anthropology,* 20: 279–309, doi: 10.1146/annurev.an.20.100191.001431.

Ong P & Azores T (1994). Health professionals on the front line. In P Ong (Ed). *The state of Asian Pacific America: economic diversity, issues, and policies* (pp139–63). Los Angeles: LEAP Asian Pacific American Public Policy Institute and University of California at Los Angeles Asian American Studies Center.

Parreñas RS (2001). *Servants of globalisation: women, migration and domestic work.* Stanford: Stanford University Press.

Portes A & J Borocz (1989). Contemporary immigration: theoretical perspectives on its determinants and modes of incorporation. *International Migration Review,* 23, 606–30.

Robertson R (1992). *Globalization: social theory and global culture.* London: Sage.

Rollins J (1985). *Between women: domestics and their employers.* Philadelphia, PA: Temple University Press.

Romero M (2002). *Maid in the U.S.A.* New York, NY: Routledge.

Romero M (1999). Immigration, the servant problem, and the legacy of the domestic labor debate: 'Where can you find good help these days?' *Univ. Miami Law Review,* 53: 1045–64.

Safa HI (1995). *The myth of the male breadwinner. Women and industrialization in the Caribbean.* Boulder, CO: Westview.

Sassen S (2008). Two stops in today's new global geographies. *American Behavioral Scientist*, 52: 457–96, doi: 10.1177/0002764208325312.

Sassen S (2006). *Cities in a world economy.* (3rd edn). Thousand Oaks, CA: Pine Forge Press.

Sassen S (1998). *Globalization and its discontents: essays in the mobility of people and money.* New York, NY: The New Press.

Thornton Dill B (1988). Making your job good yourself: domestic service and the construction of personal dignity. In A Bookman, & S Morgen (Eds). *Women and the politics of empowerment* (pp33–52). Philadelphia, PA: Temple Univ. Press.

UNDP (2007). *United Nations Development Report 2007/2008. Fighting climate change: human solidarity in a divided world.* New York, NY: United Nations Development Programme.

UNFPA (2006). *A passage of hope: women and international migration.* New York, NY: United Nations Population Fund.

United States Department of State (2002). *Victims of Trafficking and Violence Protection Act 2002: trafficking in persons report.* Washington, D.C.: Office to Monitor and Combat Trafficking in Persons, United States Department of State.

Wallerstein I (1984). *The politics of the world-economy: the states, the movements and the civilizations.* Cambridge, NJ: Cambridge University Press.

Wallerstein I (1974). *The modern world system I, capitalist agriculture and the origins of the European world economy in the sixteenth century.* New York, NY: Academic Press.

West C & Zimmerman D (1987). Doing gender. *Gender & Society*, 1: 125–51.

CHAPTER NINE

INTERNATIONAL FIELD EDUCATION AND INTERNATIONAL SOCIAL WORK: EXPERIENCES OF AUSTRALIAN AND BELGIAN STUDENTS IN THE PHILIPPINES

Nilan G. Yu

This chapter outlines the experiences of Australian and Belgian students who undertook their field education placement in the Philippines. It gives an account of the work environments and experiences that the students were exposed to and examines the opportunities presented by these international field education placements for developing competence in cross-cultural practice and international social work. Apart from being cross-cultural experiences, these placements are seen as having the value of informing international social work theory. The chapter begins with an examination of the concept of international social work and the place of field education in the training of social workers. An account of the work environment and experiences of the students will then be given followed by an examination of the potential contribution of these placements towards the development of practice skills and theory in international social work.

国际实习教育和国际社会工作：澳大利亚和比利时学生
在菲律宾的经历

这一章简要叙述了一些分别来自澳大利亚和比利时的学
生在菲律宾进行实习的经历。其内容涉及到学生们接触
到的工作环境和实习体验，并说明了国际实习为培养发
展社工学生的跨文化交流能力提供了各种良机。除了跨
文化的因素，这些实习还被视为具有指导国际社会工作
理论的价值。本章以考察国际社会工作的概念和实习教
育在社会工作者培训中的位置作为开篇，接下来对学生
的工作环境和实习体验进行了思考，最后以鉴别这些实
习机会如何在国际社会工作中有助于提高实践技能并促
进理论发展作为终结。

国際現場教育と国際ソーシャルワーク

フィリピンにおけるオーストラリアとベルギーの学生
の経験

本章は、フィリピンで現場教育実習を行ったオースト
ラリアとベルギーの学生の経験について述べている。
本章は学生がさらされている実習環境や経験に説明を
与え、異文化交流実習や国際ソーシャルワークにおけ
るコンピテンスを発達させるためのこれらの国際現場
教育実習によってもたらされる機会を検討している。
異文化交流の経験はさておき、これらの実習は国際ソ
ーシャルワーク理論を啓発するという価値を持ってい
るものとして見受けられる。本章は、まず、国際ソー
シャルワークの概念とソーシャルワーカーの研修にお
ける現場教育実習先を検討から行う。学生の実習環境
と経験についての説明は、国際ソーシャルワークにお
ける実習技術や理論の発展へのこれらの実習の潜在的
な貢献に対する検討に従って与えられるであろう。

국제 현장 교육과 국제 사회 복지 업무: 필리핀에서의 호주人과 벨기에人 학생들의 경험

이장에서는, 현장 교육 배치를 필리핀에서 실행한 호주人과 벨기에人 학생들의 경험의 대략을 다룬다. 이것은 학생들이 처한 그 현장 환경과 경험의 실제적인 예를 전해줄것이며, 교차되는 문화와 국제적인 사회 복지에 있어서 학생들의 자신감을 기르기 위한 국제 현장 교육 배치에 의하여 제공되는 기회를 점검할것이다. 교차적인 문화 경험과는 별도로, 이러한 배치들은 국제 사회 복지 이론을 알게 해 주는 가치를 가진것으로 보여진다. 이 장은 국제 사회 복지의 개념과 사회 복지사들의 훈련에 있어서 현장(現場) 교육의 설정에 관한 개념에 대한 점검으로부터 시작한다. 현장 환경과 학생들의 실제 경험들이 소개될것이며, 곧 이어 국제 사회 복지 이론과 실행 기술들의 발전을 목표로하는, 이러한 현장 배치의 기여 가능성이 점검될것이다.

This chapter draws on insights gained from the supervision of field education students from Australia and Belgium in the Philippines. The placements represent cross-cultural experience as the students, who come from two of the world's most advanced economies, find themselves living and working in what can best be described as a developing economy. These encounters between different worlds and cultures offer more than just opportunities for developing cross-cultural competence. The placements provide an opportunity for gaining global awareness and understanding. This is particularly relevant to social work practice and education that recognises how global dynamics impact on local realities. Thus, these placements find value beyond what they offer in terms of cross-cultural experiences towards what they contribute to international social work.

The contrasts between the social, cultural and educational backgrounds of the students and their placement settings provide us with an opportunity to examine relevant issues relating to international placements and practice. The insights we gain from these experiences can contribute to the building of the theory of international social work particularly in terms of the kind of practice required and the preparations needed for such practice. The focus of the discussion here is not so much what challenges the students encountered in pursuing such placements but rather the lessons and insights the placements offer for social work education and practice.

The experiences and learning of the students as they undertook field education in different physical, economic, cultural and work environments, and the lessons and insights offered by the placements for international social work practice and education will be examined. To provide the theoretical framework for the analysis of the placements, we will first look into relevant literature on international social work and field education in social work.

INTERNATIONAL SOCIAL WORK

Social work faces the challenge of developing as an international discipline, for various aims of and benefits to the profession (Hokenstad et al. 1992). The aim that gives impetus for this chapter is in examining how internationalisation in social work field education can contribute to our understanding of social problems and strengthen social work theory and practice. The recognition of the global inter-linkages of social problems forms the imperatives for international social work (Ahmadi 2003). Dominelli (2010) argues that globalisation has created the need for social workers to be capable of engaging with international issues. As increasing economic and social inequality across the world compromise the rights of the impoverished and disadvantaged, a global understanding of human rights issues and social problems is needed to enhance practice responses (Mapp 2007). It has been argued that inequality in wealth and therefore in life chances and social wellbeing is not as much an economic problem as a political one, and globalisation has put global politics to the fore (Mohan 2005). Global economic, cultural and ideological processes are also affecting social work practice and social welfare regimes around the world (Ferguson & Lavalette 2006). Ahmadi (2003) points out that, in the same way that economics and politics have transcended national boundaries, so should welfare policy and social work practice. The advance of conservative ideology across the world underscores the need for international collaboration in addressing this challenge (Midgley 2006). One front of such struggle may be in the form of international social work. In this context, there is a need to examine the various definitions of the term international social work.

There are a number of definitions of international social work. International social work has been conceived as: (1) work in international agencies, requiring a specific set of skills and knowledge, (2) social work practice with immigrants or refugees, requiring culturally-sensitive and competent practitioners, (3) interactions and exchanges between social work practitioners from different countries, and (4) practice that embodies a global perspective, enabling practitioners to transcend a local preoccupation and frame their practice within the broad, global setting (Hokenstad et al. 1992; Midgley 2001). As suggested by the foregoing, there is no agreement about what is international social work. Many authors believe that the resolution of this issue is vital to getting practitioners involved in the field of international social work and for social work schools to be able to incorporate relevant content in their curriculum (Falk 2000; Midgley 2001). Faced with this varied set of definitions that – in his view – all have merit, Midgley suggested the formulation of a broad definition of international social work incorporating the different dimensions. Hokenstad, et al. (p4) had defined international social work as 'the profession and practice in different parts of the world, especially the place of the organised profession in different countries, the different roles that social workers perform, the practice methods they use, the problems they deal with, and the many challenges they face'. This accommodates the different dimensions cited above but does not bring us closer to the resolution of the issue of definition.

Other definitions have been advanced. Healy (2001, p7) conceives international social work as 'international professional practice and the capacity for international action by the social work profession and its members'. Cox (2006, p20) offers this definition:

International social work is the promotion of social work education and practice globally and locally, with the purpose of building a truly integrated international profession that reflects social work's capacity to respond appropriately and effectively, in education and practice terms, to the various global challenges that are having a significant impact on the well-being of large sections of the world's population. This global and local promotion of social work education and practice is based on an integrated-perspectives approach that synthesizes global, human rights, ecological, and social development perspectives of international situations and responses to them.

Cox points out that 'international' should not be taken to connote that action will only be confined to the international level, arguing that efforts should be on all levels, from the local to the global – 'glocalisation' as Hong and Song (2010, p656) put it. The key challenges for international social work, according to Ahmadi (2003), are the promotion of democracy, social justice and human rights and the elimination of discrimination and conflicts.

The definition of international social work used in this chapter draws on many of the definitions given above. International social work is defined as social work practice that embodies a global perspective in the understanding of social problems and issues and in the promotion of human rights and social justice. Contextualised in a broad, global setting, such practice may be informed by interactions and exchanges between social work practitioners from different countries and may involve work in international agencies aimed towards the protection of the welfare and rights of certain populations including, but not limited to, labour migrants, immigrants and refugees. But it is the global perspective – rather than who are involved, where practice occurs or for whom practice is undertaken – that defines the character of international social work as seen here. To some extent, the definition represents what Hugman, Moosa-Mitha and Moyo (2010) refer to as borderless social work. But to use such a term would make it appear as though it was a mere category of social work, like how we can say 'it is more of a field than a discipline' (Mohan 2008, p13). Even the term 'international social work' may have the same effect. The definition put forward here implies that an international perspective is necessary for social work practice addressing many social problems. In a way, this renders the term 'international social work' superfluous because addressing many social problems in this globalised world, by necessity, requires an international perspective. In other words, it is difficult to talk about social work within the confines of the local or even national context.

International social work comes with the recognition that we live in an interdependent world. And when we talk about social justice and human rights, we have to grapple with global processes and realities. Globalisation, in its various forms, has shaped practice challenges and realities (Dominelli 2010). Beyond recognising that all social problems have a global dimension, Ife (2001) points out that, in a globalised world, all aspects of social work are affected by global issues. This has implications to the kind of social work and the kinds of preparation for social work practice needed. At the very least, the internationalisation of the issues we deal with necessitates the introduction of international content in social work education (Nagy & Falk 2000). Ahmadi (2003) notes the pedagogical and practical value of international social work, explaining that by studying and becoming involved in social work practice in other countries, social workers can learn the dynamics of social politics in such countries and learn from the experiences of others. As early as 1990, Midgley argued that social workers from economically developed countries have much to learn from social workers in developing economies in terms of working with limited resources, serving culturally-heterogeneous populations and addressing poverty.

FIELD EDUCATION IN SOCIAL WORK

Social work is defined by the International Federation of Social Workers as the profession that 'promotes social change, problem-solving in human relationships, and the empowerment and liberation of people to enhance wellbeing' by intervening 'at the points where people interact with their environments' (Hare 2004, p409). Field practice and experience has always been a key component in how professionals learn to undertake such complex work. Thus, field education (or field practice and field instruction to others) is held by many as an integral, if not, the most important part of social work education (Lager & Robbins 2004; Schneck 1995). But, while field education is widely regarded as a core component of professional social work training, there have been very few research and publications on the subject and even much less on international and cross-cultural contexts (Pawar et al. 2004). A number of these works such as those of Lough (2009), Mathiesen and Lager (2007), and Pawar, Hanna and Sheridan (2004) have been about designing and preparing for international field education placements. From these we know that cultural differences and differences in language and language proficiency between students and clients can pose a challenge for such placements (Engstrom et al. 2009; Yeom & Bae 2010) and that field education can have an emotional impact on students that needs to be considered (Barlow & Hall 2007; Litvack et al. 2010). While this chapter will lightly touch on these concerns, its main focus is to explore the potentials for such placements in contributing to international social work education and practice.

It has been noted that a good number of accredited social work programs in the US have students in international placements (Panos et al. 2004). This is likely the case for social work programs in other economically-advanced countries. What we do not know is the extent to which these placements come with the view of using such placements for the development of theory and knowledge in international social work. Globalisation requires social work education that equips students with an understanding of global problems and realities and the knowledge and skills to address the challenges they pose (Engstrom & Jones 2007). Certainly, we should be interested in how to build intercultural sensitivity and cross-cultural competence (Tesoriero 2006). But Engstrom and Jones (2007) identify at least five gains an international experience can contribute to one's practice, namely: (1) learning about different culture and behaviour, (2) experiencing being different, (3) learning different views of social welfare, (4) learning about relationships between global responses and local responses, and (5) learning about different contexts and social work practice. Placements such as those described here can serve as theoretical planks for extending the boundaries of social work practice and education in the exploration of the frontiers of international social work.

The two immediately preceding sections outlined the importance of field education in social work and the increasing recognition of international social work as an area of practice as well as an area where there is need to build knowledge. We will proceed to examine the international field education experiences of one Belgian and two Australian students. The chapter will conclude with notes on how international field education can contribute to social work education and practice.

EXPERIENCES IN THE INTERNATIONAL FIELD PLACEMENTS

In this section, I will briefly look at the experiences of three students in their field education placements in the Philippines with special attention given to specific aspects that highlight the international elements of such experiences. This account draws mainly from the experiences of two Australians, Sharon and Reece, and one Belgian, Noah. Except for Reece Gains (2010) who has published an article about his experience, pseudonyms are used in identifying the students to protect their privacy.

It was not only the poverty but the gaping inequality in the Philippines that struck the students, with Sharon marvelling in her end-of-term report 'how people from two different worlds can exist within the one country' with a 'phenomenal' discrepancy in wealth. Coming from countries where wealth inequalities are not as stark, this became one of the more prominent parts of their experiences of field education placement in the Philippines. A brief account of the placements of the three students – their practice setting, the work they undertook and some of the highlights of their experiences that have relevance to international social work – are given below.

Sharon and her work with children of migrant workers

Sharon was placed in a non-government agency called Kanlungan Centre Foundation. The word *kanlungan* in Filipino means shelter.

The agency is committed to providing support for the mostly female Filipino migrant workers and their families, especially those who are victims of illegal recruitment, human trafficking, and workplace abuse. They are engaged in direct service, policy advocacy and research. Their direct service programs include feminist counselling, legal assistance, welfare assistance, education and training, the provision of temporary shelter and community organising and development.

Labour migration became more and more pronounced in the Philippines since the 1970s along with the advance of globalisation. Filipino labourers started flocking to certain countries, first in the tens of thousands, now in the millions, as the global economic structure started to weaken the local economy and make local jobs harder to find and financially uncompetitive. For several decades now, successive Philippine governments have been openly promoting labour export as a key strategy in propping up the local economy as billions of dollars in remittances tip the balance of payments in its favour to a significant extent. This is being done even as some have pointed out the negative social consequences of labour migration on the workers themselves, their families and their children (Diega 2007; Guan 1999).

At the start of her placement, Sharon was exposed to the various facets of the work of Kanlungan. She attended staff meetings and accompanied staff in various undertakings including participating in mass action campaigns and a three-day visit to the agency's rural program site some seven hours by bus from Manila. In consultation with her agency and academic supervisors, it was decided that she be assigned to work with children of migrant workers to address a perceived gap in the agency's wide range of services. It was noted that labour migration also affects children but most of the interventions have so far been directed towards the migrant workers or the family as a whole. Children, she noted, also experience certain problems that need to be addressed. Specifically, children have to contend with the absence of an adult carer and the social implications this has on them. Upon her suggestion, Sharon was tasked to develop and test an intervention to address some of the needs of the children and prepare a program proposal based on this that would allow the agency to obtain funding to institutionalise such intervention. Sharon designed and organised a number of workshops intended to enable the children to learn about labour migration, reflect on their experiences as children of migrant workers and deal with some of the issues they face. These workshops were designed in consultation with her agency supervisor and were conducted with the assistance of other agency staff. The outcomes were then used to inform the development of a program proposal used in seeking program funding.

Sharon's reflections revolved around the development of professional skills and cultural competency, including the lessening of the pain and trauma in others. As part of Kanlungan, Sharon had come face-to-face with what she referred to in her end-of-term paper as 'confronting' and 'traumatic' issues surrounding human trafficking and international labour migration. Her notes in relation to the term 'international social work' mainly dealt with awareness and understanding of situations and problems in another part of the world and the value of cultural competence. Sharon's work with children (as opposed to, say, direct service with victims of human trafficking or policy advocacy work) may have, to some extent, limited the opportunities and extent to which she could reflect on the global dynamics that generate and sustain the phenomenon of international labour migration. But her field education experience still provided some opportunities for learning about international social work.

Noah's immersions with progressive organisations

In consultation with his Belgian academic supervisor, Noah had decided and arranged beforehand that his field education placement be in the form of immersions with some of the country's most prominent national organisations. These organisations included a national human rights advocacy group, a national women's movement, a national farmer's coalition, a national worker's union and a national alliance of urban poor who all identify themselves as progressive organisations but who are regarded by many members of the Philippine military as fronts of the underground left. Since their inception, these organisations have always had an adversarial stance towards the government but they have since gained representation, albeit marginal, in the national legislature.

The immersions came in the form of two-week exposures to various aspects of the work of the selected organisations. His experiences in these groups were varied. For example, he spent his time with the national women's group integrating with the family and community of a group member. In another organisation, he trekked to a remote upland village to observe a situational assessment mission.

As part of his exposure in the human rights advocacy organisation, he joined a team assigned to visit a woman confined in a military hospital. The woman was in the hospital for the treatment of wounds sustained from what the military reported as an encounter with underground combatants. The team's mission was to document the case of the woman. They were denied access to the hospital and were instead interrogated as to their purpose, background and mission. In the days that followed, the military arranged a press conference where they identified the student as a supporter of the leftist movement and called for his deportation. Confronted with what seemed like a real possibility of him being deported, we started to identify contacts from within the military whose support could be solicited and the human rights advocacy group held its own press conference to give its side on the incident. But in those tense few days, the physical safety of the student was never a concern considering that the military had pursued a legal course of action, indicating that the military did not feel the need to employ the extra-legal and extrajudicial tactics as they have been known to use by some human rights watchers. He was able to continue his placement but his activities had to be scaled back to some extent. The host organisation which provided him accommodation asked him to move out and transfer so that they could distance themselves from the controversy. The national farmer's organisation begged off from its commitment to host the student explaining that they could not afford to take the heat generated by the student's brush with the military. The experience showed the student how sensitive human rights work in the Philippines can be.

While it may seem that the military had overreacted considering what we know about the intent of the group, a colleague was quick to point out that it would be naive not to recognise the legitimate concern of the military considering that Belgium is one of the key sources of support for the kinds of groups thought to form part of the network that feed the underground communist movement. The human rights group with whom the student undertook the fact-finding mission has had a history of confrontation with the military. In other words, in hindsight, the response of the military should have been anticipated. The situation of human rights in the Philippines and the work that needs to be done in this area also provide a challenge for international social work.

Reece's work with disability

Reece was placed with KASAMAKA, a non-government organisation with the vision of a barrier-free society. KASAMAKA is an acronym that, when read in Filipino, literally means 'you are included'. The agency's main work has been in community-based rehabilitation of people with disabilities. Their interventions include health check-ups and the development of community organisations that can administer community-based rehabilitation programs and support services including the production of assistive devices based on alternative technology using mainly paper and locally available materials.

As part of the contracting process with the organisation, the student – in consultation with his agency supervisor who also was the agency director, and myself, his academic supervisor – explored the possible work that he could take on, taking into consideration the agency's needs and his knowledge, skills and capabilities. The organisation's core strength was in community-based rehabilitation which included initiatives for the development of self-employment skills and opportunities. But as the three of us studied the scope of the organisation's work and assessed this against its stated vision, it became apparent that there was a gaping hole between what the organisation was doing and what it intended to do as articulated in its vision statement. We noted that the organisation talked about developing a barrier-free society without addressing the barriers posed by discrimination and exclusion in mainstream employment. Noting that the student had experience with work in employment access, we agreed to have the student focus on program development work towards the organisation's engagement with work in access to employment for persons with disabilities. The student soon found out that he was not only venturing into something that the organisation was not yet involved in but, as it turned out, also something that the organisation was not yet prepared to deal with.

The student found out that the staff of the organisation, while speaking of a barrier-free society and rights-based approach in promoting the welfare of persons with disabilities, was not prepared to engage in promoting access to mainstream employment among such persons. In view of the situation, his work included intervention at the organisation level to raise the awareness of the staff about the issue of access to employment among people with disability. Apart from having experience in employment work, the fact that he had a disability himself in the form of dyslexia, (Gains 2010) gave the student the credibility to deal with community members and the agency staff themselves on the matter. A highlight in his work was a staff workshop where everyone initially indicated that they were already living in a barrier-free society (Gains 2010). When he asked them if they wanted their organisation to be engaged in promoting access to mainstream employment for persons with disabilities, a number of them dismissed the idea. This was from a group of staff that counted among them three with various forms of disabilities who had experiences of being discriminated against in employment and transportation. A female staff member explained that not too many employers were keen on employing her given her physical deformity. A male staff member recounted how some bus drivers would speed off as soon as they see him inching towards their buses on his polio-stricken legs. But part of the resistance from some of the staff to the proposed work in employment apparently came from the view that the organisation was ill-equipped – financially and human resource-wise – to handle this potential program area. The initial resistance of the staff itself indicated that there was work to be done starting with the staff of the agency. Specifically, there was a need to raise the consciousness of the staff about issues of employment as it relates to people with disability. According to his agency supervisor who was then the executive director of the agency, it was as much a learning experience for them as it was for the people with disability that they were aiming to serve. Apart from this intervention with the staff, a workshop was also organised among persons with disabilities to explore the idea with them. The student had excellent facilitation skills and so that was not a problem for the workshops but, as one can imagine, there were language difficulties considering that the student only spoke English and the staff and community members he worked with spoke and were most comfortable with Filipino. The language issues notwithstanding, he successfully completed his placement with the help of some agency staff who assisted in facilitating meetings and group activities and his interactions with community members. The results of the workshops informed the development of a funding proposal drafted by the student and submitted to an international funding agency right before he finished his placement.

International field education placements like these provide learning opportunities to develop a framework for social work practice informed by a critical understanding of the global dynamics of social problems and issues necessary for action that links the local with the global. Such dynamics are widely recognised in labour migration (Guan 1999; Sills 2007). Though much of Sharon's reflections focused on her experience 'Coming into a different ... context', working within an 'unfamiliar system', and the 'shocking' conditions so many people live in, she also talked about how international labour migration 'is truly embedded into the lives and families of many Filipinos' and how different life is in Australia compared with the Philippines. Arguably, a more direct engagement with labour migration issues such as if she was working with migrant labourers rather than their children would have brought to the fore issues relating to how her own country and other developed economies systematically draw out migrant labourers from the Philippines and similarly situated countries. A little less obvious but strong link may be gleaned from the situation of the disabled persons Reece worked with. Of course, a localised view could simply place these persons as being among the disadvantaged in their local communities and countries where Reece's reflections have so far centred. Reece talked about how the poverty he saw around him challenged his own privilege as a Westerner (Gains, 2010, p3). But he had started going beyond this in his work in promoting access to employment among disabled persons, recognising the structural barriers they faced. While his limited engagement did not allow him enough time and theoretical frame to appreciate the larger context, the significance of structural barriers could readily be extended with the recognition of how the Philippines form part of the bottom of the global capitalist order. Noah's engagement with national organisations of peasants and workers exposed him to the links between the conditions of some of the most disadvantaged sectors of the country and the national economy, seen in the context of the international global order. His experience with human rights work highlighted the significance of linkages between governments as well as social movements in the Philippines and economically advanced countries, including how governments and social movements in Belgium contribute to the human rights situation in the country. His field notes include the view of the Philippines as a neo-colony and the implications of this to the everyday lives of people that form the basic sectors of Philippine society. As to what kinds of interventions are needed in response to the problems facing the populations the students worked with, much of it would have to come from a differentiated analysis of the issues involved. Many of the issues are complex and would require a thorough analysis that may partly be informed by the theoretical and ideological frameworks of the agencies they work with. It is not my intent to outline an idealised framework for international social work practice here. Such a task is simply beyond the scope of this chapter and any attempt to synthesise a single approach from such varied practice contexts discussed here would invariably be problematic in the sense that the various practice issues confronted in these placements simply cannot be lumped together. I am also not arguing that the field placements of the three students optimally explored and utilised the opportunities provided by the placements for learning about international social work. In fact, it cannot even be said that this was the aim we had in mind when we worked together during these placements. Sharon, for one, acknowledged that she did not have an opportunity 'to work in all intervention systems'. This being their first international field placements, we focused on what may be referred as more basic concerns for international social work education which include exposure to different social and organisational contexts and cross-cultural competence. There are logistical and theoretical limitations to what can be covered in one semester of field education placement. I am certainly not arguing that I have exhaustively explored here all the possibilities for learning about international social work. What is being argued here is that there exists such opportunities in these kinds of placement which can and should be considered in the teaching and learning process.

INTERNATIONAL FIELD EDUCATION AND INTERNATIONAL SOCIAL WORK

These experiences of the three students provide us a glimpse into what can be done and what can happen within the context of international field education placements in social work. These international experiences are significant in at least three ways. For one, they involve students from one national context working in another (very different) national context. Secondly, they involve what Midgley (2001) refers to as contacts and exchanges between social work practitioners from different countries, with the students being given the opportunity to interact with social workers in their agency, social work educators and other social work students. In these, we find the value of international field education placements for the development of culture competence and an international perspective to the extent that they provide students with knowledge of realities and practices outside their own local and national contexts. With such an experience, students can learn about the realities of others and how to relate and work with them in the practice of social work. While cultural competence in one cultural context is often not transferable to another, many of the skills needed to gain such competence in new cultural settings often are. And understanding of poverty beyond what poverty is in their own local contexts certainly equips students with a broader understanding of the kind of issues that can and need to be dealt with in the practice of social work. By

themselves, these are valuable gains towards the development of professionals who are afforded by the experience a broader range of skills and
understanding of the world and the profession that otherwise would
not be possible. But international field education placements have a
more substantial significance in terms of the definition of international
social work advanced earlier.

International field education placements can provide an
opportunity to develop what Midgley refers to as 'a global awareness'
that enables social workers to 'contextualise their role within a broad,
global setting' (Midgley 2001, p25). Beyond providing opportunities
to develop cultural and basic practice competence through exposure
to different cultural and social contexts and exchanges with other
practitioners from other parts of the world, such placements can
provide an opportunity to develop a critical understanding of the
global dynamics of social problems and issues – such as with Sharon
coming from a receiving country of migrant labourers – and, perhaps,
a framework for action that links the local with the global. Work with
children of Filipino migrant workers scattered in many parts of the
world provides an opportunity to gain some insights into the dynamics
of the global economic order, particularly how developed countries –
Australia and Belgium, among them – draw in international labour
migrants from developing economies. Breaking barriers to employment
for persons with disability in a country like the Philippines would
highlight the challenges in ensuring access to employment in a country
situated in the lower half of the global capitalist order. The promotion
of human rights can point to how the same global political economic
order contributes to the human rights situation in countries like the
Philippines including the funding and arming of government and
insurgent forces and, equally important, the fostering of political
economic environments that create social unrest (Guan 1999; Sison &
De Lima 1998). Such insights into social realities and problems would
point toward particular directions for social work practice that would
be markedly international in scope. As to what these actions should be
is beyond the scope of this chapter. Suffice it to say that the need for
workshops for forlorn children of migrant workers would be endless

if the global economy continues to squeeze developing economies of their human and natural resources and receiving countries continue to regard migrant labourers as non-citizens. Human rights violations and the exclusion of at risk populations such as those with a disability would continue to abound as long as multinational capital holds primacy over human rights and social welfare in the conduct of state and international affairs. International field education placements like these can offer social workers an opportunity to gain valuable insights and develop a framework for action to address the global dimensions of social problems and issues that embody what can be regarded as international social work.

REFERENCES

Ahmadi N (2003). Globalisation of consciousness and new challenges for international social work. *International Journal of Social Welfare,* 12: 14–23.

Barlow C & Hall BL (2007). 'What about feelings?' A study of emotion and tension in social work field education. *Social Work Education,* 26(4): 399–413.

Cox DR (2006). International social work. In DR Cox & M Pawar (Eds). *International social work: issues, strategies, and programs* (pp1–23). Thousand Oaks, California: Sage Publications.

Diega A (2007). *Fast facts on Filipino labor migration.* Quezon City: Kanlungan Centre Foundation.

Engstrom D, Gamble L, & Min JW (2009). Field practicum experiences of bilingual social work students working with limited English proficiency clients. *Journal of Social Work Education,* 45(2): 209–24.

Engstrom D & Jones LP (2007). A broadened horizon: the value of international social work internships. *Social Work Education,* 26(2): 136–50.

Ferguson I & Lavalette M (2006). Globalization and global justice: towards a social work of resistance. *International Social Work,* 49(3): 309–18.

Gains R (2010). A member of the 'I' generation learns about the meaning of community in Manila. *New Community Quarterly,* 8(2): 3–5.

Guan J (1999). Filipinas as global slaves. *IBON Facts and Figures*, 22(5–6): 1–11.

Hare I (2004). Defining social work for the 21st century: the International Federation of Social Workers' revised definition of social work. *International Social Work*, 47(3): 407–24.

Healy LM (2001). *International social work: professional action in an interdependent world*. New York: Oxford University Press.

Hokenstad MC, Khinduka SK & Midgley J (Eds) (1992). *Profiles in international social work*. Washington, DC: National Association of Social Workers.

Hong PYP & Song IH (2010). Glocalization of social work practice: global and local responses to globalization. *International Social Work*, 53(5): 656–70.

Hugman R, Moosa-Mitha M & Moyo O (2010). Towards a borderless social work: reconsidering notions of international social work. *International Social Work*, 53(5): 629–43.

Ife J (2001). Local and global practice: relocating social work as a human rights profession in the new global order. *European Journal of Social Work*, 4(1): 5–15.

Lager PB & Robbins VC (2004). Field education: exploring the future, expanding the vision. *Journal of Social Work Education*, 40(1): 3–11.

Litvack A, Mishna F & Bogo M (2010). Emotional reactions of students in field education: an exploratory study. *Journal of Social Work Education*, 46(2): 227–42.

Lough BJ (2009). Principles of effective practice in international social work field placements. *Journal of Social Work Education*, 45(3): 467–80.

Mapp SC (Ed) (2007). *Human rights and social justice in a global perspective: an introduction to international social work*. New York: Oxford University Press.

Mathiesen SG & Lager P (2007). A model for developing international student exchanges. *Social Work Education*, 26(3): 280–91.

Midgely J (2006). International social work, globalization and the challenge of a unipolar world *Journal of Sociology & Social Welfare*, 33(4): 11–17.

Midgley J (2001). Issues in international social work: resolving critical debates in the profession. *Journal of Social Work*, 1(1): 21–35.

Midgley J (1990). International social work: learning from the Third World. *Social Work*, 35(4): 295–301.

Mohan B (2008). Rethinking international social work. *International Social Work*, 51(1): 11–24.

Mohan B (2005). New internationalism: social work's dilemmas, dreams and delusions. *International Social Work*, 48(3): 241–50.

Nagy G & Falk D (2000). Dilemmas in international and cross-cultural social work education. *International Social Work*, 43(1): 49–60.

Panos PT, Cox SE, Pettys GL & Jones-Hart E (2004). Survey of international field education placements of accredited social work education programs. *Journal of Social Work Education*, 40(3): 467–78.

Pawar M, Hanna G & Sheridan R (2004). International social work practicum in India. *Australian Social Work*, 57(3): 223–36.

Schneck D (1995). The promise of field education in social work. In G Rogers (Ed). *Social work field education: views and visions* (pp3–14). Dubuque, IA: Kendall/Hunt.

Sills SJ (2007). Philippine labour migration to Taiwan: social, political, demographic, and economic dimensions. *Migration Letters*, 4(1): 1–14.

Sison JM & De Lima J (1998). *Philippine economy and politics*. Manila: Aklat ng Bayan Publishing House.

Tesoriero F (2006). Personal growth towards intercultural competence through an international field education programme. *Australian Social Work*, 59(2): 126–40.

Yeom HS & Bae H (2010). Potential issues in field practicum student exchange between Korea and the USA. *International Social Work*, 53(3): 311–26.

CHAPTER TEN

COMMUNITY ENGAGEMENT: MANAGERS' VIEWPOINTS

Patricia Hanlen

Managers are invaluable for their support of fieldwork placement for social work students. This chapter examines factors that influence managers' decision-making towards student placement provision, a role which has traditionally been overlooked in the literature. Understandings were gained from fifteen non-statutory managers gathered in a qualitative study in New Zealand. Māori and non-Māori managers were interviewed twice, with a three month interval between data gathering. Four themes of organisational, cultural, student and relational factors are considered for their influence on provision. Findings suggest the importance of student quality and their ability to make connections with local indigenous communities and reciprocity in relationships between educational institutions and social service agencies.

从经理的角度看社区伙伴合作关系

实习机构经理为社工实习生提供了大力的支持。经理的角色往往在有关文献中被忽视。针对此现象,本章节讨论在社工实习过程中影响机构经理做决策的主要因数。十五位来自新西兰非政府组织的经理参与了此项定性研究,从他们的角度探讨了本论题。毛利裔和非毛利裔经理先后两次被采访,采访间隔的时间为三个月。经理们

认为，在协助实习的过程中，他们做决策的原因来自四个方面：机构，文化，实习生和人际关系。研究表明，社工实习生应该积极与本地土著社区建立良好的伙伴关系，而他们本身的性格和能力将会有助于实现这个目标。此外，实习生也应该努力促成教学单位与社区服务机构间的相互合作关系。

コミュニティ契約 —実習管理者の視点—

実習管理者は、ソーシャルワークを学ぶ学生の現場実習の支援において非常に重要な存在である。本章では、先行研究では伝統的に見過ごされてきてしまった要因、すなわち、学生の実習準備に対する、実習管理者の意思決定に影響を与える要因について検討する。その理解はニュージーランドにおける質的調査で収集された、特に法律の定めるところではない15人の実習管理者から得られた。マオリ族とマオリ族ではない実習管理者は二度インタビューを受け、それらのデータ収集の期間は３ヶ月間であった。組織的、文化的、学生、および関連要因の以上四つの主題は実習準備に影響を与えたものとして検討された。結果、学生の質と、学生が地元固有のコミュニティとのつながりを持つ能力、および教育機関と社会サービス機関との関係性における相互関係の重要性が示唆されることとなった。

지역사회 참여: (실습 기관) 관리자의 관점

관리자는 사회복지를 공부하는 학생들의 현장 실습 교육 지원에 있어서 매우 중요한 역할을 한다. 이 장은 학생 현장 실습을 제공하는데 있어서 관리자의 의사 결정에 영향을 미치는 요소들을 살펴볼 것인데, 이러한 역할은 전통적으로 관련 문헌에서 간과되어 왔다. 이와 관련된 정보를 얻기 위해, 뉴질랜드 비 정부 기관에서 일하는 15명의 관리자들을 상대로 질적 연구(qualitative study)를 수행하였다. 자료를 수집하는 동안 3개월 간격을 두고 그 관리자들을 두 번씩 인터뷰 했으며, 그 중에는 마오리(뉴질랜드 원주민) 관리자들도 있었다. 현장 실습을 제공하는데 있어 관리자에게 영향을 끼치는 것으로 조직적, 문화적, 관계적 및 실습 학생과 관련된 요소, 이렇게 네 가지 주제로 고려될 수 있다. 이 연구 결과는 학생의 자질과 그들이 현지 토착 지역 사회와 자신을 연결할 수 있는 능력, 그리고 교육 기관들과 사회 복지 단체들간 상호 협력적인 관계가 중요하다고 제시하고 있다.

Fieldwork placement of social and community work students is dependent on the voluntary good will of managers of social service agencies to support and resource it. Social work educators and students have always recognised and valued fieldwork placement as an essential component in the social work curriculum and students relish the challenge. The contribution of fieldwork placement is prized for its role in growing student skills, knowledge, and competencies as they learn to marry classroom learning with the realities of agency practice. Social work educators would hope that the student completes placement feeling inspired to be the very best social workers they can be in the future. Fieldwork placement has been described by Doel and Shardlow (1996) as the 'heartbeat of social work' (p24). Although the placement experience is a universal expectation of schools of social work, shortages of 'suitable' placements have been identified by educationalists in many countries. The educator's expectation is that social service organisations will reinforce 'the purpose, values and ethics of the profession' (Zastrow 2003, p25). The traditional expectation is that the agency will provide for day-to-day and formal social work supervision of the student as they learn about social work, develop professional competence and learn agency practices. Noble et al. (2005) state that despite rapid increases in social work and social welfare programs and increased numbers of students there is a decrease in the actual numbers of agencies willing or able to undertake partnerships with universities.

Social work fieldwork coordinators ask agency managers 'Will you take a student on placement?' This chapter addresses how non-statutory managers responded to such a question. The non-statutory sector contains a range of smaller placement providers, sometimes referred to as the 'third' sector, largely dependent upon government subsidies. The constructed term of manager, refers to a designated leadership and decision-making role of the person responsible for the smooth running of the organisation and its activities. Non-statutory managers have often been invisible in social service roles, often described as 'agencies' in the fieldwork placement and supervision literature. It is argued that both this sector and non-statutory managers within it are vitally important to the sustainability of this central component of social work education.

This chapter draws upon themes gathered from an interpretative qualitative study in New Zealand. Thirteen non-statutory managers were interviewed twice with a three month interval between each interview although two were unavailable for the second interview. Managers were drawn from a randomised sample of managers of non-statutory social service organisations. Two thirds of the managers in this study came from small- to medium-sized social services (under 12 full- or part-time paid staff). Many managers had previously acted in the dual role as both the student administrator, and social work supervisor. This focus on non-statutory social services was chosen because it is a large group of placement providers for social work students in New Zealand rather than simply statutory managers. These managers, Māori and non-Māori, employ 'over half of the social work workforce as opposed to just over one third employed in the government sector' (Social Workers Registration Board 2007, p16). Given that large numbers of students receive their practice learning from social workers employed in non-government agencies, this study is likely to have relevance beyond New Zealand, as international standards encourage 'a partnership between the educational institution and the agency' regarding field education (International Federation of Social Workers 2003, 3.3.10) Distillation of the data from 24 interviews indicates that in regional locations in New Zealand, the majority of student placements stem from polytechnic, and to a lesser extent *wananga* (tertiary institutions based on Māori philosophy), educational institutions rather than universities. Although much of the literature refers to university–agency relationships the results are more relevant to polytechnics and *wananga*.

The random selection of the sample resulted in fifteen participants, ten of which were women and five were men. As almost half the participants were Māori, it was culturally appropriate for participants to receive collegial support during the interview process. Working with indigenous people in New Zealand requires not only recognition of the connections with the land, but any research relationships include the notion of reciprocity.

TRADITIONAL MODEL OF FIELDWORK PLACEMENT

The traditional model, sometimes called the apprenticeship model, 'reflects the one-to-one relationship, implying one student assigned to one supervisor in one location' states Cleak et al. (2000, p161). Today the traditional model is the most prevalent form of integrating learning with practice and developing student competencies in Aotearoa New Zealand and Australia. No money changes hands with this model, with formal negotiation often beginning with a verbal and written contract, when the manager agrees to take a student on placement and educate him/her into practice. Alternatively a staff member takes on the role of supervisor, particularly in large social service agencies. Time limited learning contracts are agreed to and signed at the onset of the practicum, contracts designed by the schools of social work for implementation. The placement may conclude with an event organised by schools of social work to recognise contributions made by agencies towards the learning gained by students on placement.

The present study was conducted within the context of the traditional, or apprenticeship model of fieldwork placement, where there are usually three major roles identified in the literature: the student supervisor, the student and the placement coordinator from the school of social work. Under the traditional model it is expected that either one internal supervising social worker or a contracted external supervisor takes responsibility for the student's social work learning on placement for a contracted period of time. At times, the school may contract an external supervisor for short periods if an agency cannot provide student supervision. Although external supervisors can offer an objective view, external supervisors are disadvantaged if they do not fully understand the way the services operate. Whether the student placement is in the traditional setting of a social service agency or working in the wider community, for example at times of a disaster, the location of the student's learning still has to be managed and supervised. The manager of smaller organisations may also be the supervisor of a student on placement as well as carrying overall responsibility for administrative systems alongside equal responsibility for a student's learning, happiness and wellbeing while they are hosted in their organisation, as was found in the study reported here.

The managers also carry the responsibility and risk a student may bring to the workplace. It is the manager of a social or community service agency who holds the legitimate authority to say 'yes' or 'no' to students on placement. Although the supervisory role is vital to the success of fieldwork placement, it is argued that the manager is equally important as it is they who have the overview, the control over the time, workload, material, electronic, technological and people resources to expend upon students.

The word 'manager' carries and creates meaning and from a postmodernist viewpoint, the role itself is socially constructed. The methodological framework focuses on a constructionist approach and the use of systems ideas along with the concept of students contributing voluntary work, unpaid, as they learn in an unfamiliar organisation. Constructionist methodology places a focus on the role of managers within the structure of non-statutory organisations, managers that have the authority and power within the structure to sustain or reject such a system of student learning. Systems epistemology assisted with understanding the principles of circularity of information exchange and interactional systems, assumptions, patterns, forms and types of organisations and how power, ethics, change and stability in social systems provide sign posts (Bilson & Ross 1999).

Student characteristics

The study from which this chapter is drawn revealed that there was a demand for 'quality' students, that is, those students seen by managers as possessing sufficient intelligence, skill, commitment and motivation to contribute to the service delivery. Understanding was sought from these managers as to how personal, social, or psychological factors about students might influence their decision-making. The managers studied were seeking students with sufficient competence and a compatible value system to fit into and contribute to the work of the agency. They expected them to come partially informed about the agency's purpose and the social needs it was addressing. Managers' willingness towards placement provision is likely to be influenced by memories of good or bad experiences of past student placements. Goodwill is generated by students who create cohesion with the agency staff, and fit comfortably with its culture and organisational purpose. Student enthusiasm, observation, learning, action and reflection as they developed into emerging professionals appeared to impact on managers' willingness attitudes. Cooper (2000) too argued the importance of training, socialising and moulding students into the agency culture and contended placement must be supported by strong student monitoring.

Although the schools of social work generally instigate and shepherd the placement process, the agency managers were clear about their expectations of student abilities and ethical behaviour. Non-statutory managers in the study, in response to a question about whether internal or external organisational factors influenced their decision-making on the student placement question, placed emphasis on student competencies. Overall, they were looking for attributes such as social maturity and advanced training, students interested in agency work and students who matched their ethnicity or religious preferences, although there was flexibility over the latter. Other skills and values identified from the data included the ability of the student to listen well; students who were encouraging, helpful, caring, passionate, respectful and able to work with difference and open to supervision. Managers had expectations of ethical behaviour such as trustworthiness; honesty, keeping of confidentiality and being able to 'fit' into the agency value system. Such students were likely to be seen as an asset, and therefore an influence on managers' future willingness towards provision of a place.

The data synthesis into the literature would suggest that the more advanced students were in their study, the more likely they were to display a wider range of skills and knowledge to support and benefit the organisation, therefore more likely to be considered as 'earning their keep'. The results enrich a statement by O'Connor et al. (1998) in that managers gave primacy to students who showed initiative, thereby contributing to the fulfilment of agency service contracts. Similarly, Rogers et al. (2003) state that self-awareness, adaptability, flexibility, critically reflective and intellectually and personally prepared practice as professionals are desired attributes of students preparing to be helping professionals. It would appear that a double bonus presents itself, when time and energy investment is rewarded if the student on placement is suitable to fill a current or pending employment gap.

Avoidance of risky students

It would appear that managers were more likely to remember 'risky' students of the past and resolve in the future to avoid students who were likely to drain time and energy from the organisation and themselves. Managers did not like students who had: serious dependency issues; unacknowledged and unaddressed child abuse histories; their own children in care; students who were protected with violence orders by the Courts; or those who were subject to legal restraining orders. Serious convictions, unaddressed health or physical fitness issues or drug and alcohol concerns were student issues managers also did not wish to invite into their organisation. Such grave matters were seen to deter and detract from the fieldwork experience as intense feelings of the student could override the focus on learning. Risky students were also seen as posing a threat to the good name of the manager, the staff and the organisation. Managers wanted to avoid 'disastrous students' as described by one manager. Issues of conflict, power struggles, and disharmony within the organisation were seen as time consuming and as risks to the delivery of the service to clients. Some managers were unwilling to spend their time sorting out conflicted student relationships, 'baby-sitting' students or 'passing the [student] parcel' around the staff, with 'less than satisfactory' students. Similarly, students with mental health or substance abuse problems, ethical violations, illegal activities and disrespectful classroom behaviour were cited as causes to terminate Master of Social Work students from a program (Jarman-Rohde et al. 1997).

Risk to placement sustainability was created by students who lacked confidence or alternatively were 'loose cannons', that is, those who talked indiscriminately and were more likely to break client confidentiality. Such breaches of confidentiality or unethical or incorrect decision-making by students were seen by managers as posing a risk to client wellbeing. If student relationships with a supervisor became unworkable, this too was seen as a signal that complaints from clients might eventuate. Most managers in the study were aware of student risks and placement 'failure' indicators, gained from previous experiences of students. These indicators of a 'problem' student appear to be identified by staff and shared within the team, prompting the development of strategies to avoid escalation of fieldwork placement failure. These managers wished to avoid having to put such strategies in place, by being fully informed about student characteristics and curriculum provision prior to the placement selection interview. Managers expected frequent monitoring at placement commencement when issues were more likely to arise. These managers knew they could select for preferred student characteristics, as there were many competitors for placement provision.

Dearsley (2000) also found that graduates were not well prepared for child protection work and that their training on child abuse was minimal. Additionally, Napan (1997) reported that there was a dislike for the idea of students practising on clients because their lack of experience and those with an inquisitive nature might add to clients' burdens, which suggests that students must be advanced in their study prior to placement.

Placement matching process

Every school of social work has difficulty in placing students, either because of placement scarcity or insufficient opportunity for matching student characteristics with availability of places. Students who are difficult to place, such as those students who have significant child or adult care responsibilities, or challenging personalities, pose a dilemma for fieldwork placement coordinators. The coordinator may be faced with the obligation to place enrolled students and not wishing to generate harm to the school's good name or be faced with a conflict-ridden or failed placement through mismatches. In order to avoid regrets, resentment and the lotteries of the past, managers were seeking full information and student selection interviews well before placement commencement. They wished to gain information similar to that required of a job applicant. Coordinators would have to know students sufficiently to be able to promote a student's worth and ensure students quality. The problem, of course, is that 'quality' is socially constructed and very difficult to define or assure. Further, Rogers et al. (2003) described how important it was that field educators or supervisors intervene early if issues arise before damage is done to collegial relationships and conflict escalates in the practicum. The managers in this study expected a robust matching and selection process to take place as they did not want to have to admit a selection mistake to their staff, or to justify an unpopular decision to disillusioned staff. Unwillingness to offer placement positions results when the transactions costs are too high or when known benefits of provision are outweighed. The process becomes one of de-motivation, loss aversion and risk aversion (Gleitman-Fridlund & Reisberg 2000) or as March (1997) said, it leads to 'uncertainty avoidance' (p123). This in turn is likely to lead to planning in advance of the request for placement, not to take a student. Therefore, managers are more likely to think about risk, rather than the advantages students bring, if their experience of previous students has been unfavourable to themselves or their staff.

Coordination processes and the nurturing of relationships between organisations primarily fall to the school's placement coordinator, a role which Hay, O'Donoghue & Blagdon (2006) say needs clarification. Shardlow and Doel (2005) identified the coordination role as mediation of student needs with the requirements of the agency. The coordination role requires the support of the manager, the services of a student supervisor and staff goodwill for the placement duration. The negotiation by the coordinator requires arrangements for the student to transition from an educational system into a service delivery system. Organisational systems do vary in terms of technological, social, cultural, organisational, managerial and educational ways. Managers' responses are influenced partly by who requests the placement, the way the question is asked, credibility and status of the person asking, and the timing of the question to the organisation. The expectations of the managers in the study far exceed coordination tasks and responsibilities and fail to do this position of external engagement, justice.

Cultural knowledge

Students able to work with local indigenous communities were valued by many of the managers in the study under focus here. Māori managers indicated the importance of either seeing curriculum vitae which contained tribal affiliations, or the early opportunity to ask students about their family and tribal connections. The skill to work with difference, make relationship connections with clients and the wider community with whom they worked was valued. Therefore, Māori managers sought students who knew their own family genealogy. By extending links, students were seen as being able to build on relationships with local tribes and sub-tribes to improve tribal disconnection and dysfunction while addressing social issues. Students were selected on individual merit and 'someone who is loving, kind and firm'. Māori managers focused on student learning; learning that would be returned to their people and community. Their hospitality was offered freely and generously with expectations for a mutual relationship of gifting. The majority of Māori managers favoured a *mana enhancing* reciprocity approach (Ruwhiu 2001) to student placement. 'Mana is about the power and prestige of *tangata whenua*, [people of the land] and the respect that is accorded to them ... it may increase or decrease in response to the actions of others and to changing environments' (Ruwhiu 2001, p116). In the present study, the student is seen as a gift coming from the community, via the school, where managers and staff would in turn gift their basket of knowledge to the student who is expected to return such learning back to the local community, particularly to enhance and improve their peoples' wellbeing.

231

ORGANISATIONAL PRESSURES

One of the barriers to placement is the internal and external pressures on social service organisations. These pressures lead to variation in responses to requests from fieldwork coordinators. As a manager metaphorically described, the student is not to think of themselves as being a passenger on holiday, but rather going on an ocean-going liner where the seas will be rough. The research identified factors ranging from pressures as a result of globalisation and market forces, through to international and local competition for placement. The findings offer support for the idea that social service managers in New Zealand appear to be accepting the continuance of a resource-poor environment. When a decision is made to provide a placement, it seems that the non-statutory managers that were in my study are resigned to making the best of material resources offered. Material constraints were viewed as something the organisation could overcome, while staff resourcing for fieldwork placement was a key organisation issue influencing provision. Hay, O'Donoghue and Blagdon (2006) found that placement resources were lacking within agencies, which they felt restricted the development, maintenance, and recognition of the relationship and training which subsequently impacted in a negative way on the quality of student places provided.

Contracts to deliver a social service with government assistance are lobbied for by agency managers in competition with one another. Discontent with the government contracting process with social services in New Zealand and competition between providers is seen by Aimers and Walker (2008), as a one-way process of market activity which places agencies in danger of losing their autonomy and contact with their community. Sanders and Mumford (2010) believe the manageralist dialogue still holds dominance within social service management and pressures managers' judgment. In New Zealand, government contracts barely cover 70% of the income needed to sustain current services, with no room to grow said a manager outside the study (pers. comm., 12 November 2008).

Non-statutory organisations cannot escape the influence of economic factors on provision. The economic environment in which social services function pressures organisational thinking, management and staff and service delivery; factors argued by Maidment (2001) as influencing teaching and learning on placement, a concern reported by Jarman-Rohde et al. in 1997. The notion of placement provision as voluntary work was a new realisation for some managers that emerged during the study. Supervision of student placement is voluntary work on top of paid work for the social worker, unacknowledged by payment and not contracted for through service contracts with government. The results from this study suggest that managers were resigned to their position of lack of money in their government contracts or from the schools of social work, in exchange for providing a placement. There was awareness that other professions received payment and a few managers had received payment for international students on placement, but they accepted such disparity. This lack of payment was not seen as a factor influencing willingness to provide for a student placement, even though the sector was seen as under-resourced for service delivery. The broader question arises as to why social work education is out of step with other professions in terms of financial acknowledgement? A New Zealand comparison made with teacher education students on placement with Waikato University, where money changes hands, although 'pitiful', the Early Childhood Placement Co-ordinator (pers. comm., 29 April 2010) indicated that it was increasingly difficult to find placements because of teacher workload, which suggests that heavy work load, is a factor for this sector also.

Managers appear to be seeking students who could fill pending or planned staffing vacancies. Staffing is a major organisational factor which appears to fluctuate with stable and unstable environments and therefore impact on placement provision. This in turn affects transactions with others such as placement choices in a competitive environment. The current study findings indicated the occurring themes of workload pressures on agencies, insufficient support from schools, and ambivalence over contracts with schools, with some similarities to findings by Doel and Shardlow (1996).

Competition between education providers for placement

Interpretation of the present study findings leads to a picture of a highly competitive market for placement provision in the provincial cities and towns. Competition for a placement with the agency was a major factor contributing towards unwillingness to provide, as it was too difficult for these non-statutory managers to provide for more than one student at a time. In the research study, these managers juggled a multiplicity of loyalties, in a sea of competition for placements, not only from social services but occasionally from overseas. If that was not enough, competition for placements came from outside the social service sector as well as within it.

Competition for places comes from other training providers such as early childhood course providers or mental health training providers. This 'outside' competition suggests that there is a shortage of placement providers within those arenas and social services are seen as alternative choices for students from other disciplines. The students are crossing organisational boundaries when a placement is obtained for them, so competition for placements can mean that the first caller at the organisational door, may be the only one for whom it is opened that year. Many writers, such as Healy (2000) and Fook (2002) identified competition as a factor in influencing scarcity of placements, but the study in focus extends this understanding by identifying the extent and source of the competition. It also focused on how managers are realising the extent of the pressure to make their choices and the possibility of making early selections or commitments to favoured providers. Such pressure is likely to result in a selection of students who provide them with the least risk or cost, and most benefit to achieving the agency purpose. Some managers noted high staff turnover with some staff leaving the sector. Such staff turnover raises the question as to how far the pressure on social workers to respond to social needs has extended. Is it fair to ask busy social workers to carry extra work generated by students crossing boundaries into organisational space and is the sense of contributing to the long-term development of the profession sufficient reward in itself?

Supervision and organisational workload

The majority of managers in my research study carried out the role of both manager and supervisor of social work students, so there was little need to find a supervisor from the staff. In these dual roles managers did not release themselves from their core duties. This lack of reduction in duties counter what Hay et al. (2006) noted, in that reduction in the supervisor's regular workload was necessary to contribute fully to the placement learning. Additional work was seen to potentially hinder willingness towards provision by Hay et al. (2006), who found 70% of supervisors and students agreed there was a need for this release from core duties by supervisors. It is argued that workload reduction is the ideal, but in reality it appears that such reduction is not feasible or a realistic expectation of schools of social work, given the workload in social service agencies. If the manager had not undertaken the supervision of the student, they consulted with staff to find an internal supervisor. Walsh-Tapiata and Ellis (1994) questioned the insufficient recognition, support and status given to the task of student supervision. The managers in the New Zealand study generally felt external supervisors may lack understanding of operational matters and how the organisation functioned. Preference was indicated for internal supervisors over external ones, because of their depth of organisational knowledge, advantageous to student learning. Additional scrutiny of the agency from an 'outsider' may also be considered an unwelcome unnecessary pressure. Demographic and policy shifts could lead to loss of supervisory staff for students which may mean managers look for 'ready to go' mature students, advanced in their study to fill gaps, relieve workload pressures on the agencies and the need for supervisors. Given the number of competing factors influencing managers of non-statutory social service organisation, the findings suggest that at times managers may have been willing to provide, but did not have the capacity to do so, so saying 'no' to a student placement did not necessarily mean the closing of the door permanently to schools of social work.

Inter-organisational relationships and reciprocity

In the present study the subsidiary question was asked as to whether practical changes to the traditional placement model would influence provision and whether the model met agency needs. The traditional fieldwork placement model of seasonal contact was seen by many managers as an 'on again, off again' relationship between schools of social work and non-statutory social services. All managers in the study under focus, called for relationship development from the traditional 'placement season' to an all-year-round placement building relationship model. Understandings gained leads to an annual process cycle of 'greet, train and support, then thank agencies' model unfolding across the calendar year, rather than the period designated by the school for student placement in their agencies. Drawing on systems theory of inter connected systems, an annual arrangement will put more energy into relationship maintenance so an 'equilibrium state' (Payne 2005) is achieved. For practical purposes it is concluded that schools of social work need to compact their lists of potential providers to facilitate manageable relationships. As Hardcastle and Powers (2004, p298) identify, '100 units of social structures has a density potential of 4,950 relationships'. Hardcastle and Powers (2004) state that coordination and control of social networks (such as social service agencies) need to be reachable and central with size, density, segmentation, frequency and types of exchanges affecting the function of relations and structural positioning. It is suggested that lists of potential placement agencies held by schools of social work be controlled by profile with segmentations devoted to fields of practice in defined geographical locations for student matching purposes. This current study found management goodwill, fluctuating commitment dependant on organisational factors and a wish for a sustainable tangible all-year-round relationship as key considerations for continuation of collaboration.

As Maidment (2001) propositioned, relationships in the practicum were influenced by communication, goodwill and agency commitment to social work education. Relationship building through placement liaison visits, by student placement coordinators or staff, appeared not to contribute significantly to school–agency connections, although these were considered important for the students' needs. Reciprocity in relationships is an important factor influencing managers' willingness towards fieldwork placement. It is relatively easy to argue that relationships are at the heart of all human interaction. Allan (2000) identified the need for partnerships, collaboration and flexibility in arrangements, maximisation of resource sharing and the fostering of effective relationships between various parties. So too, it is argued here that management roles, status and expectations play a part in professional relationships at various levels, as identified by Compton et al. (2005). However, relationship building is an area in need of significant improvement to enhance agency willingness and participation (Maidment 2001). As Ishisaka et al. (2004) identified, collaboration and partnership greatly improved people's lives therefore these are capable of moving institutions such as a university, polytechnic or *wananga* to a larger sense of purpose.

The findings from this New Zealand study indicate that managers also wanted direct involvement with the university and access to pertinent literature relevant to staffing needs. The principle of *whanaungatanga* [relationships] from Māori culture, a binding of individuals to wider groups, affirms respectful relationships in what Ruffolo and Miller (1994) called a mutually benefiting reciprocal exchange process. Thematic analysis and synthesis of data suggests that managers are asking for more regular meetings coordinated by and at the educational institutions, to work out what might be shared interests and exchanges, other than money. Ideas suggested for greater cohesion, trust and participation by managers were research activity outcomes which were related to their field of practice. Information updates; free entrance to courses; loan of material resources; and accesses to services, such as a library, were suggestions for reciprocity from the present study. A literature matching system could be developed before placement commences and gifted to the agency, or alternatively integrated into student task allocation whilst on placement.

The managers in the New Zealand study sought chances for professional liaison for themselves, professional development for their staff and greater opportunity to contribute to classroom teaching and informal liaison with the schools throughout the year, rather than just during the placement season.

CONCLUSION

Schools of social work have been resource dependent upon non-statutory social services manager's goodwill to host their students for many decades. New understandings of factors influencing the non-statutory manager as a key stakeholder in fieldwork placement have been discussed in this chapter. Managers have the overall responsibility to control the process, the resources and for the student's overall wellbeing whilst on fieldwork placement. Competition for student placements, heavy workloads and managers' expectations of work ready students have been considered as factors influencing the nature of managers' responses to the question of fieldwork placement provision. Managers require sufficient information about students prior to placement to assist them to make decisions. Reflection upon past decisions about previous students influenced the managers' willingness or unwillingness towards fieldwork placement provision. Limited knowledge of students or their cultural connections, combined with organisational instability, could position managers to say 'no' to a place, alternatively positioning them to make risky decisions, or leave them to hope for low adverse consequences following their decision to provide a student placement. With constant change in local and global environments, fieldwork placement will remain an ongoing challenge to all stakeholders.

REFERENCES

Aimers J & Walker P (2008). Is community accountability being overlooked as a result of government-third sector partnering in New Zealand? *Aotearoa New Zealand Social Work. Review edition*, 20(3): 14–24.

Allan J (2000). Maintaining the partnerships between educators and practitioners. In L Cooper & L Briggs (Eds). *Fieldwork in the human service: theory and practice for field educators, practice teachers and supervisors* (pp145–59). St. Leonards, NSW, Australia: Allen & Unwin.

Bilson A & Ross S (1999). *Social work management and practice: systems and principles* (2nd edn) London, United Kingdom: Jessica Kingsley Publishers.

Cleak H, Hawkins L & Hess L (2000). Innovative field options. In L Cooper & L Briggs (Eds). *Fieldwork in the human service* (pp160-74). St Leonards, NSW, Australia: Allen & Unwin.

Compton B, Galaway B & Cournoyer B (2005). The ecosystems perspective and the use of knowledge. In *Social work processes* (7th edn) (pp30-35). Australia: Brooks/Cole.

Cooper L (2000). Teaching and learning in human services fieldwork. In L Cooper & L Briggs (Eds). *Fieldwork in the human service: theory and practice for field educators, practice teachers and supervisors* (pp10-25). St. Leonards, NSW, Australia: Allen & Unwin.

Dearsley P (2000). Statutory social work, but is it really social work? *Social Work Review*, 12(2): 8-13.

Doel M & Shardlow S (Eds) (1996). *Social work in a changing world: an international perspective on practice learning.* Aldershot, England: Ashgate Publishing Ltd.

Etzioni A (Ed) (1969). *The semi-professions and the organization.* New York: Free Press.

Fineman S, Sims D & Gabriel Y (2005). *Organizing and organizations.* (3rd edn). London: Sage Publications.

Fook J (2002). *Social work critical theory and practice.* London: Sage Publications.

Gibbs A (1999). Effective inter-agency partnerships. *Social Work Review*, 15-17.

Gleitman H, Fridlung A & Reisberg D (2000). *Basic psychology.* (5th edn). New York: Norton.

Hay K, O'Donoghue K & Blagdon J (2006). Exploring the aims of social work field education in the registration environment. *Social Work Review,* 18(4): 20-28.

Healy K (2000). Women as managers of non-profit community services: what future? *Women in Welfare Education,* (4): 35-49.

International Federation of Social Workers (2003). Global qualifying standards for social work education and training. [Online]. Available: www.ifsw.org/p38000255. html [Accessed 16 May 2011].

Ishisaka H, Farwell N, Sohng SL & Uehara E (2004). Teaching notes: partnership for integrated community-based learning: a social work community-campus collaboration. *Journal of Social Work Education*, 40(2): 321–35.

Jarman-Rohde L, McFall J, Kofar P & Strom G (1997). The changing context of social work practice: implications and recommendations for social work educators. *Journal of Social Work Education*, 33(1): 29–47. [Online]. Available: www.eric. ed.gov/ERICWebPortal/search/detailmini.jsp?_nfpb=true&_&ERICExtSearch_Se archValue_0=EJ539584&ERICExtSearch_SearchType_0=no&accno=EJ539584 [Accessed 16 May 2011].

Joyce E (1998). Practice teaching: what's in a name? *Social Work Review*, (1): 23–25.

Maidment J (2001). Teaching and learning social work in the field: student and field educator experiences. *Social Work Review*, 13(2): 2–6.

March J (1997). Decision making in organizations. In D Pugh & D Hickson (Eds). *Writers on organizations* (pp121–25). Thousand Oaks, California, USA: Sage Publications.

Napan K (1997). The contact-challenge method in pursuit of effective teaching and learning of social work practice. *Social Work Review*, 4(1&2): 43–47.

Noble C, Heycox K, O'Sullivan J & Bartlett B (2005). Work-based practica: real learning or just your usual job? In P Camilleri & M Ryan (Eds). *Advances in Social Work and Welfare Education*, 7(1): 98–109.

O'Connor I, Wilson J & Setterlund D (1999). *Social work and welfare practice.* (3rd edn). Melbourne, Australia: Addison Wesley Longman.

Payne M (2005). *Modern social work theory.* (3rd edn). Houndmills, United Kingdom: Palgrave Macmillan.

Robbins SP & Barnwell N (1998). *Organisation theory, concepts and cases.* (3rd edn). Sydney, Australia: Prentice Hall.

Rogers G, Benson G, Bouey E, Clark B, Langevin P, Mamehur C & Sawa R (2003). An exploration of conflict in the practicum in four professions. *Women in Welfare Education*, 6: 26–50.

Ruffolo M & Miller P (1994). An advocacy/empowerment model of organizing: developing University-Agency partnerships. *Journal of Social Work Education*, 30(3): 310–17.

Ruwhiu L (2001). Bicultural issues in Aotearoa New Zealand social work. In M Connolly (Ed). *New Zealand social work: context and practice*. Auckland: Oxford University Press.

Sanders J & Mumford R (2010). *Working with families: strengths-based approaches*. Wellington: Dunmore Publishing.

Shardlow S & Doel M (2005*). Practice learning and teaching*. (2nd edn). Basingstoke: Macmillan.

Social Workers Registration Board (2007). *Social Workers Registration Act (2003) Review Report July 2007 Presented to the Minister for Social Development and Employment Pursuant to Section 104 of the Social Workers Registration Act 2003*. Wellington: Social Workers Registration Board.

Walsh-Tapiata W & Ellis G (1994). Have you supervised a student lately? *Social Work Review,* September: 38–41.

Wearing M (1998). *Working in community services: management and practice*. St. Leonards, Australia: Allen & Unwin.

Zastrow C (2003). *The practice of social work: applications of generalist and advanced content*. (7th edn). Pacific Grove, CA: USA: Thomson Brooks/Cole.

Chapter Eleven

From Alaska to New Zealand: lessons from an international social work placement

Kathryn Hay, Mathew Keen, Marjorie Thomson and Janet Emerman

The placement of international social work students into fieldwork experiences in other countries entails a level of complexity not realised in traditional in-country student placements. Drawing on a case study of an Alaskan student's placement in a New Zealand statutory health agency in 2010 and an analysis of relevant literature, this chapter will examine several of the key issues pertaining to international social work placements. Firstly, the chapter will outline the roles, responsibilities and priorities of the four primary stakeholders: the international university; the student; the field educator and the host university. Subsequently we will consider the challenges and opportunities faced by each stakeholder as well as the issues faced in meeting the requirements of the social work professional associations in both the international and host countries. Recommendations regarding several aspects of the placement process including: establishing; monitoring; assessing and debriefing the placement, will be outlined with the intention of assisting others who may be considering similar placement experiences. Finally, a discussion of the advantages and disadvantages of international social work placements in local contexts from the perspectives of the four stakeholders will offer information and knowledge applicable to equivalent stakeholders in other country and social work contexts.

从美国阿拉斯加到新西兰：美国学生的海外实习经验

与选择本地做实习的学生比较，海外社工实习生需要面对一系列不同程度的挑战。本章节以一位来自美国阿拉斯加州的社工学生2010年在新西兰政府健康部门的实习经历为例子，结合有关文献分析海外实习成功与否的重要因数。本章首先讨论四个海外实习参与方各自的角色和责任，以及各方所发挥的不同重要性。这四个参与方包括：派遣海外实习生的大学，海外实习生，海外实习导师，以及接收海外实习生的大学。接下来笔者将讨论各参与方所面对的挑战和机会，这包括实习是否符合海外国和实习生所在国的社工行业协会规范要求。　为确保实习的顺利进行，笔者提出几点建议：选定实习地点，监督和评估实习过程，以及报告总结实习经历。这将为日后考虑选择类似实习地点的学生提供参考。最后，四个参与方将会从他们的角度讨论海外实习的利与弊。这将对其它国家有类似海外实习项目的参与者提供信息和经验。

アラスカからニュージーランドへ

国際ソーシャルワークを学ぶ学生を他の国で現場経験させるために現場に配属することは、従来の国内での実習では気づかれない一定の複雑性を伴う。2010年におけるニュージーランドの法によって定められた保健機関に配属されたアラスカからの実習生についてのケーススタディと関連文献についての分析を利用し、本章は国際ソーシャルワーク実習に付随する問題のいくつかの解決の手がかりとなる課題について検討する。はじめに、本章は国際大学、学生、現場教育者とそのホスト大学の主な4者の利害関係者の役割、責任と優先すべき事項のアウトラインを示す。次に、我々は国際的にもホスト国の両者におけるソーシャルワーク専

門機関の要求を満たす上で直面する問題同様に、それ
ぞれの利害関係者が直面している課題や機会について
検討する。実習の設定、モニタリング、アセスメン
ト、実習報告を含む実習過程の幾つかの側面について
の奨励は、類似した実習経験を念頭に置いている他の
者への援助を意図する形で示されるだろう。最後に、4
者の利害関係者の視点からの地元の状況下での国際ソ
ーシャルワーク実習の利益と不利益についての議論
は、他の国やそのソーシャルワークの状況下の同等の
利害関係者への応用可能な情報と知識を提供する。

알래스카에서부터 뉴질랜드까지: 외국 현지(現地) 상황
에서 사회복지 해외 현장 실습을 통한 교훈

사회복지를 공부하는 학생들이 다른 나라에서 현장 실습
경험을 하는 것은 어느 정도의 복잡한 특징들을 수반하는
데, 이것은 전통적인 국내 현장 실습 교육에서는 인식되
지 않던 것이다. 이 장에서는 2010년도에 뉴질랜드 정부
보건 기관에서 현장 실습을 한 알래스카 학생의 사례 연
구와 관련 문헌의 분석 자료를 인용하면서, 사회복지 해
외 실습 교육과 관련된 몇 가지 중요한 현안들을 살펴볼
것이다. 첫 번째로, 이 장은 주요 이해관계자의 역할, 책
임 그리고 우선 순위들에 대해 간략히 설명할 것이다. 주
요 이해 관계자로는 외국 대학교, 학생, 현장 실습 지도
자, 그리고 현지 대학교가 있다. 그 다음으로 각 이해 관
계자들이 직면하는 도전과 기회뿐만 아니라 국내외적으
로 사회복지 전문가 협회에서 요구하는 요건들을 충족시
키는 것과 연관된 현안들을 살펴볼 것이다. 그리고 관계
수립, 감독, 평가 및 실습 보고를 포함한 현장 실습 과정의
여러 측면과 관련하여 몇 가지 권고 사항이 간략히 기술
될 것이다. 이 부분은 비슷한 환경하에서 현장 실습을 하
려는 다른 학생들에게 도움이 될 것이다. 마지막으로 외
국 현지 상황에서 이루어지는 해외 실습 교육의 장단점을
앞의 네 부류의 이해관계자 관점에서 논의가 될 것이다.
이 논의는 다른 나라 또는 다른 사회복지 환경 안의 동등

한 위치에 있는 이해관계자에게 적용될 수 있는 정보와 지식을 제공할 것이다.

While field education presents specific significant challenges for all parties involved in the practicum experience, international placements add another level of complexity. As Lough (2009, p472) cautions, 'Although the possible advantages of international placements are many, they must be properly implemented to achieve these effects. If executed poorly, these experiences could negatively impact both students and host communities'. A study considering international placements for social work students involved in accredited US courses between 1997 and 2002, noted a reduction to 21.1% of the 94 courses providing international placements from the 29.1% found in an earlier study (Panos et al. 2004).

In 2010 a Masters of Social Work (MSW) student from the University of Alaska Anchorage (UAA) travelled to New Zealand to undertake her final practicum in an inpatient mental health service in Palmerston North Hospital. Palmerston North is a provincial city, the 7th largest in New Zealand, with a population of approximately 80,000. The hospital is a base regional facility which offers extensive inpatient and outpatient services. The placement was extremely successful from the perspectives of the four key stakeholders although many important lessons were also learned throughout the practicum process. This chapter will present these key learnings with the intent of contributing our experience and knowledge to the limited scholarship on international placements.

THE CASE STUDY

Janet Emerman, Clinical Professor, is the Field Education Coordinator for the Bachelor of Social Work (BSW) and MSW Distance Field Education Programmes at the UAA and has been involved in field education for fifteen years. Her role is to place, orient, monitor and evaluate students and placement agencies mostly in Anchorage, Alaska for BSW students, but also throughout the state of Alaska for Distance MSW students. Organising a placement to NZ was somewhat unusual and proceeded differently to the other domestic placements in the School of Social Work at the UAA. Very few social work students at the UAA endeavour to undertake an international placement for the following reasons: 1) the majority of the social work students are mature with families and work commitments thereby restricting their flexibility to travel to another country for the practicum; 2) the UAA School of Social Work does not offer extensive financial aid and adding the costs associated with an international placement to the University fees is prohibitive for most students; 3) few social work students seriously consider doing an international placement. In the last decade fewer than ten students from UAA School of Social Work have requested such placements and the School has not developed extensive connections or processes or actively promoted the concept of international placements. That said, the UAA School of Social Work has flexibility in its MSW program and can offer block placements (540 hours of placement in one 3.5 month semester) and distance-delivered classes so students can continue to stay abreast of their sequence of classes and with their graduation cohort. However, international block placements are only considered in the final year of the MSW and then preferably in the first semester when the concurrent course load would more easily accommodate such an intense experience.

Margie Thomson, a mature final year MSW student, first discussed the concept of a placement in New Zealand (NZ) with her fieldwork coordinator three years before the placement was due to occur, and began preparing in earnest 18 months prior to the anticipated start date. Margie had lived in NZ previously and was specifically interested in undertaking her placement in this country, due to her positive previous experiences and her interest in indigenous social work practice. Her employment and family situation allowed for her to be gone for the length of time necessary to complete the block placement. Margie contacted field education staff in the NZ university social work programs requesting support for her in seeking a placement, in which she would work with a diverse population, and also work in a clinical setting. In particular, Margie was interested in having a placement that would provide her with the opportunity to learn clinical skills, and to learn in a multidisciplinary and multicultural environment. Margie was looking for a field instructor who was strong in clinical skills and was willing to mentor her and assist in her professional growth.

The Director of Field Education at Massey University, Kathryn Hay, responded to Margie's initial email by requesting a Curriculum Vitae; further information as to why an international placement was being sought; and affirmation from the UAA School of Social Work as to Margie's suitability for a placement in NZ. These requests were met swiftly and appropriately and Kathryn agreed to continue considering the possibility of a placement for Margie. Many requests for international placements are sent to the Massey University social work program although these are rarely followed through. In the past ten years, three international placements have been organised and hosted by the social work field education at Massey University staff. The coordination and monitoring role for the host university has varied in each circumstance and on occasion staff have been paid to organise an international placement and arrange external supervision for the student during the practicum period. In this case example, no financial transactions occurred between the UAA and Massey University in regard to organising Margie's placement.

Mathew Keen, Senior Psychiatric Social Worker in the Acute Inpatient Mental Health Service at Palmerston North hospital, and MSW graduate from Massey, is an experienced practitioner and field educator, and regularly takes both undergraduate and masters social work students on placement. He was approached to consider taking Margie on placement due to this expertise and commitment to field education and the learning of students. This was Mathew's first experience of an international placement.

PRE-PLACEMENT PLANNING

The planning of this placement was critical for all of the four key stake-holders. As mentioned, Margie began planning for this placement well in advance. This was necessary for both personal and professional reasons. Firstly, Margie needed to budget for the experience so that she could maintain financial commitments in Alaska and also afford accommodation and living costs in NZ. Professionally Margie needed to ascertain support from the UAA School of Social Work and ensure she could meet the requirements of her practicum paper in another country and also be deemed suitable for a placement in NZ from the perspective of the host university.

In Alaska, the student and university social work staff discussed the requirements of the placement and the logistics of distance learning and attending classes via the Internet. NZ university staff agreed to approach a possible placement agency on the condition that Margie would begin reading social work publications from NZ so as to increase her understanding of the local context, and especially working appropriately with Māori, the indigenous peoples of NZ. Although Margie indicated her preferences for having her placement in specific fields of practice and client groups she was also informed that the decision would be primarily based on agency and field educator availability and suitability for an international placement. In particular, a qualified, experienced practitioner preferably registered with the NZ Social Workers' Registration Board or a member of the professional association, Aotearoa New Zealand Association of Social Workers was required to be a field educator (see Cleak & Wilson 2007 for an Australian perspective on this issue). This standard is in line with usual practicum practices in NZ. Margie did indicate her interest in the health sector and given the vast experience of several social workers in the local hospital being field educators Kathryn sought a placement in this agency in the first instance. Once a placement in the mental health field was approved, Margie also read material pertinent to that field and the broader health sector in NZ.

Importantly, at the outset of this pre-placement stage, staff at UAA School of Social Work and Massey University agreed that the primary purpose of this placement was to advance Margie's social work learning and expertise, not just to have a cross cultural experience. This emphasis continued throughout the placement and ensured the focus remained on achieving the learning requirements of the practicum paper and Margie's own professional needs. It was apparent throughout this pre-preparation stage that the student was highly motivated to come to NZ;

well organised and prepared to commit her time to meeting the requests and requirements of the host university. The friendly and respectful communication between the UAA, the student and Massey University created goodwill and a sense of openness that further encouraged the host university staff to agree to find a suitable placement for Margie.

An Affiliation Agreement was required between the UAA and the NZ hospital and whilst there were no difficulties in reaching agreement, the process took considerable time due to staff turnover, different holiday schedules and vacations, and complicated emails back and forth. The student had personal health insurance coverage and she purchased professional liability insurance that could cover her for the duration of her time in NZ; in addition the host site offered Honorary Staff privileges. The professional indemnity insurance was significant as the UAA malpractice liability insurance does not extend to students undertaking practicum in another country; in addition the accident insurance may also not have had international coverage. Other legal practicalities that were the responsibility of the student included police vetting, an appropriate visa, a current passport and medical clearances. As part of the pre-placement organisation, the host university had also stipulated that a placement would need to be in Palmerston North so that it would be in close proximity to the University. This pre-requisite arrangement was specified so that a known agency and field educator could be approached and also as a precautionary measure in case the placement did not work out as successfully as planned and staff at the host university could be nearby to intervene if necessary. Furthermore, Margie needed suitable accommodation in NZ that was affordable, appropriate and also accessible in terms of transportation. As a provincial town, rental accommodation is reasonably priced in Palmerston North and staff at the host university were able to provide Margie with some possible affordable rental options. Again, the use of email and internet was beneficial and accommodation was able to be confirmed quickly and easily online.

Course materials from Alaska, including requirements and expectations, assignments and evaluation standards, were forwarded to the host university in NZ early in the pre-placement stage so that the

UAA requirements could be considered prior to approaching agencies for a placement. Through email, staff at the two universities were able to clarify how placements in each country generally proceed, the learning expectations and assessment processes. It was apparent that processes and the vision for placement being a learning experience more than a cultural exchange were similar and this enabled a high level of trust to be established. Due to this relationship and that an experienced agency and field educator were to be used, the UAA decided that the usual face-to-face site visit between the student, a University staff member and the field educator would not occur, but would instead be held telephonically.

The actual setting up of the placement was straightforward with Kathryn contacting the Professional Advisor (Social Work) of the hospital, discussing the situation, forwarding information on Margie and agreeing to oversee the placement if anything untoward occurred. Mathew, as prospective field educator, was immediately interested in the concept of an international placement and the new learning and challenges it would entail. Once the placement was confirmed, contact between the student and the field educator was instigated through email. On reflection, Skype conversations would have also been beneficial at this matching stage of the process so that the relationship could have been further developed prior to the placement start. More relevant material was sent to the student to read before her arrival and the host university agreed to meet Margie and take her to the agency on her first day of placement. Again, in hindsight more information pertaining to the NZ health context; a job description for the student position and examples of the work the student was to be involved in would all have been beneficial prior to the student's arrival.

Practicum

The placement began in September 2010. Having an experienced field educator proved critical to the success of the placement. Mathew was prepared with an orientation package for Margie to begin her placement and this oriented her to not only the agency, its staff and its work but also to the wider Palmerston North social work community. Specifically, the orientation documentation included a list of acronyms and psychiatric

251

terms; hospital policies and procedures; a position description and a supervision contract. Mathew was clear in his expectations of Margie and her role as a student in the mental health setting. In addition, he was constantly seeking to nurture Margie's skills and strengths and further these in the placement setting. The focus on advancing her professional knowledge and abilities, rather than just surviving the placement experience, remained a bedrock of the placement throughout.

Although Mathew was invited to attend the UAA field educator orientation electronically, this was not possible due to the time difference between the two countries. The materials were sent to him instead. While the UAA was prepared to provide 'outside field instruction' if that had been necessary, in retrospect, given the severity of the clinical situations Margie worked with, having an experienced on-site field educator was an absolute necessity.

Throughout the practicum, Margie attended weekly seminars of three hours duration using computer technology (eLive, a computer-based enhanced teleconference technology). This enabled her to keep in contact with her peers and provided her seminar instructor with a way of monitoring her practice and growth. These seminars were in addition to her 540 practicum hours. The weekly seminar was an important support to the student as it was a time to connect with fellow students and share similarities and differences in their practicum experiences. In many ways, this allowed the student to reflect on the cultural aspects of living and working in another country. Her fellow classmates expressed that they also benefited by being exposed to social work in the context of another culture. Margie shared her experiences about the Mental Health system in NZ and the focus on biculturalism and the high consideration for the indigenous people of NZ through these weekly seminars, as well as maintaining an online blog, which chronicled the several month practicum.

The absence of a site visit by a university member has already been noted as a change to usual practice. In other international placements site visits may occur depending on the particular student and their needs and abilities; any challenges in the placement; and the relationship with the host university. It is of note that if serious difficulties had arisen during the placement then staff at the host university were available to visit and undertake negotiations and mediation as required on behalf of the international university. Having these measures in place provided reassurance for all of the key stakeholders but were unnecessary in this particular case study.

Several political and institutional differences were apparent throughout the practicum. The student was required to advance her knowledge and understanding of relevant government policies and procedures. In particular the welfare system of NZ presented a complex web of benefits and assistance that Margie needed to navigate quickly and efficiently so as to ensure positive outcomes for clients. The nuances of the NZ health system also provided Margie with considerable new and specific learning. The differences in the Alaskan and NZ MSW programs were also highlighted. Aspects of the placement experience were more challenging than in most Alaskan placements, although with the support of a knowledgeable and experienced field educator like Mathew, students in the advanced generalist degree program may have been given a similar placement opportunity. In spite of the differences in curriculum, Margie's advanced professional knowledge and skills, gained throughout the placement, is to a large extent transferable into other sectors in the Alaskan context.

POST-PLACEMENT

The student felt that some of her initial goals and objectives changed throughout the placement. For example, learning and mastering the role of the clinician was the initial role that she had chosen; however once situated in her practicum site, it was acknowledged that the role of the psychiatric social worker on this hospital ward was more of the role of a discharge planner. However, Margie's learning requirements were all met and exceeded. Due to her existing knowledge and skills she was gradually given substantive opportunities in the area of clinical work. These opportunities were possibly more extensive in scope than if she had undertaken a practicum in her local context, as many Alaskan agencies are becoming increasingly driven by third party payments and liability issues and thus limit the role of a practicum student.

From the perspective of the student, her learning needs and hopes for a supportive field educator and agency were exceeded. The high level of professionalism and passion for social work of both the field educator and the student enabled the establishment of a mutually positive relationship. Common interests in the active and reflective integration of social work theory into the practice environment and critical reflective practice further enhanced this relationship. The field educator's openness and availability created a climate that invited deep discussions about situations on the ward, ethics and values.

At the UAA, on her return to Alaska, Margie was reunited with her fellow students and she participated in common debriefing processes. In hindsight, a more organised way for Margie to share her experiences and learning would have been beneficial for Margie, the UAA School of Social Work staff and other students. The student will be contributing an article on her international placement in the UAA School of Social Work annual newsletter to be sent out throughout the state of Alaska. In the future the School will think ahead of time about how to capitalise on a student's international experiences and share them with a wider audience than the students in her cohort and her online classes. The initial focus, that the international placement had to be primarily intended to be more about the social work learning experience than just a cultural exchange has been affirmed, as the complexity and the richness of the experience from a social work perspective, and the importance of cultural sensitivity (which required some advance preparation) was realised.

FURTHER REFLECTIONS

On reflection several factors can be identified in this case example of an international placement that ensured a successful placement. The student had to show a high level of commitment and motivation in planning the placement and therefore she was well prepared before the placement began. Margie endeavoured to present herself in the best light to the host university so as to improve her chances for having an international placement and to be a positive 'ambassador' from UAA and Alaska. This meant she had to ensure her Curriculum Vitae and supporting documents were up to date and of a high standard. She also read a substantial amount of material pertaining to the national and social work context in NZ thereby being more prepared in this way than some students undertaking a placement in their local environment.

Contacting the potential host university over a year in advance of the placement start date was important as considerable time was required for relationships between the parties to be established; understandings of the placement processes and outcomes to be shared and decisions as to whether the student was suitable for an international placement to be made. Furthermore, confirming a placement can often take time, even with local placements, and connections and negotiations needed to occur. Whilst electronic communication may be instantaneous, this does not guarantee rapid responses to emails and in this case study the timely communication was exemplary. From the UAA School of Social Work perspective, the realisation that planning needed to begin very early was affirmed as everything took longer to get through the necessary approval processes. In addition there could have been many more complications regarding insurance and liability if this placement had not been in a country and within a system that had provisions for most of these needs. The student took the time to begin to research social work in New Zealand, Mid-Central District Health Board, journal articles concerning the Māori peoples and the Pasifika people living in New Zealand as well (Nash et al. 2001).

Having an experienced field educator provided a level of reassurance to the student, the international university and the host university. Having supervised many students previously meant that the field educator was more aware of the likely learning requirements and appropriate learning goals for the placement. This experience also meant the field educator was more comfortable with working with the student's current strengths and building on these so as to ensure her professional development.

The personalities of the key stakeholders, and particularly the student, were another crucial factor for the success of this placement. The open, honest and respectful initial communication, through email, from the student to the host university laid a positive foundation for ongoing contact. Excellent English written skills and the fact that the student had previously resided in NZ, therefore understood the local context to some extent, contributed to the decision to consider placing the student. Moreover the student was willing to locate and read additional material pertinent to the NZ social work context and was timely in all her email responses. Having appropriate mechanisms and processes in place for allocating students to social work agencies is part of a broader process of risk management and the host university was aware of ensuring the student, whom they had never met or known, would not prove to be a risk to the clients or the agency in which she was placed. Maintaining a positive professional relationship with the agency in which the student was to be placed was also critical so as to not jeopardise future placements. Margie was therefore asked questions about her history, previous placements, reasons for seeking an international placement and criminal record. Confirmation of the trustworthiness and endorsement of the suitability of the student was also requested and granted from the UAA. Margie's learning goals, prior to the placement, were also requested before the placement was confirmed. It was clear that her goals were compatible with what the agency could offer, were realistic and were transferable to the NZ context.

Agreeing to work with a student motivated to do an international placement provided the UAA with some key opportunities: 1) encouraging more students to reach for something outside of their comfort zones as this international placement illustrates a very successful example of a growth-oriented experience; 2) as a well-established department used to doing practica in a particular way, this placement provided a chance for growth in existing internal policies and practices. The current distance-delivered component to the graduate program enables the servicing of the rest of the state of Alaska but was also flexible enough to enable it to be stretched and work at a real distance; 3) in helping Margie prepare, in exploring mental health delivery in NZ and in hearing about her experiences while in NZ, UAA staff and students were able to do some 'comparing and contrasting work' and learning too.

In this case example of an international placement, no disadvantages for any of the stakeholders have been identified. As the UAA has a distance delivered component within the MSW program, Margie was able to keep in sequence with her classes and attend these from anywhere with computer Internet access. The substantial time difference between Alaska and NZ did, however, mean that Margie was subjected to some very long hours. Being overseas and involved in an intense experience has possibly set Margie off-stride in respect of her mental involvement and momentum in other courses on her return to Alaska, although this is a trade-off she is prepared to accept. The expense of such an experience is also a key consideration for other students interested in embarking on an international placement further emphasising the importance of considerable prior planning and preparation.

CONCLUSION

Alaska was the second-to-last state to become one of the United States of America; it is non-contiguous to the other mainland, connected states; it is very sparsely populated and experiences extreme weather conditions; and it is very diverse in ethnic and racial backgrounds in its population. Because of all this, residents tend to proudly identify with the state and with a sort of pioneer identity, sometimes to the exclusion of more global connections and interests. An international placement, both for the practicum student and also for others she is in contact with, truly does broaden horizons and allow for a more global view of the world (Healy 2001; Lough 2009; Noble 2009). For a social work student, the advantages are almost endless. Learning about another country's indigenous peoples and history provides a rich opportunity to compare and contrast with the Native peoples' experience in Alaska. Despite tremendous distances between these areas of the world, there are strong similarities in issues, strengths, and problems, and much to be learned by studying another region's approach to cultural diversity (Noble 2009). Economically and politically there are many differences to learn from in how the two regions handle macro issues: poverty, government involvement and regulation, welfare, service delivery. Professionally there were many opportunities to learn from service provision in the areas of mental health and addictions. While the UAA School of Social Work found it was not organised to make the most of these learning opportunities both while Margie was abroad and upon her return – another lesson learned is that the university needs a mechanism for sharing the information she learned to make sure others would also benefit from the experience.

From the perspective of the host university in NZ thorough pre-placement planning and specific requirements, including where the placement was to occur, both geographically and in terms of the agency and field educator, meant the placement launched from a solid foundation. Building relationships, as far as possible, with the UAA School of Social Work and the student was critical in this early stage of setting up the placement but would have also been essential had any difficulties in the placement arisen. A clear correlation between the vision and learning requirements of practicum in both social work programs also assisted with meeting the expectations and learning needs of the UAA and the student. The role of the host university outside of the pre-placement stage was minimal in this case study. Previous and future international placements may require further time, energy and expertise by the host university staff if there are any placement issues. Also, whilst not an issue in this case example, international placements may increase the competition for placements already experienced in NZ. The needs of domestic students seeking excellent placements must be prioritised and not be threatened by requests from overseas students.

For the field educator, the challenges lay in not having met or interviewed the student seeking placement; and of no experience with the UAA School of Social Work and its processes and documentation. Any apprehension in this case was absolutely unnecessary. While participation in the UAA field educator training and preparation session was not possible (it was going to commence at 6am on a Saturday NZ time); the information pack, CD and emails made everything very clear; and the phone conversation with the staff contact at UAA School of Social Work was very positive.

Prior experience in placements with Massey University and confidence in the Massey University field education coordinator, along with the support from Mid-Central District Health Board (DHB) social work leadership, made the process and preparation significantly less stressful than it could have been. Of significance in the success of this placement, was the exceptional support of the team at Ward 21 and throughout Mid-Central DHB's mental health services.

However, none of this would have been possible without the exceptional professionalism, and commitment to excellence consistently demonstrated by the student. Her focus and hunger to learn, to experience and to reflect on – and integrate the experiences and the knowledges informing them – this is a joy for a field educator. Margie had a focus on integrated practice and readily engaged frameworks for this (Connolly 2007; Fisher & Somerton 2000; Keen & O'Donoghue 2005). She brought a professional awareness, a construct of practice with a focus on strengths and social justice within an ecological frame of reference, and a commitment to engaging in supervision, of sharing and exploring her narrative (O'Donoghue 2003). Margie maintained a perspective of the placement as a factor in her professional training and development that actively acknowledged and affirmed cultural diversity, not as a 'cultural exchange', but recognised and endeavoured to engage in bicultural practice and become culturally competent to practice with Māori and other ethnicities, as required by the NZ Social Workers' Registration Board (Aotearoa New Zealand Association of Social Workers 2008; Noble 2009).

From the student's perspective, this international placement was a valuable opportunity to actually practice concepts and skills learned in the classroom. It was an important challenge to adapt to, and become part of, an unfamiliar organisational culture, as well as the larger diverse ethnic culture. One example was the requirement for the student to abide by the American National Association of Social Work (NASW) Code of Ethics, and compare and contrast these standards to other social work values and ethics in different parts of the world. This type of international experience proved valuable in adapting to the inevitable changing professional and cultural environments to be experienced throughout one's professional career. By accepting and adapting to the challenge of the unfamiliar professional, cultural, and ethnic 'territory' of an international placement, the student not only extends their comfort zone, but also grows in their professional skills and self-awareness. Not only did this international placement become the highlight of the student's formal training, but it led to the realisation that this was not the culmination of an educational process, but rather the beginning of 'real world' professional clinical practice.

REFERENCES

Aotearoa New Zealand Association of Social Workers (2008). *Code of Ethics.* (2nd Revision). Christchurch: Author.

Cleak H & Wilson J (2007). *Making the most of field placement.* (2nd edn). Melbourne: Thomson.

Connolly M (2007). Practice frameworks: conceptual maps to guide interventions in child welfare. *British Journal of Social Work,* 37: 825–37.

Fisher T & Somerton J (2000). Reflection on action: the process of helping social work students to develop their use of theory in practice. *Social Work Education,* 19(4): 387–401.

Healy L (2001). *International social work: professional action in an independent world.* Oxford: Oxford University Press.

Keen M & O'Donoghue K (2005). Integrated practice in mental health social work. In M Nash, R Munford & K O'Donoghue (Eds). *Social work theories in action* (pp80–92). London: Jessica Kingsley Publishers.

Lough BJ (2009). Principles of effective practice in international social work field placements. *Journal of Social Work Education,* 45(3): 467–80.

Nash M & Munford R with Hay K (2001). *Social work in context.* Palmerston North: School of Sociology, Social Policy and Social Work.

Noble C (2009). Social work and the Asia-Pacific: from rhetoric to practice. In C Noble, M Henrickson & I Young Han (Eds). *Social work education: voices from the Asia-Pacific* (pp7–29). Carlton North, VIC: Vulgar Press.

O'Donoghue K (2003). *Restorying social work supervision.* Palmerston North: Dunmore Press.

Panos PT, Pettys GL, Cox SE & Jones-Hart E (2004). Survey of international field education placements of accredited social work education programs. *Journal of Social Work Education,* 40(3): 467–78.

RESPONDING TO THE POLICY ENVIRONMENT

Chapter Twelve

Social work field education in Taiwan: past, present and future

台灣社會工作專業教育與實習教育的發展

Betty Y Weng

首先，將討論近年來，台灣新設立了許多社會工作系，造成社會工作系畢業生大量的增加，影響公部門與私部門的就業市場。同時，也將討論1997年通過的社會工作師法。其次，將呈現從以前到現在的社會工作實習時數、安排及相關規定。第三部分，自從社會工作師法通過將近15年來，新的國家社會工作師考試的報考資格即將在2013年開始實施。這些新的資格規定將會如何影響社會工作教育，尤其是社會工作實習教育。最後，將提出對未來社會工作實習教育的發展方向與建議。

An increasing number of social work departments and students have emerged in Taiwan since social work was first established. This has resulted in a significant increase in the number of graduates, and has had an effect on job markets in both the public and private sectors. The impact of the 1997 Social Worker Act is discussed. Secondly, the number and arrangement of hours required for social work field education in four-year programs both historically and in the present are presented. Thirdly, in the 15 years since the enactment of the Social Worker Act, new entry requirements for the National Social Worker Examination have been developed, and will be imposed in 2013. How these new field education requirements affect social work education, and field education in particular, are discussed.

Finally, future perspectives and recommendations about social work field education are presented.

台湾社会工作专业教育与实习教育的发展

首先，将讨论近年来，台湾新设立了许多社会工作系，造成社会工作系毕业生大量的增加，影响公部门与私部门的就业市场。同时，也将讨论1997年通过的社会工作师法。其次，将呈现从以前到现在的社会工作实习时数、安排及相关规定。第叁部分，自从社会工作师法通过将近15年来，新的国家社会工作师考试的报考资格即将在2013年开始实施。这些新的资格规定将会如何影响社会工作教育，尤其是社会工作实习教育。最后，将提出对未来社会工作实习教育的发展方向与建议。

台湾におけるソーシャルワーク現場教育

ソーシャルワークが台湾で初めて確立して以来、ソーシャルワークの学部や学生の数が増加してきた。これは卒業生の数の決定的な増加の結果へとつながり、官民両者における労働市場へ影響をもたらした。本章では、まず1997年ソーシャルワーク法の影響について議論している。二つ目に、従来と現在における4年間のプログラムにおけるソーシャルワーク教育に必要とされる調整と時間数について示している。三つ目に、ソーシャルワーク法が制定されて以来の15年間、ソーシャルワークの国家試験のために新たな受験資格要件が開かれており、2013年までに実施される予定である。これら新しい現場教育の要件がソーシャルワーク教育にどのように影響を与えるのかについて、そしてとりわけ現場教育について検討する。最後に、ソーシャルワーク現場教育に関する将来の視点と推奨される内容が提案されている。

台灣社會工作專業教育與實習教育的發展

타이완 內 사회 복지 현장 교육 : 과거, 현재, 미래

타이완 내에서 사회 복지가 최초로 설립된 이래로, 사회 복지 학부 (學部)와 학생들의 숫자가 현저히 증가되었다. 이러한 현상은 졸업생들의 증가를 가져왔으며, 민간 부문과 공익 부문 모두의 직업 시장에 영향을 주었다. 먼저 1997년 사회 복지사 법령의 효과가 논의된다. 둘째로, 과거와 현재의 4년제 프로그램에서, 사회 복지 현장 교육을 위한 필요시간 수와 배정이 논의된다. 셋째는, 사회 복지사 법령의 시행이후 15년이 지났으며, 새로운 국가 사회 복지사 시험 자격 요건이 생겨 났으며 2013년에 도입될 것이다. 이러한 새로운 현장 교육에 관한 요구들이, 어떻게 사회복지 교육과 특히 현장 교육에 영향을 주는지를 논의한다. 마지막으로 사회 복지 현장 교육에 관한 미래적 관점과 권고 사항들이 발표될 것이다.

台灣在1997年4月公布施行「社會工作師法」，迄至2011年已有14年。這14年來台灣社會工作專業制度有很大幅的改變與發展。「社會工作師法」實施之前，也就是1997年以前，台灣只有11所大學院校設有社會工作及相關科系(含社會福利系)。14年之後，已有26個大學院校設置社會工作或相關學系，2009年大學部的畢業生人數有1,783人；2010年核定招生人數為2,160人(台灣社會工作教育學會　2011)。從這些數字看來社會工作系的學生數還在增加中。

社會工作是一個重視實務工作的科系，因此，實習教育就成為在養成教育中非常重要的一環。在過去的10多年來，台灣培育社會工作專業人才的社會工作科系，在數量上在有很大幅度的成長，但是社會工作實習教育，可能因為所佔學分數不多的原因，並未受到學術界或實務界的關注。從有關社會工作實習教育的研究、著作或文章少之又少可以清楚得知，學術界很少做實習相關的研究，就更難寄望實務界來進行這方面的研究。

教育、考試與任用應是連結在一起的。資格或任用的考試，包括：報考資格、考試科目、考試範圍等等，都將影響教學。本文將探討在1997年通過「社會工作師法」後，對社會工作專業教

育、社會工作專業發展、社會工作者的就業，尤其是社會工作實習教育等方面的改變與影響；以及2007年「社會工作師法」修訂通過，將在2013年1月1日開始實施的新修訂版本，對社會工作實習教育的影響又是如何？也將在本文中討論。

社會工作的專業發展

雖然1997年才通過「社會工作師法」，但是台灣的社會工作專業早在1970年代之前就已有少數醫院及民間福利機構聘用社會工作人員，只是人數十分有限。1972年，台灣省政府訂定「台灣省各省轄市設置社會工作員實驗計畫」，翌年，才開始於基隆、台中、台南、高雄4省轄市試辦兩年。經過評鑑，效果良好，乃在全省普遍實施，此為社會工作員制度建立之始(許水德，2005)。當時由台灣省政府開始推動社工員實驗制度，係以「約聘僱人員」的身分任用，開始讓社工制度在縣市逐漸生根。

直至目前為止，也僅有台北市、高雄市及新北市家庭暴力及性侵害防治中心具有社會工作員的正式職缺，其餘縣（市）社會工作員仍是「約聘僱」身份。除此之外，就只有通過2008年起舉辦的公職社會工作師高考通過的人員也能夠分派到政府部門成為具公務員身分的社會工作師(公職王，2011)；公職社會工作師報考資格需具社會工作師資格，也就是通過社會工作師考試以後才能報考。但是各級政府部門的職缺仍然掌握在各級政府手中，如未釋出正式編制，社會工作員即使考上，亦無法被任用。因此，目前受聘於各級政府的社會工作員絕大多數都是「約聘僱」身份。

社會工作員是推展社會福利服務的重要關鍵，沒有充分的專業人力再好的福利政策與福利服務措施均無法落實在需要的民眾身上。近20多年來，台灣地區社會環境、人口與家庭結構急遽變遷，例如：單親、隔代教養、繼親及新移民家庭大量增加；外籍勞工、老年人口快速增加等，促使各項福利政策與法規的重新修訂，例如：兒童及少年福利法、身心障礙者權益保障法、老人福利法、就業服務法等。因應社會民眾需求的新法令也一一順利通過，例如：家庭暴力防治法、性別工作平等法等。這些社會變遷及新通過的各項法令需要更多專業的社會工作者來提供質與量兼備的各項福利服務。

但是，20餘年來，台灣公部門的社會工作人力配置並未受到政府重視。根據2002社會福利績效考核總報告(內政部，2002)，全台灣地區社會工作員820名，平均每位社會工作員需服務27,324人；2009年社會福利績效考核結果，各縣市政府編制內社工師/員有1,080人，平均每位社工員需服務13,671人；每位社會工作員平均服務人數相較於2002年確實有明顯減少，但是負擔之沈重仍遠超過其他先進國家的社工服務量。　長久以來，成立於1989年的「台灣社會工作專業人員協會」致力於倡議合理的社會工作人力配置。2010年政府通過「充實地方政府社工人力配置及進用計畫」，這項計畫預定自民國100年至105年增聘1,000多名社會工作人力，並將6成的人力以正式編制的方式晉用，不但增加地方社會工作人力，並保障社會工作人員的勞動權益，幫助降低兒童少年保護及家暴社會工作人員的流動率(台灣社會工作專業人員協會，2010)。中央將提供地方政府40%的人事費用，全力解決社會工作人力長期不足的問題。但各地方政府首長是否願意撥出60%差額的人事費用來補充轄內的社會工作人力，目前尚不得而知。這項計畫若能實現將能解決長期以來政府部門社會工作員人力缺乏的問題。

根據內政部統計資料，2005年台灣地區有3,686名專職社會工作員，其中公部門有1,207名，私部門有2,479名(內政部，2005)；2009年有6,232名專職社工員，其中1,947在公部門，4,285在私部門(內政部，2009)。從前項統計數字可以發現，自2005年起專職社會工作員增加了69.3%，公部門增加了61.3%，私部門增加72.9%。公部門與私部門都有大幅度的成長，私部門增加的幅度更大於公部門；除此之外，2009年開始有180名專職原住民社會工作員。2010年公部門專職社會工作員增加到1,590人(王順民2010)。根據台灣社會工作專業人員協會(2011)，台灣地區目前大約有七千多名社會工作員。可見，近年以來，由於台灣地區社會快速變遷，社會也出現許多引起社會大眾關注的社會案件，帶動了公部門與私部門對於社會工作專業的重視，從上面專職社會工作員數量增加的速度可以清楚得知。就公部門的社工人力，上面所提到的編制內的社會工作員與專職社會工作員數量上的差異是因為有些專職社會工作員不是編制內的員額所致。單純論人力應以專職社會工作員數為參考。

社會工作專業教育發展

台灣的社會工作教育曾經相當長的一段時間附屬在社會學之下，1980年代是社會工作系追求主體性，並自社會學系中獨立出來的黃金10年(社論，2007)。在附屬於社會學系的這個階段中，由於社會學較重理論研究與社會工作較重實務的學門，在性質上的差異常引發衝突。這種因「學理」與「應用」二分所引發的衝突，也曾是英國社會學與社會行政之間的爭議 (詹火生，2007)。

台灣社會工作教育最先獨立設系的是私立東海大學在1979年設立大學部，又在1984年與1994年分別設立碩士班與博士班。爾後，輔仁大學與東吳大學也隨之設立社會工作系。這樣的開端之後，大多數新設系所就都把社會工作與社會學分開來。在1989年中正大學設立社會福利碩士班，又在1992年設立學士班與博士班。1990年代新設系所時，社會工作就非唯一選擇，文化大學與玄奘大學選擇設立社會福利系。除了社會工作系與社會福利系之外，台灣地區尚有希望能顧及兩個專長的科系，例如：暨南大學「社會政策與社會工作學系」、高雄醫學大學「醫學社會學與社會工作學系」、中山醫學大學的「醫學社會與社會工作學系」、陽明大學「衛生福利研究所」及靜宜大學的「社會工作及兒童少年福利學系」等。

社會工作在1997年「社會工作師法」通過後，澈底與社會學分流！(詹火生， 2007)。社會學的學生，除非修過社會工作所要求的二十個學分的核心課程，否則被完全摒除在社會工作師的應考資格之外。也就是說，連報考資格都不具備。2007年「社會工作師法」修訂通過，將在2013年1月1日開始實施的新修訂版本，其內容規定就更嚴，包括：至少要有45個專業學分及至少要有400個小時的專業實習，才具備應考資格。自此，社會工作專業自主性與獨立性就更明確了。

1997年以後，系名裡具社會工作者學校就有26所；這個數字尚未包括已設立有相關科系的學校，例如：老人福祉學系、老人服務事業管理學系等。自2004年起每年台灣地區社會工作系大學畢業的學生超過1,005名(教育部高教司， 2010)，2010年6月大學畢業的有1,783名，2010年9月核定招收學生數為2160名(台灣社會工作教育學會， 2010)。可見，社會工作大學部的畢業生人數是在逐年增加中。現在每年就多出約1,800名社會工作系畢業生投入

台灣社會工作專業教育與實習教育的發展

社會職場。每年社會工作職場中並未能創造那麼多的新職缺，雖然並非所有的畢業生均投入社會工作行業(沙依仁， 2002；周怡君、鍾秉正， 2006)，但是仍可見職缺的增加遠少於每年投入職場的畢業生。由此可見，求職的競爭將越來越激烈，換句話說，有些畢業生很可能找不到社會工作專業的工作。

為加強社會工作教育，培育社會工作專業人員，社會工作教育界之三十多位社工教授們共同發起成立『中國社會工作教育學會』，於1992年正式成立。爾後，於2000年正式改名為「台灣社會工作教育學會」。「台灣社會工作教育學會」的主要任務有：一、關於社會工作教學改進事項；二、關於加強社會工作調查研究事項；三、關於增進社會工作實習事項；四、關於健全社會工作專業制度事項；五、關於社會工作刊物、書籍出版事項；六、關於社會工作訓練及研討會事項；七、關於社會工作國際交流事項；八、關於其他符合本會宗旨事項等八大項。從「台灣社會工作教育學會」任務的第三項就能得知學會十分關心社會工作實習的相關事項(台灣社會工作教育學會， 2011)。
學會有個人會員與團體會員兩種，個人會員多為在社會工作系任教的教師，而團體會員則各大學的社會工作系。從學會的任務可以很清楚知道，學會希望在社會工作教育的教學、實習、健全社會工作制度、研究、訓練及國際交流等方面長期努力。

社會工作實習教育狀況

實習是課程的一種或是學習的型態，它強調理論或知識的實務應用(Horejsi & Garthwait, 2002)。大部分的專業教育，例如：醫學、護理、法律或社會工作，都運用實習來協助學生學習如何應用知識與一般原則在特殊或真實狀況與問題上。社會工作教育目標在使學生能夠學以致用(learning for practice)(曾華源，1995)，以提供服務給需要的人，否則社會工作教育將空有理論。專業知識與判斷是建構在從在職訓練與實習所獲得的技巧與支撐這些技巧的抽象知識與理論間的連結而來(Watson, Burrows & Player, 2002)。社會工作是一門應用科學，實習教育就更顯重要。
雖然社會工作實習制度是各校各自辦理，也各有差異(胡中宜，2001；曾華源，2002)。劉可屏、王永慈(2002)在檢視各校

社會工作實習制度後認為：社會工作實習在不同學校或系別的意義與目的待釐清；社會工作實習的基本要件與標準有待明確訂立；社會工作的實習規畫應來自整體教育考量。梁鳳玲、何振宇及黃韻如(2003)從實務界的觀點認為：實習學生過多，使得實習機構無法依據學生實習興趣做分配；實習機構品質難以控制與掌握，無法提供一致的社會工作專業訓練；實習機構與學校間缺乏完善的溝通與協調；督導缺乏完整的訓練與督導知能。有關社會工作實習的研究實在不多。但是從有限的研究中可以看出，學校在實習教育上有須進一步釐清的教育目標；而在接受學生實習的機構也有須克服的技術上的困難。以下將從社會工作教師與接受社會工作學生實習的實務機構的角度分別指出社會工作實習值得探討的議題。

為了能夠配合2007年修訂通過的「社會工作師法」的規定，目前大多數的社會工作系有三段實習課程，分別在大二、大三升大四的暑假及大四上學期；每個階段分別為二學分。實習一是進行實習準備、自我探索及社會福利機構參觀；實習二在暑假，是每天至少8小時的機構實習，為期6-8週；實習三是每週至少12小時的機構實習，至少為期12週。全部實習時數不得少於400小時，各校間的實習相關規定多少會有些出入。有些學校規定三段實習都是必修；有些學校規定實習一與實習二是必修，實習三是選修；有些學校規定實習三可以用方案實習的方式進行(翁毓秀，2009)。

在1997年「社會工作師法」通過之前，各系具備的社會工作實習的相關規定，遠超過「社會工作師法」裡的規定--要至少有三個學分的社會工作實習學分才能達到報考社會工作師的資格規定。1997年「社會工作師法」規定的報考資格是：不論是相關科系畢業或是非相關科系畢業的報考者均須修習至少20個社會工作學分，並至少有3學分的社會工作實習。1997年「社會工作師法」的通過對當時社會工作系的實習規定並未產生影響(因為所有社會工作系的規定都超過標準)，倒是使沒有社會工作實習經驗者無法取得報考資格。

2007年修訂通過，並將在2013年實施的「社會工作師法」報考資格的規定，除了提高社會工作專業學分為45個學分，更一口氣把實習時數提高到至少400小時。2007年的修訂明顯提高了社會工作的專業知識與實務操作上的專業要求。

台灣社會工作專業教育與實習教育的發展

「社會工作師法」對社會工作教育及實習教育的影響

長久以來，社會工作課程就規定核心必修課程，Hudson(2000)認
為社會工作教育是尋求「一致的概念架構」來引導實務，而實務
界也努力尋求「標準化的處遇模式」，以提高社會工作者提供服
務的有效性。「社會工作師法」中規範的專業證照制度對應考資
格的限制，實際上就是要求標準化的課程，同時，也就是認為這
是專業化制度過程裡必須的。本小節將分別討論「社會工作師
法」的實施對台灣社會工作教育整體影響及社會工作實習教育的
影響。

對社會工作教育的影響

台灣地區早期的社會工作專業發展都有賴政府主導。但在解嚴
之後，專業社團組織紛紛陸續成立，專業制度的建立與發展就有
賴整個專業社群的共同努力，包括：學術界、專業人員團體、實
務界等。「社會工作師法」的通過也是在專業社群的共同努力下
通過的。好不容易通過的「社會工作師法」對社會工作教育的影
響如下：

1. 是會「考試」？還是「會做社會工作」？

雖然實務工作經驗五年以上可以減少三科(人類行為與社會環
　　境、社會研究法與國文)考試科目，但是對於每天忙於服務個
案的實務工作者而言，準備紙筆測驗的考試卻是件苦差事，而且
成果不佳。每年的考試錄取率偏低不說，錄取者卻常是大學應屆
畢業生或碩士班學生，使得實務工作界對考試制度怨聲連連，更
埋怨學校教育培養出「只會考試的機器，拙於專業技能的人」(
莫藜藜，　2007)。從專業的角度看，我們希望會考試，也要具備
專業技能，才能夠有效的服務需要協助的對象。

2. 考試領導教學?

系上考慮開設課程時，往往會思考這是社會工作師考試的考試

科目，我們最好要開設，否則學生沒辦法參加考試。因此，各系的課程結構都十分相似，這與教育部評鑑希望各系能各有特色，似乎有衝突之處。2007年修訂的社會工作師考試科目45個學分，各科若多於3學分，也只能以3學分計。換言之，同一科目名稱，若只開2學分，就不能算在社會工作師考試資格的學分裡；如果某系同一科目開設4學分，在社會工作師考試資格上也只能算3學分。

雖然系上開設課程科目名稱相同，但是教學內容可能差異很大。「台灣社會工作教育學會」希望協助各校對於「社會工作師法」規範的核心課程能夠有較一致性的基本內容。在2010-2011年間，分別邀請在學科教學上有豐富經驗的教師負責收集社會工作系各學科目前的教學狀況。分區邀集各系教師以焦點團體的方式收集教學相關資料，並將在2011年3月公開舉辦研討會進行討論。會後將把結果分送各系之作為各科任課老師參考。社會工作教育學會這樣做，也是回應學會的第一項任務--關於社會工作教學改進事項(台灣社會工作教育學會 2011)。

3. 社會工作學分班的開設

由於2013年即將開始實施2007年修訂通過的版本；也就是新的報考資格將從20學分增加到45學分，實習小時數也將提升到400小時。新版本的報考資格嚴格許多，使得許多有意成為社會工作師的人希望能趕在新法實施之前能夠報考。有些設有社會工作系的大學因此開設社會工作學分班以滿足這些人的需要。這種情況就成了因應考試的非正規學制下的專業教育。這與補習教育不同，因為學分班會授予學分證明，能夠以學分證明報考社會工作師。

對社會工作實習教育的影響

實習在社會工作教育是非常重要的一環。2007年修訂的「社會工作師法」規定的報考資格中對社會工作實習的規定從三個學分改為400小時。這樣的改變對社會工作實習教育可能的影響包括：

1. 學校安排學生實習的困難

提高實習小時數當然是希望學生能多學一點實務經驗。自1997年以來，社會工作系大幅度增加的狀況下，安排學生在機構實習成為不容易的事。因為每個學校都須幫學生安排機構實習，學校增加了、學生也增加了，但是實習機構可能沒有增加那麼快，因此，學校可能產生安排上的困難。

2. 學生的機構實習準備

大學階段的社會工作教育應是通才教育，但是一般學校的實習二或實習三的機構實習都是要學生專注在某個社會工作領域。學生如何準備機構實習，常是機構與學生的困擾。目前只有醫務社會工作(medical social work)實習明確要求學生一定要修習過「醫務社會工作」這門課才能申請，其他領域就都沒有明確要求。如此，學生在申請時不清楚機構要求甚麼基本知識與技巧，機構也常會感到送來的學生怎麼甚麼都沒準備。

3. 有關實習機構方面的困難

機構都是免費接受學生實習，機構本身需付出人力、空間、資源與時間來帶學校送來的實習生，特別是督導人力。機構是否有督導學生實習的人力與能力是學校安排學生到機構實習的重要考慮因素。雖然福利機構或組織不少，但是有能力接受學生實習的機構並不充裕，換句話說，機構可能在不得已的狀況下接受過多的實習生(梁鳳玲、何振宇及黃韻如，2003)。同時，實習機構的品質也具相當的差異，這也不是學校可以掌握的。在延長實習時間的要求下，勢必造成機構沉重的負擔。

4. 有關學校實習教學方面的困難

學校教師本身的過去實務經驗與持續的實務經驗對社會工作教學效果是很重要的(莫藜藜，2007)。學校教師在社會工作實習中擔任學校督導的角色與責任，自身的實務經驗對擔任學校督導是很重要的，也是很有幫助的。相當多的學校教師本身缺乏實務經

驗，但是礙於系上工作分配，不得不擔任學校督導的角色，造成教師無法有效指導學生，學生也失去了一個接受機構外部專業督導的機會。

對社會工作實習教育的建議

1. 建構本土化的社會工作實務理論

Lam（2004）及Lightfood 與Gibson （2005)都曾針對社會工作的學習方式及對特殊服務對象的教學提出幫助學生整合概念的方法。台灣地區也須開始針對目前的複雜社會問題與文化背景逐步開始建構適合於台灣地區的社會工作實務理論。當然這並非是件容易的事。

2. 加強學校與機構間的溝通與協調

目前學校與機構間的互動不外乎調查是否接受實習生、安置學生、寄送實習資料等行政作業上的來往。學校與機構間可以針對所有學生實習相關的事務進行溝通協調會議。協調會議的內容可能包括：實習時間、機構與學校督導的期待、機構的規定、學校的規定、先修課程、實習期間的聯絡方式、實習前的專業準備等等。
機構與機構間可能會有不同的相關規定也可藉由協調會議分別與學校進行溝通，以增進學校與機構間對學生實習的共識。學校與機構更可藉由長期的溝通，除了穩固學生實習資源外，同時，促進學術界與實務界的交流。

3. 提昇學生實習前的準備

學校須協助學生作實習前的準備應包括：了解自己的興趣與志願、對機構性質的了解、實習面試的準備、實習計畫書的撰寫及相關先修課程等。實習前協助學生做好周詳的準備，能夠讓學生順利進入實習場域，降低學生與實習機構在期待上的落差。學校在實習一的課程內容中，除了實地參觀福利機構外，上述的準備

工作內容都需要確實協助學生達成學習前準備。

4. 對實習機構的建議

實習機構可以在學生實習前協助學生了解機構性質、機構理念、機構的服務內容與服務對象及機構裡的社會工作員之工作內容。學生對機構的了解可以幫助學生正確找尋實習機構，也能夠在學生到達實習機構時，較符合機構的期待。

實習教育是整合概念、理論與實際操作的機會。機構須指派具督導能力的機構督導來督導學生。學生在實習期間才能得自於督導的帶領與教導，節省許多自己摸索的時間。一對一的督導過程是需要大量的督導人力的，但是這種「學徒制」的安排較能夠深入了解實習學生的需要。同時，督導也是一個很好的專業楷模，提供學生直接模仿的機會。

2007年修訂的「社會工作師法」延長了實習時數，讓學生有更長的實地學習的機會，也加重了實習機構的負擔。機構督導在教導實習生的過程也能夠有「教學相長」的收穫。

5. 對學校實習教育的建議

近十幾年來社會工作系大量的增加及2007年修訂的「社會工作師法」延長了實習時數，都使學校在安排學生實習上增加了難度。學校在規畫社會工作實習應考量整體社會工作教育的觀點，須建立明確的目的與基本要件(劉可屏、王永慈，2002)。同時，大學部、碩士班與博士班的實習應該各有各的實習目標與規劃，碩士班以上的實習應以培養督導人才為實習目標之一。

對於學校實習督導也須能配合教師的實務經驗與興趣，才能對學生實習有具體幫助。學校督導人力不足時，可以聘請實務經驗豐富的實務工作者充當學校督導。

結語

社會工作實習教育是以實際操作的過程來幫助學生整合社會工作概念或理論的過程；也是抽象社會工作概念藉由實際操作而達到

具體化的過程。社會工作實習教育對應用科學的社會工作而言，是非常重要的。

台灣地區社會快速變遷，單親、隔代教養、貧窮、外籍配偶、家庭暴力、偏差行為兒童少年、人口快速老化等等問題層出不窮，再再挑戰社會工作教學。社會工作實習教育是檢視學校裡的社會工作教育是否能夠滿足社會福利機構直接面對服務對象所需要的社會工作專業技巧的機會。

台灣地區的社會工作發展早期因為學校教師多在美國接受教育，因此所講授的內容具濃濃的美國專業文化色彩，可能的原因是台灣長期以來與美國的關係，當時國內對歐洲國家較為陌生，所以出國留學生多前往美國。在當時，還有留學生前往鄰近的日本留學，但確是相當稀少。爾後，許多教師自歐洲英國或德國留學返國，使得學校教師逐漸出現歐洲社會福利的思想色彩，其中留學英國的多以學習社會政策方面為主。近年來，本土栽培的博碩士漸漸在大學裡授課，使得社會工作教師的學習背景更加多元。教師們在豐富的知識來源環境裡，努力教育訓練社會工作專業人員，以面對社會快速變遷帶來的種種複雜的社會問題。實習教育就是一個檢視教學成果的絕佳機會，學校裡的教學必須是要能滿足社會的需要的。

參考書目

內政部 (2002). 社會福利績效考核總報告， sowf.moi.gov.tw/29/91年考核報告.pdf。

內政部 (2005). 社會福利績效考核總報告， sowf.moi.gov.tw/29/94年考核報告.htm

內政部 (2009). 社會福利績效考核總報告， sowf.moi.gov.tw/29/98年考核報告.htm

台灣社會工作專業人員協會 (2010). 社工人力尚未補足，同志仍須 努力！～社工專協邀您一同監督地方政府增聘社工人力進度！， www.tasw.org.tw/p1-news-detail.php?sn=530

內政部 (2007). 變遷中的社會工作專業教育，社區發展季刊 (120)1-7。

王順民 (2010). 關於社會工作專職人力擴編與納編的論述思考，國家政策

台灣社會工作專業教育與實習教育的發展

研究基金會，www.npf.org.tw/post/1/8190

公職王 (2011) 公職社工師介紹，www.public.com.tw/StudyZone/public/newpublic/socialworker/about.asp

台灣社會工作專業人員協會 (2010). 社工人力尚未補足，同志仍須

努力！~社工專協邀您一同監督地方政府增聘社工人力進度！，www.tasw.org.tw/p1-news-detail.php?sn=530。

台灣社會工作教育學會 (2011). 學會任務，cswe98.pixnet.net/blog/post/25498795。

台灣社會工作教育學會 (2010). 台灣社會工作教育學會第12期會訊。，cswe98.pixnet.net/blog/post/25498795。

沙依仁 (2002). 社會工作專業教育之現況及發展，社區發展季刊 (99)，5-23.

社論 (2007). 變遷中的社會工作專業教育，社區發展季刊 (120)，1-7.

周怡君、鍾秉正 (2006). 社會政策與社會立法，台北：洪葉文化事業有限公司。

許水德 (2005). 台灣社會福利工作之回顧，社區發展季刊（109）。

胡中宜 (2001). 從全面品質管理觀點建構社會工作實習制度，社區發展季刊 (99)，314-319.

翁毓秀 (2009). 國內相關社工系實習規劃一覽表，未出版。

教育部高教司 (2010) www.edu.tw/high/itemize.aspx?itemize_sn=587&pages=0&site_content_sn=1237。

莫藜藜 (2007). 台灣社會工作學科教育的發展與變革的需求，社區發展季刊 (120)，30 - 47。

曾華源 (2007). 建構服務品質為導向的台灣社會工作專業制度，社區發展季刊 (120)，106 - 14。

曾華源 (1995). 社會工作實習教學—原理及實務。台北：師大書苑有限公司。

詹火生 (2007). 台灣社會工作專業發展的經驗與展望，社區發展季刊

(120)，21 - 29。

賴兩陽（2007）．社工師法對專業制度的影響與爭議：1997～2007，社區發展季刊（120），67 - 84。

劉可屏、王永慈（2002）．我國社會工作實習課程的規劃與實施，社區發展季刊（99），51 - 72。

梁鳳玲、何振宇、黃韻如（2003）．入口閘道還是交流道?—實習與

社會工作教育的對話，社會工作專業教育—現況與展望學術研

討會，實踐大學，社工師公會全國聯合會共同舉辦。

Horejsi CR & Garthwait CL (2002). *The social work practicum*. Boston, MA: Allyn & Bacon.

Hudson CG (2000). At the edge of chaos: a new paradigm for social work? *Journal of Social Work Education,* 36(2): 215-30.

Lam D (2004) Problem based learning: an integration of theory and field. *Journal of Social Work Education,* 40(3): 371-90.

Lightfood E & Gibson P (2005) Universal instructional design: a new framework for accommodating students in social work courses. *Journal of Social Work Education,* 41(2): 250-69.

Watson F, Burrows H & Player C (2002). *Integrating theory and practice in social work education.* London: Jessica Kingsley Publishers.

CHAPTER THIRTEEN

A HISTORICAL CHANGE IN SOCIAL WORK EDUCATION AND THE PROBLEMS OF PRESENT PRACTICUM EDUCATION IN JAPAN

日本における社会福祉実習の展開と課題

桜美林大学大学院　教授

Mazakasu Sirasawa

白澤政和

日本におけるソーシャルワーク教育での実習の歴史的変遷と現在の実習教育の課題

日本のソーシャルワーク教育での実習の変化は、社会福祉士の養成システムの変化そのものであると言える。1988年の「社会福祉士及び介護福祉士法」の成立および2008年の「社会福祉士及び介護籠福祉士法」改正の２つの時点で、学生への実習教育での教育水準を高めるために、ソーシャルワーク実践に関する時間が増大し、実習受け入れ機関の実習指導者の資格要件を作り上げてきた。　現在の新しい制度のもとで、実習担当教員と実習指導者の両者は以前以上にソーシャルワーク教育で実践的な方法や手法を有するよう資格化された。新しい制度のもとで、実習指導者資格を有す

る者が学生の実習にあたることになったが、実習指導
者が十分に量的に整っていない状況にある。

The change in the Japanese practicum in social work education can be
understood as a change in the qualified social worker's training system
itself. There are two relevant Acts to consider, the National Qualification
for Social Workers of 1988, and the Amendment Act of 2008. These acts
expanded the required hours for the social work practicum and raised the
required qualification for practicum supervisors at the placement agencies.
These were done in order to raise the educational standard for students.
Both practicum supervisors in universities and placements were required
to have practical methods and techniques in social work education, even
before the new system. It required that a qualified supervisor be in charge
of the practicum; however there are not enough qualified people available.

日本社会工作教育的历史变迁和目前社工实习存在的问题

在日本社会工作教育和实习过程的演变意味着国家开始
将重点放在实现社工专业资格的课程上。两项法案与此
演变过程有紧密联系。第一项是1998年的专业社工资格
认可；而第二项是其2008年时的修正案。这两项政策延
长了社工实习的时间并提高了对实习机构导师各方面的
专业要求，尤其在学历上。这些改变的目的在于提升学
生教育实习的质量。即使新政策实施之前，无论是大学
实习课程的老师，还是实习机构的导师，都需要有一套
教授和指导学生的方法和技巧。学生实习需要有资质的
导师来负责，然而现实中并没有足够称职的人员来满足
这一要求。

일본에 있어서 사회 복지 교육의 역사적 변화와 현재의
실습 과목의 문제점들

사회 복지 교육에 있어서 일본의 실습 과목의 변화는, 자
격있는 사회 복지사 훈련 시스템 그자체의 변화라고 이해

될 수 있다. 이것과 관련된 두개의 법령을 고려해야 하는데, 그것은 1988년의 사회 복지사를 위한 국가 자격 법령과 2008년의 수정 법령이다. 이들 법령들은 사회 복지 실습 과목를 위한 필요 시간 수를 늘렸으며, 배치 기관들의 실습 과목 감독자들에게 요구되는 자격 요건을 높였다. 이러한 조치들은 학생들을 위한 교육적인 표준을 높이기 위한 것이었다. 대학들과 배치기관들 양쪽 모두의 실습 과목 감독자들은, 새로운 법 체계가 시행되기 이전부터도 요구되어 왔지만, 실제적인 방법들과 기술들을 가질 것이 요구되어 졌다. 새로운 법 체계는, 자격있는 감독자들이 실습 과목의 책임자가 되는것을 규정하고 있다. 하지만 이러한 자격을 갖춘 사람이 부족한 실정이다.

社会福祉実習は、ソーシャルワーカーを養成していく場合の講義科目を実践と繋げていく要となるものである。そのため、社会福祉実習をいかに質的・量的に充実させるかが、ソーシャルワーカー養成の鍵となる。

　ただ、社会福祉実習の充実に対して、個々の養成大学等が実施してきた部分や、日本社会福祉士養成校協会や日本社会福祉教育学校連盟（2003年12月の社団化に伴い日本社会福祉学校連盟に改組）が実施してきたこともそれなりに評価はできるが、大きくは専門職制度の法的改革と合わせて充実してきたといえる。その意味では、日本のソーシャルワーカー養成の推進は大学自らの改革によるよりも、国の意向で他律的に進められてきた側面が大きい。それは、日本のソーシャルワーカーは国家資格でもって人材養成されてきたことが大きく、この資格の責任を担う厚生労働省が主体になって、養成している大学や養成校協議会の意向を確認・協議しながら、展開してきたといえる。

1.　日本における社会福祉実習教育の展開

(1)社会福祉士制度創設前での実習の位置づけ

　1997年に社会福祉士の国家資格ができた際に、「社会福祉実習」は180時間、「社会福祉実習指導」は90時間とされた。また、実習施設の範囲が決められ、多くの社会福祉系の施設や

相談機関が実習施設として指定された。当初は、病院等の相談機関は実習施設外であったが、その後一般病院も実習施設として認められ、順次実習機関の拡大が図られてきた。

　この社会福祉士制度が出来る以前のソーシャルワーカーを養成する大学での実習内容や実習時間には全く基準がなく、個々の大学の意向に委ねられて実習が行われてきた。そのため多様であったが、ほとんどの大学は社会福祉士制度が出来た時点で、相当実習時間を増やす結果となった。また、これに合わせて、実習実施機関も確定することになった。

　この社会福祉士というソーシャルワーカーの国家資格ができる以前にも、大学でソーシャルワーカー養成教育は実施されており、こうした大学は自主的に日本社会福祉学校連盟を組織し、ソーシャルワーク教育を行なってきた。

　日本の社会福祉教育は、社会福祉制度や政策の研究や教育として始まった部分と、ソーシャルワーカー養成教育が混在して進められてきた。そのため、日本社会福祉学校教育連盟が毎年定期的に刊行しているニュースレターを見る限りでは、ソーシャルワーカー養成の観点からみれば、最も議論されなければならない実習のあり方の議論はほとんどなされていない。当時の日本の社会福祉教育を、国際ソーシャルワーカー連盟の副会長から、「school of social work」ではなく、「school of social work theory 」と批判された経緯もある。

　当時（財）大学基準協会が「社会福祉学教育に関する基準及びその実施方法」を示し、社会福祉系の大学はソーシャルワーカー養成に必要な科目が示されているが、その中には実習も位置付けられていた。ただ。これについては、「実習の効果を高めるためには、実習指導教職員の充実、実習は遺族施設の条件の整備が前提になるが、それぞれの大学の置かれた条件をもとで最大限の努力をすべきである」とし、個々の大学の自主努力に委ねられていた。

　社会福祉士の資格制度についての議論が始まった時期から、実習に対する関心が高まってきたと言える。社会福祉士制度ができるに先だって日本社会福祉学校連盟は1987年に全国社会福祉協議会•社会福祉実習のあり方に関する研究会と合同で『社会福祉士養成のための「社会福祉施設実習」のあり方に

ついて』の提言を行っている。ここでは、実習についてのガイドラインが示され、①大学と実習施設との契約、②実習指導教員と実習指導者の確保と要件、③実習前教育の実施と配属学生の選抜方法、④実習時間数、⑤実習の実施計画の作成と実習後の評価の実施、⑥実習教育実施上の必要経費、についてであった。これらのことが、社会福祉士及び介護福祉士法の成立時の議論となり、社会福祉士制度ができた時点の検討内容となった。

(2)社会福祉士制度創設時の実習の位置づけと課題

1987年に社会福祉士および介護福祉士法により社会福祉士制度ができた際には、「社会福祉実習」は180時間が位置付けられ、「社会福祉実習指導」は90時間と定められた。また、120時間の「社会福祉演習」が位置づけられ、座学による諸科目と実習を結びつける役割を果たすことになった。実習施設については、子ども、障害者、高齢者の社会福祉施設や相談機関が指定された。施設や機関の実習指導者は、「社会福祉士の資格取得後、3年以上相談援助業務に従事した経験のある者」とされた。
　大学側の実習担当教員については、以下の5つの要件のどれかを満たす者とされた。

　①教授、助教授、講師
　②専修学校の専門課程の専任教員として、当該科目を3年以上担当した経験のある者
　③大学院において、当該科目に関する研究領域を専攻した者で修士又は博士の学位を有する者
　④社会福祉士資格取得後、5年以上ソーシャルワーク業務に従事した経験のある者

　以上のような基準が国から示され、一定の社会福祉実習の基準が作成されたことは大きな成果であり、画期的なことであったといえる。しかしながら、これらすべての基準は、大学以外の専門学校には厳格に適応されたが、大学においては、監査の

基準ではなく、参考基準に留まることになり、どこまでこうした基準を取り入れるかは、個々の大学に委ねられることになった。その意味では、個々の大学の自主努力で実習教育がなされてきた。ほとんどの大学はこのような基準で実施してきたが、一部の大学については、基準を超える水準で実習を行っている場合もあれば、基準を満たさない大学もみられた。

　このことは、全ての大学において一定水準の社会福祉実習を担保できていなかっただけでなく、社会福祉実習は国家試験の試験科目にはなく、全体として実践能力のある人材養成にはなれていないという反省があった。その意味では、社会福祉実習については、さらなる改善が求められていた。

2. 日本における社会福祉実習の現状と課題

(1) 2007年の「社会福祉士及び介護福祉士法」改正による社会福祉士像の特徴

　1987年に社会福祉士制度ができ約20年を経過したが、さらに実践能力をもった人材養成が急務であるとの認識から、2007年の「社会福祉士および介護福祉士法」改正で社会福祉士教育全体の見直しが行われた。社会福祉士の実践能力を高めることが大きな目的であったことから、社会福祉実習教育の内容の改革が大きかった。

　2007年法改正の前提として、社会福祉士は、以下のような3つの役割を担える人材の養成をすることとなった。

　①福祉ニーズを抱えた者からの相談に応じ、必要に応じてサービス利用を支援するなど、その解決を自ら支援する役割
　②利用者がその有する能力に応じて、尊厳を持った自立生活を営むことができるよう、関係する様々な専門職や事業者、ボランティア等との連携を図り、自ら解決することのできないニーズについては当該担当者への橋渡しを行い、総合的かつ包括的に援助していく役割
　③地域の福祉ニーズの把握や社会資源の調整・開発、ネットワークの形成を図るなど、地域福祉の増進に働きかける役割
　そのために、社会福祉士の教育に求められることとして、

以下の6つの知識や技術を教授していくこととなった。

　①相談への対応や、総合的かつ包括的にサービスを提供することの必要性、その在り方などに係る専門的知識
　②虐待防止、就労支援、権利擁護等の関連サービスに関わる基礎的知識
　③利用者の自立支援の観点から地域において適切なサービスの選択を支援する技術
　④サービス提供者間のネットワークの形成を図る技術
　⑤地域の福祉ニーズを把握し、不足するサービスの創出を働きかける技術
　⑥専門職としての高い自覚と倫理の確立や利用者本位の立場に立った活動の実践

　そのために、新たなカリキュラムでの総時間数を1,050時間から1,200時間に増やし、「就労支援サービス」、「成年後見制度」、「更生保護制度」など、社会福祉士の活動分野の拡大にも配慮した科目が新設された。これら新しいカリキュラムについては、表1の通りである。

(2)社会福祉実習のシラバス
　新しいカリキュラムでは、従来通り「社会福祉実習」は180時間、「社会福祉実習指導」は90時間となった。これについては、社会福祉士養成校協会は、各大学の同意を得て、「社会福祉実習」については360時間とする意見をまとめたが、現状では困難であると判断され、量的な充実を図ることはできなかったが、質的な充実が図られることになった。
　まずは、「社会福祉実習」や「社会福祉実習指導」についてシラバスが定められ、これに基づき、実習や実習指導が行われることになった。これにより、一定水準の社会福祉実習が担保できることになる。
　「社会福祉実習」は、①ソーシャルワークに関する知識や技術について具体的・実際的に理解し実践的な技術等を体得すること、②社会福祉士として求められる資質、技能、倫理、自己に求められる課題を把握し、総合的に対応できる能力を習得

すること、③関連分野の専門職との連携のあり方及びその具体的内容を実践的に理解すること、を目的にしている。実習学生が実習指導者から指導を受ける内容として、具体的に以下の8点が示されている。

①利用者やその関係者、施設・事業者・機関・団体等の職員、地域住民やボランティア等との基本的なコミュニケーションや人との付き合い方などの円滑な人間関係の形成

②利用者理解とニーズの把握、支援計画の作成

③利用者やその関係者（家族親族・友人等）との援助関係の形成

④利用者やその関係者（家族・親族・友人等）への権利擁護や支援（エンパワメントを含む）の実施とその評価

⑤多職種連携をはじめとするチームアプローチに基づく支援の実際

⑥社会福祉士としての職業倫理、施設・事業者・機関・団体等の職員の就業などに関する規定への理解と、組織の一員としての役割や責任についての理解

⑦施設・事業者・機関・団体等の経営やサービスの管理運営の実際

⑧実習施設が地域社会の中の施設・事業者・機関・団体等であることの理解と、具体的な地域社会への働きかけとしてのアウトリーチ、ネットワーキング、社会資源の活用・調整・開発に関する理解

以上の内容を、実習を介して学習することで、ソーシャルワークの機能を具体的に体得することになる。これらの学習を実習指導担当教員は巡回指導等を通して、学生及び実習指導者との連絡調整を密に行い、学生の実習状況について把握し、実習中の個別指導を十分に行うことになる。

「社会福祉実習指導」は、①学生が実習の意義について理解すること、②個別指導や集団指導を通して、ソーシャルワークに関する知識と技術について具体的かつ実際的に理解し、実践的な技術を体得すること、③社会福祉士として求められる資質、技能、倫理、自己に求められる課題を把握し、総合的に対

応できる能力を習得すること、④具体的な体験や援助活動を、専門的援助技術として概念化・理論化し、体系立てていくことができる能力を涵養すること、を目的にしている。そのために、相談援助実習を効果的にすすめるため、実習生用の「実習指導マニュアル」や「実習記録ノート」を作成し、実習指導に活用することとされている。また、実習後には実習内容の達成度を評価し、必要な個別指導を行うことになるが、その際に評価基準を明確にし、評価に際しては実習先の実習指導担当者の評定はもとより、実習生本人の自己評価についても考慮し、実習指導教員が行うことになっている。

　この「実習指導」では、以下の10の内容を指導することになる。①実習の意義、②実際に実習を行う実習分野（利用者理解含む）と施設・事業者・機関・団体・地域社会等に関する基本的な理解、③実習先で必要とされる相談援助に係る知識と技術に関する理解、④現場体験学習及び見学実習（実際の介護サービスの理解や各種サービスの利用体験等を含む）、⑤実習における個人のプライバシーの保護と守秘義務等の理解（個人情報保護法の理解を含む）、⑥「実習記録ノート」への記録内容及び記録方法に関する理解⑦実習生、実習担当専任教員、実習先の実習指導者との三者協議を踏まえた実習計画の作成、⑧巡回指導、⑨実習記録や実習体験を踏まえた課題の整理と実習総括レポートの作成、⑩実習の評価全体総括会、である。

　以上、「社会福祉実習」や「社会福祉実習指導」の厚生労働省から示されたシラバスを示してきたが、これらの内容が実習教育の中に含められることになり、ソーシャルワークの具体的な学習が可能となった。

(3) 社会福祉実習教育の変化

社会福祉士を養成する大学は180時間が実習時間の目安であり、一部の大学では180時間以上の実習を行なっている場合もあったが、他方180時間に満たない実習をしている大学も存在していたことも事実である。さらには、実習の内容も施設ではソーシャルワーク実習というよりは介護実習の要素が濃い場合も多くみられた。また、実習機関の実習指導者や実習担当教員

289

にも大きな差がみられ、実習内容に大きな質の差が見られた。

　こうした中で、2007年の「社会福祉士及び介護福祉士法」改正により、教育カリキュラム全体の見直しを踏まえ、実践力の高い社会福祉士を養成する観点から、実習に関する教育内容についても充実が図られることになった。

　社会福祉実習については、大学により教育内容にばらつきが大きいとの指摘を踏まえて、大学にも実習の教育内容や時間数等について、一定の基準が課されることになり、厚生労働省からの監査を受けることになった。同時に、その基準は、今回の法改正で、実践能力を高める観点から強化され、充実したものとなった。

　実習担当教員の要件については、以下の3つの内の1つが満たされる者となった。

　①実習を5年以上担当した経験のある教員
　②社会福祉士資格取得後、5年以上相談援助業務に従事した経験のある者
　③①や②でない場合には、厚生労働大臣が定める基準を満たす講習会の課程を修了した者

　これは、従来の実習担当教員では、大学の自主性のより教員を配置することが出来たが、教員は、5年以上の実務経験を有する社会福祉士や5年の実習教歴を有する者が原則となった。これら以外の者については、実習担当教員講習会の受講が義務付けられ、実習指導ができる資質が求められることになった。同時に、実習担当教員は、従来から、1人の教員が実習指導できる人数は20人以下であったが、この教員の内で1人以上は専任の教員であることが条件として追加された。

　実習指導者については、従来からの3年以上の実務経験を有する社会福祉士であることの条件に加えて、実習指導者研修を受講することが義務化された。そして、実習施設について5名まで実習生を受け入れることであったが、1人の実習指導者に5名までの実習指導ができることになった。

　以上の社会福祉実習教育について、従来は一定の基準に過ぎなかったが、2007年の改正で、上記の要件を大学についても

満たすことが義務化された。但し、これらの基準は2012年4月までに準備するよう経過措置がとられている。そのため、この実習教育改革の成果は、現状では全体としては十分つかめない状況にある。

(4)新カリキュラムによる実習のパイロットスタディの結果

新たな社会福祉実習は2012年4月から本格的に始まるが、それに先立ちいくつかの大学では、試行的に新たな実習を試みている。ここで紹介するのは、日本福祉大学が編入生を対象に、新カリキュラムに基づく実習をパイロットスタディとして実施した結果を示しておく。

　この試行事業は、学生41人を対象に、それぞれ同一の実習施設で4週間の実習を実施し、その間に実習担当教員が巡回指導を2回実施し、別個に帰校日を2日設け、実施したものである。具体的な実習目標を「対人ソーシャルワークの現場とそのプロセスを実践的に学ぶ」こととし実施した。

3.　実習の過程としては、まずは実習事前教育を実施し、実習指導者・実習担当教員・実習学生の間で調整を行い、実習施設側の実習プログラムと実習学生の実習計画書のすり合わせを行っている。実習中では、1週目は実習施設を理解する現場実習、2週目は様々な職種の仕事を理解する職種実習、3週目以降はソーシャルワーク実習と区分されている。実習中には、個別支援計画（短期目標・長期目標）の作成と実施、個々の段階でのふりかえりと自己評価表の活用、帰校日での実習担当教員の全体でのグループスーパービジョンと個人スーパービジョン実施が行われている。実習終了後には、実習学生・実習指導者・実習担当教員の間で合同検討会を実施し、支援計画の振り返りと表2の表をもとに効果測定を実施し、最終的には実習担当教員が評価を行っている。

　その結果、新カリキュラムでの実習の評価として、以下の3点が指摘された。

　ソーシャルワーク実習の内容が明確になった。ソーシャルワークの個別支援計画の作成は、ミクロの視点をおさえなが

ら、本人のストレングスや家族や地域・社会のメゾ・マクロの視点を実習生が体得することができた。

　個別支援計画の短期目標と長期目標の作成で、社会資源の開発といった視点が醸成された。

　実習・演習・講義がつながり、ミクロ・メゾ・マクロのソーシャルワークの視点がもてるようになった。

日本の社会福祉実習の課題

日本における社会福祉実習の展開や現状について示してきたが、実践能力を高めるべく実習の改革については、新カリキュラムにより本格的に実施される段階にある。これについての評価は今後に待たなければならないが、一定の成果が得られものと予想できる。

　ただ、この実習についても、実習指導者には研修会への参加が義務づけられており、2012年から本格実施する際に、実習施設が十分に確保できるかの不安がある。そのため、実習指導者研修会が各地域で活発に実施されている状況にある。

　一方、2007年の社会福祉実習改革は実習の質を高めるものであったが、実習時間を中心にした量的な改革が残されている。既に、実習時間を拡大することについて大学等の合意を得ており、個々の大学が自主的に実習時間を拡大していき、最終的には法的な整備を図っていくことが求められている。

　（註）本論文では、社会福祉士制度を中心にして実習制度について述べてきた。日本では、精神保健を対象とする精神保健福祉士という国家資格が1997年に作られた。この資格についても、社会福祉士制度とほぼ同じような実習制度の変化を辿ってきている。

表1　　　　新カリキュラムの科目
【人・社会・生活と福祉の理解に関する知識と方法】計180時間

（1）人体の構造と機能及び疾病	30
（2）心理学理論と心理的支援	30
（3）社会理論と社会システム	30
（4）現代社会と福祉	60
（5）社会調査の基礎	30

【総合的かつ包括的な相談援助の理念と方法に関する知識と技術】計180時間

（1）相談援助の基盤と専門職	60
（2）相談援助の理論と方法	120

【地域福祉の基盤整備と開発に関する知識と技術】計120時間

（1）地域福祉の理論と方法	60
（2）福祉行財政と福祉計画	30
（3）福祉サービスの組織と経営	30

【サービスに関する知識】計300時間

（1）社会保障	60
（2）高齢者に対する支援と介護保険制度	60
（3）障害者に対する支援と障害者自立支援制度	30

（4）児童や家庭に対する支援と児童・家庭福祉制度	30
（5）低所得者に対する支援と生活保護制度	30
（6）保健医療サービス	30
（7）就労支援サービス	15
（8）権利擁護と成年後見制度	30
（9）更生保護制度	15

【実習・演習】計420時間

（1）相談援助演習	150
（2）相談援助実習指導	90
（3）相談援助実習	180

５．評価表

日本福祉大学

◆学生はこの欄のみあらかじめ記入しておくこと	学 籍 番 号	実習生氏名	実習担当教員名

　ご指導いただいた実習生について、以下の評価尺度に基づき、ご回答ください。なお、本表は、出勤簿と一緒に実習終了後２週間以内に、社会福祉実習教育研究センター宛にご送付ください。

評価尺度	4	3	2	1	E	記入例
	十分できた	ある程度できた	あまりできなかった	できなかった	経験していない	4・③・2・1・E

評 価 項 目	評価尺度
１．実習施設の運営理念と事業内容を理解している	4・3・2・1・E
２．実習施設に所属するさまざまな職種の役割、業務内容について理解している	4・3・2・1・E
３．ソーシャルワークを担う職種の役割、業務内容について理解している	4・3・2・1・E
４．専門職の倫理・価値を実践的に理解する	4・3・2・1・E
５．ソーシャルワークで用いる援助技術を理解する	
1）利用者との援助関係の築き方を理解する	4・3・2・1・E
2）他職種との連携、チームワークを理解する	4・3・2・1・E
3）利用者主体の支援方法と利用者の権利擁護の仕組みを理解する	4・3・2・1・E
６．個別支援計画を作成する	
1）アセスメントに必要な情報を理解する	4・3・2・1・E
2）アセスメントの方法を理解する	4・3・2・1・E
3）支援に活用可能な社会制度・施策や地域の社会資源について理解する	4・3・2・1・E
4）個別支援計画の作成方法を理解する	4・3・2・1・E
5）適切な個別支援計画を立案する	4・3・2・1・E
6）立案した計画の根拠を説明する	4・3・2・1・E
７．実習施設が地域社会でどのような機能や役割を果たしているか理解する	4・3・2・1・E
８．総合評価	4・3・2・1

ソーシャルワーカーとしての適性を含めて、本実習生についての総評を具体的にお書きください。

実　習　期　間		出席日数	欠席日数	遅刻日数	早退日数
年　　月　　日〜　　年　　月　　日					

実習指導者名		施設種別	
実習施設名			

所　在　地	〒　　　　　　　　　　　　　TEL.

代　表　者職名・氏名	公印

Supervision
From frameworks
to practice

Chapter Fourteen

Ways of thinking about field education and supervision: building a critical perspective

Carolyn Noble

This chapter will outline how a critical standpoint informed by a social justice and human rights perspective can be embedded into the field education curricula, with particular relevance to the supervision process. The insights gained from a critical standpoint will explore how knowledge is produced and passed on, privileging some cultural groups and disadvantaging others and can then inform a critical pedagogy aimed to challenge and then address social disadvantage and inform social change strategies. The implications of addressing difference and including multiple voices in the field education curricula is, it is argued, applicable for use in social work programs seeking a cultural relevance in the way their field program is developed and implemented.

思考实习教育和督导的一些方法 – 建立一种批判性的观点

本章将概述一种批判性的观点如何能够被嵌入到实习教育的教学安排中。这种观点源于社会公正和人权并与督导过程有着特殊的关联。此观点会使一些文化群体受益但会相应地给其它团体带来负面影响。它将探索知识是如何产生及传授，进而产生一种以挑战和强

调社会不公正行为为目的的批判性教学。这种教学同时对社会变革方针具有指导性作用。尽管存在着争议，这种在实习教育课程中寻求文化意义上的差异并涵盖多方呼声的做法可以应用于社会工作教学项目中，以寻求一种实习教学计划赖以实施和发展的文化上的相关性。

現場教育とスーパービジョンについての考え方

本章は、社会正義や人権の観点から啓発される批判的視点がどのように現場教育のカリキュラムの中に取り込まれうるのかについて、とりわけスーパービジョンのプロセスとの関連において述べる。批判的視点から得られたこの洞察は、いかに知識が生み出され、伝達され、ある幾つかの文化グループに特権を与え、他の文化に不利益を与え、そしてそのことで困難に立ち向かうことを目的とした批判的教育を啓発し、そうすることによって社会の不利益を呼びかけ、社会変革戦略を啓発するのかについて探求する。現場教育のカリキュラムにおいて差異を呼びかけることの影響や複数の声を取り入れることは、議論されており、現場プログラムが発展して要件を満たすという方法に基づいて文化的な関連づけを探求するソーシャルワークのプログラム内においての利用に適している。

현장 실습 교육 및 감독에 관한 사고 방식 - 비평적인 안목을 기름

이장에서는, 사회 정의와 인권적 관점에 의해 형성된 비평적인 입장이, 특히 감독 과정에 적합성을 둔 현장 교육 과정에 어떻게 접목될 수 있는가에 관한 윤곽을 말 할 것이다. 비평적인 입장에서 얻어진 이 통찰력은, 어떻게 지식이, 어떤 문화 그룹에게는 혜택을 주고, 또 다른 이들에게는 불리함을 주면서 만들어지고 전해지는지, 그리고 이

통찰력은, 도전을 위한 비평적인 교수법을 제공해주며, 사회적인 이점(利點)을 확인하게 할 것이며, 또한 사회 변화 전략에 관한 정보를 제공 할 것이다. 차이가 있음을 인정하는것과, 현장 교육 과정에 있어서의 다양한 목소리 를 포함하는것의 의미는, 논쟁의 여지가 있지만, 현장 프 로그램의 개발과 실행에 있어서, 문화적인 적합성을 중시 하는 사회 복지 프로그램에 적용 가능하다.

Field education's *raison d'être* is the integration of theory with prac-tice and this process needs curricula that constructs and then directs its educational and professional goals. It also needs to be cognisant of the more ambitious goal to educate social work students towards an analysis of oppressive power practices directed against certain peoples and socio-ethnic-religious groupings in the society as well as explore strategies to help with their liberation. Critical theory can provide the construct while a critical pedagogy grounded on an educational vision of social justice and equality of rights can provide the direction (Kincheloe 2008). So what is critical theory and how does it inform a critical pedagogy? The next section begins to address these questions.

WHAT IS CRITICAL THEORY?

Focused on understanding and exposing the profound impact of neo-colonial and neo-capitalist structures in shaping knowledge, critical theory stands in direct opposition to the new liberalism of capitalist pro-duction and its global, national and local enterprises (Kincheloe 2008). In adapting the ideas and constructs from the Frankfurt School, Marxist and neo-Marxist ideas, theories of democracy, feminist tradition, post-colonial and critical multiculturalism, critical theorists have debated, analysed, reconceptualised and extended its efficacy and relevance for many years now (Giroux & Pollock 2010; Apple 2009; Kincheloe 2008; McLaren & Kincheloe 2007). Until recently attempts at its application have focused on education and schooling (Apple 2009; **Brookfield 2005;** Giroux 2005). Now social work has joined this enterprise and begun to adapt many of these ideas for *its* theory and practice (Mullaly 2010; Dominelli 2009; Allan et al. 2009; Webb 2006; Noble 2004).

As a metanarrative critical thinking takes as its starting point that assumptions about reason, order, predictability and social nature are just that – assumptions. These assumptions and their associated behaviours, attitudes, biases and prejudices need to be critically interrogated with a variety of lenses such as gender, age, ethnicity, ability, sexuality and class for a clearer understanding of their impact and consequences (Hooks 2010; Mullaly 2010; Kincheloe 2008; Fraser 2008). This critique is essential as these assumptions carry a huge ideological impact and influence in the sociopolitical arenas as well as shaping behaviours, attitudes, biases and prejudges of individuals and communities. Who is privileged from these sociopolitical and cultural relations is also vitally important to explore (Mullaly 2010; Kincheloe 2008; Fraser 2008, 1997). This critique is not confined to Western thought but is applicable to all cultures where hegemony based cultural practices, ethnic-religious beliefs or patriarchal and colonial relations influence how individuals and communities act, think and conform – to what seems like the 'natural order' (Zajda 2010a; Hooks 2010; McLaren & Kincheloe 2007).

The 'natural order' from whatever sociopolitical and cultural standpoint you might be located, is argued to be constructed – constructed and then protected by the dominant gender-colonial-ethnico-religious-political groupings who, over time set the structure, create and sustain the symbols of interaction and ways of being and acting in the society that favour its own interests, thus determining who gets the privileges and who is excluded from power and influence in public and private life (Mullaly 2010; Fraser 2008, 1997; McLaren & Kincheloe 2007). In Western societies (such as Australia and Aotearoa New Zealand), for example, not only were different groups of citizens (such as women, working class people, people from Asia, the Pacific, differently able people) absent from the dominant discourse, they were found to have been directly or indirectly oppressed, discriminated and excluded from the politics of power and influence and, consequentially any meaningful participation in society and a satisfactory quality of life (Allan et al. 2009; Cheyne et al. 2005). This active exclusion results in inequality and injustices along gender, class, age, sexual orientation, cultural, geographic and language lines. Other countries are identifying the same exclusionary tactics and results (Dominelli 2010; Lyons et al. 2006). The global influence of social work is seen to be active in promoting open conversations about the impact of capitalist, colonial, ethnic, social and political oppression and its consequences in countries where programs are developing (Dominelli 2010).

In exposing this oppression critical theorists posited that if individuals and groups know how and by whom they are oppressed then they are free to act in their own interest and towards their own and others' emancipation (Freire 1985; Giroux & Pollock 2010; Hooks 2010). It is argued that individuals are not free if they do not question how knowledge is produced and by whom, and know how this influences how they act as they do and for what purpose and for whose gain. That is, an unexamined life is not to exercise control over your own destiny (Freire 1985). A critical thinker asks questions such as who, what, when and why of the origins, structures, and effects of social beliefs and how these are maintained in the system. This quest is carried out with a passionate drive for clarity, accuracy, conscious reflection and fair mindedness (Freire 1985; Kincheloe 2008).

Critical theorists highlight the centrality of people's agency, i.e. their capacity to be actively involved in the process of social change. Focusing on both individual and human agency social change is viewed as an intentional, identifiable and attainable process and an important part of praxis aimed towards a particular outcome. Linking personal experiences with awareness of domination encourages those affected by oppressive ideologies and social symbols and practices to take action, to resist and eventually transform social conditions toward more socially just outcomes (Fraser 2008; Friere 1985; Mullaly 2010; Webb 2006). In essence, knowledge is power. Critical theory holds the possibility that repressed groups, such as women, indigenous peoples, migrants, asylum seekers, the old and the young and sexually different, will, through challenge, struggle and emancipation (either individually and or collectively), attain greater control over their lives and their humanity.

Critical theory, then involves the notions of critique, resistance, struggle and emancipation set within a desire to expose repressive power relations and the many ways the dominant group construct particular concepts as 'facts', 'reality' and/or 'common sense' to justify their domination and exclusion (Hooks 2010; McLaren & Kincheloe 2007). When applied to educational practices its primary aim is to demystify canonical knowledge, create pedagogical opportunities for critical reflection and empowering moments, and to explore and expose the ways in which relations of power and domination oppress people, and explore and describe its impact on their lives (Apple 2009; Brookfield 2005; Hooks 2010; McLaren & Kincheloe 2007). Creating a set of conditions from which a critically informed praxis might emerge takes us into deep waters with the provocations it elicits.

Some results of this deconstruction are emerging with improved benefits for some groups of people. Women, gay and lesbian people, and some culturally and linguistically diverse communities have, to a greater or lesser extent, benefited from this critique. As a result, many have been able to find a voice in the body politic. For example feminists have constructed a discourse about how male privilege, supported by male violence and misogynistic policies and practices discriminates against and oppresses women and non-privileged men and continually acts against their interests (Dominelli 2009; Mullaly 2010). This privilege was shown to be supported by political, social, commercial, military, cultural, spiritual, and legislative institutions, contemporarily and historically. This feminist critique was able, with targeted social, cultural and political action, to claim a space for women's vision to take shape in the dominant discourse, opening up many different representations of being a woman. Likewise, Indigenous peoples identified previously defined places of marginalisation as sources of resistance and hope. In retrieving their histories, sense of community, stories relating to land and dreamtime, as well as their languages and social practices indigenous peoples have remade themselves against the colonising practices of the 'West'; the 'Anglo' and the 'Christian male' (Battiste 1998; Hanohano 1999; Harrison 2011).

Grounded in notions of social justice and equality of rights, critical theory's potential for use depends on a shared notion of social justice and human rights, to inform the philosophical basis of the new sociopolitical and cultural context.

Social justice

Social justice is both an analytical and practice-based framework and one that stands out as a singularly important perspective, especially in social work where social justice concerns are seen as central to its emancipatory mission (Allan et al. 2009; Dominelli 2009; Mullaly 2010; Webb 2006). Linked with ethical positions of non-judgementality, respect for differences, empathy and client respect, social justice can be seen as a moral or philosophical activity, that is, giving individuals or groups their 'due' within society (Allan et al. 2009; Ferguson et al. 2005; Webb 2006). While it can be claimed by any political persuasion, those with a redistributive agenda (Rawls 1971) are mostly associated with its use. The debate as to whether it is possible to construct a reasoned set of criteria against which to determine, objectively and universally, just what is 'socially just', or what is a person's rightful 'due' must address the issue of whether social justice is merely determined by power, or the lack of it, or by changing the broader political, economic and cultural influences (Mullaly 2010; Ferguson et al. 2005) A search for definitions might shed some light here.

While there are many starting points a beginning position comes from Mick Dodson, former Aboriginal & Torres Strait Islander Commission's (ATSIC) commissioner who stated:

> Social Justice is what faces you in the morning. It is awakening in a house with adequate water supply, cooking facilities and sanitation. It is the ability to nourish your children and send them to school where their education not only equips them for employment but reinforces their knowledge and understanding of their cultural inheritance. It is the prospect of genuine employment and good health: a life of choices and opportunity free from discrimination (ATSIC 1993).

This egalitarian view argues that a just society cares for all its citizens equally – all citizens have access to the same rights and opportunities. The prevailing social structures are pressured to promote and enact social policies that enable access to basic rights, resources and services for all citizens regardless of superficial differences such as economic disparity, class, gender, race, ethnicity, citizenship, religion, age, sexual orientation, disability, or health (Mullaly 2010; Zajda 2010a). This includes the eradication of poverty and illiteracy, the establishment of sound environmental policy and equality of opportunity for healthy personal and social development. It implies social justice is definable, desirable and achievable and that an individually based philosophy of social justice will enhance the life chances of everyone, irrespective of group membership or social positioning (Ferguson et al. 2005; Fraser 2008). Also referred to as distributive justice (Rawls 1971, in Mullaly) this concept assumes a rational and humanistic approach to the delivery of economic goods and services and where a social contract about the legitimacy of redistribution is adopted and enacted by the state. Associated with challenging poverty, agitation for social justice can take an individual, group and community-based or structural approach.

Zajda (2010a) and Allan et al. (2009) also argue that the concept of social justice should extend beyond the notion of the oppressed individual to offering a vision of a heterogeneous public that acknowledges and affirms group differences and fosters the inclusion and participation of all groups in public life irrespective of their class, gender, ethnicity, age and sexual preference. Acknowledging that there are multiple sites of oppression associated with these social divisions that create multiple forms of disadvantage, Mullaly (2010) argues that an analysis of social justice should move from the individual focus to a structural analysis of the politics of power. In attending to a more equitable distribution of goods, services and life opportunities without attending to the social practices that created the inequality is, it is argued, misdirected and probably futile (Mullaly).

In essence social justice should not only include expanding access to goods and services, but to actively promote equality by increasing participation in government decision-making and the extension of equal legal and industrial and political rights for those excluded by barriers of access. The challenge is to overturn the power politics that created this injustice. Redistribution of social resources, including wealth and power by social policies should be associated with a socially just society, a society which treats individuals as the same because of their common humanity. Only a theory that has oppression as its central concern can achieve this outcome (Mullaly 2010). However, in the end it is the individual who wears the brunt of discrimination and the success of a just society depends on whether individuals, regardless of their social positioning are benefited or violated in terms of their needs and rights.

Questions

1. How should social justice be defined?
2. Is exploring social justice issues important in the education of social work students, why?
3. Does social justice need to be addressed in the micro and macro, simultaneously?
4. What is the place of social activism in social work?
5. How might it be achieved?
6. How should concerns about social justice be prioritised in teaching social work students?
7. Does the pursuit of social justice in social work alter or limit its scope of its activities?
8. What challenges emerge?
9. How might these challenges be addressed? And to what end?

HUMAN RIGHTS

Increasingly social justice is being coupled with human rights discourse to provide a unifying framework for analysis and action. Although notions of human rights might be implicit in concepts of social justice, implicitness is not enough. Ife (2010) argues, rather than treating notions of human rights as self-evident and non-problematic, as if the concept of human rights naturally exists outside the politics of agency and social structures and human and social arrangements, we must understand them as discursively negotiated and constructed. The articulation of human rights as discursively constructed i.e. as not static, unchangeable or existing 'naturally' as part of a shared humanity but articulated as a result of historical, cultural, social, political, economic and intellectual processes of dialogue, discussion and exchange, means that a fixed definition is difficult.

However there is some agreement about what might constitute basic human rights that belong to everyone regardless of their national origin, 'race' or ethnicity, culture, age, gender or class. Mostly individually based, these human rights include right to vote, right to free and unfettered assembly, right to speech, to dissent, right to a fair trial and equality before the law, right to citizenship, privacy, self-expression, safety, right to civic participation and freedom from discrimination based on age, gender, race, religious affiliations as well as freedom from harassment, torture, and coercion (Casey 2010; Friedman 2010; Ife 2010). Seen as basic civil and political rights there is a general consensus that these rights must be protected to ensure a fully functioning democratic society (Friedman 2010; Ramcharan 2010). More contested and complicated is the notion of economic, social and cultural rights of peoples, such as the aged, children, people with disabilities, single parents, women, people suffering from physical and mental health problems as well as those without housing, adequate education, employment and experiencing dislocation as a result of global, national or regional restructuring. Ife refers to these set of rights as second generation rights, the first being the basic rights listed earlier.

Ife (2010) then adds a third generation of rights – those that are concerned with collective rights such as right to economic development, land, cultural and environmental rights, and right to belong to a stable, cohesive society, with access to clear air, uncontaminated water and food and the right to reach human potential, however that may be defined. A human rights discourse that unites peoples in their humanity provides a basis for resisting oppressive practices stemming from structural inequalities and power imbalances. By identifying what divides people in their access to equality and opportunity leaves unsaid what unites them as well.

Human rights theorists (Carey 2010; Friedman 2010; Ife 2010; Ramcharan 2008) want to bring together issues of poverty, gender, exclusion, discrimination, structural oppression, displacement and disadvantage as issues of concern for all humans, not only those experiencing their effects. Condemning oppression, discrimination or abuse is a human rights issue and should be discussed as such (Ife 2010: Ramcharan 2008; Ferguson et al. 2005).

Questions

---

1. Is a human rights discourse important and/or necessary in the education of social worker?

2. Why are some people denied human rights that others take for granted?

3. How does a rights discourse accommodate difference?

4. How can a human rights perspective inform a critical stance in the education of social work students?

WHAT ARE CRITICAL PEDAGOGIES?

Critical pedagogies take their roots from Freire's (1985) 'pedagogy of the oppressed'. Many silenced voices have emerged since his thesis of focusing on the illiterate poor in South America and critical theorists have developed many applications and departures of analysis (**Brookfield 2005; Kincheloe 2008**). Criticising the hegemony of Western pedagogies as oppressing the political struggle for liberation, Freire's work has been extended to include a feminist, anti-racist and postcolonial discourse (**Brookfield 2005**; Hooks 2010, McLaren & Kincheloe 2007). However, there are several enduring concepts that remain pertinent, in particular the notions of freeing up spaces for the silenced voices to emerge and to educate for a critical consciousness (McLaren & Kincheloe 2007). Central to this process is a critical reflection on how people learn, the contexts in which knowledge is imparted and for what purpose and in whose interests. This critique is undertaken in order to awaken possibilities of human and social agency so that critically informed actors can then act in a way that serves the interests of the wellbeing of the many (McLaren & Kincheloe 2007; Zajda 2010b). Importantly a critical pedagogy cannot be understood outside the framework of critical theory.

While embedded in notions of social justice, human rights, democracy and the equal participation of all citizens, critical analysis is most effective when teachers and learners view all actions or human agency as ambiguous, complex, oppressive, steeped in issues of control and power dynamics and assumes that the dominant social and political world will always work exclusively for its own interests. Crucial also is that teachers and learners learn to review their assumptions through as many different theoretical and experiential lenses as possible (Kincheloe 2008).

Educationally critical pedagogies construct curriculum knowledge that is responsive to the everyday knowledge as lived histories and places a strong emphasis on breaking down disciplines of knowledge construction by initiating interdisciplinary conversations. Encouraging an open dialogue with as many voices as possible, critical pedagogies incorporate aspects of difference and diversity as important elements of teaching and learning. In this analysis the dominant and the many subordinate cultures struggle for ascendancy and meaning in what is called a contested, discursive space (Fraser 2007; Kanpol 2004). The classroom is seen a living laboratory for this contestation.

FIELD EDUCATION AND SUPERVISION: BUILDING A CRITICAL PERSPECTIVE

Having provided an overview of critical theory and its links with concepts of social justice and human rights and a general summary of what underpins critical pedagogy I want to explore its application for use in field education and supervision. I want to encourage supervisors and students (learners) to look at the complex relationship between professional practice and the assumptions and theories that underpin it and then to think critically about their practice for use in the supervision sessions. Such critical thinking within the context of supervision will enable practitioners to think reflectively about their teaching and work for social change as part of their praxis. In addition to exploring how student social workers might understand the world, the same critical reflection and analysis can be used in exploring the teaching of field education in the classroom as well as the nature of supervision, the supervisory relationship, the organisational context and demands and the stories from practice that form much of the supervisory focus.

In fact thinking critically challenges the belief that professional knowledge is fixed, discreet, predictable and predictive (Noble & Irwin 2009). Critical reflection incorporates critical theory and results in developing a critically reflective practice for use when supervising students, setting their goals and creating a learning environment where students will be able (hopefully) to experience transformational learning as an educational experience and outcome. Questions that begin the process by exploring the social construction of knowledge might be:

Questions

1. What constitutes knowledge?

2. Whose knowledge is privileged?

3. How is such knowledge produced and disseminated.

4. What strategies are available to challenge knowledge construction.

5. Is this construct important for the teaching of theory and practice of field education and supervision?

6. If so, how might it be adapted?

WHAT IS CRITICAL REFLECTION?

Essentially a critical pedagogy is created by the constant use of critical reflection, where reflective practice becomes a political and social responsibility (Bolton 2005). The intent of critical thinking is to understand, explore and experience the social world reflexively. It creates a 3D vision (Kincheloe 2008) to see through the walls of power that mask the structures that shape social, political and cultural life. Reflection also demands a willingness to make public one's private dilemmas, uncertainties, frustrations, and biases which directly challenge the assumption of professionals knowing how to act, why, for what purpose and to what end. Its epistemology draws lost and subjugated knowledge to surface and fill the classroom and shape the curricula in ways that is responsive to the diversity of students' background and their cultural knowledge, heritage and traditions. The lived experience of students in the classroom is also a focus and, of course the experiences of service users/clients who are the ultimate beneficiaries of this process. This new knowledge, if accepted can create a new vision, new information and new ways of being in the world.

Critical reflection is offered as a way of making sense of the gap between 'espoused theories' and the 'theories in use' when confronted with the 'messy, indeterminate and problematic situations of the complex realities of practice'. Linking knowing 'that' (technical) and the 'how' (practice and emotion) with personal and professional growth, critical reflection has become a valuable tool for use in practice and education as well as supervision. Underpinning its use is an assumption that deep and transformative learning is essential for professional practice where deep learning is seen as a desire to grasp the main point/issue, make connections (in a myriad of ways) between the public and the personal, the ideal and the reality, the obvious and the hidden and draw conclusions as to the authenticity of the situation. This activity then becomes transferable across new settings and enterprises. Transformational learning is applied to the highest level of learning where the learner is prepared to abandon preconceptions and re-examine their assumptions not only about the subject matter, but themselves and the nature of knowledge as well (Bolton 2005; Brookfield 2005).

By definition critical reflection is never ending; a continuous cycle in which experience and reflection are inextricably linked in order to transcend usual patterns of thought to enable a critical stance to emerge (Bolton 2005). An important distinction is made between 'reflection in action' and 'reflection on action' (Bolton 2005; Schön 1987). The former is immediate and concerned with adapting strategies which are short term, while the latter takes place after the event as a systematically structured, deliberative and logical analysis and is more likely to create greater professional autonomy and ethical judgments as a result (Brookfield 2005).

CRITICAL THINKING AND REFLECTION – SHAPING A CRITICAL PEDAGOGY

So how do we illuminate a critical pedagogy, one that threads critical theory within its praxis? We have already begun to outline the key questions that can inform this process, now we need to explicate this in a way that is accessible for its use in field education and supervision.

It is challenging to design a framework where no one position becomes dominant and where a balance between each is maintained. Importantly we need to make teaching and learning approaches flexible, responsive, reflective, and evolving as well as lively and enjoyable in order to bring as much variety as possible into the teaching/learning relationship and to avoid ritualistic, superficial and automatic responses. Therefore the focus on teaching should incorporate a consideration of the following:

In the classroom: ideas for exploration for social work field education

1. Developing a political imaginary by
   - Exploring with students the many diverse ways of seeing and interpreting the world from a moral and political neutrality; to a threatening place; or with a social justice perspective and more compassionate ways of relating, so that
     - Different kinds of human concerns and differences are articulated and unrecognised or unfulfilled desires come to the fore.
     - New voices (previously suppressed) are heard
     - New forms of outrage and indignation are expressed, as a result of their hidden voices, which result in a
     - Multivoiced community of learners emerging in an ongoing, continuous dialogue throughout their learning process.

2. Adopting a no 'privilege' bearer of oppression or suffering by
   - challenging and then reconstructing the position of oppressor/ oppressed to include multiple axes of oppression, victim and privilege
   - recognising that there is no single axis around which relations of power and domination, struggle and resistance are plotted
   - recognising the multi-fields in which struggles for freedom, justice, dignity and fuller realisation of self are played out
   - exploring how sites of struggle have their own dynamic, character and possibilities
   - identifying how one's own perspectives might influence the situation
   - asking questions about the dominant aspects of 'white' or the 'dominant' culture
   - exploring issues and problems from as many difference perspectives as imaginable
   - exploring the cultural capital all students bring to classroom and harness this new knowledge for use in practice (Brookfield 2005; McLaren & Kincheloe 2007; Noble 2003).

3. Experiential and didactic educational materials used in unpacking the social construction of knowledge include:
   - self-disclosure (both teacher and learner)
   - reflections on oppression (personal and political)
   - attention to language and behaviours (and what is coded in these exchanges)
   - involving teacher/learner equally in the process of discovery and self-actualisation
   - exploring student diversity in the classroom where multiple identities are recognised
   - engaging critically with readings and class discussions, including the use of
     - metaphors and poetry
     - narratives and films
     - critical incident analysis and reflective writings as teachable moments (Bolton 2005; Fook, Ryan & Hawkins 2000; Noble 2003).

In the field: ideas for exploration for social work field education

For supervisors it would include reflecting on the particular interpretations of the relationship, the work of supervision, the structure, the context and associated tasks and assessments as well as making explicit the interpretations, assumptions, knowledges, behaviours in self, organisation, communities of practice and work with clients and how these are mediated by language, discourse, and power relations. This means democratising the supervision process and, at the same time, valuing differences in interpretations, experiences, and learning.

Questions

---

1. What kind of supervision praxis will help treat learners fairly, with compassion and tolerance while, at the same time accepting differences and encouraging learning?

2. How can you set up learning that is context relevant and not context dependent and encourage critical reflection?

3. How can you set up learning that doesn't occur in a cultural vacuum but is self-reflective of current issues, context and politics of power?

4. How can you actualise adult learning principles in setting up the learning goals and evaluation and assessment criteria?

5. How can the supervisor as well as the learner set up learning opportunities that allows for in-depth analysis of each other's work in a reassuring environment?

6. How can the supervisor and the learner take risks in their learning from each other and change their practice as a result in a reassuring environment?

Further reflective practice is learning that explores the teachable moments by examining and reexamining what happens in our interactions with others (students, supervisors, colleagues, university-based teachers and clients); by asking what we think happened; what we meant to happen; what prevented the desired outcome and what motivated our intentions and actions? There are many different schemas to identify how we learn and these questions are offered not as a fixed list but to start the process of reflection and provide further opportunity to accept, rebuke or strengthen your approach.

For students the idea of fostering a critical pedagogy is to enable significant and deep learning to occur while in the practice context- one that changes both the student and the supervisor in meaningful ways by what is learnt. So that taken-for-granted assumptions, feelings, thoughts, actions are made more discriminating and insightful as a result (Giles et al. 2010). Some more questions to guide student work include:

Questions
1. What just happened in this interaction?
2. What do you think happened, and make explicit your thinking behind this answer?
3. What were the assumptions underlying this interaction, particularly regarding the politics of power and identify those which are problematic?
4. Why are they problematic?
5. Can you identify a new theory from campus-based study that will give you answers to why this is problematic and hence undesirable?
6. Is it possible to rework what happened in light of this reflection? If so do so now
7. What new learning has emerged as a result of this reflection?

It should be clear from this exercise that a definite and authentic 'end' position is not possible, all that is possible is constant questioning and reflection, a lively, ever changing dialogue that resonates in the moment, is linked with the cultural interrogation of past histories and critiqued within the current dominant power expressions and the emerging assumptions that are produced. Critical reflection begins the process of challenge or deconstruction that takes us on the journey of discovery and ongoing analysis.

All learners approach their learning with a flexible network of ideas and knowledge shaped by prior learning experiences (Fook et al. 2000; Noble 2003). Field supervisors can help students learn while they also explore new and relevant processes to advance their own learning and professional development. This learning is best conceived by exploring a critical pedagogy and where critical reflection is informed by a critical analysis. Examples of how to construct a critical pedagogy have been peppered throughout this last section of this chapter.

CONCLUSION

This chapter has outlined the basis of a new framework for field education and supervision linked to the emancipatory project of social justice, human rights and critical theory's attention to interactive and reflective ways of knowing; connections between structural domination and self-reflectivity; and recognition of possibilities of personal and social change – by exploring a critical pedagogy.

I have demonstrated how teaching and learning critically regards practice and theorising as interrelated. Students are introduced to analyses and concepts that will help them create alternative visions for social, political, cultural, and economic relations and a critique of inherited privilege. This approach is distinguished by a greater commitment to a democratically informed redistributive justice for the citizenry. Private problems are seen as public, structurally produced and inherited. Outcomes and processes are linked. Developing a critically reflective teaching and learning opportunity for students in the very context where they are acquiring their professional skills, values, ethics and practice knowledge is a valuable developmental process for students and supervisors alike. If social work is serious about social change and individual and community empowerment then developing a critical focus should pervade the field education curriculum.

REFERENCES

Aboriginal and Torres Straits Islander Commission [ATSIC] (1993). *Closing the gap – annual report 1993–1994.* Canberra, ACT: Australian Government Publication.

Allan J, Briskman l & Pease B (2009). *Critical social work: theories and practices for a socially just world.* Crows Nest, NSW: Allen & Unwin.

Apple M (2009). *The Routledge international handbook of critical education.* Hoboken, NJ: Taylor & Francis.

Battiste M (1998). Enabling the autumn seed: toward a decolonized approach to Aboriginal knowledge, language and education. *Canadian Journal of Native Education*, 22(1): 16–2.

Bolton G (2005). *Reflective practice: writing and professional development.* London: Sage.

Brookfield S (2005). *The power of critical theory for adult learning.* Maidenhead: Open University Press.

Carey S (2010). *The politics of human rights: the quest for dignity.* Leiden: Cambridge University Press.

Cheyne C, O'Brien M & Belgrave M (2005). *Social policy in Aotearoa New Zealand.* (3rd edn). South Melbourne, VIC: Oxford University Press.

Dominelli L (2010). *Social work in a globalised world.* UK: Polity.

Dominelli L (2009). *Introducing social work.* UK: Cambridge.

Ferguson I, Lavalette M & Whitmore E (2005). *Globalisation, global justice and social work.* London: Routledge.

Fook J, Ryan M & Hawkins L (2000). *Professional expertise: practice, theory and education for working in uncertainty.* London: Whiting & Birch Ltd.

Fraser N (2007). *Adding insult to injury.* London: Verso.

Fraser N (1997). *Justice interruptus: critical reflections on the 'postsocialist' condition.* NY: Routledge.

Freire P (1985). *The politics of education: culture, power and liberation.* South Hadley, MA: Bergin & Garvey.

Friedman L (2010). *Human rights.* Detroit, MI: Greenhaven Press.

Giroux H (2005). *Cultural worker and the politics of education.* (2nd edn). Hoboken: Routledge.

Giroux H & Pollock G (2010). *The mouse that roared: Disney and the end of innocence.* Lanham, Md.: The Rowman & Litttlefield Pub.

Hanohano P (1999). The spiritual imperative of native epistemology: restoring harmony and balance to education. *Canadian Journal of Native Education*, 23(2): 206–19.

Hoffman S-L (2010). *Human rights in the twentieth century.* Leiden: Cambridge University Press.

Hooks B (2010). *Teaching critical thinking: practical wisdom.* NY: Routledge.

Ife J (2010). *Human rights from below: achieving rights through community development.* Port Melbourne, VIC: Cambridge University Press.

Kanpol B (1994). *Critical pedagogy: an introduction.* London: Westport & Garvey.

Kincheloe J (2008). *Knowledge and critical pedagogy: an introduction.* Dordrecht: Springer.

Lyons K, Manion K & Carlsen M (2006). *International perspectives on social work.* UK: Palgrave Macmillan.

McLaren P & Kincheloe J (Eds) (2007). *Critical pedagogy: where are we now?* NY: Peter Lang.

Mullaly R (2010). *Challenging oppression and confronting privilege: a critical social work approach.* Don Mills, Ontario: Oxford University Press.

Noble C (2004). Transforming social work education to respond to the challenges of the new economy. *Advances in Social Work and Welfare Work Education Journal,* 6(1): 77–90.

Noble C (2003). Discursive scholarship in anti-racist/cross-cultural social work education. *Advances in Social Work and Welfare Work Education Journal,* 5(1): 98–108.

Pease B & Fook J (1999). *Transforming social work practice: postmodern critical perspectives.* St Leonards, NSW: Allen & Unwin.

Ramcharan B (2008). *Contemporary human rights ideas.* Hoboken: Taylor & Francis.

Schön D (1983). *The reflective practitioner: how professionals think in action.* NY: Basic Books.

Webb S (2006). *Social work in a risk society: social and political perspectives*. NY: Palgrave Macmillan.

Zajda J (2010a). *Globalization, education and social justice*. Dordrecht: Springer.

Zajda J (2010b). *Global pedagogies: schooling for the future*. Dordrecht: Springer.

Chapter Fifteen

Learning opportunities of social work group supervision and peer learning

Rob Townsend, Natasha Long and Robyn Trainor

This chapter aims to explore the opportunity for professional development and learning through group supervision and peer learning during social work field education and practicum. The essential questions are: what are the teaching, learning and supervisory relationships and processes that support group supervision and peer learning and how does group supervision assist with student learning needs during social work student practicum. This topic has extensive relevance in the Australian, Asian and Pacific contexts as social work education expands in countries such as China, Cambodia, Philippines and Malaysia and as higher education reform in Australia and New Zealand means that social work professional courses are likely to expand in context and size. Social work practicum in a range of urban, regional and rural contexts and in all cultural locations can be improved by models of group supervision and peer learning that brings together students, clinicians and field educators in diverse learning relationships.

在小组督导和同学间经验交流的过程中进行学习

此章意在探究在社会工作教育与实习过程中通过小组督导及同学间的相互学习而带来的认知和职业发展的机会。其探讨的主要问题是：教，学和督导这三方面应

该怎样配合？如何确保小组督导和同学间的经验交流有效地进行？在社工专业学生实习的过程中，小组督导是如何满足学生的学习需要的？社会工作教育在中国，柬埔寨，菲律宾和马来西亚等一些国家的不断扩展以及澳大利亚和新西兰的高等教育改革所带来的专业课程在环境和规模上扩大的可能性使这个论题在澳洲，亚洲以及太平洋地区具有广泛的意义。无论在城市，乡村，其它区域或者是任何文化环境里，社会工作的实习教育均可以通过小组督导和同学间相互学习的方式得到促进和提高，因为这种方式可以把学生，督导人员以及实习教育工作者在多样性的学习关系中结合在一起。

ソーシャルワーク・グループ・スーパービジョンの学習機会と自助グループ学習

本章はソーシャルワーク現場教育と実習期間中のグループ・スーパービジョンと自助グループ学習を通して専門家育成のための学習の機会について調査することを目的とする。きわめて重要な論点は、何がグループ・スーパービジョンと自助グループ学習を支えている教え、学習であるのか、また、スーパバイズを受ける関係、プロセスはどういったものであるのか、そしてどのようにグループ・スーパービジョンがソーシャルワークの学生の実習期間中に、学生の学習におけるニーズを助長させるのかということである。この論題は、ソーシャルワークの教育が中国、カンボジア、フィリピンやマレーシアなどの国々に広がるにつれ、オーストラリア、アジアや太平洋のそれぞれの背景事情において広範囲な関連性を持ち、そして、オーストラリアやニュージーランドにおいて高い教育改革が行われるにつれ、ソーシャルワークの専門職課程がその素地と規模をより拡張することを意味するであろう。都市、地方、そして田舎といった背景の事情、また全ての文化指定地区の範囲において行われるソーシャルワーク実習は、様々な学習の関連性という意味において学生、

医療従事者、そして現場教育者をつなげるグループ・ス
ーパービジョンや自助グループ学習のモデルによって
改善されるだろう。

사회 복지 그룹 감독 하기와 동료 학습을 통한 학습 기회

이장은 사회 복지 현장 교육(現場 教育)과 실습 과목을 이
수하면서, 그룹 감독 하기와 동료 학습을 통하여, 직무 개
발과 학습을 위한 기회를 탐구하기 위함이다. 핵심적인
질문 사항들은, 가르침과 배움은 무엇이며, 그룹 감독하
기와 동료 학습을 지원하는 감독적인 관계와 그 과정은
무엇이며, 그룹 감독하는 것이 사회복지 실습 과정에서,
학생들의 학습 요구를 어떻게 도와 주는 것인가 하는것
이다. 이 주제들은, 호주 아시아 태평양 지역 실정에 있어
서 광범위한 적합성을 갖고 있다. 사회 복지 교육은 중국,
캄보디아, 필리핀, 말레이지아에서 확장되고 있으며, 호
주, 뉴질랜드에 있어서의 보다 높은 교육 개혁은, 사회복
지 직업 과정의 질적, 양적 확대를 의미한다. 도시및 지방
그리고 시골과 같은 환경적 배경을 가진곳과, 모든 문화
적 장소들을 염두에 둔 사회 복지 실습 과정은, 그룹 감독
하기와 동료 학습의 모델들에 의하여 향상되어 질수 있으
며, 이 모델들은 학생, 임상의(臨床醫), 그리고 현장 교육
자들을 다양한 배움의 관계 속에서 결속시킨다.

There is limited contribution within current literature regarding social
work group-based supervision and peer learning. Over the last decade,
there has been some advancement in the establishment of instructive
and developmental approaches to group supervision. The difficulty of
many students to identify and integrate theory into practice has resulted
in the creation of varied models of supervision that purposefully
emphasise theoretical learning and implementation. Learning about
and implementing social work theory into practice is an integral part
of social work education and there seems to be limited evidence of the

actual methods of teaching and learning theory within the supervisory process.

There are challenges for students on field education placement and social workers professionally in developing understanding and integrating the practice of supervision at an organisational level, particularly in the current climate of business models and bureaucratically driven organisational contexts in the welfare sector (Hugman 2001). Supervision that includes supportive, educative, administrative and critically reflective features can be regarded as an extra pressure at an individual and agency level. If supervision is not practiced and valued at an organisational level, then supervision can become task management, rather than being integrated as a developmental, professional and ethical component of social work and agency practice (Noble & Irwin 2010). The practice of social work within current Australasian and Pacific contexts is fraught with challenges, particularly within a welfare sector that is continually pressured to provide more service for less funding, and organisational cultures that are competitive and budget driven (Hugman 2005). This organisational practice culture can influence the importance students place on supervision and the way they think of themselves as social workers and practicing professionals (Healy 2000).

Gaining knowledge and practice from learning in human services organisations is commonplace for social work professional education. In Australian social work courses, structured field education programs exist to enable students to develop recommended standards of practice that are congruent with the requirements for professional practice according to the Australian Association of Social Workers (AASW 2010). Social work students are formally placed in a variety of human services and social work related organisations to enable them to develop professionally as future social workers, and be supported and supervised during this period. Field education is designed to enable the achievement of social work education goals and gives students the opportunity to integrate their professional practice skills and theoretical knowledge in an experiential learning environment (Rothman 2000).

While the specific details of social work field education programs vary across institutions and internationally, the inclusion of field education as core curricula in social work education is a minimum standard advised in the IASSW and IFSW document 'Global Standards for the Education and Training of the Social Work Profession' (IASSW & IFSW 2004, p5). The duration of field education is not specified, but it is indicated that field education should be *sufficient in duration and complexity of tasks and learning opportunities to ensure that students are prepared for professional practice* (IASSW/IFSW 2004, Standard 5, p5). In the Asia-Pacific region, field education programs are also part of the curricula in the Philippines, Hong Kong and China, Sri Lanka, India, Korea and New Zealand (Noble 2004). The detail of how each field education program is delivered will vary at each institution and in each country.

The AASW (2010) states that Australian social work students must undertake and successfully complete a minimum of at least 980 hours (140 days) of fieldwork placement in at least two different fields of practice over a two-year period; highlighting the importance of field education as a core component of social work education. In addition, formal supervision must be provided by a social work qualified field educator with a minimum of two years full-time practice experience and eligibility for full membership of the AASW. According to AASW and Australian university clinical and professional education guidelines, a minimum of 1.5 hours of structured supervision must be provided to students for every five days of placement, this can be formal or informal and delivered in an individual or group setting (AASW 2010, 4.3.3.a.ii).

Universities throughout the Australasian and Pacific region are currently developing new professional social work courses and field education programs. All universities throughout the Australasian and Pacific regions will have their own responses to the concerns that Australian universities have about the obligation to ensure students on field education placements are supervised by a qualified social worker. The AASW standards are used here as an example that closely reflects the IASSW/IFSW Global Standards (La Trobe University 2010) and are the standards known in most detail by the authors. The obligation for structured social work supervision has become increasingly difficult over recent years due to the increase in student numbers and a lack of social work qualified field educators, and has resulted in the need for universities to fund external supervision for students in agencies where no qualified social workers are located. Group-based student supervision and peer learning has been established and trialled at fieldwork placement organisations as a way to provide students with necessary supervision and support. This alleviates the pressure of resources for the placement organisation and is more cost effective to universities (Grinter 2006).

CURRENT RESEARCH AND ISSUES IN GROUP SUPERVISION

Studies from Australia, Japan, China, Canada and New Zealand have revealed that students can be grouped together in agencies and/or on projects that allows for more significant peer learning (Hashimoto 2010; Hair & O'Donoghue 2009; Koon-chui Law & Xia Gu 2008; Townsend & Jordan 2010). Social work field placements take many forms in an international context. Hashimoto (2010) provides a comparison between field work programs in India and Japan and concludes that as the social work profession proliferates into culturally and politically diverse regions, that students' active participation in effective field action projects and programs is essential to all contexts.

Hashimoto (2010) argues that this active participation is dependent on excellent relationships between schools of social work, their students and human service organisations. These connections allow for dynamic field placement programs and projects to be devised. She also argues that schools of social work and local human service organisations need to be open to students' initiating new projects and programs. Koon-chui Law and Xia Gu (2008) argue that in the emerging context of social work in China, the shortage of a range of social work agencies and programs means that opportunities are limited for students to engage with programs and projects that they are interested in and this leads to students taking up field education opportunities that are not satisfying or not completing their degree.

From 2006 through to 2010, social work researchers at La Trobe University Bendigo conducted evaluations of group supervision facilitated with local agencies throughout this period of time. These were small-scale qualitative evaluations utilising formative and summative evaluation methodology to facilitate open and in-depth discussion regarding the experiences of students involved in group supervision.

All social work students involved in the group supervision processes at several placement host organisations were invited to participate in the project. In total, 20 students on social work field education placements within local and international human service organisations participated in focus groups and interviews. Semi-structured student focus groups and interviews generated information and discussion for the evaluation of student experiences of group supervision. Qualitative data analysis incorporating elements of content and thematic analysis were used to identify emerging themes to link with the literature. The research findings identified a number of factors which impacted on the supervisory and learning opportunities offered by group supervision. Four broad topics were reported by students as being positive factors to the supervisory and learning opportunities.

Peer support: participants reported that group supervision facilitated the opportunity for students to provide valuable support to each other. This support was achieved in three ways: being connected and located close to each other in the same placement host agency, by sharing their experiences of placement with student peers, and by the continuous development of peer relationships and networks with other students.

Peer learning: students reported that peer-based learning was achieved as a direct result of the group context in which the supervision was based. Three main ways were identified as facilitating peer learning: through the comparison of similar placement related experiences between students, through sharing knowledge and information with others, and from direct interaction with peers.

Practice relevance of the group context: it was reported by participants that group supervision provided learning opportunities relevant to practice via the group environment in which supervision was provided. Two main ways were recognised in which this occurs: students were supported at a greater level within the context of a familiar group environment, and the group supervision offered influential learning opportunities to students by stimulating connectedness between group members.

Student learning needs: students were able to identify the progress of their individual learning objectives through participation in the group supervision. Group supervision allowed for the facilitation of peer-related learning that was identified as a positive contributor to student learning needs in two ways: the informal structure of the supervision sessions allowed the peer aspect of the group to flourish, and the teaching processes of the group supervision were able to be scrutinised from the students' learning needs perspective.

The relationship between social work students, schools of social work and human service organisations is very complex with all stakeholders in this social work education process having their own standards, motivations and processes for negotiating and managing field education programs. This recent Australian research also revealed that students voiced discontent with supervision in all its forms including: a lack of advanced planning and training in supervisory relationships, complex and slow communication processes between all stakeholders, a lack of a common understanding about one-to-one and group supervision, power relationships between universities and students on placement and the lack of engagement of host agency staff in all supervision processes (Townsend & Jordan 2010). This discontent is widespread in many social work professional education programs across the Australasian and Pacific contexts (Hashimoto 2010; Hair & O'Donoghue 2009; Koon-chui Law & Xia Gu 2008; Townsend & Jordan 2010). Reflections by the authors and some of our students of social work field education in different contexts during the research process highlight the similarities in experiences of social work field education in a range of Australasian and Pacific contexts such as; Australian Indigenous placements, Cambodian placements and regional community-based human services placements.

Cross-cultural social work field education

Having trouble processing the emotion and inaction – struggling a little bit ... my task supervisor would not talk about it with me. I know it's here all the time (social injustice/death of children/human misery) and will be when I leave – but for some reason instead of giving me greater purpose and drive to address social issues I just feel useless! There is no normal, no benchmark; the spiritual context is full of conflicting values and interpretations. The way they looked so defeated – their silence was deafening, so is everyone else's. I'm OK … just a bit stuck (Student on field education in Cambodia).

The most stark illustration of the limitations to current social work field education programs is that of social work programs, projects and supervision situated in Indigenous and cross-cultural contexts as described by Hair and O'Donoghue (2009). They argue that culturally relevant social work supervision be informed from social constructionist ideas through

> the recognition of plurality and diversity of knowledge, an emphasis on collaboration, the engagement in various relational forms such as dyadic, group and in-session supervision, increased sensitivity to power and the politics of empowerment and disempowerment in supervision and an explicit recognition of the influence of the social and cultural context within which supervision is immersed. (p77)

1. Students, who participated in the La Trobe University research, revealed that their university studies and field education preparation left them ill-prepared for Indigenous cultural contexts in Australia and Cambodia. The students also revealed that Indigenous human service agencies had very little knowledge and experience of the specifics of social work field education and those relationships took a long time to develop during placement time. Language, culture, community and organisation are all concepts that we teach and learn about; however the specific Australian and Cambodian Indigenous contexts caused distress for students because of the lack of a local cultural educator and mediator to provide direct knowledge and support. The fact that no-one was able or willing to take on the role of cultural educator and mediator resulted in students utilising each other as a peer learning experience to debrief about, educate

and question their practice in these contexts. The Australian and Cambodian Indigenous human service contexts were unaware and unprepared for the structure and level of documentation required by the placements as guided by the AASW and as such were unable to plan for the elements required.

2. Students revealed that peer learning was the most beneficial of all these processes but placed added pressure on the students to become informed about culturally relevant social work practice in specific Indigenous and cross-cultural contexts. One student revealed that:

> [T]he opportunity to implement critical peer reflection is immense and despite how extensively people may have travelled, the unique challenges to being a student in a foreign country are a great learning opportunity if explored within a supported, safe relationship. Also consider your support team – it may be your supervisor or liaison person that provides the main support, but who else could be on your team if needed – a friend back home, University staff, someone in the agency or country that might provide informal support.

SOCIAL WORK SUPERVISION

Supervision is generally experienced as a didactic interaction, often with an administrative focus that is based on a managerial agenda and individual supervisory requirements (Nilsson 2008). In contrast, group-based student supervision varies greatly; the group setting consists of more than two students and one group facilitator. The experience of supervision can often be viewed as a top-down process, and although group supervision is likely to provide a more equitable environment, there is still the potential for relationships based on power issues to surface. Regardless of the type of supervision provided, evidence suggests that organisational and administrative efficiency based on managerialism dominates the realm of supervision (Alston 2007; Baker 2010). Supervisors have a responsibility to manage students' fieldwork placements and ensure the provision of orientation, supervision, and assessment. The experience of supervisors needs to be adequate to ensure a supportive and reflective supervision style; as opposed to the potentially prescriptive and authoritarian style that inexperience may produce (Nilsson 2008). Students may have preconceived perceptions about supervision and the facilitators' role; therefore it's important to address the barriers and stressors that give rise to supervision not being another form of the teacher-student relationship.

Regardless, supervision needs to meet the interests of the human service agency, the university, and students from diverse backgrounds and as such may only be effectively achieved if the facilitator is knowledgeable about the connection between all three stakeholders (Bogo & Vayda 1998). The relationship between the field educator and the student needs to be built on a foundation of trust or the potential for conflict regarding power imbalances may result (Wilson 2000). Supervision needs to be provided to students in a way that teaches reflective practices, theoretical knowledge and professional culture. It has been widely debated that supervision would be more productive if it was viewed as both a developmental and learning relationship (Cleak &Wilson 2007; Nilsson 2008).

The professional practice of social work supervision within Australasian and Pacific contexts relies on the development of practice, knowledge and relationships within specific cultural and organisational environments (Tsui 2008). Each country and even regions within countries have very specific cultural and organisational factors that influence how social work professional education and fieldwork can be negotiated. Language, cultural customs and gender all need to be considered when coordinating, monitoring and evaluating social work field education. The explicit and implicit use of critically reflective analysis and integration within supervision relationships and process creates opportunities to explore the impact of these relationships, power and structure at an individual, group, community and political level (Noble & Irwin 2009).

Supervision is generally described as an arrangement between a supervisor and one (or more) supervisee that provides the opportunity for the review of work and reflective acknowledgement between principles, practice frameworks and future planning (O'Connor et al. 2003). Supervision allows for engagement with the social work profession, particularly in relation to active professional development, reflection and continued education. The effectiveness of supervision is dependant on the quality of supervision supplied and the contribution of the participants involved in the process. If supervision is effective, the experience for the supervisee can be transitional and transformative. Supervision is vital for the continuation of professional development and the current managerial context in which supervision is delivered is threatening the potential growth and learning opportunities that are necessary for both workers and students entering the human services profession (Noble & Irwin 2009).

The 21st-century context

The requirement of student supervision in twenty-first century social work has become a constraint on many organisations due to increasing student numbers and gradual changes in social work education curriculum and fieldwork responsibilities. This has impacted on the availability and willingness of human services organisations, particularly in rural and regional areas and countries where social work is a 'new' profession, to host social work students due to resource availability and cost issues (Alston 2007). In particular, the implication of increasing student numbers has caused concern about the viability of providing sufficient supervision for students (Cooper 2007). Research investigating the transitional experience from student to practitioner found that supervision significantly assisted graduates to identify and confront anticipated expectations and challenges (Agllias 2010). This is congruent with the fact that the experience of social work field education differs from one student to another and the expectations of individuals, the hosting organisation, the university and supervisors can cause specific conflicting problems and challenges.

Recent qualitative studies have found that the benefits of field education were significant to employers, host agencies, students, and to the profession as a whole. Supervisors acknowledged that they are required to contribute significant portions of their time when supervising students; however the benefits received regarding their own professional development outweighed issues of time and cost (Barton et al. 2005). In 21st century culturally diverse and managerial contexts across the Australasian and Pacific region, the strain on all types of human services organisations accepting social work students for fieldwork have been alleviated by universities employing creative strategies to provide the supervision requirements of the field education program. This is particularly so in countries where social work professional education is new and where relationships between universities and human service agencies have yet to be developed.

Individual supervision

In most human services, professional supervision is commonly delivered on a one-to-one basis. One evaluation of individual supervision for supervisees revealed the elements of being taught how to counsel and the conceptualisation of their casework. In contrast, supervisors emphasised providing feedback to the supervisee as a crucial element of the supervisory process (London & Chester 2000). Distinctive supervisory strategies are often employed in individual supervision sessions to address the goals and objectives of the process for both the supervisor and the supervisee. The responsibilities of a supervisor may include promoting skills and knowledge; providing feedback and evaluation; modelling effective problem-solving; promoting ethical behaviour; and providing due-process information (Nilsson 2008, p2). The responsibilities of the supervisor and the type of individual supervision provided depend on the experience of the supervisor and the needs of the supervisee. Professionals who supervise social work students on field education have different aims and focus in supervision, and student education can be unique to the individual depending on supervisors' ability to utilise a variety of supervisory approaches and discuss differences regarding power and culture (Cooper & Maidment 2001).

For social work students on placement, supervision is likely to be experienced as learning and reflective processes, with field education providing the opportunity where skills, affect, behaviour and self-awareness are developed (Cooper & Maidment 2001, p42). Students given the opportunity to reflect on feelings and assumptions will develop skills to cope with the unpredictable nature of the work they do and the clients they deal with. This will also encourage engagement with their supervisor and assist in building a supervisory relationship aimed at meeting the learning goals to be achieved during placement (Ellis 2000). However, power imbalance in this dyadic relationship can cause resistance and vulnerability that impact on the effectiveness of the supervision (Itzhaky & Ribner 1998; Noble & Irwin 2009).

Peer learning

Peer learning provides the opportunity for experiences to be shared in an honest, open, communicative and informal environment, which can enhance peer connection and networking. Established to provide support, peer learning is not hierarchal and is less formal compared to traditional group supervision formats (Bernard & Goodyear 2009). Reciprocal peer learning involves students communicating in a collaborative way to engage in reflection; whilst simultaneously developing skills in communication, collective responsibility, exploration and cooperation (Boud et al. 1999). The experiential learning that ensues allows individuals to challenge each other more deeply in a trusting, supportive and often reflective setting. In many contexts the concept of peer-based learning circles (Brennan & Brophy 2010) is now an integral part of philosophies and processes of adult learning. Widely utilised in adult community education, vocational training and citizen initiated discussion groups, learning circles are structured processes whereby peers meet together to discuss a topic utilising shared experiences and this sometimes results in collective and individual action around specific issues as agreed by the group. Learning circles and group-based peer education is specifically utilised in Indigenous community contexts across the Australasian and Pacific contexts and would be more acceptable in many ways in Indigenous community contexts than so called mainstream and urban contexts.

This concept has usefulness for peer-based group learning in social work in that adult education and learning circles philosophies encourage students to meet as peers and take control of some of their supervision with a sense of power over their actions. Peer group learning allows for more than just a 'debrief' and promotes a possibly deeper connection with peers through a shared learning process. Research with undergraduate students in a Masters of Occupational Therapy course found that when students can support each other and receive coaching from their peers, their clinical reasoning, self-confidence and performance can be significantly optimised (Nelson et al. 2010). Peer group learning is not generally reliant on one specific facilitator but if unstructured has the risk of lacking purpose and clarity, and may possibly lead to commitment challenges where people lose interest (Flood et al. 2010). The role of a leader to elicit the supervision process can reduce the pressure and anxiety of participants, giving students the opportunity to openly express themselves in a less formal setting. Peer learning can also be self-structured, but this also produces concerns about whether supervision focuses on professional social work practice or merely building friendships; therefore, requiring careful preparation and planning (Flood et al. 2010; Grover 2002).

Peer group learning is susceptible to group dynamics, in that different personalities and individual needs may impact on the learning process, and more dominant people may impede on the ability of submissive individuals to meet their own personal objectives (Cleak & Wilson 2007). In peer learning there is still a need for participants to be accountable and to limit the peer group size and be selective of participants, as some students' learning style may predispose them to one-to-one supervision as opposed to learning and supervision received in groups. These limitations can be overcome by including more specific theorising, discussion and experience in the role of building relationships in groups as part of the social work field education experience. Group work has lost its prominence in many social work curricula however; there is a place for group work theory and practice in the realm of social work field education in all Australasian and Pacific contexts particularly if group supervision and peer learning becomes useful for addressing the concerns about providing adequate supervision when qualified practitioners are not available.

There is a need to prepare social work students for field education with skills in building relationships in group settings whether they be task teams, supervision groups or peer groups and networking. Social work field education seminars need to provide theoretical materials and case examples and adult learning frameworks for social work practice and the roles and skills required for students to participate in this model. Students should be encouraged to use the seminars as a forum for practising and exploring their group work skills including developing skills in leadership, facilitating, mediation and role definition. This will ensure that students have the skills to empower themselves in group situations like task teams, group supervision, peer learning and networking.

Group supervision

For human services agencies, group supervision is an economical and time efficient way in which students on social work placement can receive necessary guidance and support from both peers and a group facilitator (Baird 2008). Group supervision is a process where people have the opportunity to teach, learn and receive beneficial elements of supervision, from each other and a facilitator, through dual-directional interaction (Cleak & Wilson 2007). The structure of group supervision generally consists of two or more students being supervised by one group facilitator and often involves top-down processes which can lead students to initially see supervision as a power relationship. Issues of group dynamics must be recognised and facilitated or they will impact on the effectiveness of group supervision objectives.

Research into field instructors' perceptions of group supervision found that effective supervision can be particularly challenging when people in the group know each other well and have conflicting past experiences and different perspectives on issues, or when students are unknown to others in a group and feel they are suppressed in expressing their opinions (Sussman et al. 2007). However, other research suggests that when group supervision is planned and structured, the teaching opportunities available in this setting encourages accountability by the participants and the facilitator; which supports the student, the facilitator and the agency (Zeira & Schiff 2010).

The learning achieved through group supervision has the potential to impact significantly on the students' professional education, allowing them to interact with like-minded individuals with whom they share commonalities regarding development, extended learning, progressive learning and exploration of knowledge (Baruch 2009; Nelson et al. 2010). Trust, accountability, cohesion, motivation, and commitment are key ingredients identified by Coulton and Krimmer (2005) to reduce anxiety and provide a supportive, reflective and explorative supervisory experience for students. The results of another study assessing the group supervision experiences of students on placement found that participants wanted more supportive, open and honest communication; more reflection on practice; and a greater element of education and exploration (Baker 2010).

Limitations in supervision

For social work students experiencing supervision which encompasses the elements of administration, education and support, the encounters can contribute significantly to current and future professional development (O'Connor et al. 2003). However, regardless of the type of supervision provided, there are limitations that will affect the supervisory outcomes for both students and supervisors. For the supervisor and students the process of supervision needs be built on foundations of trust, confidentiality, support, professionalism and mutuality (Pack 2009). Students need to be motivated and committed to achieve an agreed purpose for supervision. Possessing a willingness to collaborate and contribute to their own learning, development, assessment, and reflection; and self-evaluation will encourage active participation (Itzhaky & Ribner 1998). A new framework of social work field education supervision that is flexible and encompasses group supervision and peer learning is one that can suit developed and developing social work field education programs in all Australasian and Pacific contexts.

A 21ST-CENTURY MODEL FOR SOCIAL WORK GROUP SUPERVISION AND PEER LEARNING

In addition to the student feedback from the recent La Trobe University research on group supervision, other examples of group supervision and peer learning are also evident and two recent examples also from La Trobe University include the following. Students participating on field placements in different states or regions in a country can be connected for group supervision and peer learning by email. In 2008, six social work students from La Trobe University Bendigo were placed in different Australian states/territories and participated in group supervision and peer learning where email was used as a tool to connect the students with the university and with each other. As well as peer support and collaboration from a lecturer in the social work program, students participated in different learning tasks and reflections which they shared with the members of the group. This was successful in terms of connecting students and extending learning opportunities and support. This type of group supervision and peer learning, connected virtually by communication technology could be extended even further in terms of supervision opportunities for students in different countries experiencing similar fields of practice.

In Cambodia in 2010, Australian social work students completed their field education in Phnom Penh with different agencies but chose to live together in one accommodation complex in order to remain in regular contact. The students had different field placement tasks in different parts of the region with different supervisors and multidisciplinary teams that were complex in nature. The students were able to come together at the end of the day and debrief their experiences with each other as students without fear or favour. The learning for these students often occurred during these times of reflection and also in subsequent emails with friends, family and academic staff about their experiences the prior day or week. The learning for all concerned about social work field education in countries like Cambodia is that this peer learning *must* become a recognised part of field education rather than something that might be facilitated by students' themselves.

The recent research conducted by La Trobe University, the literature and the authors' own experiences suggest that a model of supervision during field education that incorporates both social work educator facilitated group supervision and peer lead learning has merit in the current educational environment. Figure 1 represents an integrated

Figure 1: An integrated model of group supervision for social work field education

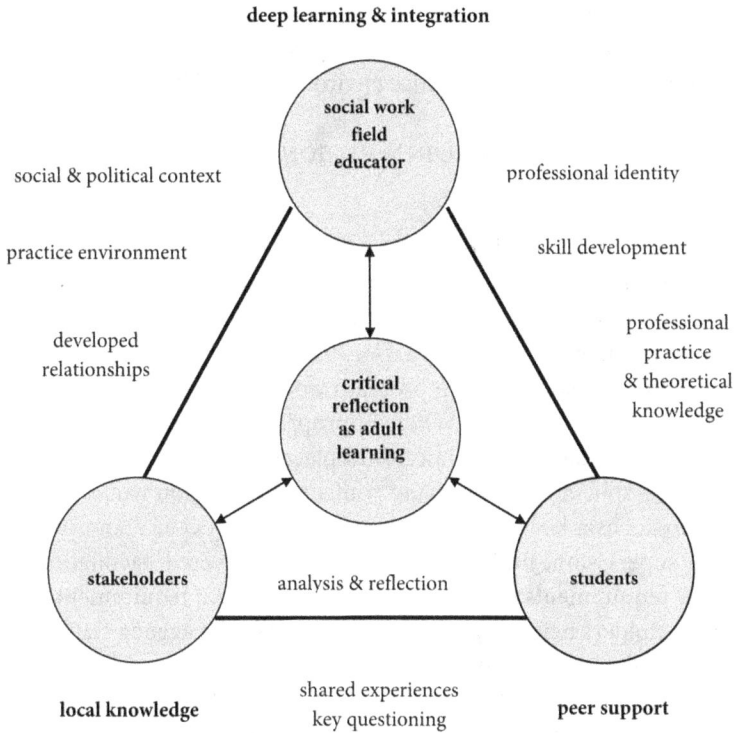

model of group-based field supervision as discussed to this point. The model is based on a process-centred method and demonstrates the expanding layers that contribute to the teaching, learning and supervisory processes occurring within the group supervision. This diagrammatic representation of the model emphasises links that can impact and influence all the levels of group supervision. The diagram highlights the significance of the people involved; field educators, stakeholders and students, and the different elements that each bring to the group supervision process; deep learning and knowledge, local knowledge and peer support. At the centre of the group supervision model is critical reflection as a process to explore shared experiences, to question and to develop skills, knowledge and professional identity. Other elements that influence the group supervision model include the social and political context, the practice environment and key relationships.

EXAMPLE OF THE MODEL IN A REGIONAL AUSTRALIAN CONTEXT

In order for the model to come to life, an example of the use of the model from a regional Australia context could be helpful. In the regional context of Australian social work field placement, well before social work placements commence, a University social work staff member, involved in a Field Education program would liaise with staff members at local regional agencies. Where appropriate and relevant, especially in Indigenous and cross-cultural field placements, a person considered knowledgeable in the culture and context of the region would be identified to act as a key resource. Discussion would occur about the style of the supervision, timing of sessions, topics covered, facilitation, the AASW requirements and the University assessment requirements, with all stakeholders being engaged in this process. The agency staff person and the cultural and contextual 'specialist' would suggest/add aspects as relevant. For example, in an organisation that has many sites it may be considered important that the place of the group supervision and peer learning sessions be rotated through sites or where it is considered important for ongoing cultural input it may be suggested that group supervision be co-facilitated by the field educator and a member from the cultural community, for example, an Indigenous community.

An agreed structure to complement the implementation of this model in an Australian regional context would consist of: group-based supervision weekly, with one week being formal field education facilitated by a social work field educator, using professional resources as reminders of social work theories and drawing on 'specialist' knowledge as required. The other week would be group-based peer learning and supervision facilitated by agency supervisors and students. All students would be encouraged to attend every session whether in person or via video-conferencing or Skype as a form of relationship building in a practice setting as per adult learning philosophy and practices (Brennan & Brophy 2010).

Given that the framework of critical reflection is central to the proposed model, developing an awareness of critical reflection in practice is essential for social work students in field education. Critical reflection is currently being incorporated by many universities into professional education programs and by many human services agencies in relation to supervision and it is a skill that needs to be practiced by students in readiness for placements. Having a clear understanding of how to utilise critical reflection in practice will assist students to gain the most from their placement experience and from their supervision experience.

As noted earlier in the chapter, students are not always clear about why they are required to be 'supervised' on placement or what supervision is. Most university curricula in Australasian and Pacific contexts would address the theoretical aspect of supervision; however, students often experience the 'practice' of various forms of supervision for the first time during their first placement. It is at this stage that students begin developing understandings of supervision in practice and therefore it is important that field educators assist positively in this development. Providing a learning environment that values learning from peers, while involving agency staff, university staff and other social work field educators, along with the encouragement of a critically reflective framework for discovering 'self' in the context of the agency, the environment and social work practice, would provide a flexible, and more reliable starting place for exploring social work supervision.

CONCLUSIONS

The research and model presented in this chapter are relevant for Australasian and Pacific contexts. Using the model in each national, regional or urban context allows for the acknowledgement of the roles of groups of local professionals from a variety of professions and agencies and links social work students who have common areas of their field education placements, and utilises the role of the qualified social work educator. All three aspects of the model; students, human services and cultural stakeholders and field educators combine to ensure that various forms of critical reflection are an essential component of all field education programs and not ad hoc.

Group supervision and peer learning as social work field education practice extends the learning benefits of field supervision beyond the didactic of social work student and social work supervisor. It acknowledges that there are many stakeholders in each rural, regional, urban or international program of social work field education. The model presented here proposes that social work group field education supervision can be more effective than current modes because it provides the opportunity for learning about social work programs in local contexts that acknowledge the professional, social, cultural, community, political and economic frameworks of 21st century global social work professional practice.

Acknowledgements

The authors would like to acknowledge Kathy Jordan and Melinda Delves who worked as research assistants on the La Trobe Rural Health School field education evaluation project and all the social work students and staff who contributed their experiences in 2006 and 2010.

References

AASW (2010). *Australian social work education and accreditation standards.* Canberra, ACT: Australian Association of Social Workers.

Agllias K (2010). Student to practitioner: a study of preparedness for social work practice. *Australian Social Work,* 63(3), 345–60.

Alston M (2007). Rural and regional developments in social work higher education. *Australian Social Work,* 60(1): 107–21.

Baird N (2008). *The internship, practicum, and field placement handbook.* (5th edn). New Jersey: Pearson Education.

Baker S (2010). An exploration of rural social worker's experiences of supervision. Unpublished thesis. School of Social Work and Social Policy, La Trobe University Bendigo: Victoria, Australia.

Barton H, Bell K & Bowles W (2005). Help or hindrance? Outcomes of social work student placements. *Australian Social Work,* 58(3): 301–12.

Baruch V (2009). Supervision groups in private practice: an integrative approach. *Psychotherapy in Australia,* 13(3): 72–76.

Bernard J & Goodyear R (2009). *Fundamentals of clinical supervision.* (4th edn). New Jersey: Pearson Education.

Bogo M & Vayda E (1998). *The practice of field instruction in social work, theory and process.* (2nd edn). Toronto: University of Toronto Press.

Boud D, Cohen R & Sampson J (1999). Peer learning assessment. *Assessment and Evaluation in Higher Education,* 24(4): 413–26.

Brennan M & Brophy M (2010). Study circles and the Dialogue to Change Program. *Australian Journal of Adult Learning,* 50(2): 411–18

Cleak H & Wilson J (2007). *Making the most of field placement.* (2nd edn). South Melbourne: Thompson Learning Australia.

Cooper L (2007). Backing Australia's future: teaching and learning in social work. *Australian Social Work,* 60(1): 94–106.

Cooper L & Maidment J (2001). Thinking about difference in student supervision. *Australian Social Work,* 54(1): 41–52.

Coulton P & Krimmer L (2005). Co-supervision of social work students: a model for meeting the future needs of the profession. *Australian Social Work,* 58(2): 154–66.

Ellis G (2000). Reflective learning and supervision. In L Cooper & L Briggs (Eds). *Fieldwork in the human service: theory and practice for field educators, practice teachers and supervisors* (pp227–38). St. Leonards, NSW, Australia: Allen & Unwin.

Flood B, Haslam L & Hocking C (2010). Implementing a collaborative model of student supervision in New Zealand: enhancing therapist and student experiences. *New Zealand Journal of Occupational Therapy,* 57(1): 22–26.

Gardner F (2006). *Working with human service organisations.* New York: Oxford University Press.

Grinter C (2006). Student social work supervision: what learning and supervisory opportunities are offered by a student supervision unit. Evaluation Report (Unpublished). School of Social Work and Social Policy, La Trobe University Bendigo: Victoria.

Grover M (2002). *Supervision for allied health professionals.* In ML McMahon & WA Patton (Eds). *Supervision in the helping professions: a practical approach* (pp273–84). Frenchs Forest, NSW: Pearson Education Australia.

Hair HJ & O'Donoghue K (2009). Culturally relevant, socially just social work supervision: becoming visible through a social constructionist lens. *Journal of Ethnic & Cultural Diversity in Social Work,* 18: 70–99.

Hashimoto Y (2010). Indian social work education and their competitive field work programme: comparative study of India and Japan. Paper presented at the Joint World Conference on Social Work and Social Development, Hong Kong SAR (July).

Healy K (2000). *Social work practices: contemporary perspectives on change.* London: Sage.

Hugman R (2001). Post-welfare social work? Reconsidering post-modernism, post-Fordism and social work education. *Social Work Education,* 20(3): 321–33.

Hung SL, Ng SL & Fung KK (2010). Functions of social work supervision in Shenzhen: insights from the cross-border supervision model. *International Social Work,* 53(3): 366–78.

International Association of Schools of Social Work [IASSW] & International Federation of Social work [IFSW] (2004). *Global standards for the education and training of the social work professional.* General Assemblies of IASSW and IFSW, Adelaide, Australia.

Itzhaky H & Ribner D (1998). Resistance as a phenomenon in clinical and student social work supervision. *Australian Social Work,* 51(3): 25–29.

Kadushin A & Harkness D (2002). *Supervision in social work.* (4th edn). New York: Columbia University Press.

Kadushin A & Harkness D (1985). *Supervision in social work.* (2nd edn). New York: Columbia University Press.

Koon-chui Law A & Xia Gu J (2008). Social work education in mainland China: development and issues. *Asian Social Work and Policy Review,* 2: 1–12.

La Trobe University (2010). *Clinical & professional education student manual: social work & social policy.* Melbourne, VIC: La Trobe University Pty Ltd.

London Z & Chester A (2000). Less assessment and more suggestions please: factors contributing to effective supervision of counsellors at different experience levels. *Australian Social Work,* 54(4): 47–53.

Melnick J & Fall M (2008). A Gestalt approach to group supervision. *Counselor Education and Supervision,* 48(1): 48–60.

Nelson A, Copley J & Salama R (2010). Occupational therapy students' perceptions of the multiple mentoring model of clinical supervision. *Focus on Health Professional Education: A Multi-disciplinary Journal,* 11(2): 14–27.

Nilsson D (2008). *Making the most of supervision.* Australian Association of Social Workers Victorian Branch Newsletter: Victorian Social Work (AASW Ltd.).

Noble C & Irwin J (2009). Social work supervision: an exploration of the current challenges in a rapidly changing social, economic and political environment. *Journal of Social Work,* 9: 345–58.

O'Connor I, Wilson J & Setterlund D (2003). *Social work and welfare practice.* (4th edn). Frenchs Forest, NSW: Pearson Education Australia.

Pack M (2009). Clinical supervision: an interdisciplinary review of literature with implications for reflective practice in social work. *Reflective Practice,* 10(5): 657–68.

Rothman J (2000). *Stepping out into the field.* Massachusetts, USA: Allyn & Bacon.

Sussman T, Bogo M & Globerman J (2007). Field instructor perceptions in group supervision. *The Clinical Supervisor,* 26(1): 61–80.

Townsend R & Jordan K (2010). *Student social work field supervision: learning opportunities offered by group and peer learning.* La Trobe University, Australia: Social Work & Social Policy (Bendigo), La Trobe Rural Health School, Faculty of Health Sciences.

Tsui M (2008). Adventures in re-searching the features of social work supervision in Hong Kong. *Qualitative Social Work 2008*, (7): 349–62.

Wilson J (2000). *Approaches to supervision in fieldwork*. In L Cooper & L Briggs (Eds). *Fieldwork in the human services* (pp26–40). St Leonard, NSW: Allen & Unwin.

Zeira A & Schiff M (2010). Testing group supervision in fieldwork training for social work students. *Research on Social Work Practice*, 20(4): 427–34.

CHAPTER SIXTEEN

USE OF SELF IN PRACTICE: A FRAMEWORK FOR INTEGRATING PERSONAL AND PROFESSIONAL KNOWLEDGE

Jay Marlowe and Shirley-Ann Chinnery

Providing assignments that promote critical learning opportunities and encourage social work students to reflectively engage with 'self' whilst on placement represents a core component of field work education. This chapter discusses how the Eastern-informed practice of mindfulness can help students attune to connections between the diverse elements of knowledge through a 'use of self' assignment. By incorporating how students conceptualise the linkages between theory, self and practice, this assignment promotes the critical inquiry of their field placement experiences that encourages them to consider the complexities of social work praxis alongside their own histories and background. A framework for the development of such an assignment is presented as a means of facilitating students to integrate the use of embodied knowledge (i.e. of mind, body and emotion). Learning to use awareness mindfully offers a promising approach for both domestic and international students looking to cultivate a more informed use of professional and personal self in field education contexts.

在实践中运用自我：怎样将个人和专业知识相结合

鼓励学生利用学习机会和进行自我反思。本章讨论如何
运用东方思维的正念来帮助学生理解一个关于自我反思

的方法。学生需要将各种社工理论知识与自我反思相结合进行联想分析。

本章讨论如何实践东方思维的正念来帮助学生理解一个关于自我反思的方法。学生需要将各种社工理论知识与自我反思相结合进行联想分析。通过思考理论，自我，和实践的联系，学生将会更好的理解他们在实习过程中所会面对的问题。同时，鼓励学生用自己的人生阅历来透析实习中遇到的复杂情况。作者同时会提出一个理论框架。这个理论框架将自我反思（例如，头脑，身体和情感）和所学的理论和知识相结合。学习谨慎地运用认知意识可帮助本地和海外学生在实习教育的环境中塑造出一个更专业，更个性化的社工形象。

実践における個人の役立て方：個人としての知識および専門家としての知識を統合する枠組

現場実習の期間中、批判的に学習する機会を促進させるという課題を課し、ソーシャルワークを学ぶ学生に対し、「自分自身」と向き合うことを助長させることは、現場教育の核となる構成要素であるといえる。本章は、東洋の洗練された配慮のある実践を、「自分の役立て方」についての課題を通して、どのように学生が知識の中の多様な要素間の関係をつなぎ、調和させるのに役立たせていくのかについて議論する。学生がどのように理論と自身、そして実践とをつなげ概念化するのかということを統合することによって、この課題は、彼らの経歴や素生に寄り添いつつ、複雑なソーシャルワークの実践について彼らが思慮深くなり自信がつけられるような現場実習の経験に対し批判的な疑問を促す。そのような課題を発展させるための枠組は、学生に、一体となった知識（精神、身体、感情など）の役立て方を統合するということを学生に促進させる手段として現れている。注意深く自己認識を行い

学習することは、現場教育の背景において専門家およ
び個人の、より洗練された役立て方の開拓、発見を期
待しうる方法を提供する。

실습에 있어서의 자신의 사용 : 개인적이고 전문적인 지
식 통합을 위한 기초 작업

비평적인 학습 기회를 장려하는 과제를 제공하는것은, 사
회복지과 학생들에게 '자신'의 참여를 반추하게하는 한
편, 현장배치는 현장 실습 교육의 핵심 요소이다.

이 장에서는, 동양에서 알려진 주의 깊은 인식의 실행이,
학생들로 하여금 '자아의 사용' 과제를 통하여, 어떻게 지
식의 다양한 요소들간에 연결 되는지를 이해할수 있게 도
와준다. 어떻게 학생들이, 이론과 자신 그리고 실습 사이
의 연계를 개념화하는 것을 채택함으로써, 이과제는 그
들의 현장 배치 경험에서의 비평적인 탐구를 촉진 할 것
이며, 이러한 경험들은, 그들 자신의 역사와 배경과 함께,
사회 복지 실행의 복잡성을 고려하게 할 것이다. 이러한
과제의 개발을 위한 기초 작업은, 구체화된 지식 (마음과
신체와 감정의 예)의 사용을 통합 하도록, 학생들을 촉진
하는 수단으로써 제공된다. 주의 깊은 인식을 사용하기
위한 학습은, 교육 내용에 관한 분야에 있어서, 보다 많이
알려진 전문가적이며 개인적인 활용 방안을 발전시키려
고 노력하는 국내외 학생들에게, 또 다른 하나의 접근 방
법을 제공한다.

This chapter introduces a 'use of self' assignment for social work students preparing for a field placement. We construe 'self' as being the
subjective identity of the practitioner which comprises a number of key
considerations such as one's developmental history, personal qualities,
social location (relating to status and power) and cultural background.
This awareness is increasingly important in the Asia-Pacific region as
the migration and movement of people highlights the rich diversities

represented across ethnicity, culture, spirituality, world view, gender, sexuality and many others. Thus, becoming aware of how these attributes and histories shape one's perspectives and actions is an imperative for critical self-reflection in social work education and practice (Dewane 2006; Heydt & Sherman 2005; Reupert 2009; Ward 2010; Wong 2004). Urdang (2010) notes the difficulties that students encounter in learning the 'how' of critical self-reflection in the absence of practical methods for achieving it. She argues that social work educators can remedy this circumstance by developing teaching strategies that equip students with an accessible understanding of critical reflection. In response, this chapter introduces a 'use of self' assignment that was developed to find practical ways of encouraging critical self-reflection in field education contexts. This assignment is informed through mindfulness practice and is further discussed once the challenges of fostering reflective practice in social work education have been presented.

THE CHALLENGES OF REFLECTIVE PRACTICE IN SOCIAL WORK

Creating and preserving a space for critically reflective practice is a core component of professional social work. However, numerous writers now recognise that the volume of work, time pressures, resource deficits, and procedural demands common to social work practice environments often mean that the space for reflective practice is compromised by the perpetual demand to do more and more (Gibbs 2001; Harrison & Ruch 2007). Mandell (2008, p240) highlights this practice reality in her observation that 'outside of social work educational settings, most practitioners have little access to truly useful guidance concerning self-monitoring and reflection'. As a result of the organisational constraints confronted in practice, reflective supervision is regularly displaced in favour of a task-focused instruction. Common to this focus is the sacrifice of professional process in deference to the demands of organisational compliance. Such supervisory oversight can limit a student's opportunity to integrate and apply their use of professional knowledge in field placement contexts.

These developments have worrying implications for social work students as the supervisory relationship is meant to provide the facilitated space to assist them to develop their professional understanding of practice (Beddoe & Worrall 1997). In the absence of reflective supervision, students may come to mistakenly identify organisational procedure for professional practice (Ruch 2007). Observing practitioners engage with practice in ritualised, prescriptive and task-focused ways can further entrench this perception. Similar findings about the limits of incorporating and fostering reflective practices within field contexts have been reported by other educators (Bower 2005; Ruch 2007; Urdang 2010, Ward 2008). In fact, some of our students' past evaluations of their field education experience have questioned the need for professional education that involves critical self-reflection given the high level of task-based requirements (i.e. just do what you're required to do).

Whilst there are clear challenges in these contexts, there is also broad literature in social work education that acknowledges the necessity of reflective practice (D'Cruz et al. 2007; Redmond 2006; Ruch 2002; Urdang 2010; Yip 2006). Reflective processes are generally understood to involve the conscious critique of one's practice experience in order to obtain new insights about one's actions and the ability to apply this information to future social work practice. Integral to this process is the critical examination of one's own assumptions, beliefs, areas of privilege, biases and perspectives on knowledge. Each of these aspects is vital to facilitating the development of professional and personal awareness (Chow et al. 2011; Fook & Askeland 2007; Rossiter 2007).

A fundamental supposition within much of the (primarily Western-based) literature on critical self-reflection is that students will come to understand the reflective process through rational means (i.e. through the use of reasoning and logic). Whilst conceptual maps are helpful guides to orient students to the importance of reflective practices (for example, see Dempsey et al. 2001; Fook & Askeland 2007; Redmond 2004, 2006), these models often fall short of being able to represent the non-rational components of experience itself (i.e. tacit assumptions, intuitive insights, and attention to other sensory feedback). Mindfulness has the ability to transcend this boundary as its focus enables people to make use of the wisdom that emanates from direct experience (i.e. arising from mind, body and emotion). The experiential process associated with mindfulness practice therefore makes it a useful teaching tool in developing students' capacity for self-awareness of mind (what they are thinking), body (what physical sensations they are experiencing) and emotion (what they are feeling). Learning to use this information in conjunction with formal professional knowledge supports the development of practice wisdom. Practice wisdom is a core component of critical self-reflection and is a much needed attribute for the conscious use of self in social work practice.

MINDFULNESS IN SOCIAL WORK EDUCATION

Interest in the application of mindfulness approaches and perspectives to social work practice has grown rapidly in recent years. Mindfulness derives from the Eastern philosophic tradition of Buddhism, dating back some 2,500 years (Nhat Hahn 1987). It is conceptualised as an embodied practice which involves paying attention to emergent sensory information across the domains of cognition, sensation and emotion – all in the present moment (Kabat-Zinn 2003). Meditation is a key element of its practice. For the full potential of mindfulness to be realised, it must be experienced and not simply conceptualised as an intellectual activity (Hick 2009a; Siegel et al. 2009).

Social work is a relative newcomer to the use of mindfulness. The benefits from mindfulness-based activities such as thought clarity, lowered levels of emotional reactivity and an enhanced sense of wellbeing have generated considerable interest amidst professional communities (Brown & Ryan 2003; Carmody & Baer 2008; Christopher 2006; Dorjee 2010; Linehan 1993; Siegel et al. 2009). Over time, professionals in these contexts have conceptualised numerous mindfulness practices into discrete teachable skills for secular use (Baer & Krietemeyer 2006). To date, social work educators have drawn on the skills of mindfulness to promote the following:

1. Fostering critical consciousness in students (Hick & Furlotte 2009; Wong 2004)

2. Developing an array of clinical aptitudes and attitudes (Gockel 2010; Hick & Bien 2008)

3. Enhancing professional identity (Birnbaum 2005; Mishna & Bogo 2007)

4. Initiating self-care as a professional necessity (Berceli & Napoli 2006; Birnbaum 2007; Birnbaum & Birnbaum 2008; Ying 2009)

5. Use as pedagogy (Lynn 2010; Sherman & Siporin 2008)

6. Critique of inclusion in social work (Debaene 2009)

7. Facilitate reflective practice in emergent practitioners (Chinnery & Beddoe in press).

The value of mindfulness is that it provides students with an experiential approach to learning and a practical way of interpreting it. Experience is known to be a powerful constituent of the learning process (Boud et al. 1985; Schön 1987). Mindfulness offers a bridge to perception that guides novice learners in processing experience (internal and external) through noticing and paying attention to mind, body and emotion. This integrative function supports the growth of another developmentally significant and contemplative form of *praxis* – the ability to reflect on action in practice and use this learning to inform future practice (Schön 1987).

The awareness skills of mindfulness can foster praxis by encouraging students to be actively self-aware through the development of an 'observing mind' (Siegel 2009). This entails the ability to be actively engaged in a practice event while at the same time bringing one's awareness to the activity as it unfolds. Acquiring an observing mind involves the use of a number of mindfulness-awareness skills which require students to incorporate a stance of curiosity and non-judgemental attitude to their experiences (Germer et al. 2005). Students are encouraged to suspend the judgement of their feelings, thoughts or sensations in favour of remaining aware of what is happening for them in the present moment. This process is accomplished by having students notice what thoughts, feelings or sensations are immediately present during the designated activity. Learning to apply this skill in the field may contribute to greater levels of student resilience as it offers an opportunity to orient oneself to practice in an engaged and proactive manner. This outcome is an indisputable benefit for practitioners entering the social service sector given the high rates of attrition and burnout associated with the profession (Collins 2008; Kim & Lee 2009; Littlechild 2008; Lloyd et al. 2002; Stanley et al. 2007).

Learning to integrate conceptual knowledge related to theoretical approaches and models alongside one's emergent sensory experiences (of mind, body and emotion) through the skills of mindfulness offers students a practical platform from which to launch their skills of reflective practice. It is within these learning contexts that a 'use of self' assignment has been developed to address the challenges of practically incorporating critical reflection as an educational and professional fieldwork tool.

USE OF SELF ASSIGNMENT

The 'use of self' assignment template was designed in response to addressing the challenges of fostering student self-awareness in field education contexts. Over the course of a field placement, students are required to complete four of these assignments. Doing this assignment multiple times in relation to their different social work experiences (i.e. conducting assessments, interviewing, working with colleagues, supervision or engaging with the community) provides a framework for students to think about their personal and professional selves on increasingly practical and conceptual levels. The opportunity to complete several of these assignments also evidences student progression of the use of self throughout the field placement. Our intention in having the students use the template that follows is to help them construct a framework for professional practice that is available for their continued use, during and beyond, the practicum. The template is divided into seven sections.

Use of self in practice template

1	The event or situation (briefly) described is (250–500 words)
2	I have chosen this event or situation (internal dialogue, immediate reaction, etc.) because (250–500 words)
3	The aspects of 'self' I brought to:
	a the preparatory phase of practice were
	b the intervention/interaction phase were
	c the adjournment/ending phase were (150–300 words)
4	The aspects of self that I need to make more 'use' of in performing the following practice tasks: (500–800 words)
	a technical
	b conceptual
	c interpersonal
	d intrapersonal
	e reflexivity
5	I have reflected upon the impacts of this situation in relation to … (myself, agency, client, etc.) (150–300 words)
6	a The aspect(s) of the practice task that most challenged me, personally and professionally were
	b The aspects of the practice task that I felt most confident about, personally and professionally were: (150–300 words)
7	The plan I need to develop to engage with the challenges I have identified is: (50–150 words).

The seven sections of the 'use of self' assignment are now discussed below. Each part of the template is discussed separately to further outline the expectations associated with this assignment. Brief student excerpts from this assignment are used to illustrate how they critically and reflectively evaluated their field placement experiences. These excerpts are anonymised and three students were selected for their insightful reflections whilst on placement. They have provided their consent to share this written material.

Part one: discussing the event or situation

The first part of the assignment is where the student briefly outlines the particular practice event or situation. The intent of this section is for the reader to be able have a context to critically assess the student's learning and reflective work associated with the event.

Part two: why was this event chosen?

This section is where the student articulates why they have chosen this particular event or situation and why it was meaningful for them. It is also here that the student can record their immediate thoughts and reactions to this situation. For example, did the student feel upset or excited? Did the experience involve anger, deep reflection or ambivalence? Students may also note how this experience (if relevant) relates to their own personal and family history. There can be a number of reasons why a particular event was chosen as it could have stimulated new reflections about:

1. How supervision can be effectively used whilst in the field

2. The relationship of theory to practice

3. How professional practice can impact upon one's personal life

4. The identification of and need to unpack previously unexplored assumptions.

Thus, students identify with their field experience and note why this focus is important to them and their development as an emerging social work practitioner. The student's narrative below is a case in point. It relates to the place of ethics when there was a tension between supporting client self-determination and the awareness that doing so could compromise the professional responsibility of ensuring a client's wellbeing:

> My initial reaction to this case and its ongoing development was to
> observe as carefully as possible but withhold my analysis. My immediate
> reaction [to the event] pertained to the ethical dilemmas it raised. The

tension was provided in retaining the client and family as service users, versus administering professionally correct opinion and potentially saving the client's life. This could and would be a very difficult and volatile procedure. I wondered whether from a social work perspective, with an emphasis on human rights and structural equality, we had a mandatory claim to be very honest in our dealings 'what we believed we knew'. This is because the onus of professional knowledge and its distribution is a social work issue as knowledge ownership concurs with power ... Were we as practitioners involved in the 'just profession' still responsible to be honest with information and therefore with the notions of power? I think so, though many of my other colleagues did not.

The student's description of the event suggests that she is positioning herself mindfully by adopting a stance of curiosity and non-judgement (i.e. being inquisitive about this experience without judging it). Her stated intention to withhold analysis further indicates that she is consciously working at *being* an impartial witness of the experience. To achieve this outcome, the student needed to orient to the experience with an open and flexible use of mind. The questions raised by the student as she dialogues her experience capably reflect this quality of mind. Moreover, her discussion demonstrates that as she grapples with significant issues around the practice event, she is learning to integrate both personal process and professional knowledge in practice. In realising this outcome the student has drawn on a number of interlocking mindfulness skills and attitudes.

Part three: recognising the 'aspects of self' from this event

The focus of this section is for students to demonstrate how they engaged with the particular event over a period of time. It is also here that students are encouraged to consciously identify the diverse forms of experience relating to mind, body and emotion as previously discussed. The preparatory phase involves students discussing how they prepared for the event. This may include reading the relevant literature about the work in which the agency specialises, doing mindfulness exercises to prepare for an interpersonal interaction with a client and/ or writing about what they were feeling, thinking and doing. The intervention/interaction phase requires the student to conduct a similar analysis about what they were feeling, thinking and doing during the event as it was happening (again relating to mind, body and emotion). The adjournment/ending phase requires the student to document the professional and personal impacts that they experienced following the selected event.

As noted earlier, teaching students to access multiple levels of awareness is important as there is a danger that action (i.e. *doing*) becomes the sole focus of intervention in the practice context with little, if any, time given to reflective practice (i.e. *being*). Another student's comment below demonstrates that she is starting to develop a sense of professional identity which involves the integration of both personal and professional qualities and skills.

> During the interaction phase with the client, I used both personal and professional aspects of self. The personal aspects that I brought with me into this situation included an open and flexible attitude, being honest with myself and the client, being non-judgemental and willing to get to know the client. On a personal level, I could appreciate the client's anxiety and her craving to use drugs in a social setting. My own difficulties in the past with anxiety helped me empathize with the client's situation. I also believe very deeply that people can and do change. I also strongly believe in the efficacy of mindfulness as both a tool to assist people with their difficulties and a means to facilitate the process of change. Reflecting on this situation I have discovered that I believe that my personality and life experience can be used in a positive way to facilitate change without transference necessarily occurring and interfering professionally. I think this belief underpinned my whole interaction with the client, which was moderated by my mindfulness and professional use of boundaries and ethics. Although I did experience confusion about how best to work with this situation, my trust in people's innate insight into their own lives and difficulties helped me to relax and allow the situation to unfold.

This student has actively used a number of the awareness skills of mindfulness (e.g. flexible use of attention, present moment focus, non-judgement, patience, kindness to oneself and curiosity). Using the three focal points of the preparatory, intervention/interaction and the ending phases helps students to identify how they use their personal and professional selves over time.

Part four: the 'aspects' of self that need more use in the associate practice task

This section is divided into five distinct areas related to practice and helps students to unpack and identify what, in particular, needs greater attention for better future practice. The following areas are briefly defined below with an expectation that students include relevant social work literature to support their analysis.

- *Technical* – Students attempt to identify the specific practice skills that need further work or examination in this section. Examples of the technical might include asking different types of questions (open ended, scaling, circular, etc.) in an interview. Much of this section would be focused on particular micro skills that might need further refining and practice. Secondly, the technical may also relate to the need for greater organisational knowledge such as knowing more about particular policies, procedures and agency history.
- *Conceptual* – this section encourages students to articulate what theory/model or approach helps to inform how the student responded to the event or situation and how this theory (or a different one) might be used in ways to better ensure that theory and practice are explicitly linked.
- *Interpersonal* – What aspects of self does the student need to make more use of in order to improve the interpersonal encounter with individual clients, families, groups or communities. Examples could include empathic processes where students need to try to understand *and* communicate this understanding to clients to check if they are correct. It could also include a discussion on the awareness of one's body language, moving to different phases of an interview or how to discuss a particularly taboo topic with a client.
- *Intrapersonal* – This area requires that students identify what they were feeling in the interpersonal interaction and how these feelings

could impact upon their work with clients. This exploration includes a discussion on their emotions, bodily awareness and cognitions and how they can use this awareness to inform future practice.

- *Reflexivity* – This section is related to the intrapersonal but more specifically encourages students to relate self to knowledge by getting them to think about how their own socially constructed meanings (on homelessness, addiction, abortion, illness, happiness, family violence, etc.) can influence how they interpret and respond to client situations.

Having these five different areas encourages students to think about the complexity associated with social work practice. It means thinking about how particular social work practice micro skills (technical) can be concurrently examined within one's own personal, social and cultural backgrounds (which may include intrapersonal and reflexive examinations). Once students start writing about these five different areas, they often find linkages between them and this highlights the need for an integrated analysis from their experiential encounters.

PART FIVE: THINKING ABOUT THE IMPACTS OF THIS SITUATION

This section focuses more specifically on empathy and getting the student to reflect how this situation has had an impact on the agency, client system and themselves. Students are encouraged to try to understand a client's and/or the agency's perspective. This student's excerpt about working with family violence illustrates how being present to one's personal experience can lead to self-awareness:

> When I first walked into the room I was shocked that someone could hurt this beautiful woman because she was heavily pregnant. I wondered about counter-transference having been a mother myself. Was I over-identifying with this young lady? I told myself, 'Ok now you know you are having these thoughts and feelings'. I noticed them and anchored to my breath and sat listening.

In this instance, the student used her personal insights to proactively make sound use of self and empower her client in a difficult practice situation. In broader contexts, another student demonstrates the complexity of social practice when personal, professional and multi-disciplinary systems coincide:

> As a social worker, I felt more intensely about the agency's responsibility with the knowledge about the family's problem than the other represented professions. This is because I also see it as ethical that we do all that we can to genuinely assist the client in terms of being client centred. Other professionals were more ambivalent saying: 'it's the family's problem'. I voiced my concerns in this area and feel that was my responsibility to share my perspective, without posing a problem to team equilibrium or culture. I think that many who have heard my thoughts may not totally agree with me but at least they can see some sense to them. I have used the team feedback to continue to explore both my understanding of social work in a multidisciplinary team, and, the meaning and relevance of a social justice framework for practitioners today.

The student's response to the experience is thoughtfully considered and non-reactive. She adopts a learning stance from which to review her experience further and identifies a range of informational sources to support this exploration. Her development in professional use of self is unmistakable. She has been able to contribute to a team discussion, maintain emotional regulation in the face of disagreement with her perspective and has gone on to explore this experience reflectively and reflexively.

Part six: recognising challenges and strengths

This section is an opportunity for students to further signal any areas related to professional practice that would benefit from ongoing development and importantly, to acknowledge the strengths and what went well in the experiential event.

> Personally, I felt most confident in the intrapersonal task relating to my openness and availability which allowed me to connect with the client.

> I didn't know what would happen but I felt confident that my openness would be helpful for both myself and others. Professionally, I felt most confident in being able to use mindfulness; both for myself where it helped me remain non-judgemental of the client and, also, as a technique I could offer the client to help her work with her anxiety.

A critical part of identifying effective social work practice is not just being aware of what did not go well or what needs to be improved but also to highlight how the student's emerging professional skills have helped work towards positive outcomes. This student's comment attests to this claim.

Part seven: the plan for future practice

It is here that students need to articulate how they will take the particular practice experience and the ensuing reflective exercises built into this assignment to inform how they will use this information to guide their praxis in future social work encounters. The student's text below illustrates this process:

> To help integrate my professional boundaries with my personality, I need to continue to practice working with them. Spending time at this field placement will provide me with this practice opportunity. I have a strong feeling that this personal/professional balance will be one that I will work with my whole career. On a practical level, I need to continue to revise the code of ethics to help myself be clear what my professional boundaries are. Over the next week, I will revise the code of ethics at the end of each day and reflect on how well I incorporated them into practice to see clearly where my personality and professional boundaries meet and separate. It will also help me to see my inner and outer world and detach from my biases so that I can create space between myself and what is best for the client.

Before students write their 'use of self' assignments

Before students go out on their field placement and write the first 'use of self' assignment, they are prepared for undertaking this work in the context of a safe and supportive classroom. In this teaching environment, students learn that it is both appropriate and expected that they engage with their prior assumptions and experiences to realise that the personal and professional can sometimes be powerfully linked. Mindfulness skills have been used to support this learning.[1] These skills assist students to deconstruct what is happening within themselves (mind, body and emotion) to be aware of how self impacts on others and how the students themselves are also impacted (both personally and professionally) through interpersonal encounters.

One such preparation for field practice students is the construction of their own genogram, among other preparatory activities. The genogram is a well-used social work tool which involves the diagrammatic representation of one's family of origin (Hartman 1978). Typically the structure incorporates at least three generations to assist in the detection of a family's structure, composition and relational patterns and themes (McGoldrick et al. 2008). Family of origin work is an essential process in helping students to critically think about their own assumptions, strengths, resiliencies and vulnerabilities. These personal aspects of self inform the relational skills and qualities an emergent practitioner will take with them into practice (Ruch et al. 2010). Much of this self-knowledge often operates beyond a conscious awareness, but it may exert a powerful influence in the development of working relationships with clients, colleagues and others in the wider systems of practice.

The use of genograms with students prior to going out on a field placement can also help raise their awareness about their own personal, relational, developmental and social histories. This groundwork provides the foundational setting for students to begin thinking about their personal and professional selves in field education contexts. Students are actively encouraged to consciously reflect on their genogram work as it relates to their interactions with relational partners in the field and to consider this information critically. This may include questioning:

---

1 An earlier small pilot project was carried out with ethics approval trialling the use of these skills in the classroom. Some preliminary results from this research have been published (Chinnery & Beddoe in press).

1. How might my experiences, family background and personality influence how I engaged with this person/people?

2. What assumptions, feelings, attitudes and thoughts were present?

3. How did I position myself in the relationship with my client?

As students become increasingly comfortable and skilled to use self-reflection in the classroom environment, it provides a valuable tool for evaluating one's actions in a field placement.

DISCUSSION: THE 'USE OF SELF' ASSIGNMENT

The 'use of self' assignment was developed to assist students in the complex exercise of integrating theory, practice and reflection whilst in the field. Scaffolding their learning in this manner is important as opportunities for facilitated reflection in field education contexts are often compromised due to the constraints endemic to the supervisory field relationship as previously discussed. The Eastern-informed practice of mindfulness can help students to realise how their personal and professional selves interact with the different client systems of individuals, families, groups and communities. This awareness necessitates an ability to integrate the use of embodied knowledge of the mind (what one is thinking), body (what one's senses are experiencing) and emotion (what one is feeling). Having this awareness provides the student with a greater ability to monitor self and evaluate how he/she influences and is affected by interpersonal interactions.

The need for integrated experiential learning is the primary focus of the 'use of self' assignment. It is often here that it becomes possible for students to envision what family systems theory looks like when working with a family or how strengths-based approach can practically be applied when working in the area of addictions. The field placement experience provides an opportunity to realise how the micro-skills of interviewing (establishing rapport, asking open questions, conducting assessments, etc.) can be used in relation to each student who has their own unique personality, cultural background and reflexive positioning. This assignment therefore encourages students to locate their own social and cultural backgrounds (and the meanings embedded within them). The active 'use of self' is predicated on the development of conscious awareness. Mindfulness practices that inform the 'use of self' assignment cultivate student capacity for critical self-reflection by teaching them to be present to their experience in each moment as it unfolds. Using attention in this way leads to the development of an expanded awareness which facilitates insights about self, others and the broader environment that may otherwise go unnoticed. Conditioning one's awareness, in this manner, is a first step toward growth of contemplative skills for practice (Mishna & Bogo 2007).

The 'use of self' assignment sets out a practical framework that students can use to scaffold the experiential skills of mindfulness to advance their development in the skills of reflective practice for the field. Repeated use of this framework enables the student to embed a structure for reflecting on the 'use of self' that they can subsequently experiment within their ongoing pursuit of critically reflective practice. It encourages students to engage with their experiences from a stance of curiosity, and as much as possible, to learn to reflect on their thoughts, sensations and feelings from a non-judgemental perspective. These aptitudes instil a disposition of open-mindedness and self-compassion (Ying 2009).

Novice practitioners need an abundance of each of these qualities in order to support critical inquiry and to be kind to self in the learning process (Hutcherson et al. 2008). As with all new skill learning, frustration, self-doubt, anxiety, scepticism, (in some cases) anger and irritation at the difficulties associated with critical self-reflection, are regular student experiences. The student voice below signifies some of the difficulties experienced in early practices.

> I found this very difficult, I had a lot of thoughts running around about how I 'should' be breathing, how I 'should' be sitting and all the other things I 'should be doing'.

Learning to *be* in the present moment is one of the initial challenges encountered by students as they come into contact with the reflective experience (Chinnery & Beddoe in press). This discovery provides an important reflexive lesson as it brings students, through direct experience, to an awareness of the qualitative difference between the modes of 'being' and 'doing'. Moreover, mindfulness practices can be used at any time in practice because all that is required for this activity is to be able to connect to the present moment (Hick 2009b). The student voice below demonstrates this development:

> To become more aware of how the use of self impacts our relationships, we need to regularly reflect on our own individual practice. Through this experience I now have a much better understanding of why we need to do so much work as professionals around our personal use of self in practice and also why we need to regularly critically reflect on our performance in a way that is non judgemental and being kind to ourselves.

Becoming clear about one's own history and its impact on self better places student social workers in a position to be able to distinguish their own 'experience' from that of their clients. Professional relationships are benefited by this explorative work as it reduces the potential for the occurrence of counter-transference (Flaskas & Amaryll 1996) and may include the further development of healthy boundaries in practice relationships. It also promotes social awareness as students come to realise that their perspectives are culturally embedded and that their social location related to status and power are powerful constituents in the formation of self. Such insights can support students in their realisations about how the self of the practitioner is shaped by both developmental and contextual histories and how these histories in turn may maintain, perpetuate or trigger conditions of oppression/discrimination in the practice context. Whether the insights made are minor or significant, they are facilitated through the expanded awareness developed in conjunction with the 'use of self' assignment. These levels of awareness herald the foundational steps towards the inclusion of reflective practice as a career long professional activity.

Conclusion

As social work practitioners and educators in the numerous contexts, countries and cultures that we find ourselves, we are professionally required to find ways of ensuring that critical reflection and self-awareness are given the attention they warrant. The importance of reflective processes is paramount in the increasing context of limited supervision opportunities for both students and practitioners. It is in this environment that mindfulness approaches provide students with the necessary awareness skills in preparation for professional practice.

Learning to use one's growing awareness in action is an important step for the active 'use of self' in the field. As students become familiar with mindfulness approaches (which inform the 'use of self' assignment), they are enabled to understand that their knowledge, beliefs, assumptions and experiences are affected by multiple influences. This level of analysis maybe further extended to include an examination of personal experiences, social relations and structural entities specific to a given time, place and context. The 'use of self' assignment provides a practical approach that can help shift student perceptions and insights in useful ways as they come to realise how their thoughts, feelings and sensations can impact on both themselves and those they work alongside. The importance of this student awareness in field education contexts signals the need for further research that can greater inform our pedagogical knowledge to fostering critical self-reflection.

The 'use of self' assignment provides a practical framework for students to integrate professional and personal knowledge. The Eastern-informed practice of mindfulness offers an approach to address this learning and presents an opportunity for social work educators across the Asia-Pacific region to consider how it might be best applied in their particular contexts. By incorporating ways for students to conceptualise the linkages between theory, self and practice, this assignment promotes the critical inquiry of their field placement experiences, assisting them to consider the complexities of social work praxis alongside their own histories and backgrounds.

Acknowledgements

We would like to thank Liz Beddoe and Catherine Deeney for providing helpful comments in the development of this chapter We would also like to recognise Tricia Bingham for her assistance in the library, Sue Osborne for her editorial assistance and three anonymous social work students for their generosity in sharing excerpts from their 'use of self' assignments.

References

Baer R & Krietemeyer J (2006). Overview of mindfulness and acceptance-based treatment approaches. In R Baer (Ed). *Mindfulness-based treatment approaches: clinician's guide to evidence base and applications* (pp3–27). San Diego, California: Elsevier Academic Press.

Beddoe L & Worrall J (1997). The future of fieldwork in a market economy. *Advances in Social Work and Welfare Education*, 2(1): 54–63.

Berceli D & Napoli M (2006). A proposal for a mindfulness-based trauma prevention program for social work professionals. *Complementary Health Practice Review*, 11(3): 153–65.

Birnbaum L (2007). The use of mindfulness training to create an 'accompanying place' for social work students. *Social Work Education*, 1–16, doi:10.1080/02615470701538330.

Birnbaum L (2005). Connecting to inner guidance: mindfulness meditation and transformation of professional self-concept in social work students. *Critical Social Work Journal*, 6(2). [Online]. Available: www.uwindsor.ca/criticalsocialwork [Accessed 16 May 2011].

Birnbaum L & Birnbaum A (2008). Mindful social work: from theory to practice. *Journal of Religion & Spirituality in Social Work: Social Thought*, 27(1): 87–104.

Boud D, Keogh R & Walker D (1985). Promoting reflection in learning: a model. In D Boud, R Keogh & D Walker (Eds). *Reflection: turning experience into learning* (pp18–40). New York, NY: Nicols Publishing Company.

Bower M (2005). Thinking under fire. In M Bower (Ed.), *Psychoanalytic theories* for social work practice (pp3–15). London, UK: Routledge.

Brown K & Ryan R (2003). The benefits of being present: mindfulness and its role in psychological well-being. Journal of Personality and Social Psychology, 84(4): 822–48.

Carmody J & Baer R (2008). Relationships between mindfulness practice and levels of mindfulness, medical and psychological symptoms and well-being in a mindfulness-based stress reduction program. Journal of Behavioral Medicine, 31(1): 23–33.

Chinnery SA & Beddoe L (in press) Taking active steps towards the competent use of self in social work. Advances in Social Work and Welfare, 13(1).

Chow AYM, Lam DOB, Leung GSM, Wong DFK & Chan BFP (2011). Promoting reflexivity among social work students: the development and evaluation of a programme. Social Work Education: The International Journal, 30(2): 141–56.

Christopher JC (2006). Teaching self-care through mindfulness practices: the application of yoga, meditation, and qigong to counsellor training. Journal of Humanistic Psychology, 46(4): 494–509.

Collins S (2008). Statutory social workers: stress, job satisfaction, coping, social support and individual differences. British Journal of Social Work, 38(6): 1173–93, doi:10.1093/bjsw/bcm047.

D'Cruz H, Gillingham P & Melendez S (2007). Reflexivity, its meanings and relevance for social work: a critical review of the literature. British Journal of Social Work, 37: 73–90.

Debaene R (2009). Mindful social work? Social Work & Society, 7(2). [Online]. Available: socialwork.net [Accessed 16 May 2011].

Dempsey M, Halton C & Murphy M (2001). Reflective learning in social work education: scaffolding the process. Social Work Education: The International Journal, 20(6): 631–41.

Dewane C (2006). Use of self: a primer revisited. Clinical Social Work Journal, 34(4): 543–58.

Dorjee D (2010). Kinds and dimensions of mindfulness: why it is important to distinguish them. Mindfulness, 1: 152–60.

Flaskas C (1996). Understanding the therapeutic relationship: using psychoanalytic ideas in the systemic context. In C Flaskas & A Perlesz (Eds). *The Therapeutic Relationship in Systemic Therapy* (pp35–52). London, UK: Karnac Books.

Fook J & Askeland G (2007). Challenges of critical reflection: 'nothing ventured, nothing gained'. *Social Work Education*, 26(5): 520–33.

Germer C, Siegel D & Fulton P (2005). *Mindfulness and psychotherapy*. New York, NY: Guilford Press.

Gibbs JA (2001). Maintaining front-line workers in child protection: a case for refocusing supervision. *Child Abuse Review*, 10(5): 323–35, doi:10.1002/car.707.

Gockel A (2010). The promise of mindfulness for clinical practice education. *Smith College Studies in Social Work*, 80: 248–68.

Harrison K & Ruch G (2007). Social work and the use of self: on becoming and being a social worker. In M Lymbery & K Postle (Eds). *Social work: a companion to learning* (pp40–50). London, UK: Sage Publications Ltd.

Hartman A (1978). Diagrammatic assessment of family relationships. *Social Casework*, 59:465–76.

Heydt M & Sherman N (2005). Conscious use of self: tuning the instrument of social work practice with cultural competence. *The Journal of Baccalaureate Social Work*, 10(2): 25–40.

Hick S (2009a). Mindfulness and social work: paying attention to ourselves, our clients, and society. In S. Hick (Ed). *Mindfulness and social work* (pp1–27). Chicago, Ill: Lyceum Books, Inc.

Hick S (2009b). *Mindfulness and social work*. Chicago: Lyceum.

Hick S & Bien T (2008). *Mindfulness and the therapeutic relationship*. New York, NY: The Guilford Press.

Hick S & Furlotte C (2009). Mindfulness and social justice approaches: bridging the mind and society in social work practice. *Canadian Social Work Review*, 26(1): 5–24.

Hutcherson C, Seppala E & Gross J (2008). Loving-kindness meditation increases social connectedness. *Emotion*, 8(5): 720–24.

Kabat-Zinn J (2003). Mindfulness-based interventions in context: past, present and future. *Clinical Psychology,* 10(2): 144–56.

Kim H & Lee SY (2009). Supervisory communication, burnout, and turnover intention among social workers in health care settings. *Social Work in Health Care,* 48(4): 364–85.

Linehan M (1993). *Cognitive behavioral treatment of borderline personality disorder.* New York, NY: Guilford Press.

Littlechild B (2008). Child protection social work: risks of fears and fears of risks – impossible tasks from impossible goals? *Social Policy & Administration,* 42(6): 662–75, doi:10.1111/j.1467-9515.2008.00630.x.

Lloyd C, King R & Chenoweth L (2002). Social work, stress and burnout: a review. *Journal of Mental Health,* 11(3): 255–65.

Lynn R (2010). Mindfulness in social work education. *Social Work Education: The International Journal,* 29(3): 289–304.

Mandell D (2008). Power, care and vulnerability: considering use of self in child welfare work. *Journal of Social Work Practice,* 22(2): 235–48.

McGoldrick M, Gerson R & Petry S (2008). *Genograms: assessment and interventions.* (3rd edn). New York: WW Norton & Company, Inc.

Mishna F & Bogo M (2007). Reflective practice in contemporary social work classrooms. *Journal of Social Work Education,* 43(3): 529–44, doi:10.5175/jswe.2007.200600001.

Nhat Hahn T (1987). *The miracle of mindfulness.* Boston, MA: Beacon.

Redmond B (2006). Starting as we mean to go on: introducing beginning social work students to reflective practice. In F Gardner (Ed). *Critical reflection in health and social care* (pp213–27). Berkshire: Open University Press.

Redmond B (2004). *Reflection in action.* Hants, England: Ashgate Publishing Limited.

Reupert A (2009). Students' use of self: teaching implications. *Social Work Education,* 28(7): 765–77.

Rossiter A (2007). Self as subjectivity: toward a use of self as respectful relations of recognition. In D Mandell (Ed). *Revisiting the use of self: questioning professional identities* (pp21–34). Toronto, Canada: Canadian Scholars Press.

Ruch G (2007). Reflective practice in contemporary child-care social work: the role of containment. *British Journal of Social Work*, 37: 659–80.

Ruch G (2002). From triangle to spiral: reflective practice in social work education, practice and research. *Social Work Education*, 21(2): 199–26.

Ruch G, Turney D & Ward A (2010). *Relationship-based social work: getting to the heart of practice*. London, UK: Jessica Kingsley Publishers.

Schön D (1987). *Educating the reflective practitioner*. San Francisco: Jossey Books.

Sherman E & Siporin M (2008). Contemplative theory and practice for social work. *Journal of Religion and Spirituality in Social Work*, 27(3): 259–74.

Siegel D (2009). *Mindsight: change your brain and your life*. Carlton North, Victoria: Scribe Publications Pty Ltd.

Siegel D, Germer K & Olendzki A (2009). *Clinical handbook of mindfulness*. New York, NY: Springer.

Stanley N, Manthorpe J & White M (2007). Depression in the profession: social workers' experiences and perceptions. *British Journal of Social Work*, 37: 281–98.

Urdang E (2010). Awareness of self: a critical tool. *Social Work Education*, 29(5): 523–38.

Ward A (2008). Beyond the instructional mode: creating a holding environment for learning about the use of self. *Journal of Social Work Practice*, 22(1): 67–83.

Ward A (2010). The use of self in relationship-based practice. In GT Ruch, D Turney & A Ward (Eds). *Relationship-based social work: getting to the heart of practice* (pp46–65). London, UK: Jessica Kingsley Publishers.

Wong YLR (2004). Knowing through discomfort: a mindfulness-based critical social work pedagogy. *Critical Social Work Journal*, 5(1).[Online]. Available: www.uwindsor.ca/criticalsocialwork [Accessed 16 May 2011].

Ying YW (2009). Contribution of self-compassion to competence and mental health in social work students. *Journal of Social Work Education*, 45(2): 309–23. doi:10.5175/JSWE.2009.200700072.

Yip S (2006). Self-reflection in reflective practice: a note of caution. *British Journal of Social Work*, 36: 777–88.

Chapter Seventeen

Social work student placements with external supervision: last resort or value-adding in Asia-Pacific?

Ines Zuchowski

In this chapter the contemporary global environments that frame social work education and supervision in field education are identified, with particular consideration to the specific challenges that some of the developing countries in the Asia-Pacific face. The role social work field education plays in socialising students into the profession, and the challenges this poses for placements with external social work supervision, are discussed. The benefits and complexities of these arrangements are explored, taking into account what might be learned from pondering the context of minority group social work students and the need to provide cultural safety in field education. Specifically, the context of social work education for Aboriginal and Torres Strait Islander students is considered. Consideration is given to the importance of establishing and maintaining the triad relationship of student, on-site and external supervisor. Finally, current approaches to field education with external supervision are reviewed and current and future research suggested.

以外部督导支持学生实习

这一章讨论了构建社会工作教育的全球环境以及实习教育中的督导，突出强调了亚太地区的一些发展中国家所面临的一些特殊挑战。此章还讨论了以外部督导为特色

的社会工作实习教育在使学生融合到他们的专业实习过程中所扮演的角色及其给学生在外部督导下进行实习所带来的挑战。考虑到少数族裔学生的文化背景并慎思他们在实习时可能需要的文化安全支持，本章对上述安排所带来的益处和复杂问题进行了探讨；尤其对土著居民和来自托雷斯海峡的学生的社会工作教育作了简要论述。这一章节同时考虑到建立并保持学生，内部督导者以及外部导师之间三元一体关系的重要性。最后，作者对当前以外部督导为特色的实习教育的一些做法进行了回顾并对目前和将来的研究提出了建议。

外部スーパービジョンにおける学生の実習支援

本章では、アジア太平洋の幾つかの発展途上国が直面する特定の困難に対する特有の考慮すべき事項とともに、ソーシャルワーク教育と現場教育におけるスーパービジョンを構成している現代のグローバル環境が確認されている。ソーシャルワーク現場教育が学生を専門家として養成していく中で担う役割や、外部のソーシャルワークのスーパービジョンを設けている現場実習によって引き起こされる困難が議論されている。これらの調整の利点と複雑性は、ソーシャルワークを学ぶマイノリティに属する学生の背景と現場教育における文化的な安全を提供することの必要性についてじっくりと考えることから何が学ばれるであろうかということを考慮して探求されている。とりわけ、アボリジニーやトレス海峡の島出身の学生のためのソーシャルワーク教育の背景を概説されている。学生、現場と外部スーパーバイザーとの三者関係を築き、維持していくことの重要性に対する検討が行われている。最後に、現在の外部スーパービジョンを利用した現場教育でのアプローチは再検討され、現在と将来の検討課題が提案された。

외부 감독을 포함하는 학생 배치 지원하기

이 장에서는, 현장(現場) 교육에 있어서의 사회 복지 교육과 감독의 체계를 결정 짓는 현대 글로벌 환경이 구체화 될것이며, 특히 아시아 태평양 개발 도상국의 특정한 도전들에 대해 각별한 관심을 기울였다. 학생들을 전문가로 인도함에 있어서, 사회복지 현장 교육의 역할과 외부 사회복지 감독이 따르는 현장 배치에 대한 도전 과제가 논의될것이다. 소수 민족 그룹 사회 복지과 학생들과 현장 교육에 있어서의 문화적인 안전의 필요성을 고려하면서, 이러한 여러가지 계획들의 이점(利點)과 복합성이 탐구될것이다. 특히 호주 원주민인 애보리진과 토리스 해협 섬나라 출신 학생들을 위한 사회 복지 교육의 내용이 소개될 것이다. 이장은 또한 학생, 현장, 외부 감독으로 구성되는 삼각 관계의 설정과 유지에 중점을 두었다. 마지막으로, 현재 시행되고 있는 외부감독과 함께하는 현장교육에 대한 접근 방법들이 재검토 되어질것이며, 현재와 미래를 위한 연구가 제안 될것이다.

In the field, students have the opportunity to test what they learn in the classroom; integrate theory with practice; evaluate the effectiveness of interventions; contend with the realities of social, political and economic injustice; strive for cultural sensitivity and competence; deliberate on the choices posed by ethical dilemmas; develop a sense of self in practice; and build a connection to and identify with the profession. (Lager & Robbins 2004, p3)

Professional social work associations across Asia-Pacific require social work students to be supervised by a qualified social worker during their field education placements. Different associations have different policies but in general this supervision is provided on-site by qualified social workers employed in the agency or by a worker external to the placement agency. Within social work field education the student–supervisor relationship is deemed vital and both social workers and non-social work staff participate in supporting social work student placements. Across the globe external supervision has been explored minimally in the field education literature.

Within the Australian professional context, it is common to view external supervision in social work field education as a last resort brought about by organisational and professional capacity constraints. Current economic and sociopolitical contexts often mean that staff contend with higher caseloads, increasingly cumbersome accountability requirements and limited resources. Simultaneously there is an increasing demand for social workers, a growing number of social work education programs and therefore an escalating requirement for student placements. In this chapter it is argued that the creative and careful use of external supervision brings a number of important benefits to this context. Rather than 'resorting' to external supervision only when there is an absence of a professionally qualified social work supervisor on site, external supervision is discussed as a worthy value-adding strategy for all placements. Specific benefits for the field education experiences of Australian Aboriginal and Torres Strait Islander students and for other minority group students across Asia-Pacific are provided to exemplify the valuable potential of external supervision.

In this chapter the importance of the supervisory relationship in field education is highlighted. Supervision concerns for placements with external supervision are identified and particular issues that might impact the triad relationship in these arrangements are explored. While issues concerning social work field education, external supervision and the needs of minority group students are discussed in the relevant literature, these have not been linked in literature, rather they are explored separately. External supervision can enhance current models of supervision in social work field education and particularly be used to address issues for culturally and linguistically diverse students. Overall, the chapter is guided by a concern that we need as a professional cohort ensure we respond culturally safely, competently and sensitively (AASW 2010a) to all people we are working with. Throughout, the terms field education, placement and practicum are used interchangeably.

THE CURRENT CONTEXT OF SOCIAL WORK EDUCATION

Globally, economic, social and political changes are impacting on social work practice, social work practitioners and social work organisations (Agllias 2010; Barton et al. 2005), and some of these have been identified as burnout, stress, large workload, limited resources and the impact of changing technologies (Lager & Robbins 2004). Lager and Robbins argue that the worsening of the economic situation of clients, the restructuring of the sector and the privatisation of social welfare services has resulted in students needing to cope with higher and more challenging case loads while on placement, without adequate preparation and support. Yet, with economic and sociopolitical pressures from global and local crises impacting on people lives, there is a high and growing demand for social work practitioners and subsequently field placements. Wayne, Bogo and Raskin (2006) argue that the expansion of social work programs and subsequent competition between tertiary institutions has meant that 'field placement personnel rush to contact agencies to take their students before a particular setting fills students from other schools' (p163). This competition for placements increases the pressures on field educators, university staff and students, and can impact on the provision of quality learning opportunities.

In the Asia-Pacific region there is expansive growth in the number of social work programs despite the fact that 'many countries developing such courses still face geographical isolation, limited access to mass communication technologies, barriers in languages and cultural differences as well as access to resources and stable government' (Midley 2000 cited in Noble 2009, p14). Noble (2009) outlines that social work programs in Asia-Pacific all started with shared common frameworks, and common core practice and knowledge as they were in the main developed in reference to Western curricula. This Western focus poses challenges for established programs across Asia-Pacific. Faledo, for instance, argues that 'Western cultural hegemony and cultural capital have both acted against the onset of culturally valid social work education' (2009, p152). Faleolo (2009) highlights the importance of including a culturally valid framework in social work education.

He outlines that while Pacific Islanders are culturally strong in their homelands, their cultural knowledge is seen as inferior when they migrate to other countries. He argues that, for example, Samoan-based knowledge and practice could be important to culturally competent social work elsewhere (Faledo 2009).

Accreditation requirements and social work programs are not standardised across Asia-Pacific. Currently, most countries have undergraduate university-based social work program with some master programs whereas 'Papua New Guinea, Samoa and other Pacific Island States have adopted a more vocational, non-university approach focusing on community development and work with NGOs on specific foci of their training' (Midgley 2000, cited in Noble 2009, p15). Field education is generally a component of all these models of social work education, but requirements differ depending on the country and program.

Increased competition between schools of social work, the lack of social work educated supervisors and remote and regional localities all contribute to difficulties in finding social work placements with on-site professional supervision in all regions of Asia-Pacific (Abram et al. 2000; Barton et al. 2005; Unger 2003). Similar issues and concerns were identified a decade ago in an international survey of social work schools about field education pointing to a shortage of qualified and trained field educators (Skolnik et al. 1999). Leung (2009), for example, considers social work education in China where field education is a recommendation in social work degrees, but not a compulsory component and outlines that many welfare organisations are without professionally qualified field educators for student placements. He suggests that without qualified field educators 'and formal collaboration or partnership between social work education programs and welfare organisations, social work students often find themselves unwelcome when on placement' (Leung 2009, p329). Nikku (2009) considers the context of social work education in Nepal. He argues that field education placements are of concern as students are viewed as volunteers rather than learners and that 'fieldwork supervisors are not trained in the social work education model and its reliance on professional supervision, hence there is a gap in guidance provided to students of social work' (Nikku 2009, p357). In Korea it appears that high standards of certification for field education supervisors may contribute to a shortage of qualified field supervisors and appropriate placement agencies (Yeom & Bae 2010). In Australia, the professional association requires students to be supervised by a qualified social worker during their placement (AASW 2010b). There is a requirement that field educators have at least two years professional experience and that social work schools provide them with training (AASW 2010b). A growing number of social work programs are competing for traditional social work placements. This, combined with some agencies and supervisors reluctance to take on students and pressure from some students to have placements in their place of employment leads to social work programs in Australia utilising external supervisors, as a last resort when on-site supervision is unavailable.

Research has identified the benefits of providing student placements for agencies and field educators (Barton et al. 2005). Positive outcomes associated with taking on students include the work students undertake, the field educator's own professional development including opportunities for critical reflection on practice, the representation of the agency, the potential to access new networks, and the possibility to screen for potential future employees (Barton et al. 2005). Lager and Robbins (2004) argue that social work field education can be a vehicle for practice wisdom to flow back into academia, but can also be used to support the restructure of clinical practice in interdisciplinary settings. This is supported by Unger (2003) who suggests that student placements can lead to the professionalisation of the social service community. Similarly, Rabally (1999) maintains that field education has the potential to promote organisational change and social development. Nevertheless, Rambally suggests that in developing countries a 'field for field education' may have to be established first (1999). This is further supported by Nikku (2009, p359), who states that 'Social work training in Nepal would play a vital role in the reconstruction processes of the country', but points out that social work training can be difficult when there are few social work educators, no social work courses outside the capital city, a lack of recognition of the profession, no accreditation body, the profession in its infancy and a need to Indigenise the profession. Nikku (2009) suggests that training paraprofessional social workers might be useful. The upshot is that social work and social work placements can be beneficial for supervisors, the service community and even the country, but that at times it is difficult to find appropriate field education opportunities supported by qualified social work supervisors.

Social work and Aboriginal and Torres Strait Islander people in Australia

In this context it needs to be acknowledged that in Australia social work may be an uneasy profession for Aboriginal and Torres Strait Islander Australians. First and foremost, there is the historical legacy, social work, the profession participated and was complicit in 'racist, patronising and unjust practices' (Green & Baldry 2008, p389). This historical legacy seems to be replicated in the present, at least to some extent. In Australia, for example, Aboriginal and Torres Strait Islander children are over-represented in the child protection system and current child protection intervention might negatively impact on the children and families involved. Western Australian Aboriginal child protection workers participating in a child protection summit, for instance, concluded that 'the lack of cultural healing programs and blindness to decision-makers to the importance and significance of cultural identity in child protection intervention could just be as harmful and traumatising to Aboriginal children as the experience of child abuse' (Bessarab & Crawford 2010, p191).

In Australia, we have to recognise that social work's commitment to social justice has not translated into structural equality for Aboriginal or Torres Strait Islander Australians (Green & Baldry 2008). Moreover, there is a lack of acknowledgement of social and community skills of Indigenous Australians and a dominant use of Euro-Western social work theories. Green and Baldry (2008) contend that while the AASW has set processes in motion to address some of this context, these are not sufficiently advanced and that it is important to build frameworks and theory relevant to Australian Aboriginal and Torres Strait Islander people. They argue that Indigenous ways of being and thinking need to be embraced in Australian social work and that 'it is vital that Australian social work education develops courses and practicums [sic] that reflect an understanding of Indigenous needs, approaches and world views' (Green & Baldry 2008, p396). This is supported by Gair, Thompson and Savage (2005) who recommend teaching a curricula 'that is relevant and meaningful for all Australian students and reflects acknowledgement of Indigenous ways of working and affirmation of the professional practice of Indigenous workers' (Gair et al. 2005, p61).

This needs further attention in research and discussion in the field education literature. Here it is proposed that external supervision models offer opportunities to teach and guide non-Indigenous supervisors without placing the Indigenous student into the role of the cultural expert, as is the current experience of some Indigenous students on placement (Gair et al. 2005). Later on in the chapter it is argued that external supervision can translate culturally valid ways of helping in a manner that can enrich generic social work practice. It can challenge inherently hostile colonising environments and introduce students to Aboriginal or Torres Strait Islander ways of helping as a valid part of their practice.

Supporting students in field education

The literature on field education overwhelmingly identifies placement as crucial to professional social work development (Barton et al. 2005; Unger 2003), 'a cornerstone for social work education' (Abram et al. 2000) and a critical transition point towards professional practice (Patford 2000). Field education plays an integral part of the degree where students are socialised into the profession and the ability to explore professional identity with a social work supervisor seems to be especially important in times when 'social workers are working in the new professional setting where other health practitioners are claiming similar knowledge and skills and are sharing similar clients' leading to a blurring of professional boundaries (Noble & Sullivan 2009, p91).

Research identifies that social work students are benefiting from field education. For example, Patford (2000) found that significant learning experiences for students on placement included encountering organisational constraints, regulating strong emotions, reconsidering their commitment to social work, encountering experiences relevant to academic learning and operating solo.

Yet, Maidment (2003, 2006) identified dual experiences for students on placement: first, the significant professional learning experience and, second, the coexisting experience of associated stress. Maidment goes as far as to question whether 'the work based placement arrangements now favoured ... serve to complement or even further complicate student lives and learning' (2003, p54). For students, the field education experience can be taxing, as it has the potential to challenge the students' perception of themselves. Ornstein and Moses (2010), for instance, argue that field education is a key experience challenging the students' sense of self and personal identity. Furthermore, field education is dominated by Western frameworks of thinking (Green & Baldry 2008) that can be particularly challenging for Indigenous and students of minority groups. Those students may find themselves overwhelmed and isolated from their cultural knowledge and support. This notion is revisited later in the chapter, with a particular reflection on how external supervision might help to address some of these issues.

Identifying field education in social work as complicated and challenging is echoed by Ornstein and Moses (2010), who suggest that the relationship between the field educator and student is the focal point of the field placement learning experience. Other authors acknowledge the central part the supervisory relationship plays in successful student placements (Bennett et al. 2008), yet also highlight some of the inherent challenges. For example, Karban (1999) identifies the need to acknowledge the dynamics and power in supervisory relationships. This fits with Ornstein and Moses' (2010, p103) recommendation of a relational approach to supervision that 'is defined by mutuality, shared and authorised power, and the co-construction of knowledge'.

Research exploring the desired characteristic of field educators shows that students want field educators to be 'available, respectful, responsive, supportive, fair, objective, and that are knowledgeable and able to directly communicate their knowledge and provide feedback' (Barretti 2007, p50). Further, students want field educators to 'encourage autonomy, provide opportunity to be observed, and facilitate professional development' (Barretti 2007, p51). These desired characteristics connect with the idea that students can learn from observing and witnessing field educators in action. Research highlights that 'observation of a professional holds a critical place in students' education' (Barretti 2007, p60). Yet, the reality of field education is that field educators supporting student placements might not always be available to be observed and that sometimes learning about desirable professional characteristics is reinforced by students' experiencing or observing the opposite behaviour or attribute (Barretti 2007). This is supported by Patford's (2000) findings, that show that students on placements found it difficult to access supervision and that this needs to be considered when setting up placements as at this stage of their professional development students need timely and directive guidance. In the social work practice context this guidance is potentially accessed from various sources, as both social workers and non-social work staff participate in supporting social work student placements (Barton et al. 2005).

EXTERNAL SUPERVISION IN FIELD EDUCATION: LAST RESORT OR VALUE ADDING STRATEGY?

One of the options utilised to ensure that placements are possible in organisations and settings where there are no qualified social workers, is to engage an off-site or external professional social work supervisor with the support of an internal supervisor who may not have social work qualifications. External supervision arrangements can happen in any setting. In Australia, the accreditation body allows placements with internal day-to-day supervision by a non social worker, however, 'arrangements must be made to ensure that appropriate professional formation and supervision takes place by a qualified social work field educator' (AASW 2010b, p16).

Only limited literature is available on the specific context of field education settings with external social work supervision. Some of the literature that is available points to social work educators generally assuming that the ideal placement arrangement involves a qualified on-site social work supervisor, facilitating the transmission of professional knowledge, values and skills; in other words socialising students to the profession (Abram et al. 2000). Abram et al. (2000) question this assumption and highlight the notion that social work placements without qualified social workers on staff can have advantages, including providing a broad range of experiences in emerging community organisation, a greater valuing of students, opportunities for multidisciplinary work, illustration of social work knowledge and skills in the host agency and job opportunities. Moreover, Plath (2003) argues that these placements result in employable and flexible graduates. Plath (2003) does caution that the students need to be carefully chosen and identifies a number of challenges, including lack of clearly defined social work roles, the importance of acknowledging and valuing the skills of on-site supervisors, and the complexity of a four-way process of assessment and reporting.

Overall, while there are considerations to be made external supervision arrangements can be positive and the point argued in this chapter, is that external supervision can be developed as a value adding strategy and while some information about how to do this is already available, other issues have to be explored further. First, external supervision can be a tool to build up the field. External supervision models can be a way of supporting student placement in field of practice and geographical areas where there is a lack of social workers or social services. Students can be supported in opening up those fields with the external support of qualified social work supervisors. Second, external supervision can be utilised to facilitate a more rounded assessment of students' performance. Supervision in field education has a number of functions, including supportive, administrative and educative, and sometimes it is difficult for supervisors to assess students' performance due to the blurring of these roles as a field educator (Hughes & Heycox 2005).

Third, student placements with external supervision may offer innovative avenues to help students integrate knowledge in more holistic and culturally appropriate ways. For example, students from ethnic minority groups may, during the course of their study, have come to rely on external cultural supports to survive in the academic setting of many universities dominated by Western philosophies, teaching practices and social work theories. At times these might be informal arrangements initiated by students accessing their personal networks. On other occasions, this might have been facilitated through processes of the educational institution. It is useful to consider social work field education settings with external supervision to accommodate and formalise cultural mentors or support as a valued and legitimate part of the placement experience. This could provide a model for Indigenous students, but perhaps all students, as external supervision can value add by contributing elements that might be absent for the students in the placement.

Utilising culturally relevant supervisors in field education might help include Indigenous ways of knowing and helping, and may make the social work education more meaningful for Aboriginal, Torres Strait Islander and other students. This is not necessarily new knowledge for the profession and attempts are made to redress some of these issues. What is argued in this chapter though, is that we have not got this right yet – that we have not articulated clear models finding balance, accessing culturally appropriate supervision and meeting the requirements of the AASW. While there might be local efforts to be culturally sensitive, the involvement of cultural mentors/elders or consultants in field education appears to be sporadic and in practice focuses more on building awareness of different cultures and helping culturally and linguistically diverse students adapt to Western thinking and ways of helping.

THE TRIAD RELATIONSHIP AND BEYOND

Aforementioned the characteristics of ideal supervisors included the opportunity to be observed and be available, although as noted earlier reduced human resources may mean that in reality the on-site supervisor's availability is constrained. Also discussed has been the concern that what has actually been observed is shaped by dominant Western frameworks of helping and that may mean that field education is not always culturally relevant, sensitive and competent. External supervision models can help address concerns by including cultural mentors. The question arises of how external supervision can maximise the potential benefits and minimise the challenges of social work field education? There is limited research about the triad relationship in social work field education supervision. Karban (1999) identifies a number of strategies to deal with the complexities of establishing relationships with external supervisors and highlights some important considerations: information sharing, professionalism, authenticity, rapport building and cooperation. Karban stresses that the decreased availability of the practice teacher may result in increased autonomy and objectivity and suggests that the triad of external supervisor, internal supervisor and student can offer a high quality placement experience.

Abram et al. (2000) consider the administrative, educational and supportive role of supervision and argue that these can be split. They argue that if the field educator, the task supervisor and the student are 'all actively engaged and supportive of each other, they can together provide a practitioner capable of knowledge and value guided practice' (Sheafor & Jenkins 1982, in Abram et al. 2000, p175). Abram et al. concede that research findings hold that qualified social work supervisors foster learning by imitation and a stronger professional identification, but otherwise student placement outcomes do not differ. Abram et al. propose that students' level of development should be assessed to best meet their needs. Their research points to the importance of an effective relationship between the task supervisor and the field educator and emphasised the significance of a common philosophy and values, clarification of the roles, division of labour and frequent communication. Abram et al. highlight the importance of the triad participatory relationship between the field educator, task supervisor and student. Abram et al. argue that 'in an effective triad each person involved has primary responsibility for one of several functions that a single ... social worker has shouldered alone in the past' (p183).

Henderson (2010) found that non-social work task supervisors experience power imbalances between themselves and the off-site supervisor. Henderson's findings suggest that work-based supervisors are not always treated as equal partners. This needs to be particularly noted when considering external supervision as a tool to include cultural mentors in field education. Power relationships need to be explored and addressed considering that the overall context of social work practice is dominated by Western social work paradigms. Henderson confirms the importance of regular meetings, time to communicate roles and expectations and the benefits of accessing the perspectives and experiences of two supervisors.

Henderson's paper (2010, p2) outlines the role of the on-site task supervisor as providing the main support to students on placement, 'responsible for the day-to-day supervision and accountable for the student's practice', whereas the role of the off-site field educator is to 'plan practice learning with the student to meet the learning outcomes, provide teaching and take overall responsibility for the assessment'. Likewise, models in the UK have the external supervisor assuming responsibility for practice teaching, including assessment, and the on-site supervisor assuming day-to-day responsibility for the student (Karban 1999).

Some literature discusses models for field education with external supervisors, including a number of authors proposing how students, field educators and task supervisors can be better supported to fulfil their role. Clare (2001), for instance, proposes a field education model focused on four key steps; developing a coordinated system or partnership, articulating a field education syllabus, implementing more rigorous assessment of field education placements and introducing training courses for field educators.

Maidment and Woodward (2002) present a specific model for external supervision within the framework of an ecological perspective. They suggest that the ecological paradigm acknowledges differences between the various stakeholders in field education and assists in understanding how they may interpret information differently (Maidment & Woodward 2002). The authors list seven essential attributes of external supervisors; however, it appears this model could be extended to consider the attributes and experiences of the students and/or task supervisors.

ADDRESSING CONCERNS BY VALUE ADDING

To this point it has been argued that external supervision is generally considered as the out of the norm model in field education by bringing in an 'outsider', recognising that at times it may be the only option left available to open up opportunities for development and growth. Equally it has been suggested that Aboriginal and Torres Strait Islander students on placement might not be offered a learning opportunity that fits with their learning styles, knowledge and cultural support model. Field education arrangements with external supervision could be one option of supporting minority group students, such as Aboriginal and Torres Strait Islander Australians, on placement. It could allow for the triad relationship of student, field educator and task supervisor to include a culturally relevant supervisor, either the field educator or the task supervisor that might help bridge some of the issues, help explore them and ensure the acknowledgement and inclusion of cultural relevant ways of helping. A broad reading of such a strategy might point to the positive creative inclusion of external supervision beyond this example.

Students from an ethnic minority group often undertake placements in mainstream settings to open up opportunities for networking and future employment. Many of these students, however, report being treated differentially in mainstream settings, and, 'if they feel courageous enough to discuss such issues, these students run the risk of being labelled "aggressive and confronting" by their field educator' (Razack 2000, p203). While placement for all students is often associated with anxiety and feelings of incompetence and powerlessness, 'Minority students face additional fears arising from historical treatment and present societal reality' (Razack p202). External supervision models that include the valuing and accessing of cultural expertise to guide practice and social work education could potentially help graduate Indigenous social workers and sensitise non-Indigenous students to the issues.

Culturally relevant supervisors may not always hold professional social work qualifications that are recognised by accreditation bodies, but they may help with the quest that Gray and Coates (2010) have identified, namely to challenge embedded views about Indigenous Australians and to decolonise non-Indigenous social workers. This would involve non-Indigenous social workers needing to 'give up their power and position as 'experts' in relation to Indigenous people' (Green & Baldry 2008, p398). Therefore, external supervision could involve contributing what is absent, in a broad value adding strategy.

Clark et al.'s (2010) research into decolonising field education does not specifically focus on external supervision in field education, but some of their research recommendations and findings point to the importance of culturally safe settings and the importance of creating 'ongoing dialogue about the power relationships inherent in field education experience' (p17), the importance of taking note of students' requested preferences with regards to field educators, and the importance of students' access to Aboriginal Elders and mentors in field education. The availability of culturally appropriate relational support could be accommodated through field education arrangements where there is an internal and external supervisor, either one assisting to ensure that the placement in culturally safe for the student.

While this discussion has focused on the experiences of Australian Indigenous students it is relevant to students in other areas of Asia-Pacific, especially when they may be part of a minority group in the country they are studying. Faleolo, who considers the context of Samoan social work education in New Zealand, particularly stresses the 'interlocking of various systems in which a young Samoan person is involved' (Faleolo 2009, p164) and the need to recognise the dynamic and interactive nature of social work education. He argues that relationships for Samoan students become multidimensional and points to their community orientation and their dynamic and interactive world view. He suggests further, that they 'would prefer to save face rather than ask for help' (p169). For Samoan social work students then, in particular those studying outside their homeland who are engaging in field education, consideration of inclusion of a culturally competent supervisor as part of their placement may be important. One of the possibilities to ensure cultural safety would be the inclusion of culturally valid supervisors, who may not be professionally qualified, however may become a valued part of a supervision triad.

Considering the issues highlighted above it is important to reflect on Western social work paradigms and how they impact on minority students or students in countries where Western social paradigms are foreign to local experiences and needs. Western social work practice, knowledge and theory is based within a Western perspective, so even when we look at implementing responses to structural disadvantages, such as anti-oppressive practice and cross-cultural practice this is based within 'Western epistemology which neither acknowledges nor understands Aboriginal epistemologies and, more critically, does not require anything beyond a theoretical grasping of issues' (Sinclair 2004 cited in Walter et al. 2011, p13). It appears then that culturally safe, competent and sensitive practice (AASW 2010a) needs to be supported actively by culturally relevant supervisors. Challenges about authentic involvement will be around giving up expertise and power as discussed above.

Rhonda Coopes (2009) explores how higher education institutions can offer cultural safety for Indigenous students and outlines guiding principles such as the importance of exploring the educator's own cultural heritage, recognising inequalities and barriers in education, reflecting on colonisation and 'recognising and respecting the legitimacy of Indigenous voices' (p110). This cannot be done without exploring power relationships, as has already been acknowledged as an important aspect in building effective relationships in placements with external supervision. Maidment and Woodward (2002, p101) consider 'the analysis of power and the ability to exercise power appropriately' as one of the key attribute of external supervisors. Processes that have been identified as important for building the complex relationships in placements with external supervision include information sharing, rapport building, professionalism, authenticity and cooperation (Karban 1999). We have information available on principles of practice that can be implemented and need to now ensure that we develop external supervision models that consciously explore power relationships, dominant paradigms, cultural contexts, resource availability and that challenge disempowering experiences and building safe learning environments. We need to seek to set up external supervision supports at times when there are internally qualified supervisors involved and need to ensure that field education educators, supervisors and students discuss and implement culturally safe practices.

CONCLUSION

It is clear that field education is an important, even imperative aspect of social work education, helping to prepare students to be professional social workers. Yet, field education models vary across Asia-Pacific, influenced by the lack of qualified field educators, the capacity of supervisors and organisations, and the need to expand the profession and the social work field. The supervisory relationship is important and while generally this relationship is seen as needing to consist of the student and professional field educator, this chapter has explored the possibility of a triad relationship, which would include a second supervisor who may or may not be professionally qualified, may or may not be available on site and may be a culturally relevant mentor or supervisor.

Overall, further research is needed to consider models, frameworks and how these might actually meet the needs of students, supervisors, organisations and educators. It appears useful to approach social work student placements from a standpoint that external supervision presents a valuable opportunity for the Asia-Pacific region. External supervision could assist in the development of the social service field in Asia-Pacific, in helping students learn in new environments, in responding to the expansion of social work across Asia-Pacific, and opening up the capacity to respond to concerns the profession as a whole has not been able to successfully respond to yet. Social work has been contentious for minority groups such as First Nation people and social workers in non-Western countries trying to indigenise Eurocentric social work knowledge and theories. Social work student placements with external supervision could open up new avenues to respond to some of the concerns and ensure that the profession continues on the journey of valuing, supporting and developing cultural relevant knowledge and practices.

Acknowledgement

I would like to thank Dr Susan Gair and Dr Debra Miles for their comments and support.

References

AASW (2010a). *AASW Code of Ethics*. Canberra, ACT: Australian Association of Social Work.

AASW (2010b). *Australian social work education and accreditation standards: learning for practice in field education* (4.3: 13–17). Canberra, ACT: Australian Association of Social Work.

Abram F, Hartung M & Wernet S (2000). The NonMSW task supervisor, MSW field instructor, and the practicum student. *Journal of Teaching in Social Work,* 20(1): 171–85, doi: 10.1300/J067v20n01_11.

Agllias K (2010). Student to practitioner: a study of preparedness for social work practitioners. *Australian Social Work,* 63(3): 346–60.

Barretti MA (2007). Teachers and field instructors as student role models. *Journal of Teaching in Social Work,* 27(3): 215–39, doi: 10.1300/J067v27n03_14.

Barton H, Bell K & Bowles W (2005). Help or hindrance? Outcomes of social work student placements. *Australian Social Work,* 58(3): 301–12, doi: 10.1111/j.1447-0748.2005.00222.x.

Bennett S, Mohr J, BrintzenhofeSzoc K & Saks LV (2008). General and supervision-specific attachment styles: relations to student *Journal of Social Work Education,* 44(2): 75–94.

Bessarab D & Crawford F (2010). Aboriginal practitioners speak out: contextualising child protection interventions. *Australian Social Work,* 63(2): 179–93.

Clare M (2001). Thinking systemically about fieldwork education - a third way. *Australian Social Work,* 54(1): 53–66, doi: 10.1080/03124070108415264.

Clark N, Drolet J, Mathews N, Walton P, Tamburro PR, Derrick J, Michaud V, Armstrong J & Arnouse M (2010). Decolonizing field education: 'Melq'ilwiye' coming together: an exploratory study in the interior of British Columbia. [electronic]. *Critical Social Work*, 11(1).

Coopes R (2009). Can universities offer a place of cultural safety for Indigenous students? In J Frawley, M Nolan & N White (Eds). *Indigenous issues in Australian universities. Research, teaching and support* (pp95–113). Darwin: Charles Darwin University Press.

Faleolo MM (2009). Culturally valid social work education: a Samoan perspective. In C Noble, M Henrickson & IY Han (Eds). *Social work education: voices from the Asia Pacific* (pp149–72). Carlton North, VIC: The Vulgar Press.

Gair S, Thomson J & Savage D (2005). What's stopping them? Exploring barriers hindering indigenous Australians from completing a social work degree at a regional Queensland University. *Advances in Social Work and Welfare Education*, 7(1): 54–62.

Gray M & Coates J (2010). 'Indigenization' and knowledge development: extending the debate. *International Social Work*, 53(5): 613–27, doi: 10.1177/0020872810372160.

Green S & Baldry E (2008). Building Indigenous Australian social work. *Australian Social Work*, 61(4): 389–402, doi: 10.1080/03124070802430718.

Henderson KJ (2010). Work-based supervisors: the neglected partners in practice learning. *Social Work Education*, 29(5): 490–502, doi: 10.1080/02615470903156352.

Hughes M & Heycox K (2005). Promoting reflective practice with older people: learning and teaching strategies. *Australian Social Work*, 58(4): 344–56, doi: 10.1111/j.1447-0748.2005.00231.x.

Karban K (1999). Long-arm practice teaching for the diploma in social work: the views of students and practice teachers. *Social Work Education*, 18(1): 59–70, doi: 10.1080/02615479911220061.

Lager PB & Robbins VC (2004). Field education: exploring the future, expanding the vision. *Journal of Social Work Education*, 40(1): 3–12.

Leung JCB (2009). Social work education in China: issues and opportunities. In C Noble, M Henrickson & IY Han (Eds). *Social work education: voices from the Asia Pacific* (pp307–40). North Carlton, VIC: The Vugar Press.

Maidment J (2006). Using on-line delivery to support students during practicum placements. *Australian Social Work,* 59(1): 47–55, doi: 10.1080/03124070500449770.

Maidment J (2003). Problems experienced by students on field placement: using research findings to inform curriculum design and content. *Australian Social Work,* 56(1): 50–60, doi: 10.1046/j.0312-407X.2003.00049.x.

Maidment J & Woodward P (2002). Student supervision in context: a model for external supervision. In S Shardlow & M Doel (Eds). *Learning to practice: international approaches* (pp93–109). London: Jessica Kingsley Publishing.

Nikku RB (2009). Social work education in South Asia: a Nepalese Perspective. In C Noble, M Henrickson & IY Han (Eds). *Social work education: voices from the Asia Pacific* (pp341–62). North Carlton, VIC: The Vulgar Press.

Noble C (2009). Social work and the Asia Pacific: from rhetoric to practice. In C Noble, M Henrikson & IY Han (Eds). *Social work education: voices from the Asia Pacific* (pp7–29). Carlton North, Victoria: The Vulgar Press.

Noble C & Sullivan J (2009). Is social work still a distinctive profession? Students, supervisors and educators reflect. *Advances in Social Work and Welfare Education,* 11(1): 89–107.

Ornstein E & Moses H (2010). Goodness of fit: a relational approach to field instruction. *Journal of Teaching in Social Work,* 30(1): 101–14, doi: 10.1080/08841230903479615.

Patford J (2000). Can I do social work and do I want to? Students perception of significant learning incidents during practica. *Australian Social Work,* 53(2): 21–28, doi: 10.1080/03124070008414145.

Plath D (2003). An experience based model of practice learning: international perspective from Australia. *Journal of Practice Teaching,* 5(1): 23–38.

Rambally RET (1999). Field education in a developing country: promoting organizational change and social development. *International Social Work,* 42(4): 485–96, doi: 10.1177/002087289904200409.

Razack N (2000). Students at risk in the field. In L Cooper & L Briggs (Eds). *Fieldwork in the human services. theory and practice for field educators, practice teachers and supervisors.* (pp195–204). Sydney: Allen & Unwin.

Skolnik L, Wayne J & Raskin MS (1999). A worldwide view of field education structures and curricula. *International Social Work,* 42(4): 471–83, doi: 10.1177/002087289904200408.

Unger J (2003). Supporting agency field instructors in forgotonia. *Journal of Teaching in Social Work,* 23(1): 105–21, doi: 10.1300/J067v23n01_08.

Walter M, Taylor S & Habibis D (2011). How white is social work in Australia? *Australian Social Work,* 64(1): 6–19, doi: 10.1080/0312407x.2010.510892.

Wayne J, Bogo M & Raskin M (2006). The need for radical change in field education. *Journal of Social Work Education,* 42(1): 161–69.

Yeom HS & Bae HO (2010). Potential issues in field practicum student exchange between Korea and the USA. *International Social Work,* 53(3): 311–26, doi: 10.1177/0020872809359748.

Contributors

Eileen Baldry, PhD is Professor of Criminology in the School of Social Sciences and International Studies, University of New South Wales (UNSW), Australia, where she teaches social policy, social development and criminology. She has been involved in the development of a core Aboriginal social work course. She co-publishes on Indigenous welfare and social work as well as criminal justice. She is chief investigator on numerous grants including mental and cognitive disability in criminal justice and community development. Email: e.baldry@unsw.edu.au

Dan Baschiera is a social worker specialising in humanitarianism who coordinates the Bachelor of Humanitarian and Community Studies and associated international placements at Charles Darwin University, Australia. Email: dan.baschiera@cdu.edu.au

Catherine Briscoe MSW, PhD took early retirement from the management of a social services department in the UK to lecture in social work in Singapore then became a volunteer for Voluntary Service Overseas, a British NGO, in Vietnam from 2006 to 2009. There she trained trainers in social work, was involved in the development of social work programs in different universities and consulted with voluntary organisations. She is officially retired now but is still doing consultancy. Email: catherine.briscoe@gmail.com

Michael Brosowski is the founder and chief executive officer of Blue Dragon Children's Foundation in Vietnam. His background is Arts/Education. He has a Masters in Education from University of New

South Wales. Email: bluedragon@bdcf.org
Shirley Ann Chinnery is a senior lecturer within the School of Counselling, Human Services and Social Work at the University of Auckland, New Zealand. Email: s.chinnery@auckland.ac.nz

Helen Cleak is a senior lecturer and Director of International Placements in the School of Social Work and Social Policy at La Trobe University, Australia. She teaches in social work practice, family mediation and interdisciplinary professional practice and has published a book on supervising students on placement, *Making the most of field education*, as well as a recent book, *Assessment and report writing in the human services*. Email: H.Cleak@latrobe.edu.au

Janet Emerman is Field Education Coordinator at the University of Alaska Anchorage, US, for the Bachelor of Social Work and Masters of Social Work Distance Field programs. Email: Janet@uaa.alaska.edu

Annalisa Enrile, MSW, PhD, is a Clinical Associate Professor at the School of Social Work, University of Southern California, US, and Board President of Mariposa Center for Change (a US-based multi-ethnic nonprofit organisation for women and children that aims to improve social, political and economic conditions and end inequality through an empowered sisterhood, transformative programming, grassroots organising, and strategic alliances). www.mariposacenterforchange.org Email: enrile@usc.edu

Mim Fox is the Professional Liaison Officer in Field Education in the Social Work Program at the University of New South Wales, Australia. Mim is currently completing her PhD research in 'International Field Placements in Social Work Education'. Mim has published and taught in the areas of international social work, field education, as well as social work and health. Email: m.fox@unsw.edu.au

Peter Garrity, BSW, MSW, MAASW, is a lecturer at James Cook University, Australia. Peter has over 30 years of practice experience and balances teaching with continued professional engagement. He has lectured in social work field education, theories of social work, group work, community development and social work and welfare practice. Email: peter.garrity@jcu.edu.au

Susan Green is an Associate Professor of Social Work in the School of Social Sciences and International Studies, University of New South Wales (UNSW), Australia, where she teaches within a number of social work courses with a particular focus on Indigenous social work practice at both the undergraduate and postgraduate level. Her areas of research and publication interest are on Indigenous welfare both historically and currently. Recently she has co-published articles on Indigenous social work and on decolonisation. Email: s.green@unsw.edu.au

Trish Hanlen, MNZM, RSW, MANZASW is convenor of Social Work at the University of Waikato, New Zealand. Her interests include management, non-statutory social services and child neglect. Email: Patricia@waikato.ac.nz or trishhanlen@xtra.co.nz

Kathryn Hay is Director of Field Education at Massey University, New Zealand and paper coordinator for the Bachelor of Social Work placement students. Email: K.S.Hay@massey.ac.nz

Mark Henrickson, MDiv, MSW, PhD, RSW, is a senior lecturer in social work at Massey University, Auckland, New Zealand. His research interests include HIV, sexual and gender minorities, and international social work. He is on the boards of APASWE and the International Association of Schools of Social Work (IASSW). Email: m.henrickson@massey.ac.nz

Soo Mi Jang is is an assistant professor and teaches practicum courses, field education, family violence and substance misuse at Cheongju University in South Korea. She is an experienced clinician in the health and mental health areas. Her research includes alcohol abuse and family violence as well as effective field work. Email: jsumi@cju.ac.kr

Mathew Keen is Senior Psychiatric Social Worker at Ward 21 (Acute Inpatient Mental Health Service), Palmerston North Hospital, Mid-Central District Health Board, Palmerston North, New Zealand. He has been a student placement sponsor and supervisor for many students over the past 20 years. Email: mathew.keen@midcentraldhb.govt.nz

Natasha Long is a lecturer and Field Education Coordinator in Social Work with the La Trobe Rural Health School, La Trobe University, Bendigo, Australia. Email: N.Long@latrobe.edu.au

Skye Maconachie recently completed her MSW(PQ) at James Cook University, and has a BA (major in Theatre). She is currently working with Centacare Migrant Services as a Case Manager with newly arrived refugee families in Cairns, Australia. Email: skye.maconachie@gmail.com

Jay Marlowe, PhD, is a lecturer within the School of Counselling, Human Services and Social Work at the University of Auckland, New Zealand. Email: jm.marlowe@auckland.ac.nz

Jennifer Nazareno, MSW, is a medical sociology doctoral candidate at University of California, San Francisco, and is a part-time lecturer at the School of Social Work, University of Southern California, US. She is also a Board Member of Mariposa Center for Change. Email: jnazaren@usc.edu.

Amanda Nickson: BSW, MSW, MAASW, currently works as a lecturer and Field Education Coordinator, Department of Social Work and Community Welfare, James Cook University, Australia. Email: amanda.nickson@jcu.edu.au

Carolyn Noble, PhD, is Professor Emerita, School of Social Sciences and Psychology at Victoria University, Melbourne, Australia. She is also Head of College and Academic Leader at Jansen Newman College of Counselling and Psychotherapy. She is Vice-President of APASWE. Her research is in the area of professional education, critical reflection, supervision, social work ethics, work-based learning and community engagement and theory development in social work. Email: Carolyn. noble@vu.edu.au or cnoble@jni.edu.au.

Masakazu Shirasawa, PhD, is Professor of the Graduate School of Gerontology, J.F. Oberlin University, Professor Emeritus of the Graduate School of Social Work, Osaka City University, Japan, and President of the Japanese Association of Schools of Certified Social Workers (JASCSW). He is also President of the Japanese Society for the Study of Social Welfare and the Japan Academy of Home Care, and Vice-President of the Japan Society of Care Management. As the President of the JASCSW he was instrumental in the establishment of the 'Reformed Law of Certified Social Workers and Certified Care Workers' in 2008, which aims to develop more practical social workers by enriching fieldwork practice. Email: sirasawa@smile.ocn.ne.jp

Marjorie Thomson is a Masters of Social Work student completing her final semester at University of Alaska Anchorage, US. She currently works at the University of Alaska Southeast. Email: margie.thomson@uas.alaska.edu

Rob Townsend, PhD, is a lecturer in social policy and a researcher with the La Trobe Rural Health School, La Trobe University, Bendigo, Australia. Email: robert.townsend@latrobe.edu.au

Robyn Trainor is the Loddon Campaspe Regional Integrated Family Violence Coordinator at EASE, Bendigo, and in 2006–10 was employed as a lecturer and Field Placement Coordinator in Social Work with the La Trobe Rural Health School, La Trobe University, Bendigo, Australia. Email: robyn.trainor@ease.org.au

Betty Y. Weng is Associate Professor in the Social Work and Child Welfare Department, Providence University in Taiwan. Currently, she teaches case management, program design and evaluation, social work supervision, child protective services, medical social work and social work practicum. In addition to her teaching, she is CEO of a small non-profit organisation, specialised in providing direct social work services for children and families in need. She received her MSW degree from University of Iowa, and MA degree from West Virginia University in the US. She received her PhD in Guidance and Counselling from National Chung-Hwa Normal University, Taiwan. Email: ysweng@gm.pu.edu.tw

Deborah West (BA, MSW, PhD) is Associate Professor and head of the Social Work and Community Studies Department at Charles Darwin University, Australia. Email: deborah.west@cdu.edu.au

Nilan G. Yu is a lecturer in social work and social policy of the School of Psychology, Social Work and Social Policy, University of South Australia, Adelaide, South Australia, Australia. Email: nilan_yu@yahoo.com

Ines Zuchowski is a social worker, currently employed as a lecturer at James Cook University, Australia in field education. She is enrolled in a PhD, focusing on external supervision in field education. Email: ines.zuchowski@jcu.edu.au

www.ingramcontent.com/pod-product-compliance
Lightning Source LLC
Chambersburg PA
CBHW071728270326
41928CB00013B/2599